P9-BYR-586

BRAVE MEN, GENTLE HEROES

BRAVE MEN, GENTLE HEROES

American Fathers and Sons in World War II and Vietnam

MICHAEL TAKIFF

wm
WILLIAM MORROW
An Imprint of HarperCollins*Publishers*

HarperCollins books may be purchased for educational, business, or sales promotional use. For information please write: Special Markets Department, HarperCollins Publishers Inc., 10 East 53rd Street, New York, NY 10022.

FIRST EDITION

Designed by Renato Stanisic

Printed on acid-free paper

Library of Congress Cataloging-in-Publication Data

Takiff, Michael, 1955–
Brave men, gentle heroes : American fathers and sons in World War II and Vietnam / Michael Takiff.—1st ed.
p. cm.
Includes bibliographical references.
ISBN 0-06-621081-X
1. World War, 1939–1945—Personal narratives, American. 2. Vietnamese Conflict, 1961–1975—Personal narratives, American. 3. World War, 1939–1945—Biography. 4. Vietnamese Conflict, 1961–1975—Biography. 5. United States—Armed Forces—Biography. 6. Fathers and sons—United States—Biography. 7. United States—Biography. I. Title.

D811.A2T298 2003
940.54'8173—dc21
[B]

2003044203

---

03 04 05 06 07 RRD 10 9 8 7 6 5 4 3 2 1

FOR ALFRED TAKIFF, MY WAR HERO

And in that time
When men decide and feel safe
To call the war insane,
Take one moment to embrace
Those gentle heroes
You left behind.

—Major Michael Davis O'Donnell, First Aviation Brigade, Dak To, Vietnam

From a poem written January 1, 1970. On March 24 Michael O'Donnell was killed in action.

CONTENTS

Introduction

To most Americans, World War II and the war in Vietnam are utterly contrary events. The Good War, fought worldwide, was won by a unified nation and led to a period of unprecedented prosperity at home and ascendancy abroad. The Bad War, fought in a remote corner of the globe, was lost by a nation at war with itself as much as with Communism and ushered in an era of domestic discontent and international decline.

They are utterly discrete events as well. Rarely do we consider the two conflicts together, except to define each by what it is not. For Vietnam especially, this contrast forms our framework of understanding: It is the un–World War II; it is the war without memorable, easily explained battles; the war whose rationale and ultimate military objective a series of presidents never quite succeeded in making plain. We know World War II better on its own terms. We are familiar with Pearl Harbor and D-Day. The war's rationale and objective are so clear to us that we can state them in a handful of words: respectively, "to save the world" and "unconditional surrender." Yet the ten years of war that came later, bringing combat to our televisions and turmoil to our streets, cannot help but shape the context in which we see the war waged a generation before. And so World War II becomes the un-Vietnam: It is the war in which our nation did not fail.

This dichotomy is useful shorthand, but it leaves much to be desired as a comprehensive guide to two events as complex and consequential as World War II and Vietnam, for the wars have more in common with each other, and are more connected to each other, than we ordinarily realize. To begin with, how often do we stop to note that the two conflicts were separated by only twenty years? The cataclysm that ended in 1945 was less history than it was recent memory to the nation's leaders in 1965, when they began pouring young Americans into South Vietnam. The United States would keep this domino upright or it would see a chain of them fall, until America was forced back on its heels as England had been in 1940, after Hitler's assault on the Continent's dominoes had culminated in the surrender of France. Only after fifty-eight thousand dead did Munich syndrome give way to Vietnam syndrome.

Twenty years was a lifetime to the youngsters sent to fight in the jungles of Southeast Asia, but as they made the choice to serve in Vietnam—and most of the Vietnam veterans in this book had at least some choice in the matter—the Second World War was on their minds as surely as it was on the minds of their superiors in Washington. "Before I went into the service," says Vince Way, an Army intelligence sergeant in Vietnam, "World War II was huge. It was ingrained in us that it was a grand and heroic thing that our country did and our fathers did. Military service was grand and heroic—if the country needed you, you went off to war." These young men had been raised on World War II—by their parents, their teachers, their classmates, their neighbors. And if their fathers withheld the details of combat—for many combat veterans will go decades without talking of what they have seen and done—Hollywood was there to fill in the blanks. "We grew up with John Wayne, *Sands of Iwo Jima,*" recalls Jim Coyne Jr., an

Army communications lieutenant in Vietnam. "I was brought up to understand that what we as Americans do is right."

This intimate generational connection between the two wars made comparisons inevitable from the beginning of America's involvement in Vietnam, because young men flew to a distant land expecting a war like the war their fathers had fought. When the reality of Vietnam did not match their preconceptions, they found their situation difficult to comprehend, painful to accept. Sooner or later, every Vietnam veteran in this book came to agree with the conclusion of infantry lieutenant Mickey Hutchins that "this was not my father's war." Veterans of World War II went overseas intent on doing their duty, and they returned with their idealism intact. Veterans of Vietnam went overseas with the same desire to serve their fellow Americans in time of need but found a war so unlike the just, purposeful, apparently well commanded effort in which their fathers had taken part that their high ideals yielded to cynicism about the entire enterprise. That disillusionment struck as early as the moment they stepped off the aircraft that had brought them there. For most, the process was more gradual, occurring over the first several months of their yearlong tour of duty, as they became acquainted with a war that didn't add up. And for a few, the realization did not come until after they had returned home to a broader perspective than that available to an individual soldier in the middle of a big fight. The opinions of the Vietnam veterans differ as to why the war went wrong: Our leaders made honest mistakes, our leaders made venal mistakes; we were mistaken to fight in the first place, we were mistaken to fight a war the politicians wouldn't let us win. But all the Vietnam veterans in this book, with one exception, share a fundamental dissatisfaction with the war in which they risked their lives. And that one exception, who holds that our show of force in Vietnam did, in fact, help to contain Communism, found the rules of engagement baffling and the conduct of his company commander unconscionable.

World War II veterans did not gladly send their sons to fight this new war—they knew too well the trials that awaited them. But neither did they begrudge their sons. "I guess a lot of parents didn't want their kids to go. . . ." says Mas Takahashi, a World War II Army infantryman. "But the way I see it, if you get drafted, that means your country needs you. . . . You've got to go." Like their sons, these veterans appraised Vietnam using the earlier war's standards; they had given service when fit and able, now it was their sons' turn. But as with their sons, the more they knew about Vietnam, the more damning the comparison. "If the United States had gone into Vietnam with the same resolve that we went into World War II with," says Paul Walmsley, a veteran of George Patton's Third Army, "the North Vietnamese would have been defeated in six months or less." World War II veterans do not raise fundamental objections to their own war. They quibble with the actions of this or that commander—Douglas MacArthur and Britain's Bernard Montgomery come in for particular criticism—but the imperative to fight and win World War II is as urgent to them now as it was the day they were inducted into uniform. World War II veterans and Vietnam veterans both take pride in their service in war. But the older veterans feel proud also of their war itself.

We feel proud with them, just as we share the discontent of their sons. Our accustomed ways of thinking about the wars, then, are far from arbitrary. Broadly, they conform to the attitudes of the veterans themselves—or at least to those attitudes we choose to highlight because they allow us to fit the wars into two concise, complementary narratives.

Recalling World War II, rightly, makes us feel good. We celebrate it, accurately, as a majestic national achievement. Farm boys and city kids, rich and poor, Jews and Gentiles, sons of Poland and England and Italy and Japan, blacks and whites, northerners and southerners, men and women, those sent overseas and those left on the home front—all came together as one to fight the common foes. After the warriors extinguished the evils in Europe and the Pacific, they came home heroes. They then turned to peacetime use the industrial behemoth that had armed the victorious forces, thus building for their nation the most powerful economic engine in world history and for themselves successful lives as workers, husbands, and fathers.

Recalling Vietnam pains us. We find nothing positive to celebrate; rather, we analyze the war, as pathology. We keep asking, What went wrong? as if we are coroners examining a corpse to find the one true cause of death when there are a thousand correct answers. The poor and the patriotic, we lament, left their better-off and less-committed brethren behind as they went to fight a jungle war as brutal as it was pointless. Mendacious political leadership and questionable military management, an unreliable ally and a tenacious enemy gave us an interminable war when we had expected a short one, and public support for the effort withered as the years went by and the body bags came home. In the end we turned tail and ran, leaving the Communists to their triumph, just as we would have ten years earlier had Lyndon Johnson not invested our nation's resources and prestige in stopping them, and the richest, most powerful nation in human history was humbled by a poor, agrarian country a fraction of its size. As the veterans returned, our society wanted nothing so much as to forget them and everything they stood for—not only the years of futile war, but the rest of what happened during a tumultuous time: riots in the streets, convulsions on campus, political assassinations, a presidential scandal. In turn the veterans, so we believe, isolated and disaffected, could not or would not readjust to civilian life, and so flooded society with substance abuse, homelessness, and post-traumatic stress disorder (PTSD).

All these stereotypes, and more, are true—in some measure. In World War II, Americans of all economic and ethnic backgrounds did unite to bring an end to unspeakable evil. The men who fought the war did return to fortify General Motors and build the interstate highway system. In Vietnam, the burden of fighting did fall to those not fortunate enough to succeed in higher education or devious enough to forge a plausible medical excuse. The war did not proceed as we wanted it to; its end, on the roof of the U.S. embassy in Saigon, was ignominious. Veterans did return to a society indifferent to them at best, often actively hostile. PTSD has afflicted many Vietnam veterans.

But these well-rehearsed generalizations crowd out the stories of the millions of individuals who shouldered the guns, flew the planes, and manned the ships. If we see World War II only as a great national triumph, we forget that it was also a great national ordeal. Four hundred thousand Americans gave their lives, every one of whom was someone's best friend. Jim Coyne Sr., an Army communications sergeant who served in Europe, watched his best friend's intestines spill out of his belly as he was mortally wounded. The struggles of Vietnam veterans with PTSD are well known—and they appear in this book—but shortly after the war, Arthur Way, an infantryman with the Forty-fifth Division in Sicily and Italy, nearly strangled his wife in his sleep, and Walter Kraus, a submariner in the Pacific, has nightmares to this day of the time his boat nearly sank. Americans of all origins did military service, but before Mas Takahashi joined the Army, he and his family had been interned with a hundred ten thousand other Japanese Americans from the West Coast. Veterans did come home to a hero's welcome, but Howard Baugh Sr.'s valor as a Tuskegee Airman spared him none of the indignity visited upon blacks in his native South, where Jim Crow's grip on everyday life had relaxed not a bit in the time he was gone. World War II enlisted men cooperated with their officers; fragging—the killing of officers by enlisted men—is considered a phenomenon peculiar to the mess that was Vietnam. But Gene Swanson, of the Third Marine Division, recalls two occasions on Iwo Jima when seasoned noncommissioned officers took matters into their own hands after inexperienced lieutenants refused to listen to their counsel. World War II servicemen appreciated the immensity of the stakes involved in their endeavor, unlike their counterparts in Vietnam, many of whom tell us that their only goal was to get out alive. But Al Tarbell, a paratrooper who landed in Holland with the Eighty-second Airborne Division, just wanted to get home to his family, get a good night's sleep, listen to a ball game; only after his outfit liberated a concentration camp did the war's larger aims finally become apparent to him as the reason he'd been fighting. It's comforting to think that the Allies won World War II because we were the good guys. And morale among fighting men surely benefited from their faith in their cause. But being right hardly made our victory inevitable. It took blood, treasure, technological know-how, skillful generalship, industrial might, wise statesmanship, hard work, dumb luck, and small acts of bravery on the part of millions of Allied soldiers, sailors, airmen, and Marines to win a long and savage fight against two powerful, motivated enemies. The men who won World War II were human beings; we minimize their accomplishment when we make of them plaster saints.

Likewise, to see Vietnam purely as an American embarrassment is to ignore the sacrifice and courage of those who served. Fraggings took place—they were not common, but they did take place—yet infantry grunt Michael Mace saved his platoon lieutenant's life. Men did sometimes place their own safety ahead of the fulfillment of their mission, but the Novosels—Mike Sr. and Mike Jr.—pilots of medical evacuation helicopters, braved gunfire every day to extract wounded men from ongoing battles and bring them to treatment. Mike Jackson flew his light observation plane low and slow, making it a perfect target for enemy gunners, in order to obtain the best possible view of firefights on the ground before he called in air strikes to support friendly troops. Some career officers did strive after promotions heedless of their troops' well-being, but career Army officer Mike Perkins jeopardized his standing with his superiors to give his men a few hours of rest between grueling missions in the Mekong Delta. The racial strife in the era's military is well known, but John Howe, an African American born and raised in Brooklyn, judges his treatment in the Army fairer overall than that he's found outside it. Many returning veterans found life at home alienating. But Richard Rivas, a helicopter-door gunner, found a loving wife and with her raised two successful children. Army artilleryman Scott Takahashi devoted himself to helping others as a health-care professional.

Mike Jackson, Mike Perkins, and others stayed in the military after Vietnam, continuing in service to their country and retiring at high ranks. And Mike Tarbell, a veteran of three tours in Vietnam, found strength in his Native American heritage to overcome problems with PTSD and contribute to his community as a teacher of Iroquois history. Like their fathers, the men who fought the Vietnam War were human beings; we blind ourselves to their honor when we make of them merely bundles of symptoms.

This book has its origins in a conversation I had with my father in December 1992, three weeks before his death. We were in a hospital room in Elizabeth, New Jersey, the working-class town where he had lived his entire life, save 1942–46, his years in the Army.

Dad had always loved to tell stories of his time in the service and I had never tired of hearing them, even though I'd heard each one a hundred times. But during the last year or two of his life, he returned to the subject more and more. Dad was a walking medical textbook, but his most serious illness was chronic obstructive pulmonary disorder. COPD can be a terminal disease—it was in his case—but it's not one that carries a fixed, imminent deadline, as, say, lung cancer does. Nevertheless, Dad's health had been deteriorating those last couple of years; clearly, he was taking stock.

That afternoon in the hospital, I heard some of the old stories. My favorite was about the night he was billeted in the home of an elderly French doctor. After dinner, Dad and his host argued over the need for American bombing of targets in France during the Nazi occupation, then got pie-eyed on Armagnac and marched around the table singing "The Marseillaise" and "The Star-Spangled Banner."

But as he sat on his bed in his pajamas and red-flannel bathrobe, he said something he'd never before said to me—nor, I'm certain, to anyone else. Just the two of us were in the room that day; my mother had had to leave town for the weekend, so I was filling in to help him pass the dull hospital time. "You might say," he told me, "that the war was the high point of my life."

I didn't think much about that comment right away. There was already enough to think about: He was sick; a week later his condition took a turn for the worse, and he was dying. Only in the months following his passing did I consider what he'd said. At first it made little sense. He'd been to war nearly a half-century ago, he'd never fired his weapon in anger, he'd had a reasonably successful career in business, he'd raised four children, he'd been married forty-nine years. But then I realized: Of course. What could compare to his crossing the sea—this young man who had never traveled more than a few miles from home—as one among millions around the world engaged in this grand and good enterprise? How could the rest of his life—nine to five, day after day, year after year, putting bread on the table for his growing family—measure up to sailing off to save the world?

I suppose I had always been proud of my father's service during World War II, but during his lifetime, aside from enjoying his stories—most of them amusing, one sobering—I'd paid it scant attention. I suppose I had always admired the accomplishment of all the Americans who fought in World War II. But it took my father's comment and his death for me to begin to appreciate the extent to which the lives of these now elderly men had been defined by a few years of their youth. Only then did I begin to understand why men stood at traffic intersections to collect money for the VFW, why they marched in Memorial Day parades. My father did not march in parades, probably because it was not his nature to be demonstrative, perhaps because he thought that other men, who had seen more combat, were more deserving of the recognition. But during my boyhood he took me to Memorial Day parades in downtown Elizabeth. Only after his death did I begin to imagine what must have been going through his mind at those parades and why, as the flag passed, he took off his hat and placed it over his heart.

In researching this project—talking with the veterans who appear in these pages and with many others—I've come to realize that the experience of war is no less pivotal in the lives of Vietnam veterans than in those of the veterans of World War II. War changes people. Thirty-five or fifty-five years after the fact, men may have trouble recalling the date they stormed a beach or the name of the lieutenant who led them on a patrol. But they never forget their feelings the first time they were shot at or saw a body blown apart or heard that a buddy had been killed. They never forget the sights and sounds and smells of living with death on a daily basis. When I interviewed Jim Coyne Sr. in the spring of 2000, Alzheimer's disease had robbed him of most of his short-term memory; during the couple of hours I spent at his house, I heard him ask his son, Jim Jr., the same question—"Where's Mother?"—several times. But he recalled precisely his confusion and fear the day in 1943 when he participated in the invasion of Sicily and the fierceness of the enemy he faced.

"My experience in war wasn't all that different from Jim's," Mr. Coyne told me. "It was a different experience because it was different people, but when you undergo gunfire, I don't think there's a difference." Combat deeply unites those who have taken part in it and deeply divides them from everyone else. I am not a veteran. Although I came to this project with general historical knowledge of the two wars, I knew little of the nuts and bolts of military life and even less of the hard reality of armed conflict. I've tried my best the past three years, in long hours of conversation, to understand what these men went through. But I will never be able to truly appreciate what combat is like, nor, I believe, can anyone else who has not been there. The gulf between those who have seen combat and the rest of us can be narrowed—indeed, I hope this book will help to do so—but it can never be bridged. "You recognize that character," says John Howe, "that quality, in someone who has been there and who has seen the shit." His stepfather, Pacific veteran Sonny Dunbar, states, "It's very hard to talk about this to people who haven't experienced it. . . . If a person has felt it, then they understand what I'm talking about. And not particularly the words that I put out—they can feel the feeling and the energies that come out of me. But if I'm dealing with somebody else that has never experienced that kind of thing, I can't converse with you. You don't know what path I'm walking unless you walked that path." These men—men who fought on land and on sea and in the air, in Europe, the Pacific, and Southeast Asia—know what it is to hunt and be hunted.

If I've learned anything from gathering these stories, it is that, literally, I never knew the first thing about war. All these men have taught me this lesson; here's how Sandy Walmsley, a combat medic in Vietnam, puts it: "You've got to remember that the purpose of an army in wartime will never change. It's to kill other people. You can do statistics, you can do logistics, you can market it any way you want, but the bottom line is to destroy other human lives. That is what an army is all about, and that's what a soldier is trained to do or give support to." Watching war on television and in the movies, reading about it in books, war's essence had escaped me, and I'm sure I was not alone. We can speak of war as "politics by other means," we can scan maps, discuss divisions and battalions, analyze landing zones and lines of attack, compare weaponry, pick apart strategy. But all of it—all of it—is an edifice constructed of war's elemental building block: two people, each trying to kill the other before the other kills him. This basic purpose is hidden beneath the language of tactics and objectives: Warriors must knock out a gun position, sink shipping, provide air cover. But when a platoon of infantrymen is ordered to "take that hill," they can do so only by killing or wounding the people currently on that hill, or by making the threat that they will kill or wound those people credible enough that those people will surrender or flee. Time and again these veterans told me: It's kill or be killed, it's either him or you. That killing forms the heart of warfare should be warfare's most obvious fact, and it is to the few among us who, like Vietnam Marine Steve Kraus, have found themselves "crawling through guts and brains and smoke." But to the rest of us, fortunate to have been spared that hell—we who are "the innocents," as Mike Novosel Jr. calls us—this uncomfortable truth needs to be pointed out. As I write, June 2003, American troops continue to die in Afghanistan and Iraq. Whether we endorse or dissent from decisions our leaders make, in our names, to put young Americans in harm's way, we shirk our duty as citizens if we avert our eyes from what they are about to encounter—and, if they survive, what they will live with the rest of their lives.

Civilized people will never be—must never be—comfortable with war. War marks individuals for life, war marks families for generations. Mickey Hutchins, raised a Quaker, asks the question, "What does it take to wage peace?" It's stating the obvious to call war an enormous human tragedy—the blood spilled, the treasure spent, the lives ruined. But more than those consequences of wars waged, there is the devotion of resources to preparing for wars yet to be waged. How many billions of man-hours around the world are each year devoted directly to military endeavors—the labor not only of those who wear the uniforms and fire the guns but also of those who stitch the uniforms and forge the guns? How many more hours do people of all occupations work to earn the money to pay the taxes that finance this expensive enterprise, which is, by definition, destructive?

And yet, what are we to do? George Santayana erred when he said that those who cannot remember the past are condemned to repeat it. We can take what we will from the wars our nation has fought; certainly the men whose voices appear in this book can help us to remember and to learn. But humankind will not soon give up war, and so we will continue to rely on brave men like these to bear arms when we believe our nation's interests are threatened. "Without heroes," wrote Bernard Malamud, "we are all plain people, and don't know how far we can go." These forty men have shown us how far we can go—by their pursuit not of glory but of honor, by their willingness to die for what they believed precious. And if these men are heroes, they are, as Michael Davis O'Donnell instructs us, gentle heroes. For they are not faraway superhumans, they are not strangers, but rather our fathers, our sons, our brothers, our husbands, our lovers. As a nation, as a species, we wear the face of war whether we like it or not.

I

"His death affected me greatly."

MIKE NOVOSEL SR.

MIKE NOVOSEL SR.

RETIRED CAREER MILITARY OFFICER
FORT WALTON BEACH, FLORIDA
CAPTAIN, UNITED STATES ARMY AIR FORCES, WORLD WAR II
CHIEF WARRANT OFFICER THREE, UNITED STATES ARMY, VIETNAM

From June 1944 to March 1945, American B-29s, known as Superfortresses, carried out daylight precision bombing raids over Japan with little success. High winds at thirty thousand feet, as well as Japanese fighter planes and antiaircraft artillery, frustrated American efforts to cripple Japanese war production.

On March 9 over three hundred B-29s of Major General Curtis E. LeMay's XXI Bomber Command tried a different tactic. Flying at low altitude to avoid the jet stream, flying at night to minimize the effectiveness of enemy flak and fighters, the bombers carpeted Tokyo with 1,665 tons of incendiaries. Although the targeting was anything but precise, it did not need to be: Factories were dispersed throughout the city, and in the process of setting the city on fire, the bombers laid waste to twenty-two major industrial facilities. Even so, disrupting Japanese manufacturing was not the sole purpose of the attack; American war planners intended it also to convey to the empire's population the price of continuing resistance. The signal sent was a horrific one: As many as a hundred thousand people died as a result of that one night of bombing. A quarter of a million buildings were destroyed.

Night incendiary bombings continued through March, and then in April, emboldened by new complements of P-51 fighter escort aircraft, LeMay instituted nighttime and daylight raids that dropped a carefully prepared mix of ordnance—as Michael J. Novosel Sr., a pilot of one of the attacking B-29s, explains. The raids continued into August, halted only by the dropping of atomic bombs on Hiroshima and Nagasaki and the resultant Japanese surrender.

Generally, presidential inaugural speeches are made on January 20 and then forgotten on the twenty-first. But I didn't forget John F. Kennedy's.

Kennedy was a political breath of fresh air. True, he was a politician, but he was of my generation. If you were one of the voters of that time, you saw the change that he was trying to bring about—a change in attitude, a change in doing things. I just liked what he stood for.

"Let the word go forth from this time and place, to friend and foe alike, that the torch has been passed to a new generation of Americans"—that's what I mean: that torch was now given to us, not the old fogeys; we're the new youngsters in charge of this country—"a new generation of Americans—born in this century, tempered by war, disciplined by a hard and bitter peace, proud of our ancient heritage—and unwilling to witness or permit the slow undoing of those human rights to which this Nation has always been committed, and to which we are committed today at home and around the world."

And I often want to say in addition that our generation was reared in the crucible of the Great Depression. I wish he had mentioned that. The Depression was great training—great training in survival and in getting along—for winning that damn war. Everybody that fought in World War II was the product of the Great Depression.

I was born in '22. I was not materially affected by the Depression, but I saw all around me what it did. I lived in Etna, Pennsylvania, a small town just outside of Pittsburgh. My father had his own business there: He was a shoemaker. He was born in Croatia and had learned his trade as an apprentice in Vienna. He prospered during the thirties because people were not buying shoes, they were repairing them. The people during that Great Depression would never think of throwing a pair of shoes away just because there was a hole in it.

Because we were able to sustain ourselves in quite a nice way, I wouldn't even think about missing a meal. But my mother, who was also from Croatia, always made it known at lunchtime that there was an extra bowl of soup for whoever was hungry. We knew people were hungry—we saw people living in tar-paper shacks on the edge of town. So every day someone would come to the door. But only one. There would never be a clamoring—"Hey, you gave him something, how about me?" Nothing like that. We were disciplined in those days.

The Depression welded us together. We knew that we were all in the same boat. Sure, some of us may have had a dollar or two more than our neighbor, but we didn't gloat about it. You knew you had to cooperate to get along. And this I found to extend right into the service life. The cohesiveness of a unit is amplified when people are out to help one another, not stab one another.

I made my first model airplane at the age of twelve. There were two of us that worked together on this—Louis Duderstadt, a good German friend of mine, and I. I must have made a dozen or more with him. He always completed his before I completed mine, but his were not as fancy-looking and not as detailed as mine would be. I think the models cost us a dime. It was the rubber-band variety. Later on, my younger brother and I actually made a trainer in our cellar. When I say a "trainer," it certainly had no engine. But it was an airplane we made out of wood that had movable ailerons and movable rudders, and we would pretend that we were flying this thing. He became a pilot, too. He flew P-51s in World War II, when I was flying the bombers.

My father was successful in that we were never hungry and always had a nice home to live in. But he was not wealthy enough to afford the Pennsylvania higher-educational system. I did have a scholarship to Carnegie Tech but it was only a partial one, and there was no way I could get a job that would pay me enough money to go to school. I figured that I would get an education if I went into the service. I specifically picked the Air Corps because I figured, "I can be a mechanic. And after I become a mechanic, and I've learned what the airplanes are all about, then I'll be old enough to get into flight training." Remember, I was eighteen. You had to be twenty or twenty-one to get into flight training.

I enlisted February 7, 1941, ten months to the day before Pearl Harbor.

Because I wanted to be a mechanic, I was really set back when they assigned me, without any questions being asked—and in those days you didn't ask—to administrative school to become a chief clerk. But I was the type of man who said, "It's not what I wanted to do, but since they're making me a chief clerk, I'm going to be the best one they have." I graduated near the top of the class, and I had the responsibility of paying everybody in my squadron at Shepherd Field, Texas.

That's where I was on December 7. It was a Sunday morning. I was walking down Lucille Avenue in Wichita Falls, Texas. A convertible came by with the radio blaring, "The Japs attacked Pearl Harbor!" And then the announcer said, "All servicemen have been ordered back to their barracks."

I knew it wasn't good, but I had no idea of what the implications would be until I got back to the barracks and we all started talking about it. Then the reality set in: This means that we're at war. I do remember the general consensus was, "The stupid Japs. How could they do that? We'll wax their ass in ninety days." We were voicing our own propaganda. We had had too many toys

"Made in Japan." The Japanese were known for making shoddy goods, and so *they* were shoddy and couldn't possibly stand up against us.

By this time I'd already been accepted for flight school, although there had been a problem that past summer when I'd applied. The minimum height was five foot four inches, and I thought that I *was* five foot four inches. But my friends measured me. "No, you're not five-four. You're only five-three and seven-eighths."

So Curv Miller, a learned individual from Pocono Pines, Pennsylvania, said, "I just read an article that says you're much taller in the morning when you get up than during the day when you're working. So we're going to make you lie flat. At the last minute, we're going to dress you and then take you over there to get you measured." Well, they not only kept me flat at the barracks, they even put me on a board and carried me to the flight surgeon's office. Then they propped me up and immediately told the orderly to measure me before I shrank. When he measured me, I was still five foot three and seven-eights. Of course, he wouldn't change it to five foot four. "No, no. I ain't going to do nothing like that. You're five-three and seven-eighths."

Then I saw the flight surgeon. I'm stark naked there in his examination office, and he has me turn around, I guess to check my build, my shoulders, and so on. He asked me how old I was; I told him I was eighteen. And he said, "Promise me you'll grow another eighth of an inch." I said, "Yes, sir." He changed it to five foot four, and that was it. From that moment on, I was officially tall enough. The doctor could have said, "No, you don't go," but he knew that at eighteen I still had some growing to do. I fulfilled the promise. I did grow the other eighth of an inch, and maybe a little bit more. But then, as time goes on, I'm back to where the hell I started.

I graduated from Flight School December 15 of '42. My first assignment was as an instructor at Laredo Army Airfield, in Laredo, Texas. Three of us were sent there, and we didn't like it.

We wanted to get into the war. Remember, we were only twenty years old. We figured if we were there, we'd all be aces and win the war. We certainly didn't want to be instructors. We figured that was a duty for the old-timers, because some of my instructors were from World War I.

We'd go to Nuevo Laredo, in Mexico, to let off steam. I believed in it. I guess that was my Croatian upbringing. Croatians are noted for their hard work and a good-time lifestyle. I think it makes you a levelheaded individual. We worked real hard. In the wintertime we would report for work when it was dark, and we wouldn't finish until it was dark again. We'd go back to the barracks, change our clothes, wash up, and head for town. It took at the most a half an hour to be in Mexico; we would take a bus down to the bridge and then we'd walk across. Then it was a matter of maybe two hundred yards to the Cadillac Bar, which was our headquarters.

I spent two years stationed in Laredo. During that time I went to Tennessee to learn how to fly the B-24. It was recommended that whoever flew a B-24 had to be at least five foot eight inches and 160 pounds, because it was a big airplane and it had a big cockpit. I weighed 120, and I was five-four. Again, here's this challenge, this damn big airplane. No one's going to tell me I can't do it.

When I get there, Captain Frecker looks at me and he says, "How tall are you?"

I says, "I'm five-eight."

"How much do you weigh?"

"One-sixty."

And he says, "You know what we want. Now we're going to see if you can do it."

At the end of the training, he gave me my final check ride. I still have the notation on my flight record: "Lieutenant Novosel, in spite of being of small stature, is an above-average B-24 aircraft commander." That's in black and white. But really, I could not reach the pedals. You had to be able to push all the way down on the pedals to stop. So I got cushions that allowed me to sit forward.

I went back to Laredo to become an instructor on the B-24, then was recruited to be a flight-test engineering pilot—I'd fly aircraft that had been through maintenance and repair to see if they functioned correctly.

By late '44, I knew that the B-29s were going overseas to fight Japan. I had first seen the B-29 flying in late '43 in Dalhart, Texas. Well, it was such a big airplane that I wanted a piece of it. Toward the end of '44, they were asking for volunteers, so I asked my boss about it, and he says, "No way. I can't spare you." By this time we could see that the war was going to be winding down. The emphasis on our training of gunners had lessened—there were no longer the big classes that we had, and that was because the Germans no longer had fighter planes in the air. The news from all fronts—Europe and the Pacific—was that the enemy was going backward and we were going forward. I figured, "If I'm going to be a part of this war, I better go now."

I knew that the levies were coming down for B-29 volunteers. I finally made up my mind when my boss left the base for a conference. I called the personnel major, who I knew really well, and said, "Put me down in the next levy of B-29s."

And he said, "Does Colonel Todd know about this?"

I lied. "Of course he knows about it. I wouldn't be calling otherwise."

Three days later—before the colonel came home—I was gone.

I trained on the B-29 at Maxwell Field, Montgomery, Alabama. That's where I met my copilot and then my flight engineer. We trained together as a unit there. Then the rest of the crew we met at Kirtland Army Air Field in New Mexico. It was my job to mold this group into a combat team. We had about six weeks. We got along so damn well. It's just amazing how we never had a problem. Never. We would go out and bar-hop together. We knew that we weren't supposed to fraternize together—officers and enlisted men—but if we met together somewhere in town, we certainly didn't ignore one another.

The early part of July—I guess it was around the fourth—we

flew out on a transport plane, a C-54, to the island of Tinian, in the South Pacific. Tinian was narrow, long, and flat, forty square miles in size.

We started flying missions right away. In all, we flew three bombing missions, and on each one we had seven tons of mixed ordnance. We set out absolutely to destroy Tokyo, there's no doubt about it. And we did. There was nothing of substance left. There were some concrete buildings, but they were shells. The interiors were gutted.

They had actually built the equivalent of a square block of a typical Japanese city at Eglin Field, right here in Fort Walton Beach, on what we call Range 52, and set about trying to find the best mix of bombs to destroy it. And that is where they came up with this mix of general-purpose bombs, incendiaries, and delayed action. The GPs would blow up a sufficient amount of the building material that would then splinter and be ready to be set on fire by the incendiaries. In the ensuing holocaust, the buildings themselves, some of them made of concrete, would be damaged severely. Then, when the firefighters came, they wouldn't know when the heck the delayed-action bombs would be going off.

We were flying at only about seven thousand feet, but you could just barely hear the thud of the larger bombs. I've occasionally visualized what was happening on the ground, but it's nothing that stays with me or bothers me at all. When you're in a war such as we were, a war that we knew we had to win, you're only thinking of the job that you have. In my case it was maintaining my control over my crew, making sure that I was on time—time was one of the things that were important—that I was at my proper altitude; in other words, that I accomplished my mission. That's what I was trained to do since I had started in this business. From my eighteenth to my twenty-second birthday, all I knew was war.

We certainly knew what was going on. We knew in the early stages of the war that we were losing. That's a hard thing to accept. And we were elated when we saw that we were changing this around, that we were no longer backing up, now we were advancing. A lot of people don't think about that. They think that World War II was a snap, which we, in our American way and in our American destiny, were bound to win. So there was no sweat. It was no big deal.

Demoralizing the population was probably a hoped-for result of the firebombing. We'll never know if it achieved its purpose, since we never did have to invade. We knew that we were planning to. We knew that since the war in Europe had ended, there were big movements involved with bringing troops over to these different island groupings for the jump-off to the eventual invasion of Japan. However, all that was set aside after the use of the two atomic bombs on the sixth and ninth of August.

We soon realized this meant the war was finished. We certainly knew by the time the fifteenth came around, because that's when the emperor spoke to his people about the enemy having a "cruel bomb." He was letting them know that he wanted the war to end and asked them to "cultivate the ways of rectitude."

Living in those times and being a part of the offensive against Japan, one weapon was no more powerful, in the final analysis, than another. Sure, we could come up with measurements. But it's like a serial murderer. What's the difference if the man kills twelve or if he kills twenty-six? The deed is done. You don't measure the violence of war by how many people are killed in an offensive as long as you're successful. And our success was partly due—*partly,* I say *partly*—to so many hundreds of thousands of people being killed. What is the difference between Hiroshima on one side and Dresden on the other side? The difference is the number. And then you might say the difference was how. The difference was the intensity of the heat. You'd go on and on with no conclusion except that it was a necessary act of war. If humanity can find no better method to settle differences than war, so be it. At that point it has got to be moral. This is a contradiction in terms. How can it be moral when you're killing people? And yet we believe in the morality of war. That's a strange term, isn't it? But it must be so. The United States is not an immoral nation. If it believed war to be immoral, it would not have gone to war six times in less than a hundred years.

I have faith that humanity will come up with another answer. If every well-thinking individual thinks about it, if leaders of nations think about it, they will set war aside because really—and this is no cliché—there's no winner in war, in the final analysis.

I piloted one of the 462 B-29s that flew over the battleship *Missouri* on September 2, 1945, when Douglas MacArthur accepted the surrender of the Japanese. It was the day before my twenty-third birthday. We flew at a thousand feet in eleven-ship formations—each had an inverted V of three ships leading, with a four-ship diamond on either side of the V. A mile behind them, another eleven would come. Other types of planes flew over the *Missouri* that day also. After we passed over, I flew in a big racetrack pattern and we came around a second time. That was my longest mission ever: seventeen hours and ten minutes.

We could hear everything being said on the ship—it was broadcast up to us—but at the time I was more interested in keeping my formation spot right. It was only on the last, maybe two hours of the flight, when I realized, "Hey, we were a part of history." For all practical purposes, the war had ended in the middle of August, when the emperor said, "I accept your terms, I surrender." But symbolically, this was it: The war is now over. We are victorious.

I still remember MacArthur's words on the *Missouri.* Oh, he had a command of the English language that was terrific. He talked about mankind and conflict and all that. And I remember how he finished it: "These proceedings are closed."

The war certainly matured me. It instilled in me a level of responsibility. And it was such an easy thing for me to grab hold of my responsibility. A lot of people think of responsibility as being a chore. I thought it was emblematic of my lifestyle. I was twenty-three years old when I took command of the Ninety-ninth Bomb Squadron on Tinian just after the war. I decided, "I've never done this before, but I know what I have to do." I ran the damn squadron for well over a year. And inside a couple months of taking command, I moved the whole outfit—seventeen B-29s, six hundred officers and men, all their tents, all their paraphernalia, all the maintenance equipment—about fifteen hundred miles to Luzon, in the Philippines.

My first time back in the States was in the summer of '47, when I made a flight to deliver a war-weary airplane to an airplane graveyard.

It was nonstop from Hawaii to Pyote, Texas. Well, you see stateside for the first time in two years, and you know that they're getting up in the morning, and they go to work, and when the work is done they go home, and they're probably having their beer and their cocktails, or they're playing golf, or the kids are playing softball. The everyday life back in the States—which we certainly have no way of duplicating in the Philippines. First of all, in the Philippines, it's all war-ravaged. You go to downtown Manila, everything is destroyed. You can actually get a good dinner at the Manila Hotel, but the walls are propped up with scaffolding and whatnot. And the number of times I went into Manila from Clark Field was maybe a half a dozen in a year. It was a rare occasion.

And in the Philippines, when we got beer, it was a horrible, horrible dark beer, in cans, which would usually be rusted. It was made of tiger piss, I think. But I remember that I used to see those ads with the tall, brown Budweiser bottle, and the moisture coming down. . . . Man, I used to dream about that.

That was the first thing I got in Texas. And of course a big steak. There was only one restaurant there, Pyote Joe's. We told Pyote Joe, "Give us the biggest steak you got." It was set on one of those platters that are oblong, made of thick crockery—they weigh a ton. The steak folded over every bit of that. Each of us on the crew got one.

By the time we got back to the Philippines, we found out that our unit was being disbanded. I finally got to come home to stay around the end of '47. Less than a month later, I got married to my childhood sweetheart.

I was certainly planning on a career in the service. I was stationed here at Eglin, and in the fall of 1949 they sent me to Air Tactical School at Tyndall Air Force Base, which is seventy-five miles away. I learned management principles, public speaking, principles of atomic energy, because that was new at the time. Only your cream of the crop, so to speak, is supposed to go to that school.

But in December, a week before graduation, I got word of a Reduction in Force. RIFs were something that in those days were going on with some degree of regularity, because we were still downsizing from World War II. The squadron had to get rid of two officers. When the adjutant called to tell me I was being RIF'd, I said, "Why did the CO pick me?"

"I don't know exactly," he says, "but you've been gone at school for three or four months and he figures he could get along without you."

The first day out, in February of '50, I opened a restaurant. It was a combination of drive-in and sit-down. Hamburgers, hot dogs, soda fountain, milk shakes. I hadn't had restaurant experience as such, but I'd been a mess officer.

Four months later the Korean War started. Now they really need me, but they can't have me. But then eventually I did join the reserves, and then eventually I went and served a short tour during the Korean War. I volunteered. I thought it was my duty.

They made me a test pilot here at Eglin Field. We were testing bombs, ammunition, navigational equipment.

I stayed in about half a year—the first half of '53. By then they were coming close to an armistice and I said, "In that case, if I can, I'll get out and return home." And I did so. This time I stayed in the reserves. Number one, I wanted to keep my hand in flying. The other thing was that it was a way to get promoted, and I was. I was kicked out as a captain, and five years later I was a lieutenant colonel.

By the mid-fifties, in addition to having the restaurant, I'd expanded into other businesses. But I decided to get out of them. By now I had three children, and you might say I woke up to the fact that "Damn, I've been so busy, I hardly remember when my children were born." So I started looking for a flying job, and I went to work as a commercial pilot for Southern Airways.

Then came the Kennedy assassination. His death affected me greatly. The damn funeral was something. I'll always remember that little kid of his saluting. My God, he's what, three years old? And there he is, standing straight and saluting his old man. And I thought of the words "Ask not what your country can do for you—ask what you can do for your country."

I know this might seem far-fetched to some people, but I took those words to heart. I always prided myself on being a man who really, truly put my money where my mouth is. A lot of people say, "I shoulda done this" or "I shoulda done that," and I say, "Why the hell didn't you?" I had the skill. I'll admit, this was rare. Few people could fly and instruct in all of the types of aircraft that we had, and I just happened to be one of those people. That was my desire, to help out and instruct these youngsters who would be a part of the war effort in Vietnam.

I thought it was a noble cause, and I knew we would be drawn into that war. I could see the way it was building up. As an example, flying for the airline, I had an overnight once in Mobile, Alabama. And I saw a TV special on helicopter gunships raking with gunfire a canal where the Vietcong were passing by. Well, I had flown helicopters before, and I'd never dreamed that we would use them in an attack situation. I decided to volunteer my services.

I went to the Air Force and said, "I want active duty," and they said, "You've got too much rank, we can't use you." In other words, I would upset the applecart. I'd been a lieutenant colonel for over nine years. If I came into the Air Force, right away every lieutenant colonel that has less than nine years of service would be behind me for promotion purposes, and that would upset a helluva lot of people.

They also implied that I was too old, which didn't sit well with me.

I let it go at that. But it just so happened that a friend of mine said, "Hell, if you really want to do your part, you can go to the Army, because they are desperate for pilots." And I looked into the situation and found out they were really and truly desperate—for pilots of all kinds of aircraft, helicopter and fixed-wing. To show how desperate they were, they took me on my forty-second birthday. I thought that I would be used as an instructor, in the States.

The Army made me a warrant officer, which is neither fish nor fowl. We have the enlisted men and the noncommissioned officers—the privates up through corporals and sergeants. And then we have second lieutenant and so on. Now, the warrant officer slides in between there. He is a technician. He is a specialist. My specialty as a warrant officer was flying helicopters, and I accepted that.

I was initially assigned to Special Forces, in Fort Bragg, North Carolina, practicing night insertions of troops and so on. Special Forces aviation at that time was strictly stateside; in Vietnam, Special Forces were advisers, and not aviation-oriented. So it came as a complete surprise when, at the end of '65, I got orders to Vietnam.

By now I'm convinced that this is not what I meant when I volunteered, but then I realized, well, there was nothing I could do about it. I suppose I could've gone to my headquarters and said, "This is not what I bargained for." But I never shied away from any assignment. I still wasn't expecting a combat role. No, I figured there were so many things that Army aviation was capable of, in Vietnam or anyplace. I had no idea, because I was going unassigned.

Saying good-bye to my wife was not pleasant at all. But I left her in a nice house and in a place that she liked. By this time Mike was sixteen. I told him he was now the man of the house.

I remember that she is the one who brought up the idea that I might not come back. That really shocked me, because it had never dawned on me. And when I was in combat, I never thought that I would be hit. I don't know why. Hell, I saw a lot of people that got killed. But I just had every confidence that I was not one of those people.

The day after I arrive in Vietnam, I come into the replacement depot and my name is hollered out on the amplifier, and the voice says report to the head shed. I go over there, and this lieutenant says, "I'm Lieutenant Sawyer. I'm here to take you to the 283rd Med Detachment." He takes me right away to the CO, who says, "Welcome to the 283rd Dustoff." I say, "What is Dustoff?" Didn't know there was such an entity, didn't know there was such a word. Of course it was explained to me rather quickly.

Dustoff was accepted as the call sign for medical evacuation by helicopter. Normally an outfit would change its call sign every month. But early in the Vietnam War, it was decided that having a permanent call sign would make the job of medical evacuation easier. The call sign at that point happened to be Dustoff, so that's what it stayed. The individual pilots were given call signs with a number. I was given "Dustoff 300."

I guess I was there three days and I was in combat. I liked the challenge of flying this type of mission. The fact that we were there to help and not to hurt had a certain allure. The idea that we were the only ones dedicated to this type of work was another plus. There was also a certain element of derring-do—some people were afraid of that type work. No doubt about it, people looked up to us.

We flew day and night. In the Air Force way of doing things, you can't rearm during a thunderstorm, you can't even refuel. It could be raining cats and dogs—we'd refuel. We wouldn't even shut down to refuel. You got a little water in there, you drained it off.

We picked up the wounded in the midst of battle. Every

wound that is imaginable, we were acquainted with. Traumatic amputation, nothing unusual. Serious head wounds. Sucking chest wounds—that's a wound in the chest where there is a big hole, and when the man breathes, it sucks air. So you have to plug up that hole with something. This is the one time when a pack of cigarettes was useful. Put the whole pack of cigarettes right there, it was just the right size. Our medics did that many times, because in those days just about every soldier had a pack of cigarettes.

At first it was upsetting because it was so gory. If you look back at your deck, it is awash in blood. There is not just one man bleeding; every man that you have on board is bleeding in some fashion or another. But after a while the commonality of the wounds makes them unimpressive. "Hell, okay, there is another traumatic amputation." "Oh, there is another damn sucking chest wound."

If we knew we had nothing to do for the next five or ten minutes, we would on many occasions get a fire hose and wash the blood off the deck of the helicopter. If allowed to stay any length of time, it would start smelling.

Your flying day started at 6:00 A.M. That meant that you had to be showered and cleaned up and ready to go at five so you could get something to eat for breakfast, preflight your aircraft, and make yourself available. The next thing you know, someone slips you a piece of paper, and that would start it. You might get one mission to start, maybe two or three. Then the missions would keep on coming. I don't think I ever counted how many I had in a day. Let's put it this way: In two tours I flew 2,435 missions and I evacuated 5,589 wounded.

One time we were going to play bridge—myself, Joe Fulghum, Mickey Runion, and Father Quealy. This was in what we called the First Division, First Battalion, First Medical Battalion Officers' Club—it was a corner of our tent. When Father Quealy sat down, he was facing a lot of *Playboy* centerfolds hung up on the wall. And he said, "I can't stand this, I want to change seats." He made me sit where he was sitting.

A few weeks later I was the only one of the four still alive.

Mickey Runion was a dentist. As a matter of fact, he filled my teeth. He used a dental chair with a pedal-powered drill—we had captured it from the Vietcong. If you were a dentist out in the field in Vietnam, you didn't have a dental chair or much dental equipment. You could give cursory treatment, and that was it. He was real proud that he had the ability to fill teeth.

He volunteered to go as a medic on this one mission, and Joe Fulghum was the pilot. They were brought down by enemy fire, and when they hit the ground, the aircraft immediately exploded and everybody on board was killed outright.

Michael J. Quealy was a Catholic chaplain. If he happened to be around and he saw me or some other Dustoff cranking up, he would just run over there and jump on board. The reason he did that was to console the wounded, give them last rites, whether they were Catholic or not, if he thought they were dying. The way he figured, "Well, it won't hurt none." Could have been Jewish, could have been Muslim, he'd give 'em last rites.

And so it was that there was this big battle, and he jumped on board a helicopter. And he was killed. He was just filled with bullet holes. This happened while he was giving last rites to a wounded soldier. And I'd known this man. I'd played bridge with him, helped him say mass.

I very seldom took dead bodies, but I made a special effort to haul his body out. Later I was there when they were getting his personal effects together, and one of the chaplains said, "By the way, here's four of his cigars." He liked Tampa Nuggets, and there they were. And I said, "Give 'em to me. I'll smoke 'em for him." And that's what I did.

All you could do was put it out of your mind and keep on going. Father Quealy, I'll never forget him. Joe Fulghum and Mickey Runion, the same way.

You got a dentist who's not supposed to be in combat. He gets killed. A priest, he's not supposed to be in combat. He gets killed. I was present when two nurses were killed in a helicopter crash.

It was a crazy war.

When my tour of duty ended, I knew that I was done with war. I had promised my wife that that was it, I was going back to the airline as soon as my time was up.

I had my orders discharging me. Of course, I had to have a separation physical. So I go there, no sweat. I had just had a regular physical six months before, and everything was peaches and cream. This time everything's okay except that there is a mistake apparently with my eye pressure. They check it again and say, "No, there ain't a mistake. You have glaucoma."

Oh, shit. I immediately call the Federal Aviation Administration, and I say, "Can I have a waiver for glaucoma?" And they come back, "Are you shitting me? No way." That's a grounding condition. Just imagine if the FAA had allowed me to fly with glaucoma. There is no cure, and the end result of glaucoma, left to its own devices, is you're gonna go blind. Suppose I'm just taxiing an airliner, and I scratch a wingtip. The damn media gets hold of it and says, "Blind Pilot Flying for Southern Airways." In other words, my airline career was done.

I was also grounded by the Army. And I'm really in a bad way, because the Army has the authority to discharge me on medical grounds. Or I can get something that is very rare. According to Don Bissell, a friend in the Medical Service Corps, they do not ordinarily give waivers for glaucoma. But he manages to convince the general that he should give me a waiver, and it's the only one, to my knowledge, that they ever gave for that disease. I still remember General Meszar saying, "Major Bissell says that he and the doctors have decided that you really don't have to see as well as we do." So he signed the waiver, and I signed it. And once the waiver is in, it's in. I just had to take eyedrops four times a day.

I was assigned as an instructor at Hunter Army Airfield in Savannah, Georgia. After two years back in the States, I got the word that I was ordered back to Vietnam.

I was with a different unit, the Eighty-second Medical Detachment, with a different call sign, Dustoff 88, but doing the same work, absolutely the same, in an area that I was quite familiar with. But it was a totally different war now. It had become a nightmare of paper pushers.

Let's put it this way: During my first tour, if you could picture the list of recurring reports that were posted up on every orderly-room wall, let's say it was five or six inches long. But the second time that we went there, it would've been a foot and a half or two feet. They had more than tripled the number of recurring reports—reports that had to be submitted daily, reports that had to be submitted weekly, reports that had to come in every two weeks, reports that were due monthly. Reports, reports, reports.

We actually had a "hit report," with the outline of the helicopter on the piece of paper, and you had to show where the hits were and what direction they came from, and was it from down below or up above. And then the final question, was it enemy or friendly fire. Some man made this up to keep us busy and to keep him busy shuffling his papers. If there were any good reason for the hit reports, we would've been given the results, which we never were. I mean, that is prima facie evidence it was not necessary. These were nothing more than subterfuges these people came up with to authenticate their importance. I'm talking now about people who generally were field-grade officers—major, lieutenant colonel, colonel. Sitting at their desk, air-conditioned room, starched uniform, three meals a day in a nice restaurant with white tablecloths. And there were hundreds and thousands of those bastards.

So we just faked the reports. We were taking fire all the time, but we'd say there were no hits—just so we didn't have to mess with the reports.

There was all kinds of crap. You were supposed to have a weekly safety meeting. How the hell are you gonna have a safety meeting when everybody is flying all the time? So the report would go in: "Mr. So-and-so made the safety meeting at such and such a date with so many people." It was pure invention. It had to be. Otherwise we would've gone crazy. We had to have reports on voting—your responsibility as an American soldier was to vote. So whenever there was an election, we had to have a lecture. We didn't have one, but we showed that we did. And we had a "voting control officer."

A crazy war. You would see so many opposites—so many things that were bad, then almost immediately so many things that were good. Just the fact that I could be up to my hips in a rice paddy one minute, and wearing clean clothes and drinking gin and tonic or scotch and soda an hour later.

You laughed it off. It was nothing unusual to work all day, hauling nothing but wounded, and six o'clock comes, that's it, you're off, now the night shift's on. You go home, you clean up, and you say, "I think I'll go to Saigon to the Rex for dinner"—the Rex Hotel, the top floor of which served as an officers' club. And there is a wine bar. And there is a salad bar. Up on the stage there is a combo playing Viennese waltzes. The people in Saigon left nothing to chance. You might as well have been in New York—they had everything except Gallagher's.

This one day Charlie Wilson and I have been flying all afternoon. We go into the Rex and we're lucky, because we get a table right away. And, man, it was real nice. We ordered a bottle of Mateus wine, which was our favorite in those days over there, and ordered steak all around and whatnot, a salad. And at the same time, why, here is this major that asks us, "Is it okay to sit with you, because everything else is taken?"

We're nice and gentlemanly about it and we say, "Certainly, sit down." And Charlie says, "Yeah, and have a glass of wine with us." And this SOB looks at the damn menu and reads it, and then he gets mad, flops it down on the table, and says, "Same old shit."

Charlie and I think we're in hog heaven. But this guy lives at this place. A major! Oh, hell. Charlie right away took the wine away from him and says, "What an ungrateful son of a bitch. Leave this table." Just the fact that he didn't know how nice he had it, and he showed his ingratitude: "Same old shit." He was another REMF. We saw them all the time.

There was a corruption of the spirit over there. Take the base at Long Binh. The total population went as high as fifty thousand. All support, get that. It stretched for miles. They had a Mexican restaurant. And they had a Chinese restaurant. Why they had a Chinese restaurant, I don't know, because you'd go outside and find one. They had the regular mess halls and the regular officers' clubs, where you could find everything that you needed. There were a bunch of massage parlors. Someone in the service was running these parlors. I assumed that. I didn't go there, but we knew that they existed and that they had Vietnamese girls inside. Anybody who believed it was strictly a massage parlor was really naive.

If there was any liquor that was sidetracked, it was sidetracked up there. If there was fuel that was sidetracked, it was sidetracked there. Clothing, rations. You just couldn't have a complex that big with the South Vietnamese, knowing how they operated, without graft and corruption. It was just riddled with it.

On October 2, 1969, at about six in the morning, three ARVN companies went on a clearing operation right up against the border of Cambodia. Their objective was to get rid of a training complex that belonged to the Vietcong. As they began the attack, they were hit with such ferocity on both flanks that by about eight, the forward element had advanced too far, beyond its flank protection, and was cut off.

After this initial contact with the enemy, the commander of the ARVN forces judged that he didn't have enough men to complete the job, so he made the decision to abandon the troops that were cut off and retreat. In other words, they were left to their own devices. They lost radio contact. They soon expended all their ammunition. And now they were in hiding, clutching the ground, looking for any depression they might drop into to avoid the enemy fire.

The enemy was firing at them continuously, with mortars and automatic weapons and recoilless rifles and a .50-caliber antiaircraft weapon. The enemy was well supplied with ammunition because, remember now, this was right on the border. Their main force was on the other side, in Cambodia. So the Vietcong commander could call back to the people in Cambodia, "I need this" or "I need that," and he would get it.

Our side was supported by Air Force fighter-bombers and by Army gunships. They were there when this initial onslaught took place but soon had to return back to base for rearming and refueling. I don't know how much support they gave as the day went on, but by the time I got the mission, at four in the afternoon, they had tried desperately to get these troops out somehow but could find no way to do it.

They finally decided, "The only thing left for us is to try to get a Dustoff up here." We couldn't do any better than they could. After all, we were completely unarmed, and what they needed was an armed force to go in there and relieve those troops. But get this: When they asked for Dustoff, that meant one ship. And that was me.

Of course I have to be briefed as to what's going on, and that's when I find out that nothing I need for a successful evacuation of troops is present. I don't have any cover. The troops themselves can't give me any cover, and there are no friendly troops in the area to give me cover. There are no Air Force fighter-bombers in the area to give me cover, no Army gunships to give me cover. There is no one to pop smoke to show me where they are. It was nothing unusual to have an evacuation where some of the elements necessary for a proper pickup were not there. We lived with that situation. However, to my knowledge, we had never had a case where *everything* was missing. And time was critical—I couldn't wait for support to show up.

Also, there is no one on the ground I can communicate with, because they've abandoned their radio. Besides, they're all Vietnamese troops, and I don't speak Vietnamese. When the operation started, there had been American advisers, but they'd either avoided the trap or been killed.

We did have a command-and-control ship, up above me, circling, and he could discern through his binoculars some—not all—of the wounded troops that were hiding. And every one of them that was left behind was wounded, either as a result of the ambush or the cutoff maneuver of the enemy, or later through the impact of grenades, mortars, and so on, because the enemy was really laying into them.

All right. The C&C tells me that he sees one wounded well inside the complex. This man had no doubt penetrated as far into this area as anybody else did, so that gave me the idea that he was probably the advance man, and the rest of the surrounded people were behind him. But I couldn't see any of them.

So I was asked to try to get this one man. Well, I dive down to him, and I mean I dive—the nose of the helicopter is pointed almost straight down at him. At the same time, I want to make myself a bad target, and so I maneuver like a falling leaf, zigzagging my way down.

I go from two thousand feet down to nothing in half a minute at most. And when I come down to the bottom, I stop the descent real quick and hover.

The C&C says, "You're right over top of him." And as I'm hovering, the enemy opens up on me from what we call "around the clock"—their positions that are all around me.

I expect this man to leap up and get on board. But he sees my aircraft being hit by enemy fire and he figures, "Hell, I'm safer down here than up there." And he stays where he is. Besides that, I can't see him because my rotor wash is folding the elephant grass on top of him.

It's a no-win situation, he's not getting on. So I've got to get out of there, and I do. And in getting out of there, I make a right turn without any hesitation. And that's when they really open up on me. I say to the C&C, "They're most unfriendly over here." And he says, "Yeah, you just crossed the border into Cambodia. That's where the main force is." He then convinced me that I should try again to get that one man; I did, and the results were the same. Well, it was evident that his method was not going to work. He wanted to direct me to every individual that he could spot—a nice idea, but it just was not going to work.

I decided to try something else. After talking it over with my crew, we returned to the area, but now I'm skidding on the ground in a gigantic racetrack pattern, which I figured covered all the area where our troops are.

Just kept going, never stopped. First one man stood up, and the medic and crew chief yanked him on board. And no doubt the others saw that happen, and now they got the message. So if they wanted to be saved, when they saw that I was getting close to them, they would stand up and get yanked on board. We were skidding right on the ground. I might lift up because of an obstacle, too much grass or something, but essentially I'm on the ground, and I keep moving. There is no problem in this maneuver, it takes no special skill.

Sure enough, we get about ten people on board. But ten people, that's a load. I don't mean the helicopter can't carry more, but it's crowded, and the people are all wounded.

By now I needed fuel anyhow, so I decided to take them over to a Special Forces camp nearby. Dropped them off where they really could get care, and we got more fuel. Just about half the tank—I wanted to stay as light as possible. You want mobility to maneuver better.

Returned for a second time, doing the same thing. Again, all this time we're under fire. You can feel the hits. Got a second load and extracted them. And then refueled again. We're back the third time.

Now, the third time we finally got the cover that we expected: the Air Force F-100s returned. They said that they had been detained by weather, and they couldn't take off, and they're sorry, but they're here to give me some help. I said, "Good. Hit that enemy bunker over there." And they said, "We'll do that, but you have to get out of there." It was a conflict of standard operating procedures.

I was ignoring my SOPs; I wanted them to attack this one section of enemy positions while I continued my circular maneuvering to pick up the wounded. I figured that would keep the enemy heads down. Well, they wouldn't do that, because their regulation said they cannot bomb when I'm on the ground.

To me that was silly, especially when I was the one who directed them and wanted them to hit a certain area. In a nutshell, I had more faith in their ability than they had in themselves. I had to go back up to circle, like the C&C, and watch them do their thing. Well, all their real good intentions, as far as I was concerned, weren't worth a damn, because as soon as they were finished, and they told me, "Okay, we're done, you can go down now," I went back down and nothing had changed.

Anyhow, I go in a third time to retrieve these people and pick up eight or nine. By now it's getting dark. After we make one final circuit without picking anybody up, I say, "It looks like we're through for the night."

Then my crew chief says, "We see a man behind us waving a shirt." I could continue to circle and get him as I come back around, but he's only about fifty meters away and I'm in a hurry to get this thing over with. So I hover that aircraft backwards to him. The thing was, he was real close to the enemy position, and I fully expected to be subjected to fire as I got near him. If I was hovering backwards, I thought, when the enemy opened up on me, all the projectiles would have to pass through my tail column and through the fuel cell before they reached the freight compartment where we were. By that time the bullets would be spent.

That was a good idea, right? Except it didn't work, because the damn enemy had set up a man at about my eleven-o'clock position, about thirty meters away. And the instant I came to a stop to make the pickup, the enemy soldier slid up from the grass and emptied his AK-47 at me—me personally—through the windshield. Three of the bullets hit on the inside of my seat armor on both sides of me. How the hell did that happen? I was wearing a chicken plate, but my seat was armored to deflect bullets that were fired at me from the rear and from either side, not from the front. The rounds made a big hole in the glass in front of me, and somehow or another they had to separate a little bit to be on both sides of me. In other words, they basically didn't hit me. But one bullet fragment nicked my right hand, which was holding the stick, and that caused me to pull the stick back. Also, a bullet glanced off the sole of my left foot, and shrapnel got my right leg around the knee; these hits caused my legs to move spasmodically, the left pulling back and the right thrusting forward, pressing the pedal in. All this was happening simultaneously. And the combination of the stick back and pedal forward caused the aircraft to suddenly slue to the right and up.

The man that was being pulled on board, now he slipped out. But his leg straddled the skids, and my crew chief never let loose. My copilot and I wrestled the aircraft back under control, and by the time the crew chief got the man back on board, we were sixty feet in the air. That was the end of the mission.

We made it back to the Special Forces camp, and the aircraft was severely damaged; essentially it was shot away. They knocked out two of my radios and my airspeed indicator. I told the crew chief and my copilot, "Check this aircraft out, and when you tell me that it's flyable, we're going back home."

They said, "You can't fly it home. You've got all this battle damage, and you have no airspeed indicator."

I said, "Forget about it. We don't have to know how fast we're going. I know we'll go fast enough."

We couldn't leave yet—it took at least two hours on the ground to check that aircraft out. Actually, we needed the rest. I needed the rest. This was really fatiguing, man. I know the first thing I asked for was a cup of coffee. That's all I wanted. One of the Special Forces guys got me a canteen full of it. I just sat there and sipped on that thing, relaxing. It was better than wine. It's amazing how the simplest of things, in some instances, can be so pleasurable.

The ride home wasn't dangerous. I parked the aircraft and went to the hospital and had myself examined and my wounds painted up with iodine—my whole right leg was painted, because there were about fifty holes there from the Plexiglas and the bullet fragments. They didn't bother to do anything for my hand.

I made my after-action reports. When all was said and done, it was probably 1:30 A.M. We'd been on duty since five o'clock the previous morning, and the last time I had anything to eat was that breakfast at five o'clock. We were too damn busy to eat. Just going on nervous energy.

I tried to sleep, and all I was doing was reliving the whole damn day and feeling like I was on dope. Elated. A sense of great euphoria. Especially having missed being hit all those times. There were so many things flashing through my mind. I poured myself a couple of drinks and finally did get to sleep at three o'clock in the morning or thereabouts. I intended to get up early so I could take pictures of my damaged aircraft—I wanted to have a souvenir. But I overslept, and by the time I got up and was ready to take a picture, the aircraft was gone. They had already evacuated it, taken it to the junk pile, and no one had bothered to take a picture of it.

At the time, I didn't think this mission was anything special. What I was doing at that battle site, I'd done at many other battle sites. Maybe not in that exact manner, but picking up wounded while being fired on? We did it all the time.

However, the next day, when I had a chance to talk about it to my commanding officer, I said, "I think that my crew deserves some recognition, because they worked their ass off yesterday, and they did some fine work."

And he said, "Don't forget, now, according to the system, if they get an award, you have to include yourself, since you were in charge." So I just recommended the whole crew, each of them, to get the Silver Star because I thought they deserved it, which, incidentally, was the only time I recommended anybody for a major award in that whole year.

They were all decorated. The medic and crew chief got the Silver Star. The copilot got either the Silver Star or the Distinguished Service Cross. We were all working together. I never knew that word would be filtered to General Abrams, because a Silver Star recommendation would not go to him.

But he heard about the mission, I don't know how. And he was the one—so I'm told—who recommended me for the Medal of Honor. It was over a year and a half later when I was notified of it. I received it from President Nixon in a ceremony at the White House, June 15, 1971.

I was recognized for an unusual mission that you wouldn't do every day. I knew that if I refused to do it, no one could fault me. Because nothing was in my favor. I could have refused it just for one item, and I had half a dozen. But I also knew that if I didn't take it, the people would be dead. It was as simple as that. Now, does that mean I'm worthy of a medal? I don't know. You be the judge of that yourself. I won't be the judge.

I knew my son Mike wanted to be a pilot, and I knew damn well that if he watched himself and did right he would graduate. He kept me posted as to what he was doing and who he was flying with, and I knew his instructors. He would really have to be a dumb shit to wash out. I'm not saying it was an easy course, but he knew what he was doing.

I was in Vietnam, on my second tour, when he graduated flight school, December 15, 1969, same month, same day that I did, twenty-seven years earlier.

I knew he was coming over in January. I was surprised when the assignments officer called. He says, "Your son wants to be assigned to your unit. Do you have any objections?"

I say, "No, send him right down."

To be truthful, I wasn't even thinking. It's just that the opportunity to have him there appealed to me. We'd be together. And then it dawned on me: Damn, this has all kinds of serious repercussions.

Hell, I liked to party, and now he was gonna come over, and, well, he'd be writing his mother. The goddamn letters better match up. Let's say that I write, "I've been to a party tonight. I had a good time." And Mike writes, "We were at a party. We had a good time. The place was packed with nurses."

Never were there father and son pilots assigned to the same unit flying combat together. If you think about it, this was almost impossible to occur. It took two wars. We both had to be pilots. We both had to survive a very strong training program that eliminates you at the drop of a hat. We both had to be warrant officers—under ordinary circumstances, I, the father, should've been a colonel at least, a rank I gave up to join the Army in 1964.

But more than that, the old man—me—had to be in good physical condition. Remember, by the time he graduated, I was forty-seven. I certainly wasn't old, but most people who had started flying when I did were retired by then. And of those who had not retired, most were not in physical condition to continue flying. Our situation will never happen again, I'm sure of that.

In the Eighty-second Med Detachment my second tour, I practically ran the unit. I was not the de jure commander, I was the de facto commander—with the acquiescence of the commander who had brought me over there. I was his right-hand man. If I saw something wrong, I'd correct it. If I spoke, whatever I said was his word.

But my position in the unit didn't cause a problem with Mike, because we were sensible enough to avoid it. As a matter of fact, when we first talked to each other in my quarters, I let him know, "This is a small outfit. We work our ass off here. You're gonna have all kinds of missions, and you're gonna have to take 'em one at a time, same as everybody else. There'll be no favoritism." Our personal relationship was never an issue. He never asked for anything special. He saw the duty roster, and he could read as well as anybody else.

The first two times that he flew, we were together. This was my method of bringing new people in—all the new people flew with me two times. I gave them the information that I wanted them to understand and to know. From the get-go I explained the situation sufficiently so that there was no doubt in any new pilot's mind what he was up against.

And then periodically I would fly with the new men. I alternated, made sure that I flew with all of them, just to check how they were working. That was my method of keeping control.

One thing I stressed was how you communicated. In a war zone, people get into the habit of getting excited and speaking in a very high voice. I recognized this as being not helpful. If you do it that way, then the other guy gets antsy, too. So I used to talk in a very subdued voice—to calm the situation. It pisses me off to see captains screaming into a damn microphone about some damn Iraqi plane that they're trying to shoot down. You can't even understand them. You could understand a Dustoff pilot—if he was from the Eighty-second, I'll guarantee you.

I assigned Mike to fly copilot with Rex Smith. I wanted Mike to make a good team with a good man, and Rex Smith was a good man.

One day the two of them happened to be flying in support of an operation, and I was about ten miles distant with another operation. And I heard Rex Smith come up with a Mayday—he had been hit and had to go down.

I got on the phone right away. I said, "Rex, I'll be there to pick you up in a jiffy. In the meantime try to make it to a safe area."

He makes it down okay, no problem. About a minute later, I come in there. I land right next to them, pick 'em up, and get 'em out of there.

Once the situation is all concluded, you have relief that everything's okay, and you get flippant. I said, "You guys are bothering the hell out of me, taking me away from my very important work, inconveniencing me. You owe me a drink tonight." So they paid for the drinks, and that lets everybody know that I went to pick up Mike and his aircraft commander and his crew.

I shouldn't have made them buy the drinks, because what goes around comes around. Seven days later *I'm* forced down, and Mike and Rex come to rescue *me.* Someone radios back, and by the time we get home, everybody knows about it. Con Jaburg says, "What kind of a record are you trying to set?" This was an ongoing thing with Con. When Mike came over there, he said, "Damn, that's really something, father and son in the same unit." And then, when Mike gets shot down and I save him, he says, "Isn't it enough that you're together as father and son here? Now you have to go and save him when he gets shot down!" And then, of course, when I'm down and I'm rescued by them, he starts off on it again. We had a big night, and I bought all the drinks.

Saying good-bye to Mike—oh, that was not a good scene. Neither one of us liked it. We were both in a hurry to get it over with. He flew me to Forty-fifth Medical Company in Long Binh, where I was going to rest up a couple of days before reporting to Bien Hoa for the bird home. He went to refuel, and then he came back and said, "I'm ready to go." And that was it. I didn't give him any particular advice. I'd given him words of wisdom all along, and he knew it.

We were at Bragg when Mike came home. I was a pilot for the Golden Knights, the Army parachute-demonstration team. We didn't have any special party. For one thing, he was too tired. His mother was all giddied up and thrilled to have him back, but I guess the emotion was enough to sap all of her energy, too. I remember what he said: "I didn't get any medals, but I'm here in one piece."

That was all his mother wanted. That was all I wanted.

The first tour I don't think that I came away with any idea that the Vietnam War would not be concluded to our satisfaction. That doesn't mean I thought it would end with a big victory parade; I was a realist enough to know that. When I went back for my second tour, I knew we weren't doing well, so I was more determined than ever to do all I could to help. That's the reason we flew the way we did. Then, by the time the second tour was completed, I was at a loss to explain just what the heck was going to happen. If someone had asked me, "Are we any closer to victory? Do you think we'll close this thing out in the next year or the year after?" I couldn't have told them. I would have had doubts that anybody could've concluded our endeavors over there.

We were tar-babied into that damn war. Remember Brer Rabbit from *Uncle Remus*? He hit the tar baby. His hand got stuck. How did he get out of it? He hit again. Now he's got two hands stuck. Then he puts out his feet, and they get stuck. First we had a few raids, then we had a few advisers. The advisers felt that they needed some help. We sent in a Marine division up in the northern section, sent in the 173rd Airborne. Then we sent in the First Division—the Big Red One—and the Twenty-fifth Division.

We never expected it to develop into the immense situation that it did. President Johnson thought in all seriousness that a couple of good raids would be enough to bring these people to their knees. Evidently he had not studied the problems the French endured in the years that they were fighting the Vietminh, the predecessors, if you will, of the Vietcong. It was unbelievable that the Vietminh could bring sufficient force to bear to oust the French, yet they did. We made the second effort to get rid of Ho Chi Minh and the Communists. We first tried to hold them back to the seventeenth parallel diplomatically—he had everything north of the seventeenth parallel, and we, essentially, controlled everything south of the seventeenth parallel. The division was supposed to be temporary, and an election was scheduled to be held two years later to choose the government of a unified country. When it was known that the election would not turn out in our favor, we canceled it.

I like to use the analogy of our own revolution. Suppose when George Washington had taken the sword of Cornwallis, a group of foreign pirates would've told him, "You can have everything north of the Mason-Dixon Line, but the rest is ours." What would George have done? Well, that's exactly what we did to Ho Chi Minh with the seventeenth parallel. I think you can see it was not gonna work. In the American Revolution, we were trying to get rid of the British. Ho was trying to get rid of the white man's colonialism.

It didn't matter to him if the white man was French or American. We were still white. Of course, our thinking at the time was that if he won, the place would go Communist. Yet the people were willing to take on life under the Communist system, because that way at least it would be Vietnamese Communism and not the white man's capitalism or, as they viewed it, the extension of the white man's colonial empire.

We knew that he was a Communist when we got his help against the Japanese. We appreciated all the work that he did in that regard. He helped to evacuate downed American pilots. He was an ally. When he declared the independence of his country after World War II was concluded, he quoted directly from our own Declaration of Independence.

Ho and his followers were revolutionaries with a legitimate rationale for their revolution. And they had come to the West first for assistance. If the West had been smart, if it had played chess rather than checkers, then it would have gone along with them. But when the West refused the aid, the next course of action was to go to the Communists. And the Communists said, "Did you go over to see the capitalists of the West?"

"Yes, we did, and they turned us down."

"Okay, we'll help you."

We were victimized by the mind-set of the Cold War. If it was Russian, it was no good. We had forgotten that these people helped us win World War II. As a matter of fact, history was almost rewritten. When you think about all the American World War II movies and World War II books, you very seldom see the Russian contribution.

Get this: I would say close to 80 percent of the German aircraft destroyed in that war were destroyed by the Russians. Eighty percent of the German soldiers killed, were killed by the Russians. That left the Western Allies with approximately 20 percent. There are some people in America—I'm serious—who actually believe that we could have whipped Hitler by ourselves. The attention span of the Americans, I'm sorry to say, is really short, and they absolutely do not like history. I don't know why. It is such a fascinating subject.

As a GI, as a combatant in World War II, I want to remind you that Americans used to cheer when they heard that the Russians were having a one-hundred-gun salute in Moscow for the retaking of a certain town. Why were we cheering? We knew it meant we were one day closer to the end of the war.

All this is forgotten for the sake of the Cold War. It doesn't make sense to a man who has lived through that period to see friends all of a sudden become enemies. The Vietnam War was an outgrowth of this hard-nosed attitude—on our side and on the Russian side. We should've been getting together long before that. But we didn't. We were jockeying for position, trying to outmaneuver one another. That's what brought on the war in Korea and the stalemate that it produced.

The Vietnam War lasted as long as it did because we knew that if we pulled out, we were going to be labeled a loser. So we delayed as long as we could, trying to find a mysterious panacea by which we could come out gracefully. I don't know if there was anything graceful about the way we concluded that war. We did get our prisoners of war back, and that in itself is a sad story, because we had to use them as a pawn in the negotiations. I think collectively the country recognizes the Vietnam War was a waste of effort. After all, we gave up on it. If it wasn't a waste, what else was it? If it really meant something for us, we'd still be there.

I have often asked myself if some of those guys I evacuated were so horribly maimed that they hate me for keeping them alive. I don't think they do. There might be some, but I'll have to take that as part of the system. The recovery of most of them was total, and most of them are glad that we in Dustoff were there. A while ago I got an E-mail from a "head wound" I evacuated out of a hot battle my first tour. I assure you that if I hadn't been where I was when he was wounded, and if he were forced to make that trip the old-fashioned way—being carried on a litter to an aid station—my God, he would not have made it.

This man writes to me:

> **In the summer of 1966, I was a platoon leader in B Company 1st of the 26th Infantry, First Infantry Division. On 25 August, at Bong Trang, a VC playing dead was willing to blow himself up with a grenade in order to take me with him. As I was being put aboard a Dustoff, a doctor took my CO aside and told him that I had 3 chances out of 10 to live, and the numbers were falling fast. I was bleeding from over 18 major wounds, extending from my forehead to my ankles.**
>
> **Dustoff did their job that day for me.**
>
> **In September 1969 (3 years, 1 month, 19 days later) I returned to Bong Trang as CO of A Company, 1st of the 26th Infantry.**
>
> **I've never forgotten that Dustoff came in under fire, and by doing so allowed me to continue my military career. We all incur debts as soldiers. I've tried to pay mine by passing the obligations on.**
>
> **My thanks to you and to your compatriots.**
>
> **Tom Galvin**

Getting this letter is better than any medal. You can take all the medals and shove 'em up your ass.

II

"You just go get him. Period."

MIKE NOVOSEL JR.

MIKE NOVOSEL JR.

RETIRED CAREER MILITARY OFFICER; HELICOPTER PILOT, OFFSHORE OIL INDUSTRY
FORT WALTON BEACH, FLORIDA
CHIEF WARRANT OFFICER TWO, UNITED STATES ARMY, VIETNAM

In World War II, before helicopters were used as ambulances, about a fourth of all men who fell in the field of battle were killed in action, as opposed to wounded in action. In Korea, when limited use began, the number dropped to a fifth. In Vietnam, when use was extensive, it declined to just over a seventh. Certainly, advances in medical technology and understanding helped account for this improvement, but the helicopter—as piloted by both Mike Novosel Sr. and his eldest son, Michael J. Novosel Jr.—was crucial. "Getting the casualty and the physician together as soon as possible is the keystone of the practice of combat medicine," noted an Army report on the practice of medicine in the Vietnam War. "The helicopter achieved this goal as never before."

Because my dad flew for the airlines when I was growing up, I was always around airplanes and people that flew. So it was a natural progression. That's what I wanted to do.

At the height of the Vietnam War, in '67, we moved to Savannah, Georgia, and lived on post at Hunter Army Airfield. I worked at the officers' club on the flight line, and all there was, was Army aviators. I knew the guys, and I knew which units they were from in Vietnam. I was just a kid, but I knew all that. I'd do my bartending job, and I'd get off work at five or six or seven in the evening. And then I'd play ball with the guys and drink and raise hell with 'em, because they were all my peers—twenty-year-old, twenty-one-, twenty-two-year-old helicopter pilots. It was just natural that I would go take the flight test and get accepted.

The Air Force and Navy flight schools required some college. But the Army had the warrant-officer, high-school-to-flight-school program. You had to be nineteen to take the exam, and that's how I spent my nineteenth birthday, November 19, 1968. I'd finished high school the previous June, and I didn't want to wait. I wanted to go right now. Everybody said, "You're crazier than hell."

I joined the Army in January, and after eight weeks of basic, I went to Fort Wolters to begin flight school.

All the instructors in flight school knew my dad. But it didn't go any easier. In fact, the deal was, they were harder on me because they wanted Mike Novosel's boy to be the best. Which was fine. Made me a better damn pilot. And that helped keep me alive.

I graduated flight school on the fifteenth of December 1969, twenty-seven years to the day after my dad. I got two and a half weeks off and flew over to Vietnam. I wanted to be a Dustoff pilot. I wasn't really sure where in Vietnam Dad's unit was. I could've volunteered to be sent to one of the other Dustoff units, but I just wanted to be at the same place he was. I was right at that age when, usually, kids don't like to be around their dad. But I liked being around him. I admired him.

I still admire him for the things he does, and I would even if he hadn't got the medal. He ain't afraid of nothing. He ain't. I mean, everybody's afraid of something; I'm sure he's afraid of something, too. But as far as a combat situation, he's not afraid of anything.

My dad had taught me a lot of things, like how to ride a bicycle, how to drive. And when he taught me stuff, he taught me right. I knew the same thing would happen in Vietnam. He doesn't get mad when you don't perform. He'll get mad if you don't try, but if you try, he doesn't get mad. Real patient. "Do it again, let's do it again. Let's try it again."

When I got over there, I can remember him showing me autorotations, which is how you land the aircraft when the engine's out: When you're going downward, the air going up through the rotors keeps the blades turning so that you have the ability to touch down softly. He and I went up, and he shut the engine down on me, and I did an autorotation to the rice paddy and landed there fine. Then we started doing autorotations for a beer. What he'd do is, he took a handkerchief and set it out on a bush. We took off, and the deal was that he was to shut the engine off and then land the helicopter and be able to reach out and grab that handkerchief.

We'd come around, land. He'd be stopped right at the handkerchief. I said, "Oh, shit, that was just luck, Dad." "No, it ain't," he said. "I'll do it again." And he did it again. And every time it was costing me a beer. He did it five or six times. So I finally admitted that it wasn't just luck. Then he let me do some. But I couldn't do them to that precision, no way. I can now, of course. But back then I only had, like, two hundred hours of flight time.

Those first two days flying with my dad were critical. See, in Dustoff, you had to do everything yourself. In slick units—troop-transport units—which is where most pilots were, pilots didn't work alone. They worked in groups of three and four and five. And when they'd go out, they didn't have to know how to navigate to get from point A to point B. All someone would have to do is look at the tailpipe and skids of the guy that's in front of him and follow. When he lands, you land. It's that simple. It's like being the third car on a train; that third car on the train isn't very smart.

But in Dustoff you're not following anyone. And if the weather is bad, you're the only aircraft in the sky. So you're it. You've got to navigate. You've got to make all your mission decisions. You've got to plan your fuel, everything. You've got to figure out, "Can I carry all the wounded, can I carry the load? Well then, which of them *do* I carry?"

My dad gave me training to make sure that I could do everything.

Later on, the guys told me that at first they wondered if I was gonna be some kind of drip because my dad ran the unit. But then they all found out that I'd stand on my own two feet, so they liked me and respected me. They thought that I would do the old coattail thing. But I didn't.

In Dustoff we went from firefight to firefight, from bad shit happening to bad shit happening.

According to standard operating procedure, you were supposed to wait for gunships to cover you. Hell, I had 'em maybe eight times the whole year I was in Vietnam. You got that little window of whether a guy is gonna live or die. You go in and get him, the hell with it. You can't wait for gunships, you can't wait for them to stop the firefight. You just go get him. Period.

In the Air Force, you go to a fancy room with an easy chair and eleven guys parading in front of you with their bullshit. For us it was: "We got three whiskeys (short for Whiskey India Alpha, 'wounded in action'); multiple gunshot wounds; X-Ray Sierra one zero, one zero (the map coordinates); Cornhusker 56 (the ground commander's call sign)." Period, go, good-bye.

Now, whenever my dad and I talk about Dustoff and use the term "I," actually the proper way to do it is "we," because it wasn't just one person in the helicopter. It was me, my copilot, my medic, and my crew chief. I want to make sure that they get the credit they deserve. A lot of times, the ground troops would hunker down in a hole because they were taking so much fire, so the medic and crew chief would jump out of the aircraft and run across to grab up the wounded to carry them over to the helicopter. You could see the rounds impacting all around. And all the medics could fix the helicopter, and all the crew chiefs could fix a patient. We couldn't have done the job without those guys.

We had medics—could be a twenty-year-old kid—who would have a guy that was at death's door when we got him. Then, by giving the guy an epinephrine shot to the heart, he'd have him sitting up, smiling and talking, before we got back to the hospital. Can you imagine that? And think about starting IVs in four or five different patients on a shaking, maneuvering helicopter. And loading twenty-two people in ten seconds. And not only would they do it, they'd do it faster than anyone could ever imagine it could be done because of their skill and courage. Just unbelievable what those guys could do.

We'd go wherever we had to. I was in on the invasion of Cambodia, in May of 1970. But the thing is, we used to go into Cambodia on a regular basis. If there were wounded, we'd go. And I mean to the point where when I got back: "We heard you went into Cambodia. If you went into Cambodia, we're gonna court-martial your ass." I'd swear and be damned: "No, I didn't go into Cambodia." And you'd make sure the rest of crew would tell him: "No, we never went into Cambodia." Oh, yeah, we'd go in there.

Before I got to Vietnam, I assumed that war would be almost the same as going to a ball game. That's the only way to describe it, us and them. The finality of it didn't really dawn on me, because I was just a dumb kid.

Seriously, it seemed glorious. When I got over there, I got used to seeing, literally every day, people blown to pieces. And even then it took a while for it to dawn on me. I had just turned twenty when I got there, and it was neat shit to see all this stuff happening—initially. It was neat to get shot at—initially.

When they'd start shooting, it sounded like a pot of popcorn. One, and then two or three, and then four or five, and then all hell breaks loose. That's how it goes. I'm sure what it is, the platoon leader is firing the first shot. "Don't you shoot until I shoot," he tells the squad leaders. And the squad leaders say to their guys, "Don't you shoot until I shoot." So you can hear the lieutenant shoot, then you hear the squad leaders, then the squads.

And believe it or not, what would go through my mind at that time, especially with tracers whizzing through—we used to have four or five beehives here in Fort Walton. You never knew when some of them son of a bitches was gonna sting you. That's how I felt with the bullets whizzing around me. I translated those bullets into the bees, and that gave me the ability to continue to operate.

The first time I saw a real bad wound was probably about five or six days after I got there. It was a guy with his leg blown off. It looked terrible, a tourniquet with a bloody stump. Sometimes you picked up Vietnamese where they had actually used buffalo shit to glue the leg back on. And Batman. This was a little green bottle with a picture of Batman on it and some green smelly stuff inside. I'll never forget that smell—you know how your smeller has a memory. It was a cure-all, a black-magic cure-all. You picked up Vietnamese, you'd smell the stuff all over, because they all had it on. It didn't do a damn thing. But it gave them solace, so I guess it did do something.

The way I dealt with what I was seeing was, instead of a person with a head wound, it became "a head wound." Nowadays I could look at a group of fifty wounded or hurt people and I could triage 'em in five seconds. Because back then there was a lot of them that looked bad, but they ain't bad. And you can see that right away. If they're moving around and standing up and walking around, don't worry about *them,* start looking for the ones that *ain't* moving. And then the ones that ain't moving, look to see where they're hit. And after you look to see where they're hit, see how bad it is they're hit. And then look to see, if you take them right now, are they gonna die anyway? Or do you take these over here that aren't so bad? That's a decision I was making at twenty years old.

At the time I just wanted to be good at what I did. I wanted to make my dad proud of me. Now I'm amazed. What I was expected to do, I did. I rose to the occasion.

In retrospect it crosses your mind that you're playing God, deciding, "Well, I ain't gonna take him because it's obvious he's not gonna make it." But here's the situation you're caught in: If you take this one and you don't have room for that one, both of 'em are gonna die. So you've got to get real practical. You've got to save the most you can, and that means some are gonna have to die. You can't sit there and fret over it. It's sort of like falling down several flights of stairs. You're making deals on the way down. Oh, shit, my hand's hurt. Oh, that hurts. Oh, shit, there goes my arm. Oh, shit, I don't need that arm anyway, I got another one. Making deals all the way down: That's done, all right, forget about it—now what do I got left? You can get killed at the bottom, but you don't want to get killed, so you're making deals to survive the way down. You know what I'm saying? It's a matter of being pragmatic. I guaran-damn-tee you that doing what I did will make you a practical person.

Every day, every single day after making it through that war, is a borrowed day on my life. It's a gift. No matter what happens, a bad day or a good day, every day is an extra day.

The worst wound I ever saw was a guy who got his head blown off, and his face was still there. I'll never forget it. Did you ever see a stingray sitting on a dock after you catch it, how it undulates? His face was attached to his body and was on the floor in the blood, undulating with the air blowing through it.

Every day, everybody that you're associating with is blown apart. Taking off out of an LZ that was hot—and when it was hot, you kind of dipped your nose lower to build speed fast—you'd see all the blood rushing to the chin bubble, the little glass window by your feet, and actually filling it up. You learned not to put anything on the floor, because it'd get all bloody—you hung things up on the seat or on a hook. The chin bubble had a little hole in it, but it took a while for the blood to run out. It was a gruesome sight every single day. For a whole year.

You couldn't dwell on how terrible it all was. One time we went back to our base at Binh Thuy for lunch, and I sent the crew chief over to the Red Cross to buy some hamburgers for all of us; you didn't get the medic to do it, because he was always covered in blood and you didn't want your hamburgers all bloody. The crew chief came back with a stack of three or four paper plates, and he put one in front of me, and it had somebody's foot in there. He did it as a joke. I just said, "You cocksucker."

Then, at the end of a day like that, you go out, you got a guy with a white towel standing there serving you a steak and a drink.

Fliers, in general, would drink a lot. Alcohol is a great equalizer. It's not an escape—flying's the escape. It's a brief respite, is all you can say. In Vietnam you would drink to celebrate that you didn't get killed today doing what you do. That was it totally. It ain't an escape. You're just drinking to celebrate that you didn't get killed today.

When my dad went in the Army, and even before, when he was an instructor at Fort Wolters, he was around other Army aviators and Army folks. And I'm not a mushroom, I'm hearing what they're talking about. Then, when we went to Hunter, all my friends were aviators. I can remember the camaraderie: "You're a bunch of shitheads." "They ain't worth shit." "We got our asses shot off. You guys were a bunch of pussies." "I was in the First of the fucking Ninth." Not the "First of the Ninth"—when you say it, you say it with respect.

In Dustoff we flew single shift. But if you did have other aircraft to protect you, you'd have gunships. And because gun bunnies are too dumb to navigate, you're doing the navigating and scouting, and they're just flying along behind you, fat, dumb, and happy. Gun bunnies. That's how it goes when you're sitting around: "You damn gun bunny. What the hell do you know?"

It's a mutual respect. You don't tell a guy you respect and you like that you respect and you like him. You call him an asshole.

I was living in Savannah when the protesting and all that stuff really got going—'67, '68. But they weren't demonstrating in the South. People just didn't do that.

I saw the protesting on TV, though, and I didn't like it. The thing that got me more than anything else is that most of the protesters I saw on the tube were complaining at the GIs. Of course, my dad was one of those GIs, and he was in Vietnam. And all my friends—the Army guys I hung out with at the flight line—had just gotten back from Vietnam. They weren't bad like the protesters said they were, not to me. They weren't terrible people. So it pissed me off: These demonstrators are lying. Why would they say that about these guys?

Now I'm glad they did protest, because if they hadn't, maybe we'd still be fighting that war. More people would be getting hurt. But I wasn't against the war at the time, because, being young and naive, I really thought that we were doing the right thing. It had to be the right thing, because the country was doing it. That's how I felt.

But then you see everybody getting hurt, you're wading in blood—it makes you think a little more. Your eyes are opened.

What I thought was, "This shit has got to end. What are these guys dying for?" Over there I was exposed to draftees who would quote the slogans—"Make love, not war." As a Dustoff pilot, I felt lucky to be saving rather than killing somebody. A lot of guys did things they feel real guilty over now. They're suffering today for what they did; these are the guys that have nightmares. My dad and I don't have that baggage; I feel very, very fortunate for that. I sleep at night.

I don't know about my dad's opinion, but in my opinion money talks, and it was pure corporate greed that kept Vietnam going for all the years that it went on. I think that all the big defense contractors, the day in 1973 when they realized that we weren't part of it anymore, those companies' CEOs were at home crying in their beer.

Listen to the special language for that war: Joe got "wasted." They didn't say that in World War II; people didn't get "wasted." In Vietnam people got "wasted." "Wasted" don't mean killed. It means wasted—instead of using a paper cup, you wad it up and throw it in the trash can. You wasted that paper cup. When the GIs said, "So-and-so got wasted," that's what they meant: another wasted life. Because what were we fighting for? Who knows?

"Go take that hill," and everybody busts ass and does what they can to take the hill. Then, okay, you took it. "Now let's haul ass back to base and leave the hill there." Fifty guys got killed on our side. Probably three hundred of their guys got killed. Three hundred fifty people lost their lives over this dumb-ass hill. For what?

To this day I'm glad that it's over. We're not wasting any more lives. But I'm also glad that it's over because now the Vietnamese are back as part of the world community. It's a good culture; the world lost something without it. They're not war-crazed killers. The Vietnamese are gentle people. If you get to know them, they are. I got a very high opinion of 'em. A lot of people wouldn't like to hear that, but they're really decent. Think about it. You know who stopped the killing fields in Cambodia? The Vietnamese stopped it. They didn't have to do that; it was no threat to them. But they went in there and they stopped it. After they stopped it, they went back home. "Don't do it anymore, or we'll come back." And they meant it.

They were damn good fighters. They didn't have a bunch of REMFs, because if you were a Vietcong, you were out there in the AO. You can compare what they did to the Underground Railroad in our American history or to the French Resistance. That's the best way to describe it.

The way it is to me, they put up their finest young men to go against the South Vietnamese and the Americans' finest young men. All of us were decent people, all of us. Them and us. And the only reason everyone's trying to kill each other is so that the other one doesn't kill you. Not because of hate. Because once you get to sit down and talk to 'em, they're guys like us, same shit. I got a friend here in Fort Walton, an electrician, who used to be in the NVA. When you talk, you compare. "Aw, shit, we had it worse than that." "Aw, bullshit, we had it worse." You want a leg up, you know what I mean? I don't hate him.

I knew people who were killed. While I was there, I'd hear through the grapevine who got it out of my flight-school classmates, because I had over a hundred classmates who graduated.

It hit you. It hit you deep. But you couldn't let it get you, so you delayed the grieving. I delayed my life's grieving until Jack, my son-in-law, was killed. He was also an Army aviator. He was murdered in 1998 by an antiwhite street gang while on vacation in Hawaii. I'd delayed an entire life's grieving for everybody I knew that had passed away. I always pushed it out, just pushed it out, until Jack was killed. It was a defense mechanism.

As soon as we heard, I sent my wife, Margaret, over there to Hawaii—I didn't want our daughter, Wendy, to be by herself. It was the beginning of the summer, when it's hard to get a flight; our friends at Delta made it happen.

I had to stay here and make arrangements, because this is where we were bringing him. I was here by myself, so I had a whole lot of time to think. I knew that we would have a lot of people. We had my entire family coming, and a lot of military friends of Jack's. So we wound up with people sleeping on the floor, everywhere. Both my house and my dad's house were just full of people. There was a lot of getting ready before they got here, and I stayed and worked.

But I didn't break until I was out working in the yard. A neighbor came by and asked me what was happening, could they do anything for me. And I just broke down. I don't know why. I had never, ever grieved like that in my life over anybody or anything. It just triggered it, and I don't understand. I still get very emotional about it.

I've grieved for my losing Jack. A little bit sorry for myself—that I can deal with. But what really upsets me is for the kids—our grandchildren, Josh and Breanna—because I know how close he was to the kids. He was such a great dad. To me it connects with two kids I picked up about two-thirds of the way through my year in Vietnam.

They were starting to Vietnamize the war by then, and there was a lot of terrorism going on, not against the Americans but by the Vietcong towards the Vietnamese people. And I can remember picking up a couple of little girls. I'll never forget them. I remember the hat one of them had. It was almost like a cowboy hat, but yet it was a French-fashioned hat that the Vietnamese would wear. This was just a little girl, about Breanna's age, five or so. She had on a little blue dress and she had the hat, like a little doll, and she had multiple gunshot wounds on her way home from school. The hat wasn't on her head—it was laying with her on the stretcher, and the medic held it down so it wouldn't blow away. That was a difficult, pivotal point for me, as young as I was. I realized that they were hurting little kids. At that point everything changed.

Where we were supposed to take local nationals if we happened to have a pickup depended on who they were. If they were CIDG—Civilian Irregular Defense Group—or their relatives, we would take them to the U.S. Army hospital. If they were just plain Vietnamese, they were to go to the Vietnamese hospital.

Well, the Vietnamese hospital didn't have a lot of drugs. They didn't have a lot of equipment, a lot of capabilities. More often than not, instead of fixing the wound, they'd just amputate.

So I brought the two kids to the American hospital, the Third Surg in Binh Thuy, and they had a fit: "We didn't get a call on this one." Well, I lied and said they were CIDG children. So they took them and fixed them. Later on they called the unit and said, "They were not CIDG. Why did you tell us that?"

I said, "I thought they were. I'll be damned that they weren't."

They were really badly wounded. They needed a lot of serious treatment, and they got it. But those doctors were mad at me for bringing them in.

If I had a baseball bat in my hand when they said they didn't want to take those girls, I would have smacked 'em in the mouth with it. That's how I felt. I didn't have any use for a lot of the noncombatants. Those doctors were more worried about the book and the rules than what they were there for. But then, I didn't have their job.

When those girls were hurt, I started growing up. If it's other soldiers, you could dehumanize it in your head. I mean, you've got to do something. You use humor, levity, and you also dehumanize it. It'd be different if you see an American face versus a Vietnamese face. And that's awful to say. Absolutely, I don't feel that way now. Deep down I don't think I felt that way then. I can remember sitting in a place and looking at the Vietnamese bodies lined up in body bags, beside the heliport, ready to be taken out. They're staring at nothing, and you feel for 'em. You do. You say, "Oh, shit, that's too bad." You say a little prayer for 'em. Even so, you could dehumanize it to an extent. But these beautiful little girls—it was just a bit much for me. And I see my grandkids, and I see an invasion on them that is tantamount to the same thing. It would've been easier had they been shot and they didn't live through it and didn't lose their dad. That's almost a mortal wound to these children. That's how I look at it.

Before my son-in-law was killed, I could think about my friends and relatives that have died, and there wasn't very much behind the thought. Now when I think about them, it's a whole new dimension. I had never learned to grieve; his death taught me. Why should a son-in-law's death affect me so much? I've come to figure out that it opened the channels.

I don't see it as a weakness. I think it's a strength. And I don't care if the grandkids see me cry. It was after the initial breaking down with my neighbor that I picked them up at the airport. With

Josh—he's a little older—I could hug him and stand up. But Breanna, I got on my knees to give her a hug. And I just broke down. What Breanna did was, she patted me on the back and consoled me. She's an exceptional little kid. She'll end up being a doctor, is what I think. That's what she wants to do.

When I first got to Vietnam, everything was neat. I wasn't reveling in other people's pain and misfortune or anything like that, it was just what was happening around me was so interesting. To the point where when I was off duty, I'd still fly. I was out there all the time. I couldn't get enough of it. I couldn't get enough of the feeling of elation when I successfully completed a mission, when I delivered a live person somewhere. Dustoff was a very rewarding job.

But after I picked up those little girls, the reality of everything that I'd been doing and everything that we were about—everything—just set in. There wasn't nothing neat about what happened to those girls. And at that point I started wondering about the war and why was this damn shit going on that could do this to some little kids. And that's when a lot of things became apparent to me. I'd never thought about the term "wasted," where that came from. By God, I knew now: people giving up their lives for nothing versus giving up their lives for something. And that something, that elusive something they never could quite put their finger on, that something we were trying to achieve—whatever it was, it sure as hell wasn't worth one human life.

There's a bond between people who've been in the military. I could go right now out to the bridge here in Fort Walton that crosses the bay we live on. And we got homeless people living under that bridge. I'd go out there whether I had a can of beer on me or not and sit down and talk to them. And, you understand, a lot of the homeless are Vietnam veterans. They just never made it. They're casualties. I wish that the government would look at it that way. They *are* casualties.

I could sit down with one or two of 'em, and they would be

nineteen again, and I would be twenty again, period. "Where were you?" "I was here." "What'd you guys do?" "Oh, we supported the Third of the Eleventh." We'd be right there again.

You can tell who's seen combat, too. The guy that's seen combat, he'll just have a different way of explaining things. He won't tell you things unless he's asked. A guy who has never seen combat will basically volunteer all this shit. One veteran will ask another, and then by the way he answers, you can tell. If it's some upside-down shit that just doesn't make sense, he couldn't have been there. I actually had a guy one time start telling me the story about how he and his father flew Dustoff together in Vietnam, and his father got the Medal of Honor. I just said, "Oh, yeah? Really?"

Civilians—they're the innocents. They don't know. They can't know. And I don't want to say "fat, dumb, and happy," because they may not be fat. They may be very intelligent. They may not be too happy. But basically that describes it: fat, dumb, and happy.

Say there's a group of people out there. I could look out there and tell you right off: Is the situation dangerous, do they mean us harm? I could tell by their posture if they mean harm, but the civilian in most cases would never know the difference. They may not even notice that someone has a weapon.

I guarantee you, Jack didn't look at those guys that came to get him in Hawaii in the same way that I would've looked at them. He looked at them as people who interrupted his evening; I'd have looked at them as a possible threat to kill me or my family. He wasn't a civilian—Jack got shot down in Iraq in 1994—but he was also not really a war veteran the way I am. What you expect to happen depends on how much you've seen. All the scenarios go through your head, and not in a slow fashion either. They go through your head real fast. I've seen more, I know what people are capable of. That's the difference.

I came home in 1971, January the seventh or eighth. I was happy to be back. Nobody spit at me; I would've knocked 'em in the mouth if they did. I came through Travis Air Force Base in California, and I went straight to Fayetteville, where my mom and dad were. I was lucky in that I got to come back to a military town, because most everybody was a veteran there. There was nothing special about it. I went to the Dustoff unit there in Bragg, and we were made up of guys from different Vietnam Dustoff units.

Soon after I got home, I remember turning the TV on and watching Lam Son 719 going on. It was Vietnamese running an operation with American aviation assets to it, and over a hundred helicopters were destroyed. I felt sorry for 'em, but I was glad that I had gotten out of there before that shit hit.

A lot of stuff was going on in the country. When Nixon would come on the tube, I'd flip the channel. I didn't want to see him, I didn't want to hear anything about it. I knew that I was home for at least eighteen months before I'd be rotated back to Vietnam, and I didn't want to hear about it. So I exiled myself. I was here, I was in the U.S. But I exiled myself from the news. I was full up.

To this day I still feel there's no politician worth a shit, not one. The Establishment still is a bunch of greedy, self-serving shitheads, every one of 'em, every single one of 'em. They're not worth the powder to blow 'em up. I wouldn't piss on 'em if they were on fire. The war, the atrocity that they perpetrated on us and on another group of human beings—the Vietnamese—is unforgivable. Just unforgivable.

When my father received his medal in June of '71, Nixon came down the line and shook our hands. And when he shook my hand, he said, "We've decided that the Novosels have done enough, so you're not going back."

Being a Medal of Honor recipient is pretty consuming for my dad. He goes from one event to another. I got a little taste of that this year when I was inducted into A Gathering of Eagles—it's an honor society for those that have contributed in some way to the furtherance of aviation. Of course, the reason I was inducted is having been, with my father, the only father-and-son team to fly together in combat, something that will never happen again. And if you're in this organization, you get to be the center of attention, you're the object of adoration.

I've got to tell you something, it's not a bad thing. It's nice to have people want to meet you, want to shake your hand, want to ask you about yourself. It's nice to have that feeling of being in the limelight.

Dad likes that, of course. Everybody likes that. But he's always said there's a difference between cheap shit and apple butter. He likes people to be real. And he is. He lives that way.

Obviously I love him, and obviously I'm very proud of him.

In my career my dad's fame did at times get in the way a little bit, because you had some shitheads that were very jealous. But I was a professional Army officer. I tried my best to do my best job. After Vietnam I held some very high-level jobs in the safety field, and it wasn't because I was the son of a Medal of Honor recipient. The Army doesn't put you in a high level like that if you don't earn your way into it, not as a warrant officer. You don't nepotize yourself into that.

When I retired from the Army, I moved back here to Fort Walton. I was born here, and I've always loved it here. No matter where I was in my entire life, I was coming back to Fort Walton. This is where my roots are. So this is where I wanted to come home.

We had the old house, but it was "wore out," as they say here. So what we decided to do, at first we were gonna build a duplex for my dad and me. But then they said, "You have to go in for a zoning thing, because we don't have duplexes here." So okay, screw it. We'll cut it in two, no problem. This was in 1987.

I drew up a preliminary plan and then showed Dad, and he helped me use the space better than I had used it. Everybody got what they wanted. And we went looking for a builder and had him build it.

The two houses are right next to each other, and they're mirror images. So everything in each one is the same as in the other, except on the opposite side. I can look out of my bedroom and see his house, and he can look out of his bedroom and see my house. But if you look out any of the other windows—on both houses—you won't see the house next door, because his house is forward just a little bit, and my house is turned just a little bit. So we have our privacy.

Dad is both my father and an Army buddy. There is a certain camaraderie that you have with the guys that you were in Vietnam with, this unbreakable bond. In a lot of cases, it's even closer than two guys are as brothers. And that's how it is with us. We were together in the same hellhole doing the same thing.

"Army buddies"—that just means that he's always there for you. We're our own support group. That's why they have reunions.

We don't have to. We're together all the time.

III

"We've been given this great country . . ."

LEGACIES OF NATION AND FAMILY

At Gettysburg in 1863, Abraham Lincoln reached back to the Declaration of Independence, and its "proposition that all men are created equal," to justify the war he was waging. Another four score years later, Sonny Dunbar, an African American from Brooklyn, New York, joined a military that enforced the inequality still the rule in those states whose rebellion Lincoln had defeated at so great a cost. When we speak of "American ideals," we usually take those words to mean freedom, justice, respect for the individual. We find it too painful to recognize that, until recently, the separation of black from white was also an American ideal.

When people put on our country's uniform, they do so as inheritors of traditions handed down from our common metaphorical fathers cited by Lincoln—Washington, Jefferson, Madison; to which we must add Lincoln—or by their particular fathers (and mothers) who wore the uniform in earlier conflicts.

People do not go to war unmindful of what they are fighting for.

BILL PERKINS

Retired Career Military Officer
Spokane, Washington
Captain, United States Army Air Forces, World War II

"I had two brothers in the Navy," recalls William M. Perkins, "one brother in the Army and another brother in the Air Corps. My sister was in the Medical Corps.

"All six of us lived through the war. I guess it was hard on my parents, but I never heard them complain about it."

Bill Perkins was born in 1917 in Farmington, Utah.

When I was a young boy in the early twenties, there were a lot of World War I veterans around and a lot of discussion about the war.

Most of the veterans would say how horrible it was living in the trenches, with water in the bottom and mud. Some of them talked about coming out of the trenches to attack and falling into shell craters. But the heroics were emphasized by some of the news that came out and by some of the silent movies. I think young people then thought it was glorious to be a soldier and to go to places like France and fight a war. I was enthralled with the airplanes. I thought it was the greatest thing in the world to be a pilot in one of those aircraft.

One of the old silent movies was called *Lilac Time,* about the World War I fliers in France. It showed these combat flights, and you'd see these airplanes with ex–World War I pilots in them, and you thought, "Boy, that's the place to be."

I used to read magazines, particularly the Boy Scout magazine, *Boys' Life.* It would have a lot of articles about flying. When Commander Byrd flew to the South Pole, it had articles about him.

When I was about ten years old is when Lindbergh flew the Atlantic. And that was something great, as a young boy, to learn about. After he came back from Paris, he flew the *Spirit of St. Louis* around the country and stopped at various cities. He came through

Salt Lake City, and my father took me down to see him. The place was flooded with people.

Well, Lindbergh happened to be standing by his airplane. And just as a young boy, I walked up and touched the propeller blade. One of the attendants come up and told me, "No, no. You're not to do that." Lindbergh says, "It's all right," and he come over and shook hands with me. Of course, I was so excited, about all I could do was stutter.

In those days flying was something special. These people used to come around barnstorming. They'd come to county fairs and do acrobatics and wing hopping and parachute jumping. If you were an aviator, you were acknowledged as a special person. A lot of people couldn't quite comprehend what flying was, I suppose. I heard people say, "You'll never get me up in one of those things." But others couldn't wait to get strapped in and put the helmet and goggles on.

At the age of seventeen, Bill began flying lessons. He soon earned his private pilot's license, and in September 1942 he entered the pilot-training program of the Army Air Forces.

It took us a year from the time we went in to be commissioned. Most of us were impatient to get the training completed. But you played along to get your wings and get a commission so you could eventually go out and do combat. You'd see these combat fliers coming back, and they'd be hero-worshipped. And you felt, "Boy, that's great."

You didn't realize what being in combat was.

MIKE PERKINS

Retired Career Military Officer; Middle School Teacher
Tremonton, Utah
Captain, United States Army, Vietnam

Bill Perkins stayed in the service after World War II, and in 1948 he was sent to Germany to fly the Berlin Airlift, the Anglo-American operation that supplied West Berlin after Joseph Stalin had closed all surface routes to the city, which lay deep within the Soviet zone of occupied Germany. Soon Bill's wife and son—seven-year-old William "Mike" Perkins—traveled to Germany to be near him.

They took up residence in the town of Kempten.

I played with German kids, and the Germans were very nice to us. But there were a few exceptions. We'd be downtown shopping, and some teenagers—thirteen-, fourteen-, fifteen-, and sixteen-year-old kids—would push my mother off the sidewalk. They'd spit on us and give the Nazi salute—*Sieg Heil!*—even though Hitler had been dead for three or four years.

So we had Polish bodyguards assigned to protect the American kids at school, on the bus, and other places. We called them DPs—displaced persons. I didn't realize who they were then. I do now. They were Jews.

We had one guy who was an absolute giant—he was six-foot-four or -five. He was always patting us on the head and giving us hugs. He hated Germans with a vengeance. One day, in broken English, he told us his story.

He was sitting on the school grounds with two or three of us American kids, and we asked him, "Do you have a wife?"

And he said, "I have a wife, but she's dead."

"Do you have kids?"

He brought out this old, wrinkled picture—you could barely see it. "Yeah, I have kids, but they're dead."

We went through his family. "Do you have a father? Uncle?"

"I have 'em, but they're all dead."

We couldn't figure this out.

And then he told us how the Nazis had put him on a train and transported him somewhere. As they got out of the cattle car, his mother and his wife and his sisters and his kids were taken off. He's trying to reach them, and the guards are pushing them back. That's the last he ever saw of them. I think it was he and his two brothers and his dad—I guess they were all big men, and they were shuffled off to go somewhere else.

He told us that eventually his two brothers were worked to death, and so was his father, just worked to death. Then he himself was dying—he was being nursed by one of his friends, and he figured he was gonna die in three or four days.

All of us kids are just sitting there. Even to this day, I remember that conversation under that tree. Our mouths are hanging open, and we're going, "How can this be?" We're just little kids.

He told us that he heard a roar, and an engine, and guns firing. This friend ran out to see what was going on and never came back in. Pretty soon, he said, a man in a strange uniform came in with a red cross on his helmet and knelt down beside him and talked to him in a strange tongue, which he figured out was English, and patted his head. Eventually a bunch of Americans came in—he figured out then that the Americans had come—and they hauled him outside on that spring day. He said it must've been spring—there were flowers coming up and grass.

The Americans took him to a hospital, where he was nursed back to health. Who knows what he had? Probably typhus and everything else, and he weighed ninety or a hundred pounds.

Then he told us—and this probably had the biggest impact of anything he said—"God bless America."

PERRY POLLINS
ENGINEER
LEXINGTON, MASSACHUSETTS
CORPORAL, UNITED STATES MARINE CORPS, WORLD WAR II

It's no accident that the Marine Corps is the only American armed service with a widely known "hymn." The smallest of the services, the Corps is practically a religion to many, if not most, of the people who have been part of it, including Perry and Dave Pollins.

When I met with Perry, he was wearing a Marine Corps belt buckle. I noticed a Marine Corps calendar on his wall. When we went out for lunch, he put on a Marine Corps baseball cap.

In act 4, scene 3 of Shakespeare's Henry V, *a small force of English soldiers is preparing to do battle at Agincourt against a far more numerous French foe. But when one of his noblemen wishes for more troops, King Henry rebukes him: "The fewer men, the greater share of honour."*

"The few. The proud," goes the recruiting slogan of the Marine Corps.

Perry was born in 1924.

My family moved to Cambridge, Massachusetts, when I was ten, and I grew up in what you might call a cosmopolitan area. There were Jewish families, Greeks, Polish, Irish, Italian. I met and associated with some really top-rate people in those days. Guys like Horton, who I assume was Irish; McCleod, also Irish; Klashman, Jewish; Adelson, Jewish; Katowski, a good pitcher, Polish.

We got into hassles now and then. They called me names—kike, hebe—and I called them names—mick, ginzo, wop—which would not be accepted today. But five minutes later we were the best of friends.

Patriotism reigned in those days. It was not exactly taught in school, but it was conveyed in some way, shape, or form—by saluting the flag in the morning and singing "The Star-Spangled

Banner," by celebrating Armistice Day, which is now called Veterans Day. It was a different time.

My father was in the Navy during World War I—he was a seaman in the Azores on a submarine chaser. He didn't say all that much about it.

I heard more about World War I from a former Marine, a chap by the name of Tom Drummond, who had an apartment in the same building we did. We used to sit out on the front stairs, and he'd tell us about the Second Battle of the Marne and a couple of other battles he'd been part of with the Fifth Marines. He was gassed, terribly gassed, and he had difficulty breathing, difficulty speaking sometimes. He was not exactly a recluse, but he lived alone. I can picture him right now. He was prematurely gray, almost white, probably from the dose of gas that he took.

Tanks and armor were not at the disposal of the Marines when Tom was in combat; the Marines were on foot. The Marines were shock troops, for all intents and purposes, the first ones out of the trenches. When I got down to boot camp in the Marine Corps, and they said immediately that our lives would be in jeopardy, I knew exactly what jeopardy meant.

He exemplified Marines as I later found them to be: staunch believers in their ability to stand up to anything. He impressed me as being a very gentle individual, but he must've been a fighting Marine. When you fight, you get angry. You can't help but get angry. I found that out later.

DAVE POLLINS
Sales Representative
Lexington, Massachusetts
Lance Corporal, United States Marine Corps, Vietnam

"Once a Marine, always a Marine," says David Pollins, born in 1948, "that's something you can be proud of. Not too many people can say that.

"In the Marine Corps, you're not black, you're not white. You're a little green amphibious monster that thrives on shit. It's one big family. And I don't care if you're a Marine from World War II, Korea, Desert Storm, Cold War, peacetime, whatever. It doesn't matter. You're a Marine. Right on."

My grandfather was in the Marine Corps for over thirty-five years. Between my father and my grandfather, they had a lot of stories.

Steve Cronan, my mother's stepfather, was the only grandfather I knew. He joined the Marine Corps in 1923, I believe it was. Back then they were rough, they were tough. He was in World War II with the Fourth Marine Division in the Pacific, island hopping. I want to say he was at Kwajalein. I think he was at Iwo Jima. He came out a master gunnery sergeant, which was the highest you could go as an enlisted person.

He didn't get into too much about World War II. But he did tell me he was with Chesty Puller at the Chosin Reservoir in Korea. Chesty Puller—you talk about famous Marines, he's probably the most famous. Basically, the Marines had the Army on each flank, and the Army got their asses kicked and pushed back. And that's when the enemy surrounded the Marines at the Chosin Reservoir. They fought their way out of there, and they didn't leave any dead Marines or any wounded. They brought everybody home. No offense to the Army, but they left people.

I didn't hear that much in the way of gory details from Perry before I went in. But once I did my time in the Marine Corps and I came out, the stories started coming. He saw a lot of action. Peleliu, which was probably one of the bloodiest battles the Marine Corps went through.

When I was a kid, I heard mostly funny stories from Perry—about him and his pals, what they used to do.

There was one. They were down somewhere on R&R, the whole company, and there was an Australian outfit there, too. And the Aussies and the Marines got in a barroom fight. Perry, he was a little guy, so he and a buddy got under a table. They could tell by the shoes who the Aussies were and who the Marines were. So what they would do is, they'd wrap a napkin around an Aussie's feet and yank them out from underneath him, and then jump on him and beat the hell out of him, and then get back under the table.

It's the atmosphere. It's rivalries, fun, camaraderie with your friends going through all this. You're in battle for thirty days, and your buddies get killed, and then you're back in the rear. That's part of war—you have good times and you have bad times. That's what I got out of it.

The stories both of them told made a hell of an impression. If I had to go in, I knew where I was going. Between my grandfather and my father, I had no choice. I was born and bred a Marine.

MICKEY HUTCHINS

Support Engineer, Software Industry
Concord, North Carolina
First Lieutenant, United States Army, Vietnam

Born in 1946, Mickey L. Hutchins recalls growing up in the 1950s. "They still had the newsreels that preceded the movie, and you'd see things that were left over from World War II or had to do with Korea and current events. In the popular culture of the time, the two most adventuresome kinds of heroes you would see at the movies or on TV were cowboys and soldiers. In both types of stories, the good guys always won.

"The fifties and sixties were a time of optimism. There was this feeling that we were the good guys. We had prevailed against the evil of Hitler in World War II and were prevailing against Communism. There was the expectation that that would continue."

Until I was sixteen, we lived in Winston-Salem, and we went to the Winston-Salem Friends meeting there. As I got into junior high and high school, we started studying a bit more about what it is to be a Quaker. By far, the belief of the Quakers that was the most heavily emphasized was the notion of nonviolence. The truth of the matter is, it's tougher to be nonviolent than it is to be violent, and in many cases it's harder to refuse to serve than it is to actually serve.

I learned that fact early on, intellectually, but it's something else again to have to actually face it and make the decision for yourself. You have to weigh a lot of things: your concepts of self, your concepts of citizenship, your concepts of your religious belief, where you felt God was calling you. By the time I was in college and the letter came from the draft board, I did not feel terribly called to stand up and say, "I'm a conscientious objector." I probably should have felt the need to say that—from a religious standpoint, it would have been a more consistent position to take, it would have been the truer thing to do. My church had taught me to refuse to participate in war. But I don't regret having done what I did, and if I had it to do over again, I'd probably do it exactly the same way.

Before I went into the Army, I had not been concerned enough to do very much by way of research into "Where the heck is Vietnam? Who is Ho Chi Minh? What's at stake here?" I didn't have the answer to any of those questions. The overwhelming feeling that I had, though, was that I'm not fully sure why we are in this war, but I know we're in war. And I know that my country is saying, "I need you." As a citizen of this country I had already received a fair number of benefits. The way I looked at it, if you're going to hang in there for the benefits, you've got to hang in there for the responsibilities as well, and military service is a responsibility of citizenship. A student deferment had occurred to me, but only in passing, given my grade-point average. So basically the decision came down to "Am I going to be a good citizen? Am I going to support my country?" Or "Am I going to protest? Am I going to go to Canada?" I just couldn't see myself doing that.

Not only my father, but most of my male relatives, when they had been called, they had served. I couldn't see any compelling reason why, when I was called, I shouldn't serve. It would be awful hard to look your dad in the eye and say, "Dad, I'm sorry, but this one's just not for me."

TONY RIVAS JR.

FIREFIGHTER
SAN ANTONIO, TEXAS
SHIPFITTER THIRD CLASS, UNITED STATES NAVY, VIETNAM

Antonio V. Rivas Jr. was born in 1947 in San Antonio.

"I became an altar boy at seven or eight, and I did that for ten, eleven years. But it was starting to be, like, 'I'm getting too old for this. Maybe I should do something else.'

"I had a real close cousin who was all enthused about becoming a brother, and then maybe with ambitions to become a priest. He was getting ready to graduate, and was gonna leave to go to a seminary in California. I said, 'Well, I'll go also.'

"That was the first time I ever had a man-to-man talk with my dad. He said that he'd rather see some grandchildren—typical Mexican culture. So instead of becoming a brother, I joined the Navy. And then, instead of being a really good boy, I was hell on wheels."

Tony and his brother Richard both served in Vietnam.

The whole West Side of San Antonio was a barrio. But in that barrio you had little barrios, called *colonias*—little communities within the community.

A *colonia* is about seven or eight families real close together in the same block or two. On Christmas we'd all get together at one house. On New Year's Eve we'd get together and have a little bonfire in the middle of the street—we lived on a dead end—and everybody'd be cooking.

Everybody in the *colonia* was a *comadre* or *compadre*—godmother, godfather. They were all a little bit related where we lived. The people in the back were cousins to the people across the street, and two houses down they were uncles to the people on the corner. It was a close-knit family.

The girls would grow up with the guys, and they would marry. It was all in a row; you wouldn't get out of it. I don't think I saw a white guy—an Anglo—until I went to high school. And then, in my senior year, a black guy.

One of the reasons I joined the Navy is that I wanted to get out of the barrio and see something else, because I had never gone anywhere. I didn't want to get stuck there. I didn't want to get married to one of those girls and have six or seven kids and just move down the street. I wanted to experience a different kind of lifestyle—even though we were very close in the barrio, and I do miss it now.

In the barrio everything was going down. We had gangs all over the place. Joining the service was an honor to the family, because they said, "Oh, there goes Tony" or "There goes Richard. Oh, he's in the service. The other guy, he's in jail" or "he died already because of a gang." You would see somebody with a uniform and you would say, "Wow, that guy made something of himself."

SONNY DUNBAR
RETIRED BUS DRIVER AND SUBWAY MOTORMAN
ALBANY, NEW YORK
SERGEANT, UNITED STATES ARMY, WORLD WAR II

In the fall of 1940, African Americans formed a tenth of the nation's population, but under 3 percent of the Army's. Only five black officers served in the Army, three of them chaplains. Blacks were not accepted into the Air Corps or the Marines. And blacks and whites did not serve together in the same outfits.

With America creeping toward involvement in the year-old conflagration in Europe, however, congressional leaders realized that the military could not afford to overlook a rich source of manpower. And so, when Congress passed the Selective Service Act in mid-September to reinstitute the draft, the bill included a provision banning racial discrimination. But neither Congress nor the president, despite entreaties from African American leaders, would change the military's policy on segregation within units.

Before the war and throughout it, segregation of the armed services went beyond physical separation of the races. Although some blacks served in combat roles, most were assigned to duties thought suited to their supposedly strong backs and weak minds: grave digging, mess duty, construction. Confinement to noncombat jobs did not guarantee the safety of black servicemen, however: The truck drivers of the Red Ball Express risked death by accident or German artillery in order to keep Allied tankers and infantrymen supplied as they moved across France. And the stevedores of the 315th Port Battalion, including Kenneth A. Dunbar, a Brooklyn native born in 1922, unloaded ships in contested areas of the South Pacific.

The armed forces were segregated, but at the time I never got into thinking about the political side of it. I never had a problem being mistreated in the service. There are those, I guess certain things did happen to them. But I didn't carry no anger about what went down, because my thing is, if a person is ignorant, he's ignorant. *He* got the problem. I didn't have a problem. To me the segregation was a nonissue.

Later on, as I grew older and traveled the world more, then I knew we had been shafted. I began to find that out when I was coming home to be let out of the service. On the West Coast, I noticed that the German prisoners had more privileges than I did—it was the way they walked around and the places they went and were allowed into. Some of those places, restaurants particularly, I couldn't go. I ran into that type of thing again before I got home. I was traveling back to New York with another soldier who happened to be white, or nonblack, and we went through Boston and had to walk from the North Side to the South Side to change trains. We went into a bar to get something to drink. And the bartender came up and told him that they can't serve me.

Not too much has changed since then. But we make our own lives comfortable, or not, within ourselves. It's all up to us.

JOHN HOWE

FREELANCE WRITER
ALBANY, NEW YORK
STAFF SERGEANT, UNITED STATES ARMY, VIETNAM

On July 26, 1948, Harry Truman issued Executive Order 9981, which desegregated America's armed services in accord with "the highest standards of democracy." Although some elements of the armed forces moved slowly toward meeting those standards—all-black outfits did fight in the Korean War—by the time American troops began traveling in large numbers to Vietnam, all units had long been desegregated.

Contrary to popular belief, African Americans served in Vietnam in rough proportion to their presence in the nation's population. Their share of the officer corps was another matter: In 1968 only 2 percent of officers in the combined services were black.

Blacks also died in Vietnam in rough proportion to the population, making up 12 percent of the fifty-eight thousand who lost their lives.

The biological parents of John L. Howe separated within two years of his birth in 1946. His mother soon remarried, but his birth father remained a strong force in John's life. He called his stepfather, Sonny Dunbar, Dad, and his biological father, Melville Howe, Daddy Mel.

My mother says I wanted to be a soldier from the time that I was in her womb, because she could feel me kicking when the gunshots went off at the John Wayne movies. She loved watching war movies and cowboy movies, and would even howl to John Wayne, "Kill that son of a bitch!"

I always wanted to be a soldier. I think that, like a lot of other kids who were born with fathers who came from World War II, I felt as though it was the thing to do. It was patriotic. You know, our great heroes were World War II heroes. My dad went off, and he was part of the war against evil. There was a certain reverence that was paid to veterans. I think that's part of what I, as an African American, wanted. I saw so much respect accorded to those people who fought in that war—I saw respect even in a segregated society.

In Brooklyn they'd have this event called Brooklyn Day. And every June the black churches gathered together and had these tremendous parades. They used to have their great drum-and-bugle corps and their floats and their different societies, and the kids would sit along the stoops on Stuyvesant Avenue. For black Brooklyn it was the place to be.

Brooklyn Day was celebrated by all folks, but this parade down Stuyvesant Avenue was essentially a black tradition. See, for blacks, Brooklyn Day was tied to Juneteenth Day, the nineteenth of June, which was the time in 1865 that the last African Americans received word of their emancipation from slavery. That was in Texas. So Juneteenth Day is an essential piece of Americana in terms of African Americans.

The Usher Board from the AME Church would pass by, and the board of trustees, and everybody would be decked out. But the guys who always drew my attention were the guys who came from the 369th Infantry and the 715th AAA Gun Battalion and from the 106th Infantry—all New York National Guard units. The 369th and the 715th were black units from way back in 1916. The 106th was integrated, but essentially they were black because they came from armories that were in black neighborhoods.

I can recall sitting on the stoop and seeing those guys come down the street with shiny helmets and shiny boots—they walked so confidently, those wonderful guys in their uniforms. And my father—both my fathers, my stepfather and my father—would stand up when they came by.

In our family there's a wonderful, wonderful tradition of service. My great-grandfather on my mother's side, William Cash, was a sixteen- or seventeen-year-old drummer boy in Cuba with the First U.S. Volunteer Cavalry, Teddy Roosevelt's unit. He was there when they charged up San Juan Hill—well, they walked up there very quickly, and they were helped along by members of the Ninth Cavalry, a unit of the Buffalo Soldiers. My uncle James, William's brother-in-law, served in that outfit.

William died of influenza a few years after he came home from Cuba, but Uncle James was out west with the Buffalo Soldiers, in places like Nebraska and South Dakota, and was with them when they chased Pancho Villa through Mexico. He was a wrangler; he'd take care of the horses that traveled with the outfit to provide "remounts" for the cavalrymen. His son served in the Buffalo Soldiers, too, out west, and in France during World War I. We are the custodians here in this house of the memorial citation that was issued for the Buffalo Soldiers by New York's governor, George Pataki.

I feel that I am blessed in this life. I've had two fathers, and both treated me exactly as I would expect to treat my sons and have treated my sons. Melville John Howe, my birth father, came from the town of Port-of-Spain in Trinidad and was raised in Harlem, up on Edgecombe Avenue. He was a wonderful guy. Now, his father, whose name was Frederick A. Howe—Frederick Aloysius Howe, Frederick Alfred Howe, there is some debate as to his middle name—he was a fellow who was very feisty. He had this wonderful copper hue, like a new penny, and he was dashing and robust and very athletically built. He was a policeman, and he eventually became responsible for building and maintaining all of the police stations in Trinidad. He served in World War I as a member of the British Expeditionary Force that was in France. He was at the Second Battle of the Somme.

When you serve in the U.S. military, it makes you part and parcel of American history. It makes you undeniably American. And not just blacks. You get a guy who comes here from Armenia. And he decides, "I'm gonna be in the military." Now he is as American as the next person.

We recently went to an event where they honored "Ten Nubian Men," as they call them, black men prominent in the community. They had a doctor, they had a lawyer, they had a preacher. They had a guy who was a cop, they had a businessman. They had all these different guys. But at the end I said, "You're missing one. You're missing a warrior. You're missing the guy who defends your village and your way of life." When you become a warrior, when you serve your country—it doesn't matter whether you're called or whether you enlist—you then have the right to say to people, "What have you done for your country?" Now, you can be a warrior in other ways. You can be a warrior by going into the Peace Corps. You can be a warrior by being in VISTA. You can be a warrior by working in an inner-city school. You can do all of those things. But when the rubber meets the road, those guys who have placed themselves in harm's way, and women who have placed themselves in harm's way, should be listened to. They should not be looked down upon but should be elevated to a place of honor because of what they chose to do.

My one brother who didn't serve in the military has put in twenty-five years as a New York City firefighter, and he is a tremendously courageous individual.

I was at my desk, writing, the morning of September 11, and my wife came downstairs and shook her fist at the television—CNN was on. And the phone rings and it's my brother. He's on a cell phone, and he's on his way to the Trade Center. He's calling to ask me to make sure that his children are taken care of if anything happens to him. He came out of it okay, but they lost thirteen men from his firehouse.

I was in tears. Our country was being attacked; we were being attacked on our own soil. I had friends in those buildings; I lost some of them. My office was there years ago, on the fifty-second floor, when I worked for the governor. And it was happening right next to my beloved Brooklyn; when we lived there, I used to go up on the roof of my house and see the towers. And they were going down. And here I am, armed only with my keyboard and my computer. I had been one who would place his life on the line and go in harm's way at a moment's notice, but now I was too old.

And so I began to think about the newer generation of our family. My son's in Army ROTC down at Hampton University. My brother has a son who's in Marine ROTC. I have friends, the Perez family, whose son was with the military in Europe on 9/11, getting ready to go to jump school and become a paratrooper. And I'm saying, "Is this another generation of our family and friends who are gonna be placed in harm's way?" I said, "I don't know. But it's every American's right and obligation to defend their country. We've been given this great country, and we have a duty, a stewardship to fulfill, and that's to keep our country strong."

Our family has a tradition that service is a way of life. And there is no greater service you can perform than to serve your country, particularly in time of war.

IV

"We knew right away we were going to war."

PEARL HARBOR AND THE GULF OF TONKIN

We know—to the minute—when World War II started for the United States: 7:55 A.M., Hawaii time, Sunday, December 7, 1941. Indeed, a day after Japan's brazen and massive attack on America's naval, air, and ground assets stationed at Pearl Harbor, Franklin Roosevelt called upon Congress to declare war retroactively: "I ask that the Congress declare that since the unprovoked and dastardly attack . . . a state of war has existed between the United States and the Japanese Empire." The resolution passed Congress with only one dissenting vote. On December 11, Adolf Hitler, standing with his Asian Axis partner, declared war on the United States, and the American government reciprocated within hours. America had joined the worldwide fight.

The beginning of America's war in Vietnam resists pinning down. Did it begin on May 7, 1954, when French forces at Dien Bien Phu fell to Ho Chi Minh's Vietminh, leaving the United States the effective guarantor of the West's interests in Vietnam? On January 2, 1963, when American advisers watched with dismay as 1,500 heavily armed South Vietnamese troops were embarrassed by 350 Vietcong guerrillas in the Battle of Ap Bac? On March 8, 1965, when two battalions of Marines began arriving in Da Nang?

Or did it begin on August 2, 1964, when the first of two supposed Gulf of Tonkin incidents took place? That day the USS

Maddox *was stationed in the Gulf of Tonkin, near the North Vietnamese coast, to monitor a series of covert attacks undertaken against that coast by small South Vietnamese seacraft operating under American orders. To the surprise of American commanders, three North Vietnamese patrol boats took action, firing ineffectually on the American destroyer. The* Maddox, *in concert with fighter jets from the aircraft carrier USS* Ticonderoga, *returned fire; two of the North Vietnamese boats escaped with damage, one was rendered dead in the water. Lyndon B. Johnson shrugged off the affair, taking no more than five minutes to discuss it in a meeting with his top foreign-policy advisers.*

He responded with more vigor to events that occurred two days later. On the morning of the fourth, Washington time, the Maddox *reported an electronic sighting of hostile vessels apparently preparing for another attack, threatening not only the* Maddox *but also another destroyer in the area, the USS* Turner Joy. *Robert McNamara, the secretary of defense, began preparing a list of North Vietnamese targets for U.S. retaliation. By afternoon, however, word came from the* Maddox *that the apparent sighting had likely been the result of "[f]reak weather effects on radar and overeager sonar men. . . ." But Johnson, in the midst of his bid for another four years in the White House, saw an opportunity. Striking at the North Vietnamese would inoculate him against charges of weakness leveled by his bellicose campaign rival, Republican Barry Goldwater, and would intimidate members of Congress who might otherwise oppose his domestic agenda. So, late that night, after McNamara induced the military to confirm the initial report and to make sure that the officer who had reported second thoughts recanted them, American carrier aircraft launched attacks against four North Vietnamese patrol-boat bases and an oil-storage facility. In public, the administration did not voice any doubts as to the existence of a second attack, nor did it acknowledge the coastal raids that had provoked the incident(s).*

LBJ's next move was to introduce to Congress the Gulf of Tonkin Resolution. The resolution expressed support for the president's immediate response to the North Vietnamese hostilities. But it also granted Johnson a free hand to "take all necessary steps, including the use of armed force," to protect any Southeast Asian ally. Members of the administration assured nervous members of Congress that they need not worry about the open-ended provision, as the president entertained no thought of a significant buildup of U.S. forces in the region. Johnson rammed the resolution through Congress; it passed on August 10—unanimously in the House, 88–2 in the Senate. Campaigning that autumn, he promised that he was "not about to send American boys nine or ten thousand miles away from home to do what Asian boys ought to be doing for themselves." Beginning just a few months later and throughout his term in office, as he sent more than a million American boys to do what Asian boys could not do for themselves, LBJ cited the resolution as his authority.

The Gulf of Tonkin Resolution stood until January 1971, when the Senate, increasingly aware of the falsehoods behind it, voted 81–10 for its repeal. The repeal had no practical effect, however, as Richard Nixon claimed that his position as commander in chief gave him all the authority he needed to continue prosecuting the war.

Franklin Roosevelt's casus belli was unmistakable and devastating; he asked for, and received, a nation's unqualified support. Lyndon Johnson's casus belli was manufactured and insignificant; he did not activate the reserves, he did not extend military tours, he did not end student draft deferments. Not coincidentally, support at home for World War II never wavered, while support for the war in Vietnam, though broad at first, in time decayed.

In his State of the Union address on January 8, 1964, President Johnson admirably proclaimed, "This administration here and now declares unconditional war on poverty." Lyndon Johnson did not flinch from declaring metaphoric war to achieve his vision of a Great Society, but he would never declare the real, shooting war that would cost his society its tranquillity, its confidence, and fifty-eight thousand of its children.

Since World War II, no president has requested, and no Congress has passed, a declaration of war.

GENE CAMP

RETIRED CAREER MILITARY OFFICER
SAN ANTONIO, TEXAS
CAPTAIN, UNITED STATES ARMY, WORLD WAR II
MAJOR, UNITED STATES ARMY, VIETNAM

Born in 1920 into what would quickly become an "extremely broken family," as he describes it, Eugene C. Camp finished high school in his native Fort Worth, Texas, where he lived with his father and stepmother, then traveled to San Diego, California, to stay with his mother and third stepfather. "This is when Hitler's running rampant throughout Europe. It appeared to even the most naive that we were gonna get into this thing. There were congressional debates about the draft, so I was thinking it would be best to go ahead and have a military affiliation rather than let them draft me into it. So in June of 1940, in San Diego, I joined the 251st Coast Artillery (Antiaircraft) of the California National Guard."

Three months later the unit was called to active duty in the United States Army.

From San Diego they sent us to Ventura, California, where we had a temporary camp in the ballpark. They told us that we were staging and that we were going to Hawaii to bolster the antiaircraft defense there. That sounded great: a year's vacation in Hawaii. We had a lot of people join just to go there. On the thirty-first of October, we boarded the SS *Washington* headed for Honolulu.

At first we were in a temporary camp at Fort Ruger, right at the base of Diamond Head, but we didn't stay there long. We moved out to Barbers Point, which is a promontory about nine miles—as the Zeroes fly—from Pearl Harbor. We built our own camp, Camp Malakole. We built these nice, long, one-story wooden barracks, built a beer hall and mess halls and everything.

I got promoted to corporal in July of '41, then, in November, I was promoted to sergeant.

We worked long and hard, even on Saturdays—Saturday mornings, at least. We didn't make enough money to enjoy Waikiki or the tourist-type things, but it wasn't too bad. We had movies at the bases. And there was a lot of camaraderie: We're all in this thing together, and we have to take pride in our unit.

By late 1941 I'd say that we were superbly trained. Everybody knew their job, what to do, and how to do it.

There were troops all over the island. The Army had around forty-two thousand; the Navy varied, of course, with whether the fleet was in or out. They used to say, "Bring in anything else, we're gonna sink this island."

We were the lone National Guard regiment at that time; all the other units were Regular Army. Sometimes we would go into one of the beer gardens, and they would get a little chant going:

I'd rather be a pimp in a whore's backyard
Than a chickenshit corporal in the National Guard.

That occasioned a few fistfights every now and then

In Hawaii I didn't have time to read papers or magazines much and didn't hear an awful lot of news on the radio, so I was not clued in on what was going on in the Far East, other than the fact that there were problems with Japan. But we always thought, if anything, they would hit the Philippines. They wouldn't hit us.

Everybody was really worried about what was going on in Europe. But that didn't affect us. We're out here in the "Paradise of the Pacific."

There were something like a hundred thousand Japanese on Oahu, and although they had never shown any signs of disloyalty, the higher-ups were worried that we were subject to sabotage. So they put the whole island on antisabotage alert, and we moved everything closer together so we could better guard it. And not only our guns, but the airplanes, too; at Wheeler Field and at Hickham Field, they were all lined up close together.

I had just come off a week as sergeant of the guard, and I was pretty tired. So Saturday night, December 6, I went down to the beer garden, had a couple of beers, and went to bed. I was going to sleep in on Sunday morning—the only morning that we could.

I was sound asleep in my bunk when I heard a plane come over, and a short burst of automatic-weapons fire. The plane going over was not unusual, because the Navy had a dive-bomb target off of Barbers Point, and after they practiced their bombing, they loved to buzz our barracks.

It was probably the machine-gun fire, not the plane's engine, that woke me up. And then it all seemed to happen at once. The mess sergeant came running in and said, "Get up, you guys, the Japs are on us, and they've shot Childress!" Herb Childress was a staff sergeant who bunked in the opposite end of the barracks from me; he had been wounded by this strafing plane.

We got up, and about three of us ran out onto our little porch. And just as we got out there, here is this plane making a low, slow bank around us, and it's got great big red circles on the wing. I remember it like it was yesterday. I don't know who it was, but somebody said, "Jesus Christ, that's not one of ours!" At just about that time, our air-raid siren went off, and the bugler of the guard started blowing call to arms.

We went into action. There was no panic; everybody did what they were supposed to do. My driver got what we called our "prime mover"—a five-ton Mack truck—and went over where these twelve three-inch guns were all lined up, hub to hub, and got it hooked to our gun.

The planes kept coming back, not continuously, but they strafed us off and on. We had nothing but these 1903 Springfield bolt-action rifles to shoot a fast-flying plane. We didn't really stop to do that, because our mission was not to defend Camp Malakole, it was to go down to Pearl Harbor. But when a plane starts coming over strafing and you have a rifle and some ammunition, you take a couple of potshots at it. I got off two or three rounds. They didn't cause any damage, I'm sure.

We took off for our battle positions at Pearl Harbor. We were breaking all the speed limits. That's a five-ton truck pulling that big gun. If anything had gotten in our way we would've crushed it, but fortunately nothing did. We passed through the little town of Honouliuli between Barbers Point and Pearl Harbor. We'd been through many times on work details and on practices, and the civilian population had never paid any attention to us. But this day they were all out there, giving us a V for victory. "Our boys!" "Go get 'em."

We rolled on in to our battle position inside the Navy ammunition depot at West Loch, one of the three Lochs at Pearl Harbor. The Marine guards welcomed us with open arms. We had prepared this position. We had revetments for the guns, we had ammunition storage places.

Now, there's four wheels on this gun, and they were called bogies. There's a manual jack, and you have to jack the gun up so you can undo the bogies and pull them out. Then you jack the gun back down; that sets it on the ground, and then you unfold the four outriggers. Once you get those out, then you unfold the platform that the gun crew works on, and that platform sits on top of the outriggers.

All this takes time to do. And while we're working, there's a lot of booming going on, and smoke. There is a peninsula between West Loch and Battleship Row, so we didn't have a direct line of sight into there—plus, we were so busy getting our guns ready, we weren't sightseeing. But you could certainly hear it, and you could smell it. It's burning oil that you smell. And when a round explodes, the cordite has a peculiar odor—once you smell it, you'll never forget it.

The bunker we had was open at both ends in order to get the gun in. Once we got the gun in, got the bogies out, and did all that other stuff, we were in the process of closing up the ends of the bunker with sandbags. And that's when the attack ended—two hours after it had begun.

It was a terrible disappointment and frustration that we didn't get to fire: We've been training all this time, and now here's our chance to do what we've been trained to do, and we don't get to do it.

When the attack began, there was at first disbelief: This can't happen. Where did they come from? How did they get here? And then it turned into a sense of blind, absolute rage: What are they doing? We could hear the planes going over and the antiaircraft from the ships—and they kept on doing it.

Herman Wouk, in his book *War and Remembrance,* has got a phrase I often use when someone asks me how it felt. He said something to the effect that Pearl Harbor incurred in the proud Yanks an irrational desire for frontier justice. We were mad. We were angry.

I never went down to Battleship Row to look at the damage; I really didn't want to. I saw it from a distance two or three days after the attack; that was close enough. It was still burning and smoking, there was oil all over everything. It was so devastating.

TONY RIVAS SR.

RETIRED SUPERVISOR, AIRCRAFT PART MANUFACTURING,
UNITED STATES AIR FORCE CIVIL SERVICE
SAN ANTONIO, TEXAS
SEAMAN FIRST CLASS, UNITED STATES NAVY, WORLD WAR II

Born in San Antonio in 1922, Antonio V. Rivas Sr. grew up in hard times. "My father used to play the violin. He used to go on each corner where there was a store, and he used to play there, and they would give him fifteen cents or twenty cents. He used to take us to pick cotton for three months in the summer—we were in school, and that's the kind of vacation we used to get.

"It was rough during those days, but we made it. Tamales were maybe three cents a dozen, and bread was maybe five cents a loaf. We were happy."

In 1941 he found employment through the Work Projects Administration (known originally as the Works Progress Administration), the New Deal program that between 1935 and 1943 gave work to 8.5 million Americans.

I was working at the airport digging ditches for the WPA, and I heard somebody's car radio. And people were talking: "They bombed Pearl Harbor! They bombed Pearl Harbor!" I said, "Where in the hell's Pearl Harbor?" I didn't know where Pearl Harbor was. Oh, in the Pacific, in Honolulu. "Where's Honolulu?" I didn't know where Honolulu was. In Hawaii. "Where's Hawaii?" I didn't know where Hawaii was.

We didn't have no radio at home. There used to be a barbershop right up the street, and they had a radio—we would go there and listen to the news. People trusted the barber more than anybody else. If we needed a doctor, we didn't have no money—we'd go to the barbershop. If you got a bee sting, he'd tell you, "Hey, don't forget, you use mud." Okay, we use mud. We'd ask him questions. Anything that goes on, the guy that was cutting the hair knew about it. That's the reason why we ended up there, to learn what was going on.

The people at the barbershop, the people on the streets, they were going wild—"Extra, extra, read all about it!" Everybody was thinking maybe those Japanese will come over here to San Antonio and beat the hell out of us. On the radio there was news all the time—they didn't put no music, nothing, just the news. And then later we heard President Roosevelt's speech.

Everybody was talking about it. And I said, "I'm gonna do my part. Do my part and help the United States."

MAS TAKAHASHI

RETIRED SERVICE STATION OWNER
TORRANCE, CALIFORNIA
TECHNICAL SERGEANT, UNITED STATES ARMY, WORLD WAR II

Masao Takahashi was born in Modesto, California, in 1924, to immigrants from Japan. When his mother died—Mas was three or four—his father, a migrant farm laborer, sent Mas and his four siblings to live in a Salvation Army orphanage for Japanese American children in San Francisco's Japantown.

"We went to the public schools. The grammar school was mixed—we had blacks, we had Jewish, Chinese, Japanese, Mexican, Italian. And we all used to get along good there. Then we went to junior high and high school; they were mixed, too. We all got along."

During high school, Mas left the orphanage and joined his father and brother on a farm near Stockton. "They were leasing the farm—people from Japan weren't allowed to own land then. I went to a vocational high school in Stockton, and that was mixed, too. We all played on the same football team, same basketball team.

"Before the war I didn't feel prejudice amongst anybody."

Pearl Harbor happened on a Sunday morning, so I was at home on the farm when I heard about it. We knew right away we were going to war. But I didn't think anything would happen to us. We were U.S. citizens.

I blame a lot on the newspapers. All the newspapers and the radio commentators—Westbrook Pegler, Walter Winchell—were putting all kinds of stuff out about the Japanese, that we were the enemy, that they should round us all up. They fired up the Caucasians and all the other groups.

The Caucasian people I knew weren't like that, but among the general public, it was snowballing. There were all these signs they put up in the stores: "Japs Get Out." Trying to be like they were patriots or something. A lot of the Japanese were afraid. I wasn't afraid—I was too young to be afraid, maybe.

And then Roosevelt signed that executive order to evacuate all the Japanese who lived on the West Coast. I had thought he was pretty good. But after he signed the order, I had my doubts. Earl Warren is another guy. He was the state attorney general, and then he was the governor. He wanted to get us all out of California. And he became, what, chief justice of the Supreme Court? I said, "What a farce that is."

First they rounded up most of what they called the leaders of the community. Japanese schoolteachers, Buddhist ministers, business leaders. They took them to a little jail, and then they sent them to special detention camps—Bismarck, North Dakota; Crystal City, Texas; and some other places.

General DeWitt is the one who really forced the issue. He was West Coast Army commander. He figured every Japanese was a spy. I barely knew some of the Japanese language. But they didn't try to distinguish; they just took the whole group. Here's a baby in an orphanage, and he don't have any parents. How the heck is a little baby gonna be a spy in an orphanage? But they sent 'em to camp anyway.

Some of the fishermen down in San Pedro had twenty-four hours to get out. At least we had a little notice.

You only could take what you could carry. You'd get a big sheet to throw all your stuff in and tie it up—that's it. We took mostly clothing, because you couldn't have radios, you couldn't have a camera—they took everything away.

Everything we didn't take, we lost. We had a horse, a truck, whatever we owned in the building, and the crop. My brother had this guy trying to run it after we left. He couldn't make a go of it, though. Nobody got any compensation until long after the war.

The Army was at the station to make us get on the train. They searched you to make sure you didn't have any weapons. Someone from the War Relocation Authority was there; they gave each family a number.

I didn't know where we were going to; they just put us on a train.

We ended up in Manzanar.

They picked us up in an Army vehicle, a troop-carrier type, and they took us into camp.

Manzanar is near Lone Pine, California, in the desert. Right below Mount Whitney. It's sandy, flat. Tumbleweeds. The executive order came out in February 1942; this was about a month after that, so it was springtime. But it was cold. The wind would blow.

The camp was just a bunch of tar-papered barracks. They took you to whatever block you were in and what building you were in—there were sixteen buildings in a block. I was in Block 27.

The barracks was divided into compartments, like; each one was about twenty by twenty feet. My whole family was there, except my older sister. She was married, so she went with her husband to another camp, in Arizona. Five of us—my two brothers, my younger sister, my father, and me—in one room. There were big cots, with straw in the mattress. There was not much privacy. You had to go out and use a common shower room and bathroom—each block had one.

They issued us Navy pea coats, it was so cold. They had a stove in the barracks to keep us warm. Then, in the summertime, it got hot and windy and dusty. Sand would be blowing.

I don't know how we managed, to tell you the truth. But half of the time we weren't home anyway. We were running around. Each block had a mess hall; we used to roam around the camp and go to different mess halls.

You could get a job doing different things. I had all kinds of jobs in there. I worked at the hospital cleaning the floor. I got a job driving the car around to pick up patients. I worked at the warehouse, where the supplies would come in. Then I worked at what they called the irrigation crew—we had to dig ditches out there. We didn't get much done; we used to go out and play cards.

A lot of outsiders say, "It wasn't so bad." Yeah, it wasn't so bad, because the people in there made it better. Instead of just sitting around and protesting, some of them made their own furniture, made rock gardens. They had regular Boy Scouts, regular Christmas things. It was just like a regular city. A community. They started what they called the *Manzanar Free Press*—mostly camp news—and then they started delivering one of the papers from the L.A. area. They used to have dances at different blocks. They'd have baseball, football, basketball. We took the championship of the camp when I played basketball.

Most of the teams kept where they came from, like San Fernando or Montebello, for their name. But on my team we were from all over different places. So somebody said, "You know the Japanese airplanes, Zeroes? We'll call ourselves the Zeroes."

It was just like everyday life—except the Army was guarding the place. There was a barbed-wire fence, and in front of it was a buffer zone—you had to keep that far away from the fence. There were guard towers; the guards had rifles and machine guns. I don't know why. I just couldn't understand all that.

The younger people figured out activities, but the older people were pretty much down. They were the ones that were affected the most. They really took a beating, from when they first came from Japan. They had to make their way, and they couldn't speak the language. They couldn't own land. They couldn't do anything. And now they get put into camp. What they were trying to accomplish was down the drain.

BILL KEITH
RETIRED SCHOOL CUSTODIAN
MARSHFIELD, MASSACHUSETTS
HOSPITAL CORPSMAN FIRST CLASS, UNITED STATES NAVY, WORLD WAR II

"I always wanted to join the Navy. I just liked the sea," says William J. Keith, who grew up on the Massachusetts coast. He joined the Navy in August 1940, four months after his eighteenth birthday. After boot camp he was put aboard the USS West Virginia, *a* Colorado-*class battleship commissioned in 1923. Before long, the* West Virginia *headed for Pearl Harbor. First assigned to man a five-inch gun, Bill asked for and received a transfer to become a hospital corpsman. "I'd go down to sick bay, and these guys were in nice beds. I figured it was better than sleeping in a hammock."*

The morning of December 7, I got up and pressed my uniform, because I was getting ready to go on liberty. Then, around five of eight, you could hear all this noise, you could feel the shaking of the ship. You had to go to your battle station. Mine was the first-aid station, down about the third deck. There were six lower decks altogether; I was about in the middle of the ship. They closed all the hatches and everything—we still thought it was a drill.

When you go to a battle station in a ship, every door is locked, because you don't want water coming in there. So we started getting a little bit scared. No way to get out, right? But luckily somebody opened the hatch. Freedom. I don't think it was what you'd call a real panic—nobody was yelling. But a lot of men didn't get up that ladder because everybody was stepping on each other.

I got up on the main deck, but I'm not sure how. Some things I don't remember. I don't know why.

The planes were still strafing the ship. So, to get out of the way, we hid under the turrets of the big guns.

After the shooting stopped, they announced, "Abandon ship."

I came down the ladder and jumped onto this other ship that was inside of us that didn't get really hit, the *Tennessee.* We went down a ladder from there to the water, and it was just a few feet to Ford Island. That's the island in the center that all the ships were tied around.

That night we all were given rifles, and we were in, like, foxholes. There were a lot of rumors that the enemy was going to land. That night the Americans sent some planes over from a carrier, and they were shot down. Did you ever know that? By our own gunners.

The *West Virginia* got seven torpedoes—the most of any ship—and a couple of bombs. When you stop to think of it, one torpedo can do a lot of damage, right? But if you get seven, that's a lot of explosion. It was 106 men lost from the *West Virginia*.

I found an old paper bag. I wrote "I'm safe" and mailed it to my mother. She kept it for years. But one day she says, "Well, that's old." She threw it away. Now, that would have been a good keepsake. She kept it for years and years. I wish I had it today.

GREG CAMP

RETIRED CAREER MILITARY OFFICER;
EXECUTIVE, MILITARY FOUNDATION
COLUMBUS, GEORGIA
CAPTAIN, UNITED STATES ARMY, VIETNAM

On July 1, 1964, seventeen-year-old Gregory C. Camp reported for the beginning of his education at the United States Military Academy. "The first summer at West Point, which is referred to as

Beast Barracks, is just about like basic training. The first thing you do is go in and get your head shaved, and then you go through and get all of your uniforms. From that moment on, you've got upper-class cadets that are basically like drill sergeants. Beast Barracks lasts nine weeks, until Labor Day weekend. Then you become a fourth-classman, which is a plebe. You have a whole year when you have to respond to every upperclassman."

The cadet commander of Beast Barracks is referred to as the King of Beasts. There's a July cadre—a group of upperclassmen who train you—and then they leave and an August cadre comes in. So one guy is the commander for July, and another guy does it in August. And typically they're vying to be the first captain of the corps of cadets, which is the top-ranking cadet, for their senior year. The guy who was the King of Beasts the first month I was there was named Bob Arvin. I mean, a mind's-eye image of a soldier: square-jawed, dark, handsome, everything. He had all the military presence about him. He was the captain of the wrestling team, and he was really smart: an athlete and a scholar. We thought the world of him.

After July he left for a month's vacation, but he came back a little early, because he was, in fact, selected to be the first captain. Once at dinner he came and sat at the end of the table where some of us plebes were sitting. And we hung on every word he said—he was an idol to us. He was talking to this other first-classman about the Gulf of Tonkin incident and about the fact that there would be American soldiers over there. He was excited about this—the idea that "I'm training to become an officer to go to war, and there'll be a war for me when I graduate."

And sure enough, he graduated. And sure enough, he went to Vietnam. And sure enough, he was killed in Vietnam. The gym at West Point is named after him now: Arvin Gym.

When you start West Point, they give you these name tags to stick on your footlocker, your wall locker, and anything else you need to identify. I remember when I first saw my name tag. It said, "Camp G C 68." This is in the summer of '64, and I'm thinking to myself, "Nineteen sixty-eight will never come." Every day seemed like an eternity when you were in Beast Barracks. Nineteen sixty-eight—that was like a new millennium.

So when Bob Arvin was talking about Vietnam, I honestly did not think that it was gonna impact me. I assumed it might impact him and his class, maybe even the next class. But surely if there was a war, it'd be long over by the time I graduated.

Probably about a year into West Point, that assumption changed, because every year they would bury somebody from the previous year's graduating class. And they'd bury more each year: It was unusual for the class of '65. They buried two or three from the class of '66 by the time the class of '67 graduated. They buried three or four from the class of '67 before our class graduated. Of course, only a few of the West Point graduates who were killed in Vietnam were buried at West Point, but when someone was killed, wherever they were buried, you heard about it. So by the time I had been there a year and a half there was no doubt in my mind that the war would be there when I graduated.

One of the things that brought the war home to me was, I was a Sunday-school teacher when I was there. The cadets used to teach Sunday school to the kids on post, and they'd always pair you up. So when I was a plebe, I got paired up with a junior, Denny Loftheim. We taught together for two years, and I thought the world of this guy. He was way up in his class, either a regimental commander or on the brigade staff, I'm not sure which, and he was a "star man"—if you were in the top 5 percent academically, you wore a little star on your collar. He was quite a role model for a guy like me. But he was killed and buried at West Point before I graduated.

There's a little chapel inside the West Point cemetery, and for a burial you'd go down there, and it would be very much a military funeral, with a flag-draped coffin and buglers and a firing squad. It was a sobering event for cadets who knew they were going to graduate and then go to Vietnam.

It was enormously sad. When Bob Arvin died, it sent a cold chill through the corps of cadets, because he was revered. It really shook up West Point.

V

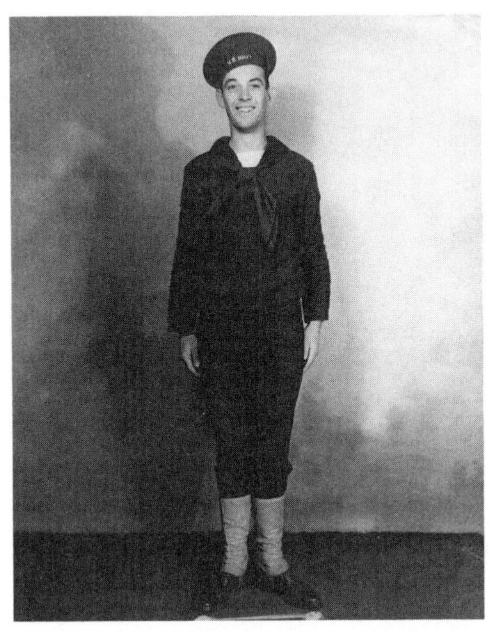

"I grew up in two minutes."

JOINING AND TRAINING

These are the times that try men's souls," wrote Thomas Paine as America readied for its revolution. "The summer soldier and the sunshine patriot will, in this crisis, shrink from the service of their country; but he that stands it now, deserves the love and thanks of man and woman."

The men in this book share a common chronology: They came of age in trying times, when their government was calling for the services of able young men. By accident of birth, the responsibility to fight—or to choose not to fight—fell upon them.

Some of them, veterans of World War II and Vietnam alike, joined the military because they believed in the endeavor to which their country was calling them. Others held no brief for the war they were being asked to fight, but instead believed simply that they could not let their country's call go unanswered. Still others had more personal reasons—to prove their manhood, to learn to fly a plane. Of course, a number joined through no choice of their own. But by the end of their initial training, all the draftees in this book—even the young men conscripted for the controversial war in Southeast Asia—came to believe in the cause they were about to join and in their destiny to fight for it.

Some veterans speak of the harried first weeks in the Army or the Marine Corps—the regimen is not so harsh in the Navy or the Air Force—as "brainwashing," and not all use the term perjora-

tively. "They do brainwash you," says Dave Pollins, who recalls the pride he and his fellow recruits took in completing boot camp and being told, at last, "Today you are Marines." Stripped of its sinister connotations, the word "brainwashing" is an apt metaphor for Army basic training or Marine boot camp. Ingrained habits of thought are washed away by Army drill sergeants and Marine drill instructors, whose voices and demeanors possess the force of water cannons. New ideas are affixed on the bare surface that remains—especially the idea of obedience. "They do, intentionally, break you down spiritually," says Mickey Hutchins, "more or less in order to get your attention. And then they build you back up in the way they want you to be—as a solid soldier. The truth of the matter is that coming in there most of us had some baggage that we needed to leave at the door, and after the first couple of weeks of basic most of us had pretty well left it. Then by the time we got to the end of those eight weeks, I think we had a pretty good idea of who was in charge. And when somebody told us what to do, we had a pretty good idea when to do it. That was a good foundation to work with."

MIKE PERKINS

TREMONTON, UTAH

CAPTAIN, UNITED STATES ARMY, VIETNAM

I graduated high school in '59, and, like most guys, I went to college. But I realized after a term at Brigham Young that this wasn't for me. I went to work in the natural-gas fields in New Mexico for a while, then went up and worked in Spokane where they were building Atlas missile sites. I did that for about a year and a half and finally said, "I'm going nowhere with my life."

I went to San Francisco and wanted to go out on a merchant-marine ship, but you had to belong to the seamen's union; I went down to the seamen's union, and they said, "Well, you have to go out and sail first." A catch-22. So finally I said what the heck and joined the Army.

I took basic training at Fort Ord, and I loved it. Most people griped about the regimentation—I thought it was great. Sometimes in the morning when they got you up, it was a pain. Other than that it was fun.

My drill sergeant was Sergeant Martin. Sure, he yelled. He did what he had to do. But I idolized the guy. He was the kind of soldier I wanted to be. He had been an airborne ranger in Korea. He was a black guy, Sergeant First Class Martin.

Toward the end of basic, he let his guard down a little bit, and we sat around in the barracks talking about what it was to be a soldier and fight in combat. "Life is not what you think it is as a soldier. It's the worst thing you'll ever imagine." But he said, "This is where you find out what people are really made of." And he was absolutely right.

He'd been in an all-black airborne ranger company. He was telling us, "We had to prove to those white boys that we were just as good as they were." And that left an impression on me about treating people fairly. He was such a good soldier and such a good example for us, I guess that's where I lost a lot of the color-consciousness that people use to look at the world.

I really idolized that man. He was killed, sad to say, about three years later in Vietnam. He was an adviser with one of the Vietnamese ranger units.

I met a lot of good people in my life that told lots of stories. I remember Mr. Waters, who I used to work for when I was putting those Atlas missiles in. He'd been a Marine lieutenant at Iwo Jima, and he was marked for life because of that. He always had that faraway stare.

I used to ask Mr. Waters about it. And he said, "I'd rather not talk about it. But I'll tell you it's not something human beings should be doing."

I said, "But you're a man who stood up and defended this country."

He said, "I'd do it again, but it's not something human beings should be doing." And *he* was right. But somebody has to stand up and do it.

ED JACKSON

RETIRED COMPUTER SYSTEMS ANALYST,
UNITED STATES AIR FORCE CIVIL SERVICE
TIPP CITY, OHIO
STAFF SERGEANT, UNITED STATES ARMY AIR FORCES,
WORLD WAR II

Edmund F. Jackson was born in Tipp City in 1924. When war came, he was a civilian employee at what is now called Wright-Patterson Air Force Base, in Dayton.

"I didn't have any idea that there was gonna be a war until we heard about Pearl Harbor. When that happened, you got aggravated to think that anybody could do that to your country. You wanted to do something about it. Kids are that way: When you're younger, you don't think of the danger that's involved."

I tried to enlist in both the Navy and the Marines, but they wouldn't take me. When I went to the recruiting office, they said that I didn't have enough molars. I hadn't taken too good care of my teeth, and I'd had some teeth pulled. They said I could get shell shock—they were pretty finicky. I didn't know how I could get shell shock from having bad teeth, but I didn't think too much about it. I just was sad that I didn't get to go.

I wound up drafted—I went in the service February 23, 1943. Everybody was crying when I left. I got on a bus in Tipp City and went to Troy and then into Columbus for the final physical they gave you. I went through the physical with flying colors, like I was the healthiest guy that ever lived. Nobody said anything about my teeth.

Ed was soon assigned to the Army Air Forces and took basic training in Clearwater, Florida. "I was thrilled to death. Flying seemed exciting and modern."

After basic training I went on to Colorado. I went to both Buckley Field and Lowry Field, which were armament schools—one of them was for pursuit armament, and the other one was for heavy-bombardment armament. They taught you about turrets and how to take .50-caliber machine guns apart, put 'em back together blindfolded, and all this kind of stuff.

After I got done there, they sent me down to Laredo, Texas, to gunnery school, and I thought, "Boy, this is really gonna be something," because usually when you came out of gunnery school, you automatically got to be a buck sergeant. You got flying pay and you got the gunner wings, and there was a lot of glory attached to it.

Laredo's where I took my first airplane ride, in an AT-6. You flew backwards in the thing. It had a little safety strap that come up from the floor and hooked through your parachute harness. You always had to have a parachute on.

When I went out there, the pilot was asking me if I'd ever flown before, and I said no. And he said, "When I rock my wings, you pull the .30-caliber around into position"—they had a .30-caliber machine gun in it—"and feed your ammunition into it. And the next time I rock my wings, start firing at the sleeve." Another plane would be pulling a sleeve, which was a long cloth tube that was used as a target.

After we took off and we got up in the air, he rocked his wings, so I stood up. Luckily, I'd had sense enough to put that strap up between my legs, because I pulled that gun around, and the next thing I know, he turned that plane over and was peeling off, going down.

Scared the daylights out of me. He finally leveled off and rocked his wings again, and I was supposed to see a sleeve out there. But I didn't see it. He had already told me that if I knuckleheaded—that means bringing back any live ammunition—the next time he took me up, it was really gonna be a rough ride. So I just started firing, even though there wasn't nothing to fire at out there as far as I was concerned.

Every once in awhile, you'd have this short round—a round that wasn't in the belt properly—and it would jam your gun. They put in different malfunctions to see how you'd react. And you'd have to get the cover plate up and get the ammunition out and try to feed it back in, then pound that cover plate back down. I didn't have any gloves on, so by the time I got back on the ground, my hand was beaten to dickens, all sore and bleeding.

When we got out, he said, "Let's go over and see how many hits you got in that sleeve." People had different-colored paint on their shells—that's how they kept track of who hit what.

We went over there, and there wasn't any holes from my shells. He said, "You sure are a poor shot."

"Yeah, I guess I am."

Well, I never saw the sleeve or the airplane that was supposed to be pulling it or nothing. I had no idea where it was. Maybe it wasn't even there. Maybe he knew it wasn't there, and he was just pulling my leg. All I knew is that I wasn't gonna bring back any live ammunition.

After that it was kind of fun, because I knew exactly what was gonna happen, and I was always ready for it—I was looking for the thing that was pulling the sleeve a long time before we ever started firing. And I was able to hit the sleeve quite a bit.

Gunnery school lasted about six weeks. All along they was washing people out for different reasons. I don't know, maybe they couldn't shoot what they was aiming at, or maybe they just got airsick.

So when I finished the whole course, I assumed that I had hit it: I was gonna get my wings. We were in formation, and they called your name, and you went forward, and they'd give you your wings and a diploma or something. And when they called my name, instead of getting wings, I was told to report to the orderly room.

We ended up with about sixteen of us in there. We were all talking among ourselves: "What's going on? What's going to happen to us? Why don't we get wings?" And that's when they called each one of us up separately and told us the reason that we didn't get them. In my case they said, "You don't have enough molars." They had pulled some of my teeth out at the gunnery school even.

I said, "What's that got to do with it?" And once again they said it had something to do with being shell-shocked.

I was really down.

After I didn't make it through gunnery school, I went down to Chatham Field, in Savannah, Georgia. I was gonna be in the ground forces of the Air Corps, in the armament section, mostly loading bombs on the airplanes and all that stuff. They had B-24s parked there, and you had to take the guns out of the turrets and clean them and take them back out to the plane and put them in. Different things like that.

After we completed our training in Savannah, they put us over to Hampton Roads, Virginia, where we shipped out on a big convoy of Liberty ships. It took us about thirty days to get to Naples, Italy, because of the evasive actions and submarines being in the area. I was stationed at a small town, Spinazzola, with the 460th Bomb Group. They made an airfield there. They had these big steel mats for the runway and for the B-24s to be parked on.

One day my name appeared on the bulletin board to report to the orderly room. So I did, and they said that I had had all the training to be an aerial gunner and they were short on aerial gunners, a lot of 'em being killed. And they wanted to know if I would volunteer to fly. I said, "Yeah, I'll volunteer."

That was either the dumbest thing I ever done or the smartest.

PERRY POLLINS

LEXINGTON, MASSACHUSETTS

CORPORAL, UNITED STATES MARINE CORPS, WORLD WAR II

In 1940, at the age of sixteen, Perry went to Montreal to join the Canadian navy. He made two runs to England aboard a Lend-Lease transport ship; on the way home from the second, a German submarine torpedoed the vessel.

The ship survived, but Perry took shrapnel in his knee. He was recuperating in a hospital in St. John's, Newfoundland, when the Japanese attacked Pearl Harbor.

The next day I told the medic in charge of the room that I'd like to go back to the States and enlist in the service. A couple of weeks later, I left the hospital. The day after that, I enlisted.

In those days civilian doctors examined us to approve our joining any branch of service. I was interviewed by a Jewish doctor. And while he was examining me, he says, "Why does a nice Jewish boy like you want to join the Marine Corps?"

My response immediately was, "I want to kill Japs."

"Well, you got shrapnel in your leg. I can make you IV-F."

"I want to kill Japs."

He signed me over.

My first dealings with a Marine DI, I'm sitting at a table in Parris Island, eating my breakfast, and all of a sudden I feel something sharp sticking in my neck.

This DI has a swagger stick with a .30-caliber slug on the end of it, sharpened to a point. He says, "You see that black shit in front of you? It's a cup of coffee." And I say yes. "Have you ever drunk that stuff before?" And I say no. "You drink that."

And he says, "Do you shave?" I say no. "Blankety-blank, goddamn it, you go back and you shave." So I grew up in two minutes—I drank a cup of coffee and I shaved, whether I needed it or not.

One thing taught us in boot camp was what they called the French bayonet system: parry, thrust, butt stroke, parry. We were up against these wooden machines that were a copy of your adversary, but they didn't stick you back. A week or so into this, a Colonel Biddle—of the famous Biddle family from Philadelphia, a big strapping guy—personally explained to us the "Biddle bayonet system." He said, "The Biddle bayonet system is based on the fact that you gotta kill the fucking enemy." He pointed out that the Japanese had a hook on the end of their bayonet. "They are very adept with it. If you parry and thrust and they get that hook under the hilt of your bayonet, you're gonna be without a rifle, because they'll just *whoosh*—and you're done for." So he said, "You see some son of a bitch running at you carrying a rifle with a bayonet on the end of it, shoot the bastard. And if you can't do that, kick him in the balls."

The discipline was demanding, it was intrusive. In the Marine Corps, when you took an order from a superior officer—noncom or commissioned—you did it. Without question you did it. They knocked you around—they kicked you in the ass, they came up behind you with their swagger stick and hit you behind the knees. Looking back, it was harsh. But, boy, it sure was persuasive.

After two months of boot camp, I was sent out to Camp Pendleton for four months—two months of radio school, plus infantry training and amphibious training.

In the Marine Corps, you did things over and over and over and over again. And if you didn't do it, they yelled at you, they denigrated you, they beat you. I think rote is the best teacher of anything. They teach you how to kill, over and over again; they teach you radio procedures, how to climb out of a landing craft on the high seas, how to get up the beach—you do it over and over and over again. Then you know how to do it.

On top of that, they keep telling you, over and over again, that the Marine Corps is the greatest fighting force in the entire world. There's nobody better than us. Period. And all of a sudden, you begin to think that way.

HOWARD BAUGH SR.

RETIRED CAREER MILITARY OFFICER
MIDLOTHIAN, VIRGINIA
CAPTAIN, UNITED STATES ARMY AIR FORCES, WORLD WAR II

"The whites in Virginia didn't want to have anything to do with us," notes Howard L. Baugh Sr., born in Petersburg in 1921. "Hotels were segregated, restaurants. Everything was separate. You couldn't drink out of the same water fountain. If you went in a place and happened to get a drink of water, they'd break the glass so that a white man would never have to drink from it. Washing it wasn't enough.

"Jim Crow was the way of life. Maybe some people got angry about it; I didn't. Maybe I didn't have sense enough to. I was born into it and I accepted it and I didn't think that it would ever change."

I wanted to fly, even as a teenager. I wanted to become a pilot, any kind of pilot. But I knew that I couldn't afford to buy flying time, because we grew up poor, so the only way I could get to be a pilot was to fly for the military services. But the Air Force—the "Army Air Corps" at that time—wasn't accepting applications from African Americans for pilot training.

Pilot training came on at the right time for me.

In January 1941, after promises made to African American leaders by Franklin Roosevelt during the previous year's election campaign, and after the filing of a lawsuit by a black college student whose application for pilot training the Army had rejected, the War Department announced the formation of an all-black Air Corps unit, the Ninety-

ninth Pursuit Squadron. Training for the pilots who would fly the Ninety-ninth's fighter aircraft would take place on the grounds of Tuskegee Institute, an all-black college in Tuskegee, Alabama, and at Tuskegee Army Air Field, to be built nearby. The first class entered the program in July 1941. Howard got to Tuskegee in March 1942.

Pilot training is tough. I mean, military pilot training. In civilian pilot training, if you're paying somebody by the hour to teach you to fly, he doesn't care how long it takes. You can fly with an instructor for fifteen, twenty, twenty-five hours. But in the military service, when there is a war going on, if someone doesn't solo in ten or twelve hours, he is eliminated. And that happened to a lot of people. Some classes had a higher rate of completion than we did in my class, but of the twenty of us starting, only four finished.

You got up early in the morning, and you came out to roll call. Then you went in and made up your bed and cleaned up. Then you marched to breakfast. Then you marched back. Then you either went to the airfield or you went to a classroom. You did that till lunch, and then you marched to lunch, and then you marched back from lunch. Then you either went flying or to ground school, whichever you didn't do in the morning.

After about five o'clock in the evening, they called it free time, but it wasn't free. There was always something to study, or you'd do some physical training. It wasn't a fun time. It was work, work, work.

In the early twenties, the Army War College conducted what's called a "staff study" to determine how African Americans could best be utilized in the armed forces.

The study concluded that African Americans were lacking in intelligence, that we had no qualities of leadership, that we thought of ourselves as being inferior to whites, that we were by nature subservient, that we were cowards who would run in the face of the enemy. It recommended that African Americans could best be used in service jobs—truck drivers and ditchdiggers and latrine diggers, anything that didn't require intelligence.

When the Tuskegee program got under way, people all over the country thought the government was throwing away money trying to train African Americans to fly airplanes. People in the military felt that way. A lot of people have come to think of the Tuskegee experience as an experiment that was supposed to fail but didn't.

The base commander when I first got down there was Colonel Frederick von Kimble, and he wasn't enthusiastic about the program. But he didn't stay there very long, and Colonel Noel Parrish took over. He was the best thing that ever happened to us. He was very much in favor of the training. He believed in what we were doing and made numerous trips to Washington, D.C., on our behalf to keep the air base going.

The local black population was very friendly to us. If they had extra rooms, they would rent them out to dependents. My wife came down there, and she stayed with a doctor and his family for a while. Then, after I graduated and could leave the barracks, we had a bedroom in the home of a nurse. Tuskegee Institute was a totally black college—faculty and students and administration. The surrounding community, where all the faculty and the workers for the school lived, was black also. It was completely separated from the white areas.

We had very little to do with Tuskegee town—we weren't welcome down there. I don't know of any specific incidents, but you could tell there was hostility, just like there was in Virginia.

It was the custom of the Army at that time to conduct itself in accordance with local laws. And Alabama law, as in many other states in the South, required segregation. You didn't have a choice. Even whites didn't have a choice.

So, even though Army regulations required that all officers belong to the officers' club, at Tuskegee we had an officers' club but the white instructors and other white personnel on the base didn't have to belong. Even in the PX cafeteria they had a section set off to the side for whites.

The people running the program never said anything about any historical significance. I think it may have been good if they had, but they didn't. And we were so occupied trying to fly the airplane and not get washed out that we weren't concerned with anything else.

History never came into it. I think people who make history, all through history, never realized at the time that they were making history.

PAUL KEITH

Consultant, Transportation Industry
Plymouth, Massachusetts
Specialist Fourth Class, United States Army, Vietnam

"Growing up," says Paul E. Keith, who was born in 1949, "I knew the historical significance of Pearl Harbor and that it was meaningful that my father was there.

"I was curious about it, but I knew not to ask him—he just seemed closed about it. He did have a drawer in his bureau that had some memorabilia—some papers, some old pictures—and I snuck in there."

I knew I was gay by the time I was six. I didn't have a label for it; it's a retroactive understanding. I suppose mentally I put on the label in my early teens. But looking back now, I knew I was different when I was a little kid.

I never was able to talk to anybody about it—in the fifties and sixties you didn't talk about straight sex, let alone anything else. Being gay was part of my negative self-image: Something's wrong with me. I'm not the tough guy like my brother, Steve, who was cocaptain of the football team, and my dad, who was at Pearl

Harbor. And it was part of what drove me to make a determination, somewhere prior to Vietnam, that whatever it was I was afraid of, I would just go straight at the monster and go head-to-head with it. Because I was tired of being afraid.

I was a kid who had nightmares a lot and would wake up screaming. I dealt with that by sneaking downstairs at midnight to watch the horror shows on TV. You deal with fear by going straight at it. I didn't like heights, so I went skydiving.

I wasn't a physical or combative person, so I signed up for Vietnam. Inside I had a feeling that if I didn't come back, that would be okay. It's not that I was suicidal. But I was either going to grow up and be tough or die trying.

I remember having a debate with my history teacher, Mr. Barclay. He was dead set opposed to any of his students going over there. He and I used to argue about it after class.

I remember telling him, "I'm hearing this, I'm hearing that. I want to go over there and see for myself."

He told me it was a damn stupid thing to do, that I should go to college and forget about that nonsense. But I wasn't ready to go to college. I think inside what I wasn't ready to discuss with my history teacher was that this thing was so scary I had to do it.

I was aware of the disputes, people flying to Canada and whatnot. To each his own. That's not what I was thinking about; it was more internal. I hate to say there was this huge thing going on in my generation and I was just picking out my personal agenda from it. But that's what I was doing. It wasn't till I got there that I actually started to formulate some ideas as to what it was about.

I went to the recruiter just before I graduated in June of '67. In fact, I had to get parental permission, because I hadn't turned eighteen yet—my birthday is June 20. After graduation my parents gave me a big going-away party, and I went up to the Boston Army Base to go through the induction process.

We had to fill out a health-and-fitness questionnaire, and I lied on it. There was a series of yes-or-no questions. One asked if you had a heart murmur, another if you had fainting and dizzy spells. Well, I did have a heart murmur, and it did cause dizzy spells and make me pass out from time to time. It was something you grow out of anyway, but I didn't want to tell the Army anything that would keep me from joining. Then there was a question I didn't expect to see: "Do you have homosexual tendencies?" I was aware that most of the people I knew were doing everything they could not to go in and probably would've been happy to check yes on some of those questions. But I checked no on all of them. I wanted to go in.

At the bottom of the form, it said that each act of perjury was punishable by five years and five thousand dollars. The homosexual-tendencies question was count one. The heart murmur was count two. The dizzy spells and fainting, count three. So three acts of perjury for fifteen years and fifteen thousand dollars, all in one day when you're eighteen years old.

When I started basic training at Fort Jackson, South Carolina, I found I liked it. I was a good soldier. I surprised myself.

I liked the challenge. Now I found something that I did well. And even though I had the drill sergeants on my case just like everybody else, I got made a squad leader. That was a big ego boost.

The military did a lot to enhance my self-esteem. The more they threw at me, the more I found I could come up to meeting it. It felt good to be good at it. I had an opportunity to volunteer for Vietnam. There's a no-brainer—that's why I enlisted.

I came out of basic training with orders for transportation AIT. I stayed at Fort Jackson, just moved over to a different brigade. My first MOS was 64-Alpha, a truck driver. I'd never even driven a car in my life.

When I graduated from AIT, I got orders for Germany. That was bullshit. I mean, they had to have mixed me up with someone else. I went down to the first sergeant's office, banging my fist on his desk.

"Private, you get your hand off my desk. What is your goddamn problem?"

"I got orders for Germany."

"So?"

"I volunteered for Vietnam."

"You are a stupid bastard. I got a hundred and sixty men out there that'd cut off a nut to take your place."

"Find one."

Looking back at it, maybe somebody who would've gone to 'Nam is alive today because he went to Germany instead. And I made it back alive, so it's okay.

MAS TAKAHASHI

TORRANCE, CALIFORNIA
TECHNICAL SERGEANT, UNITED STATES ARMY, WORLD WAR II

After Pearl Harbor the Japanese in Hawaii weren't put into camp. And a few months later they took the Japanese from two regiments of the Hawaiian National Guard and transferred them to the One Hundredth Infantry Battalion, an all-Japanese, all-Nisei unit. Nisei means "second generation." They are actually like Japanese numbers: *ichi* is one, *ni* is two, and *san* is three. So Issei is the first generation, then Nisei, and Sansei is the third generation.

Around that time a questionnaire came out, and the two most important questions were "Are you willing to serve in the military?" and "Are you loyal to the country?" I put yes and yes on the questionnaire. If you signed no/no, then they would kick you in a group and send you up to Tule Lake, a camp in Northern California. The government plan was to trade them for prisoners of war in Japan.

In January '43 they formed a larger Nisei unit, the 442nd

Regimental Combat Team, with recruits from Hawaii and the mainland. There was an announcement in the *Manzanar Free Press* that they were looking for volunteers. My older brother volunteered, but I didn't, because my father said, "Just one of you volunteer." My brother tried to volunteer for the service before the war. He tried Navy, Marines, Coast Guard—he wanted everything else but the Army. But they all refused. So now he joined the Army and went to Camp Shelby for training.

In the autumn of 1942, Mas was allowed to leave Manzanar to do farm work in Montana and Idaho; before returning to camp, he harvested sugar beets and picked apples. At the end of 1943, he and two friends received permission to relocate away from the West Coast. Joining another friend who had already left camp, they went to Detroit, where the War Relocation Authority found them employment, first in a creamery, then in a machine shop.

At the beginning of the war, they'd made my draft status IV-C, enemy alien. But when the guys from Hawaii were doing so good, then they started drafting all the Nisei and changing their status to I-A.

My brother came to visit me in Detroit from Camp Shelby—that was just before he was shipping out. And right after that I got my draft notice.

They shipped me to Fort Sheridan, in Illinois. That's where they give you your haircut and issue your clothing and make you do KP. And then they shipped us down to Florida to train at Camp Blanding.

It was all Japanese. They were coming from different parts of the country—Wyoming and Colorado and places like that. Some had been in camp, but a lot of them had not. The officers and noncoms were Caucasian.

Our cadre, they didn't know how to look at us. You'd go to these orientation things, and they'd show you a newsreel of the different battles that were going on. And there'd be some Japanese on it, a flag, and we'd raise hell: "Banzai!" And, boy, they got on our case—they were ready to court-martial us. What's the matter? You guys can't take a joke?

The One Hundred and the Four-Four-Two were already in Europe fighting. One day we were out on bivouac, and they said, "Everybody pack up and go back into camp." I thought there was gonna be a hurricane. Then, the first thing you know, they're saying, "Everybody turn in your equipment."

I said, "What's going on?"

It was because the outfit was taking so many casualties in Europe. We were getting shipped over without finishing basic.

Before going overseas, we had furloughs. They flew us back and forth—they were losing so many men over there they wanted us in a hurry.

We had papers "not to detain this man." So when I got to Manzanar, I had the freedom of walking in and out of the camp. And purposely I did that. I just walked out and came walking back in, and out and in. There was nowhere to go; it's nothing but desert out there. They stopped me, but I had these papers.

Only my father was there at that time, because my sister went to Milwaukee and my other brother was up in Utah working at a munition plant. My father and I were never too close till after the war. We never had seen each other much, because I was in the orphanage—just that brief time before the war. I didn't know if I'd make it back, so I didn't want to leave any hopes by saying I'll be back or anything. I just said good-bye.

GREG CAMP

Columbus, Georgia

Captain, United States Army, Vietnam

In 1964, when I was a plebe, we went to Shea Stadium to watch Army play Syracuse in football. That's when Syracuse had Floyd Little and Jim Nance. We didn't win, but it was a good game. And it was a big thing for a plebe, because this was the first time we were allowed off post, and we had about four or five hours of freedom after the game before we had to catch a bus to go back.

In New York City, you couldn't pay for a taxicab. You couldn't buy a drink. You couldn't pay for anything, because you had your uniform on. If you were a West Point cadet in New York in 1964, it was almost like you played for the Knicks. Everybody wanted to be your friend.

But as the war built up, that changed. It probably took a couple of years, but even by '65 I can remember it starting. And in '66 or '67, we went up to Ithaca for a track meet—I was a miler and half-miler. We had a bus that said "Army Team" on it, and when we got back after the meet, there was a bunch of graffiti on it—"Get Out of Vietnam" or "Baby Killers," stuff like that.

Then, in the spring of '68, when our first captain, his brigade staff, and a cadet color guard marched into Yankee Stadium before the start of the opening game of the baseball season, they were booed. The people threw anything they had at them—tomatoes, eggs, cups.

So it changed from the very end of an era of great respect when I started West Point to, by the time I graduated, a time when cadets were pretty much persona non grata in the public at large.

We were mad. We were really mad. We're starting to see some of our friends come back dead. And knowing that virtually every cadet that graduates is going to Vietnam within a year or two, we're seeing the public turn against us.

At this point I know personally I was still very much caught up in the administration's image: This is a noble war. We're saving South Vietnam from Communism. The domino theory. All that made good sense to me. But now the country has turned against people who are out executing the administration's policy. And I'm thinking, "This doesn't seem right."

Upon graduation, Greg chose to go into the infantry and volunteered for service in Vietnam with the First Cavalry Division.

"You're joining the United States Army. You're gonna be an infantry officer. What do infantry officers do? When their country calls them to war, they go fight the war."

After some additional schooling and five and a half months with the Twenty-fourth Division in Fort Riley, Kansas, Greg was given thirty days' leave before he was to fly to Vietnam in June 1969.

At the beginning of the month, I was just relaxing, enjoying myself. But there was this cloud that loomed bigger and bigger. The last week or so, it was almost like, I can't enjoy this anymore—I just need to go.

I spent the last few days visiting family in Fort Worth. By far the hardest part of going to Vietnam was when I finally got on the plane—I flew from Texas to Seattle, then on to Vietnam. My sister took me to the airport. She had just seen her husband off to Vietnam the day before. She had a baby boy, Timmy, probably a year old then, and was in Fort Worth to stay with our maternal grandparents while Tom was gone. He and I went and came back within twenty-four, forty-eight hours of each other.

My sister is not an outwardly emotional person. She keeps her feelings to herself. You almost never know what she's thinking.

So she was chitchatting away, like I was going off to summer camp—this was pretty normal for my sister. I hugged her and said something like, "I'm heading off." And as I went to get on the plane, I turned around, and she was bawling.

VI

"We just lived in snow."

JOHN MACE

JOHN MACE

RETIRED FARMER

BRAZIL, INDIANA

STAFF SERGEANT, UNITED STATES ARMY, WORLD WAR II

After their breakout from the Normandy hedgerows in July 1944, Allied troops raced across France and Belgium, pulling up along Germany's western frontier by mid-September.

In autumn, however, progress turned to stagnation. Operation Market-Garden, British commander Bernard Montgomery's audacious plan to strike into Germany via Holland, proved a disaster (see Al Tarbell's account in Chapter XI), and ensuing Allied operations were hampered by overstretched supply lines and shoddy generalship. So, aside from a small salient that extended just past Aachen, the front lines in the west essentially conformed to Germany's border on the night of December 15, 1944.

Despite this three-month standstill, Allied generals reckoned that Germany lay wide open before them, defended by troops deficient in number, morale, and equipment. Intelligence reports described a buildup of German forces in Belgium's Ardennes Forest, a stretch of the western front manned weakly by troops of Courtney Hodges's First Army. But Allied commanders, George Patton excepted, believed what they wanted to believe. The morning of December 16, they awoke to news that astonished them.

Two hundred thousand German soldiers attacked a front held by fewer than half that number of Americans, as Adolf Hitler threw his remaining reserves of men and supplies into an effort to inflict such serious damage on the Western Allies as to drive America, Britain, or both from the war. Then, freed from the distraction in the west, he would be able to concentrate on his enemy in the east, the Soviet Union. But the führer had underestimated the might and resolve of his three main adversaries from the war's beginning. Once again his enemy bent but did not break.

American defenses held on the northern flank of the offensive, but to the south, German men and tanks, aided by inclement weather that grounded Allied aircraft for the offensive's first seven days, managed to push forward a salient in the lines—a bulge—some sixty miles into Belgium. However, clearing Belgian skies and stiffening American spines—like that of John S. Mace, a twenty-one-year-old infantry sergeant in the Seventy-fifth Division—ruined Hitler's scheme. Fighting the Battle of the Bulge in a winter that was Western Europe's coldest in forty years, Allied forces did not finally eliminate the bulge until February 7, 1945. But by that time the failure of the German offensive had been apparent for a month. A hundred thousand Germans and eighty thousand Americans were killed, wounded, or captured in the Bulge, but the Allies had men to replace their casualties, whereas the Third Reich's cupboard was bare. At last Germany lay wide open to its conquerors, east and west.

There was a lot of farm boys who stayed out of the service, some for the duration of the war, on account of they was needed on the farm.

You can see why there was a farm deferment: for the necessity of production. They had a point system set up. If you had milk cows, you got so many points per milk cow. If you raised hogs, you got so many points per head. If you had corn or wheat or beans, you got so many points per acre. If you applied to get a farm deferment, you had to have so many points to qualify.

Daddy and Mother, as much chickens and pigs and what few cows they had, and the acreage we was a-farming, why, they had enough points I could have stayed out. I was called in to duty on the twenty-third of March of '43. Daddy took me to Rockville, the Parke County seat, and I got on a bus and went to Indianapolis to Fort Benny—Fort Benjamin Harrison. Later on, Daddy told me that after I had left that morning, he went over to the county agent's office. Daddy knew him personally; Noah Hadley was his name. And he asked Daddy, "What are you doing here in Rockville this time of the day?" We had to be up there at seven-thirty or eight o'clock. And so Daddy told him. He said to Daddy, "Lou, why did you let that boy go?"

Daddy said, "He felt like it was his duty to go."

"With the size of your farming operation, you had enough points to keep him out."

"I know. But that wasn't his desire."

I don't know as I was any more patriotic than anybody else, but I had the feeling that the service was one of the things you had to face if you wanted to enjoy your freedom. You have to serve your country, and I served with pride.

The farm boys that stayed out of the service for farm deferment and then stayed on the farm after the war was over had a big jump on the rest of us, as far as the price of commodities—grain, milk, what have you—whenever we come out.

I can't say that I really had ill feelings, but I was often reminded of it. It's something you didn't mention. Most of the time, it was just within you.

There were some, after they got out of high school, that was working public works, and they went back to the farm to stay out of the service. Then, when the war was over, they quit the farm and went again to public works. Today they still carry the name "draft dodger."

Two families up here had four boys that went in the service. One had five. And this father that had five, he'd worked diligently in the REMC—the Rural Electric Membership Cooperative—trying to get electricity out to the rural area. He was one of the people that would volunteer to go around and talk to whoever lived in a certain area to get permission to put a power line past their house and to collect the ten-dollar membership dues to join the cooperative.

The one that had the five boys in the service, he went and seen his neighbor—his neighbor had one boy. Well, he didn't need no electricity. He wouldn't even allow them to trim the trees in front of his house so the electric line could go by. They had to go across the road with the line and go past his house and then come back across the road again.

Well, when his son come up for the draft, they didn't have enough points. So he goes out and buys some milk cows, and they built up enough points to keep the boy out of the service. And as soon as he started buying those cows, he went to the REMC—he had to put in a milk machine to milk the cows with, and he had to have electricity. The REMC signed him up, and they put in electricity to the house.

By the time the war was over, his boy was in no danger of getting drafted, so he sold the milk cows and he quit milking. And his next-door neighbor that had five boys in the service, he never did forget it, and you can understand why. Today the fella and his son, they're both dead; the grandson has the farm. He and that family, I expect, are the wealthiest farmers and own the most land in the whole neighborhood.

It still carries. It carries clear down to the grandson.

I was on the first or second trainload that shipped out from the induction center in Indianapolis to Fort Leonard Wood, Missouri, to be in a new division that they were forming. It was the Seventy-fifth Infantry Division. After they had got their quota in there, we had the activation ceremonies—it was along in mid-April of '43. That was the youngest division that was ever activated—the average age was nineteen.

We had an old first sergeant in basic training, and he was a

Regular Army man with several years in the service. Galumbewski was his name. He was a little guy, but he was tougher than shoe leather. And we were put into such misery out there in the hot training area in Fort Leonard Wood that it got to where you wanted to get out and get away from there.

In July they shipped out a lot of our unit. It cut the number in our platoon to where probably we didn't have a third of the number that started.

I don't know how they picked it as far as who went and who didn't. But I went to Sergeant Galumbewski and told him that I was tired of basic training. I wanted to be shipped out right away.

I'll never forget. Sergeant Galumbewski looked at me, and he said, "Mace, you don't want to go." He didn't pick me out, and it wasn't long after that, the old first sergeant told us where those men had shipped to. They was replacements in the infantry in the South Pacific. We had heard reports in the service of how rough it was in the South Pacific, the type of fighting that took place down there—a lot of hand-to-hand combat and that. After I found out where they went, I was glad I didn't go, I'll have to admit.

Then we got in a lot of recruits, fellas that had just been drafted, a lot of them eighteen years old. And so we went through basic training again. Well, whenever you go through two basic trainings, you've had about all you think you can stand of it. After that second basic training, we went to Louisiana on maneuvers. When we went to Louisiana maneuvers, I was a private. When we came off of the Louisiana maneuvers, I was a staff sergeant. The old first sergeant had brought me up through the ranks each month.

By the time we came back from Louisiana, we got another group of new recruits. It was in the summer of '44 down here at Camp Breckenridge, Kentucky—they closed it right after the war. One of the new boys was Fred Pruite, a friend of mine before we went to the service. And Fred, he got a pass and went home, and he brought his automobile back to camp, a 1934 Ford.

One day he said to me, "I'm going home this weekend. If you can get a pass, come with me." So I got a weekend pass. We started home, and he said, "As you ought to remember, we don't have no brakes on this thing."

We drove from Camp Breckenridge, Kentucky, through Evansville and Vincennes and Terre Haute and home. And there wasn't enough brakes on it to stop it within forty feet of where you thought you were gonna stop.

Anyhow, while we was home, he traded it off and he got him a 1936 Ford, a nice one. So most nearly every other weekend, me and him would ride back and forth to home. But he got shipped overseas, as a replacement in the 106th Division, I believe, along about the end of the summer. After that I rode the bus back and forth.

Around the start of October, I came home on a weekend pass. I knew it was my last weekend before shipping out, and I had some stuff in a little old satchel that I needed to take home. For one thing, I didn't like the kind of underwear they had in the service. They were boxers. I always kept them for my inspections, but mostly I wore what I always wore, Jockey shorts. Those Jockey shorts were in the satchel. Also dress shoes. They weren't issued to us, but we were allowed to have one pair of dress shoes instead of wearing the GI combat boots all the time. I was bringing the underwear and the shoes home because I knew that when I got overseas, I'd have to wear what was issued to me. I wouldn't have room to carry anything else.

I didn't want Mom and them to know that this was my last time I'd be home. So when I got home, I shoved that little suitcase underneath the bed. But after I left, Mother found the suitcase, and she was suspicious.

At camp we could talk among ourselves about where we were going, but as far as telling your folks anything, you weren't allowed. Everything was kept a secret, on account of if you were on a troop train at night, even here in the States, there could be sabotage. That was really drilled into us.

So when I left home that weekend, my mother didn't say anything other than "See you in two weeks," or what have you. And I left them with that expectation, that I'd be back in two or three weeks for another weekend. She wrote me a letter and asked about the suitcase. I wrote back and just told her I didn't need those things anymore, and that was it.

But she suspicioned that that was my last time home.

I was never out of the state of Indiana before I went in the service, except one time I went with my grandfather just across the state line to Charleston, Illinois, to buy a tractor motor. It was all new, being away from home and that. Some of it was good, and some of it wasn't so good.

It was hard, especially to start with. But I suppose that I adapted to the military way of life about as good as anybody could've. I didn't press and gripe. That is a trait that's carried me through the years, because no matter what kind of a situation I'm in, I do whatever it takes to get through it.

In October—I'm gonna say about the fifteenth—they shipped the whole division as a unit overseas. We left from New York, and we was eight days or nine days on the boat going over. It was a big boat; in peacetime it was a luxury boat. I forget how many thousands of troops were on that boat.

Up on deck there was a big area that they had boxing and wrestling—that was the only entertainment we had. And if you wanted to box or you wanted to wrestle, then you put your name on a piece of paper and you waited. They'd match you up with anybody comparable in weight.

Of course, I was never a fighter anyhow—a boxer or a wrestler, either one, so I never put my name in. But we had fellas in the outfit that did. And sometimes you got some pretty good boxers—semi-pros, with Golden Glove boxing and that. They had a referee, and they'd go just three rounds. It wasn't supposed to get too rough.

But this one guy was a heavyweight boxer. I don't know what his name was—he wasn't even from our outfit—but I can still see his face. And when somebody'd put their name in for his weight, boy, he went in there for blood. And it got so nobody'd put their name in with that weight.

The last day we was on the ship, after the fights were over, he got out in the ring and started pacing around, going off about how nobody'd fight him, yeah, yeah, yeah. Putting on a big blow show, so to speak.

Finally there was a lieutenant jumped up in the ring. He wasn't very big. He said, "I'll fight you." All over the ship, anyplace that you could see, GIs were hanging around watching. And the big one said, "I can't fight you. You got them bars." The lieutenant said, "I'll take my shirt off. There'll be no bars on me, and don't you worry about that part of it."

So they took their shirts off, put the gloves on. I never seen such a going-over in all my life. That big guy, he'd make a swing, and that little one'd dodge him. And before the big guy knew what was going on, he just had the stuffing pounded out of him. Everybody was just a-cheering the lieutenant on, because that big guy, he was cruel. They stayed to three rounds, and that was the last fight on the boat.

We landed in Great Britain, where we stayed for a few weeks. And while we were there, we done training. Most of it was marching, just to keep you in shape and keep you irritated. Our equipment was catching up to us, and we got everything together. And then we shipped across on smaller boats to Le Havre, France. It seems to me it was on the Saturday after Thanksgiving that we unloaded.

We knew where we was headed. We knew what we'd been trained to face.

We were in a field, sleeping in pup tents, and the kitchen was feeding us till the whole division got in. Then we started to move on toward the lines. We'd move, and then we'd hit an area and wait for everything else to catch up with us before we moved on. And while we were in the process of moving, that's when the Battle of the Bulge started, with the breakthrough in Belgium.

Then things speeded up. We didn't have but very little information as far as knowing just how bad the fighting was and the weather conditions, but we knew it was a life-or-death situation.

We was on a truck till we got up close, then we was on foot. The Germans were still advancing as we got there.

We shoved right into the heavy stuff.

The first time that our particular unit came under fire was Christmas Day of '44. I couldn't tell you what the name of the town was. About the only towns that you remember are the ones you fought the hardest to get.

There were shells coming in on you. You didn't know whether they would hit you or hit your buddy or where they would hit. In Iraq or in Afghanistan, where a bomb would hit the wrong place, it's on the news. But back then it was just a guess. I didn't get hit, but I saw our own troops get hit by our own field artillery when the shells would fall short. You didn't like it, but there was nothing you could do about it. It was no one particular person's fault. It was just a different way of fighting than what it is today.

We didn't have much fighting the next day. The Germans had retreated on back; in the town, tanks was on fire, vehicles was on fire. There was dead people laying around—civilians and German troops. I remember we went by one tank, and the body was like he was hit just getting out of the tank—he was hanging over the hole.

Words can't describe the feeling that you had when you saw something like that. You feared for your life all the while. It didn't make no difference whether it was daylight or dark or what, as long as you was any way near to the front lines. Every morning you started off advancing. You didn't know, when it would come nightfall, whether you'd be alive or whether you'd be dead or whether you'd be in the hospital or where you'd be.

That was not a very good feeling.

We'd been in a wooded area for a couple, three days, more or less in a reserve position. And one night we got orders to be prepared to move out the next morning, the fifteenth of January 1945.

At four, four-thirty in the morning—way before daylight—we moved down to the town of Grand-Halleux, Belgium. From there we spread out in formation and started up across the open fields, and we came to a hedgerow.

The Germans had an outpost there, and we took them by surprise. There wasn't no shots fired. We overtook it, and the Germans gave up. There was four or five of 'em.

Some of the fellas, they said they would take the prisoners on back to headquarters, but this one guy said, "I'll take them back." And he took off with them, and he didn't go too far till he shot them all. Even though they'd given up—they'd dropped their guns—he shot 'em. This boy had got word just a few days before that his brother was killed, and he had such bitter feelings.

We started to move on, and there was a small open field there, leading to a wooded area. We got about halfway across that field when the Germans opened up on us from the woods. Of course, we fell to the ground for cover.

After it was over with, a lot of us wondered, if this one guy hadn't pulled what he did—and I'm satisfied the Germans knew what happened—would the Germans have given up instead of fighting? Of course, we were facing SS—the special, hard-core German troops. But it was always in all the rest of our minds that if he hadn't killed the Germans from the outpost, maybe the rest of them that was in the woods would've given up. Maybe those were a decoy to see whether everything would be all right.

After the war was over, people came around wanting to know if any of us had information in regard to any atrocities that the Germans had pulled on American troops. I'll never forget this one fella, a staff sergeant in another platoon. He said, "No, I don't have. But I've got one atrocity that the Americans pulled on the Germans."

"That's not what we're looking for."

There was an old Regular Army guy who'd come to us down there at Camp Breckenridge, Kentucky. He had been in the Army for a long while, was still a private. He had served a lot of time in the Aleutian Islands.

Sometimes you'd think that he wasn't quite all there. He'd just sit and mumble to himself. When we was here in Camp Breckenridge, I heard him say, I don't know how many times, "After going through all this all my life, when I get overseas and we get to fighting, I reckon I'll be the first one to get killed." Just fussing and complaining.

Well, this same day, January 15, this fella started to climb over the barbed-wire fence that went across the field we was caught in, and they shot him, and he fell over it, dead. I could never figure out why he was climbing over that fence instead of crawling underneath of it. He was off to my left, not too far. He laid there all that day, and he was still there that night when we pulled back. It's a nightmare to think back about it.

They pinned us down there in that snow all day. We were sticking up like a sore thumb out there in our ODs—olive drab, just your dark brown uniform. We never did have no what they call camouflage gear, white outfits to put on to camouflage you in snow. A lot of the troops did, but our unit didn't.

We never did get to the woods that day. If you moved, they fired on you. Consequently you just laid there.

When it was dark, we started to move back. We had one boy that was wounded pretty bad. He made it back near as far as he could, to the hedgerow. A boy by the name of Keith Williams—we always called him Willie, from Iowa—was with me, and we laid this wounded boy on an overcoat. And we were dragging him in the snow, crawling on our hands and knees, moving him behind the hedgerow to get him up to where he could get help.

When the day was over, there was eight or nine dead in my platoon, and there was, I think, seven left that didn't go to the hospital. Out of thirty-seven men. That's rough.

I had two real, real close buddies that were killed. And they weren't, I suspect, as far as thirty feet from me. We had a boy that was killed that day by the name of Jay Kimmelsman, a fine young man. He was from New York, I think, or New Jersey.

At the last company reunion that I was at, this one boy from New York was there—John was his last name—and I was talking to him. It was ten, twelve years ago, in Indianapolis. That was the first time I'd seen him since we were shipped back, split up, and sent home. He was telling me he was talking to Jay's widow or his sister not too long before this reunion, and they asked if he knew anything about Jay's death, whether he suffered long or he was killed outright or what have you. And I told John, I said, "If you see her again, you tell her that he never suffered." I said, "He was close enough to me that I seen him fall. He never suffered any because he never moved a muscle."

The other buddy killed was Kent, from Bloomington, Indiana. Just as polite and nice a fella as you could imagine. It was about a week, I suspect, before he got killed that he got a telegram from home that his wife had had a baby daughter. He was happy about it.

At that same reunion, there were three or four fellas that were in my company that had done a lot of digging and research on people. They said that they had made contact with this Kent's widow, and she never did remarry. She was still a single widow, and his girl, of course, was grown up.

I've thought different times I ought to try to locate the widow, as close as she is, and talk to her. But I just don't feel up to it. He was one of the men that I could always depend on.

I guess there's a lot of it I don't want to remember. This winter, there about the twelfth of December, we had a snow come in, and it snowed up two or three days. We had a big snow all winter long. On up about the middle of January, it was starting some more. One night I told the wife to go to bed, I'd be taking a shower. And as I went back to the bathroom on the far end of the house, I looked out and I seen the snow, and a lot of memories come back. Back there in the Bulge, when my buddies was killed, we just lived in snow.

It seems like it bothered me more this winter than it ever did. I guess just because there was snow. It was long. It stayed cold.

That day, January 15, ended my fighting in the Bulge. My feet and legs had frostbite that turned into trench foot, and that night I was sent back to the medics. They sent me on from there, and two or three days later I arrived at a hospital in Paris.

There was just no feeling in my feet. The only treatment that you could get was, you had to keep 'em out from under the covers, keep 'em in the cold. I really can't say why.

I've had circulation problems in my feet—in my late fifties it hit me. And then it has turned into arthritis and cracking of the bones and what have you. There's no question in my mind that a lot of it goes back to the frostbite.

From Paris they moved me to a tent hospital in Le Havre. The medical staff was American, but all the orderlies were German prisoners. Practically all of them spoke English—that's the reason they were using them. Up on the line, you were facing people trying to take your life, take over your country. But talking with these orderlies, they was just like we was.

We had a staff sergeant in our tent. And he went in on Normandy, walked clear through France. He was talking to a German prisoner that day, and he asked this German prisoner where he was out on line. And so the prisoner told him: such and such a spot on the St.-Lô–Paris road.

Come to find out, they had fought pretty near face-to-face. And I'm telling you, they had to hold that GI down. He just went berserk. He said, "You helped to kill my buddies." They had taken a beating in that battle. It was more than that GI could take.

It was the last days of March before they released me from the hospital and I got back to the unit.

We were in combat clear to the end of the war. We were

advancing across country and were in Fischbach, Germany, this little town that had never been shelled or tore up or anything, when we got word that the war had ended. One of the best feelings you could have.

We did occupation duty in that town for a month or so; then they shipped us back into France to a redeployment camp. We were sent back there to be reprocessed—we was doomed for the Pacific. But we hadn't left France yet when the war in Japan ended. We rejoiced. That there was in August.

In about the middle of December, it was my turn to go home. I loaded on the boat in Antwerp, Belgium, on New Year's Eve—'45 going out, '46 coming in—about eleven o'clock at night. That was my New Year's Eve celebration.

Everybody on the boat from Indiana came up here to Fort Benny to be processed out. I was formally discharged on the twenty-first of January. And then they took us into Indianapolis to the bus station. I didn't have too long to wait till I got on a bus to come home.

There was snow on the ground, the roads were slick. I was on the front seat, right behind the driver. I could just see him having a wreck before I got home.

We came down on Route 40, and just east of Harmony here, I told that bus driver, "It's not very far up now to where I get off." I was going to my grandparents' house.

He said, "Hell, I can't let you off there. I'm not allowed to get out of the bus on the road to get your duffel bag out." He had put it in a side compartment on the bus. "The only place I get out of the bus is at bus stations."

I said, "I'll tell you, mister. You stop and let me off. I don't give a damn what you do with that duffel bag." So he stopped, and I got off. But he got out and got my duffel bag for me.

It was around noon when I walked into the house. My aunts and uncles were there. Big day for rejoicing.

I wasn't there very long greeting Grandpa and Grandma, and then we took off for home. At that time Mother and Daddy lived about seven miles north of where me and Mom live now. Just a day of rejoicing.

But I still quite often think of all the fellas that didn't make it.

Mike didn't want to go into the service any worse than anybody else did, but he went. Whenever he was about ready to leave, he said, "Dad, I don't want to go."

I said, "If the country is not worth fighting for, it's not worth living in."

That was the one time I made a statement to him like that. After he was wounded and spent twenty-two months in the hospital, sometimes I wondered whether I told him the right thing or not. But I still think I did. We got a free country. And that there's the main thing.

I remember when he called to tell us he was wounded; it was on Easter morning. Where we lived up there at the farm, the telephone was in the dining room next to the kitchen, and our bedroom was on the far end of the house. About four o'clock in the morning, the phone rang. Well, anytime the phone rings that time of the night, you wonder what it is. So I jumped out of bed and headed for the phone, and of course Mother was right behind me. It was Mike, calling from a hospital in Tokyo, Japan.

Getting that call, I had a lot of memories of World War II and what I'd seen of some of the wounds people had. Not knowing to what extent Mike was wounded, I asked him if he still had both hands and both legs and feet. He said yes. That was a relief, just to know that he still had them. I still couldn't visualize the condition that he was in till two weeks later, when he got back here to the hospital at Fort Campbell, Kentucky. That was a long two weeks.

Me and Mom went down to see him. It was twenty-five or thirty boys in that ward, I reckon. We had to wear special clothing in order to go into it.

We went in, and the shock of it was pretty near unbelievable. They didn't have his leg bandaged or anything. They couldn't even cover it up. They kept it in the open air all the time. We was there a couple of hours before we started back home. I told Mikey, "It's really healed fast, Mike."

He looked at me. He said, "What do you mean?"

I said, "It don't look as bad now as it did when we first came in."

We got a laugh out of that. If you can have a sense of humor about life, it helps you through.

It was a nearly four-hour drive from here down to Fort Campbell. Many, many days we'd leave early in the morning and go down and spend a couple hours with him and turn around and drive back. It was time well spent.

We always knew when he was gonna have an operation—there were seven of them that he went through on that leg. He would be put in the intensive-care unit for so many days, so me and Mom, we'd wait till he was back on his ward and could have visitors before we would go down again.

One time that it was one of the most serious operations, we spread the word. There was a Methodist church in Lena, and a Church of Christ—we had a lot of very close friends in both. And then there was Harmony Church and the Ebenezer Church over here. We told everyone his operation would be on Wednesday. Family members, too.

After the operation, when we could go down and see him, I asked if he got any cards. And he said, yeah, he got fifty-four cards the day before he went to surgery. In one day. I said, "That helps, doesn't it?" And he said, "Yeah, just knowing that people care."

Every once in a while, I'll tell people about Mikey down there and all the cards that he got and the prayers that were said for him. I believe in the strength of prayer and the Lord. There's no other explanation but the healing hand of the Lord and the concern of so many people for his welfare that he was able to come through and still have his leg.

While I was in the service and shortly after, you started hearing about atrocities and massacres and everything that happened there in Germany and Czechoslovakia and all those countries that Hitler had taken over. And it gave you a feeling of satisfaction that what you had done didn't just affect this country, but it affected people throughout the world and made a better place for them to live in.

Just one or two or a dozen people can cause so much pain and misery for so many. It's greed and wanting pride and glory that brings it all about. It only takes a bomb a second or two to tear up something that takes a lifetime to put back.

I remember taking Mike to the airport in Indianapolis when he left for Vietnam. And knowing where he was going, and that he was in the infantry, it was pretty hard to do. But I felt that it was a person's duty to serve the country and help keep it free. It bothers me, the way people take for granted our situation and fuss about things here. As far as I'm concerned, it's the greatest country in the world to live in—otherwise, people wouldn't be trying to get in here all the time.

Of all the lives lost, and all the heartaches and the sorrows and the injuries that have taken place throughout the years, there's not one of 'em that's been in vain.

I love my country.

VII

"Somebody had to walk point."

MICHAEL MACE

MICHAEL MACE

EXECUTIVE, TRAILER INDUSTRY
SAVANNAH, GEORGIA
PRIVATE FIRST CLASS, UNITED STATES ARMY, VIETNAM

The notion of a bulge in the front doesn't occur when considering the Vietnam War because there was no front, at least not in the sense the term was understood by the men fighting World War II. American ground operations in Vietnam did not involve the movement of multiple divisions in order to capture land and occupy it. Rather, they applied much smaller numbers of troops to target not territory but the elusive foe within it. Sweeps, ambushes, search-and-destroys—all aimed at seeking out the enemy and killing him, finding his supplies and nullifying them.

If there was no front per se in Vietnam, there were nonetheless countless U.S. positions that defined the limits of friendly territory. But, unlike the offensive front of the attacking World War II Allies, the "perimeters" of the Vietnam War were defensive positions. Whether surrounding a night encampment of a platoon out on patrol, the remote firebase at which the platoon and its company regrouped between missions, or the huge air base through which the platoon's soldiers and thousands of others had entered and hoped to exit

Vietnam, a perimeter separated the relative security of the area enclosed from the danger that lay without. Even so, the enemy often breached American perimeters. The smaller the enclosure, the more vulnerable it was to enemy ground attack, but at even the largest installations, American military personnel had sometimes to dodge rockets and fend off sappers. American warriors during World War II knew who and where the enemy was. Their counterparts in Vietnam faced an enemy who was everywhere but nowhere, all around them yet often hiding in plain sight.

A foot soldier like his father, Michael V. Mace arrived in Vietnam in January 1969 to join the 199th Light Infantry Brigade, which hunted the enemy on the ground in II Corps.

I helped Dad on the farm until I went into the service. And it was a thing where we'd be talking about who was farming what ground, and he would mention to me and to my brother that someone managed to get a better jump, to get more ground and machinery, by not going into the service. That had an effect on me down the road, instilling a patriotic duty. I didn't want that label—of dodging the service—on myself.

In my mind Dad was a hero. As kids growing up in the fifties, we used to play army all the time, and we'd talk about what our dads had done. Of course, World War II hadn't been that long ago. I was always so proud that my dad had been in the service and in the Army and in the Battle of the Bulge.

It wasn't that war was glamorous. But to me it was an honor to be able to go into the military and give service to my country. Not that Dad preached that to me, by any means. And not that I ever planned on joining the military. But I always held military service in high esteem. I guess I put it on a pedestal. It was the right thing to do.

We studied Vietnam just a little bit in my high-school history class. I remember at one point in time trying to figure out where Vietnam was—it's so small on a globe that it was hard to place. But as I got to be a senior, three out of our class signed up for the Marines before we graduated in May of '66. They were all gung ho about going to Vietnam.

There was the possibility of me having to go, but I didn't think too much about it. I was wrapped up in getting a higher education and in moving from down home on the farm to downtown Chicago, where I was registered at a tech school to become a tool-and-die engineer. But after one semester I knew that I didn't want to be a tool-and-die engineer, so I came back home.

I went over to my uncle's plastic plant in Terre Haute and worked there for a few months until spring, when farming season started, and I said, "I'll plan on farming for a living." And every month more and more of my friends were being drafted.

I'd contemplated going to college and applying for deferment. And Dad said to me, "If you want, we can work out a farming deferment."

I said, "I don't want any farming deferment." I said, "I don't want any deferment. I don't think that the deferments for secondary education are fair. That's one reason why you got so many kids in school now: They took the safe haven of going to college to stay out of the draft, which I view as a coward's way." I didn't know whether it was legal or not; I just knew it wasn't right for some people to have to go and others not. That had been impressed upon me a long time ago. If your local draft board sends you a letter saying that your friends and neighbors have selected you for military service, you go, you serve your country.

My mom wanted me to join the Air Force. But at that time the Air Force had a backlog of people. The National Guard had a backlog of two and a half to three years. Mom said, "If you don't get in the Air Force, you'll end up in the infantry like your dad did."

I said, "That's probably so." And I accepted that fact.

As my friends kept going into the service, it was getting to where there wasn't anybody to run with anymore. Then, in February '68, a reality set in. Jack Krider, the first fella that was drafted from our graduating class, came home dead. He'd been a helicopter door gunner in Vietnam and been wounded twice before. After being hit the third time, he ended up dying on the hospital ship, and when he lay a corpse at the funeral home down here in Brazil, Indiana, I went to pay respects. I sensed then that I would definitely be going, and I sensed I would be wounded. I knew all this. I even sensed I'd be hit in one of my legs—I didn't know which one—and would possibly lose it.

I don't know how I knew it. I'd never even had a physical yet. But that intuition come over me at the funeral home. Totally strange.

In April I was called to Indianapolis for a physical. And when I got to the end, the guy looked at the medical papers that I'd been carrying around, and he says, "What's wrong with you?"

I said, "There's nothing wrong with me."

And he actually stopped and called attention to all the doctors. There were about six or seven of them that were processing guys at the time.

He called their attention to the fact he had somebody that didn't have anything wrong with him, because that was the rarity. I didn't catch it at the time, but when I thought about it afterward, it dawned on me that everybody else was trying to get out on some physical disability. He goes, "You're I-A then."

I said, "Well, good." And he looked at me kind of funny.

After that I never heard anything—other than I did get my Selective Service System card that classified me as I-A—until Friday the thirteenth of August. We'd just gotten back from the Parke County horse-and-pony show. That was a real happy day; we always had a good time at the 4-H fair. But Mom wasn't real happy whenever she handed the mail to me. She had this letter—I saw "Selective Service," and I thought, "This is it." Opened it up, it was my draft notice. I had been selected to serve my country. I was to report on September the fifth.

On September 5, Dad and my uncle Tub, Victor Mace, took me to Rockville to catch the bus to Indianapolis, the same as Dad had done. From the induction center in Indianapolis, we rode to Fort Campbell, Kentucky, where I took basic training.

I was proud of my achievement in basic. At the end of it, you take a test based upon everything you learned. A maximum of sixty-nine points. I managed to set a new record for Fort Campbell, Kentucky, at least in that battalion, by scoring sixty-eight and a half points. They give me a little plaque about that, and I got to be out in front at our graduation. Plus, I shot expert with the rifle. Of course, that probably wasn't too wise if you wanted to avoid getting in the infantry.

They wanted me to become an officer. I said, "Okay, I'll be an officer."

They said, "You can't be an officer and just be a draftee. You have to sign up for another year."

And I said, "I got two years. You want me to go to officers' school, I'll go. But I'm not signing up for another year in this Army." That made the sergeant mad. He was a lifer, and he said, "You'll end up in the infantry."

I said, "That's all right by me. My dad was in the infantry in World War II. That's fine."

I really believe that at that time he stamped my papers 11-Bravo, the infantry MOS.

I went to infantry AIT in Fort Lewis, Washington, for twelve weeks.

With about three weeks to go, I managed to come home for Christmas—it was for ten or twelve days. Before we left the base, they informed our whole infantry company that our names were on orders for the Republic of Vietnam; the date on my papers was the twenty-seventh of January of 1969. If we went AWOL then, it wasn't AWOL, it was desertion, and the penalty was a whole lot more severe.

At home I tried to see everyone. Knowing what was waiting, I was nervous, apprehensive, having second thoughts. There was a sense of loneliness. I'm sure that having a number of friends and cousins over there, the reality was apparent to me: If you go over to Vietnam, you have a good chance of not coming back the way you went, be it physically, emotionally, or mentally even. And I guess I stated my thoughts when I said, "I really don't want to go."

And that's when Dad told me if a country isn't worth fighting for, it's not worth living in. It was a reassuring thought: Freedom is not free. Someone pays a price. And some pay a price for the many that don't have to. Later on, when I was in college, I made that statement to another student. I said, "Maybe by me going, you didn't have to." And his response to me was, "You're a fool—you went," which was the typical reception of Vietnam veterans after they come home.

The day I left my family, it was a cold winter's day. The best way that I can describe the way I was feeling was a kind of numbness and almost an avoidance of trying to say good-bye. I don't like saying good-byes. We were at the gate, and my little sister was there. Becky was just old enough—eleven—to be confused about the whole thing. She knew that I was in the military and that where I was going was not good. But as far as really setting down and trying to explain it to her, I can't say that I did.

You really didn't know what to say. I didn't want my parents to worry excessively about me, even though, having lost my brother four years before in a tractor accident, I realized it was a big load on them knowing that I might be killed. But I drew strength from them in their support, and I guess I just had the faith that I'll be all right, and I'll see you when I get home.

I had a very positive feeling about coming back home. Not overconfident, not believing I was bulletproof, but a feeling that I would make it. For one thing, I intended to. Self-determination, okay? You do everything right, you score high on this test the Army gives you, you shoot expert—and you continue to do the best job that you can.

I still had the feeling that I'd be wounded in one of my legs. I don't have any idea why I would feel that way, that being the way things turned out. My mother has premonitions—maybe I get that from her. I'm not saying it's supernatural, other than there's a little voice in the back of your mind saying, "Watch out. Be careful."

After New Year's I was back at Fort Lewis to finish AIT. Two weeks before we left for Vietnam, we were out on bivouac and slept in snow twelve to fifteen inches deep. And I got my feet frostbitten. I thought, "This is so ironic. Frostbite before I go to Vietnam."

It didn't take long to thaw out, and it wasn't that bad. But they also said that if there were any cases of frostbite from us being out in the snow, we would be getting Article 15s written up in our record. An Article 15 is a reprimand for devious actions, for doing stuff you're not supposed to be doing. For us it was a good motivator to not saying anything, keeping your mouth shut. That came down from our platoon sergeant, and I'm sure he got orders from above.

The people in charge didn't give two hoots in hell about us. This was their way of saying, "We don't wanna fill out any paperwork. You guys are going to Vietnam anyway. You have more stuff to worry about, so stop complaining."

When it was time to leave, they loaded all of our company up at a processing center in Fort Lewis and sent us down to Oakland, California, which was an overseas replacement center. We were down at Oakland for about four or five days, and then we went from Oakland right back up to Fort Lewis. Then from there we flew to Vietnam.

On the flight over, we made the best of it—flirting with the stewardesses, that type of thing. But the reality hadn't hit yet. The reality hit when they landed the plane and opened up the door and you walked out. The stench—it smelled like a sewer. And the heat—it was like you were walking into a bake oven.

The stench was like a septic tank. You'd have half of a fifty-five-gallon barrel that they would put in the latrine, and everybody would go in that barrel. Then guys that were new in-country got the opportunity to dispose of that by burning it.

You poured diesel fuel in on top of it. And when you're burning it, it forms a crust, a burnt top layer. You had to make sure you burned all of it, so you'd have to stir it up to distribute the diesel fuel all through it. That old adage of "The more you stir shit, the worse it stinks" certainly applied. Everybody got that job. I had to do it twice. The memory of that stench is pretty vivid—something like that you don't forget. Having worked on the farm, though, I could handle it a whole lot better than some others. I mean, some guys would gag. Having been around hogs and all, why, not that I had a real good stomach for it, but it didn't make me sick.

From the replacement center, I was sent to the 199th Light Infantry Brigade. Their main base camp was located in Long Binh. I was assigned to Charlie Company, Second of the Third Infantry.

During my time in Vietnam, there was only one man in my outfit that spent twelve months there. He'd been wounded twice, but he actually DEROS'd when his twelve-month tour of duty came up. He left about two or three weeks after I got there; until then he stayed away from us new guys big time. He said, "You new guys don't know enough, and you're not gonna get me wounded." But that was the only guy like that I ever saw. The rest had six months or less. There weren't any old-timers. We went through three lieutenants while I was there.

You were either wounded or you were killed.

I was only in the field—when you went out there, you stayed. There were little fire-support bases that we might operate out of, but one of them wasn't much bigger than what Mom and Dad's house is. We would go out on ambush patrols every night.

The temperature ran about 105, 110 degrees, about 90 to 100 percent humidity, all the time. So stifling it was like you were breathing water. On top of that, you're carrying all kinds of equipment—a good eighty, ninety pounds. I always carried an M-79 grenade launcher; it was a forty-millimeter shell. I'd learned in AIT that M-16s jam. I told them I didn't want to carry that, give me something else. An M-79's what I carried.

It was exhausting. You lost a lot of weight pretty quick. I started at about 155 pounds, and I probably dropped 18, 20 pounds in the time I was there. You wouldn't eat much—maybe a can of peaches and some cookies and some hot cocoa, once a day. It was too hot to eat.

The first night that I was out in the field, I spotted three Vietnamese. And it was a thing where there were curfews, and after dark there was supposed to be no movement of any locals; if there *was* any movement, they were considered enemy. So I wanted to fire, and the sergeant said, "No, we can't do that."

I said, "What do you mean, we can't do that? What are we doing here?"

He said, "Mace, we're in a no-fire zone."

"What?"

"We're in a no-fire zone. We can't fire on anybody unless we get permission. Permission has to come from battalion."

"What the hell are we doing out on a nighttime ambush if we can't take and do what we're supposed to? This is contradictory."

"You got a lot to learn here."

"I obviously do."

I thought, "My lands, this is not what I thought it was going to be." What we had been taught was in reverse of the practical application. Not that I was so hepped up on killing anybody. But that was the job that we were supposed to do. I had been trained for five months on it. All through the training, the main motivation was to kill. That was indoctrinated, almost to a point of brainwashing. That was our main goal, to kill people, which is totally opposed to what's your normal life.

So from that first night of being out on that ambush patrol, I had a contradictory mind-set of "I was trained to do a certain thing, but now that I'm here, I can't. What do I do now?"

The officers in charge didn't know what the hell was going on.

It was a total confusion. Things made no rhyme, no reason. It finally got to where I thought, "The less we do, the better it is. Because the more we do, the more we'll end up in a firefight where someone gets hurt."

Our company commander, a captain—I've purposely forgotten his name because I had such disdain for him—was bucking for major, so he would volunteer our infantry line company for every stinking search-and-destroy mission that he could possibly come up with.

We had what was known as Kit Carson scouts helping to guide us—North Vietnamese that had surrendered. This one time the scout told the company commander, "This area is all booby-trapped. You don't want to go in there. You can go around." He didn't pay any attention to the scout, took the Third Platoon in there, and the casualties ended up being all but about seven guys. Almost thirty guys were killed or wounded because of his arrogance. He was career, doing whatever was necessary to make his way up the ladder. We had 144 in the company when I came in-country; we had 62 when I left. That's 57 percent casualties.

I heard this one guy say, after we lost most of that Third Platoon, that they were trying to collect money to put on our company commander's head. I didn't have anything to do with that, and it never came to anything, but he made stupid mistakes. Everybody makes mistakes. But when you saw a series of mistakes that cost people's lives and limbs, well, then you started handling things yourself. Fragging was one of the ways that you handled people in authority that made stupid mistakes. Now, I know the government doesn't like to hear that, but that's what happened.

There was one fragging that I knew of while I was there. It wasn't in my company; it happened back at the brigade base camp about six weeks after I came in-country. I was appalled. I thought, "My lands, that's our own man." But having experienced the stuff out in the field with our company commander, I could understand it. He didn't listen to reason. We weren't walking fast enough on point one day, so he came up, took the point himself, and walked point for the whole company—the captain, the man in charge. Which was totally irrational, because the point man was the man out front of everyone else. This captain had all these men under his command, and the life expectancy of a point man was about twenty seconds. That left him vulnerable to being separated from the men he was responsible for. That's how psycho he was.

Sometimes we'd be out on patrol at night, come in during the morning, rest, clean our weapons and all, and then go out on an afternoon patrol and come back before dark.

We did mostly sweeping operations and search-and-destroy. Searching for caches of weapons and rice. We destroyed all of it—you'd put an explosive to it. Or you'd call and have diesel fuel brought in to ruin the food. Any bunkers that we would find, we'd blow up. I'd carry C4 plastic explosives and detonator caps for that.

We didn't have any trucks—generally we walked everywhere, although we did do a few air assaults. My first air assault, they brought us into an area that was supposedly a hot LZ. I was on the first chopper coming in, and the door gunners and the chopper pilot and copilot had already given us instructions: "Don't make us throw you out of the helicopter. Make sure you jump out of the helicopter so we can get the heck out of here."

Being as enthusiastic as I was, I was sitting in the door, right next to the door gunner. He opens up when we first get close, and you can see flashes from the tree line. You know you're getting shot at.

Well, he starts to return fire. And all the other door gunners on that one side started to penetrate all along this one nipa palm line. I was the first guy on the ground—I think it was because I was so scared. I wanted to make sure I got out of that chopper—it was a whole lot bigger target to hit than what I am. I jumped out of the chopper, and I had so much stuff on I came clear up to my knees in mud. I got up and worked myself loose and turned around, and the chopper is still about five feet over my head. It hadn't even come down yet—it had to have been twelve or fifteen feet off the ground whenever I bailed out.

It seemed like two or three minutes by the time the others got down and got out, but it wasn't probably thirty, forty seconds. I ended up in the center of this whole sweep line. I didn't get close to the enemy; the people at the left end of the sweep came closer. It wasn't but maybe two or three enemy—something small. I don't think we were ever up against any large force. It was always two or three or four—half a dozen, maybe. Of course, they can do a lot of damage, that number of people.

In fact, the day that I got hit, it was either two or three snipers that had our whole company pinned down. You were lying flat on the ground and you could hear bullets going over you and hitting bushes to where they're knocking leaves off. Or hitting close enough to be knocking dirt in your face. It was very, very frightening, very scary. We were joking about pulling the buttons off the front of our shirts because they were holding us up too high.

When the shooting ended on this air assault, the sergeant came and got me. He was wanting to have me go do a body count. I said, "I'm not doing that." I said, "I'll kill the enemy. But there's not any way you're gonna make me go and count them." The body count was always a big plus for the company and for the company commander. But I had no desire to see any dead people. I didn't want that memory.

There is not a March 29 that comes around that I don't think about what happened on that date in 1969, at four o'clock in the afternoon.

That morning all of us were exhausted from the day before—we'd been on a forced march from six in the morning to about twelve-thirty at night. We'd got in mail. And I was talking with a fella from one of the other platoons, and he told me he was walking point. We were joking about it, because with the life expectancy of a point man so short, if you worried about it, you'd go nuts. And we were both happy to be getting a letter from home. Mine was from Dad—maybe the only one that he wrote me. He said he knew what it was that I was going through and what it was like being in combat and that he understood. That meant a lot.

We went on a search-and-destroy. We were in pineapple fields. About two hundred, two hundred fifty meters apart were water canals for irrigation, with banks up on each side and thick bamboo on the banks. And the enemy had dug in one-man bunkers. The company split in two. We were moving down one canal; the other half was on the next canal, on our right flank. We were blowing all those bunkers up. At one point we depleted the supply of C4 plastic explosives and all the blasting caps, and we were using concussion grenades.

To have the day go a little bit better, I was trying to make fun out of blowing stuff up. I made a game to see how many grenades we could get down in a hole—we'd end up blowing mud and dirt and bamboo everywhere. Plus, we'd joke around: Don't be making a mistake, you'll blow yourself up. Just acting like twenty-year-old kids with a bunch of explosives.

I was having such fun that our platoon leader, Lieutenant White, came back, and he says, "Let me blow some stuff up."

I said, "Lieutenant, you gotta be careful." I told him what I was doing as far as sticking my arm through the bamboo, reaching down, and then rolling the grenades off into these one-man positions. You always had to yell, "Fire in the hole," to let everybody know it was an intended explosion and not a booby trap going off. And when the grenades exploded, they would collapse the bunker wall and the bunker would flood out. By this time we had run through all the concussion grenades and were using fragmentation grenades, which you have to be real cautious with. You'll blow yourself up with the things if you don't watch out.

So the lieutenant's sitting right in front of me, and I'm watching him do this, and I'm thinking, "He's gonna sit there too long." And he pulls the pin on the grenade, sticks his arm through, and lets the spoon go, which arms the grenade. And he's sitting there watching this grenade try to roll in the hole—and it stops. And he's waiting for it to go ahead and roll down.

Well, the seconds are ticking off—a grenade goes off after five or six—so I end up grabbing him, and I roll him over. And about the time I say, "Fire in the—" it explodes. And he turns around to me, and he's just white as a sheet. He goes, "Thanks, Mace."

I say, "I'm sorry I grabbed ahold of you, sir." You're not supposed to be putting your hands on officers and throwing them around.

That was about two o'clock in the afternoon and the last time I ever talked to him. A little before four, this guy that I had joked with early in the morning, who was walking point on the other canal, tripped a booby-trapped grenade. Of course, we heard the explosion and then the chatter on the radio about the fact that the point man had tripped a booby trap. Everybody stopped in their place.

While we were waiting on choppers to fly in from the Third Field Hospital that was out around Saigon to pick that wounded man up, it was hot as can be. We all jumped off into the canal—it was black and murky. It stunk. It was really nasty stuff. But we cooled off, and it felt good for the moment.

And then they called me up to walk point. The thing of it was, there were only two of us in our platoon that would walk point: John Kevin McCombs, a good friend, from Terre Haute, Indiana, and I. Nobody else wanted to do that. I didn't really want to either, but I would. Somebody had to walk point.

McCombs had walked it all day, and I knew that he needed a break, so I took over. And there wasn't one man in that whole squad that didn't tell me to be careful, watch out for the traps. McCombs had found a number of booby traps by this time, and when I got up to the front, he goes, "You sure you—"

I said, "I'll be careful." This was only the third time that I'd walked point. About the only way you got any experience was to just do it.

I told the sergeant, "Keep the company commander off my backside. Don't be pushing me to go fast." Because I'd seen him before, wanting to push so fast that people weren't careful enough. And I said, "Don't be following me real close. If I mess up, I don't want anybody else getting hurt."

From that spot, why, I hadn't walked very far at all, maybe twelve, fifteen, eighteen feet. And just as the path along the canal started to go around this little bush, I stepped down off of the berm, and now I was apprehensive. I thought, "I need to probably fire into that bush." A lot of times we would recon by fire, to set anything off if there was a booby trap.

But I thought, "Fuck it."

I should've followed my instincts and shot around in there to see if I could set anything off, because that's right where the booby trap ended up being. You couldn't see the trip wire if you held it up between you and the sun—it was that thin—and they had it strung through the grass. My size-twelve boots tripped the wire.

The first thing that I felt was the *whoosh* of the concussion. I didn't even hear it yet. I felt the *whoosh* of the concussion blowing my helmet off, and then I hear the explosion, and I'm seeing the dirt fly up all around me. And going through my head, "Oh, my God, help me," because in that fraction of a second I realized I'd tripped a booby trap. And being so close to it, I didn't know how big it was.

What they would do is take a ChiCom grenade, tie a wire to it, and put it in a can with the pin pulled. So then when the wire pulls it, it slips out, and the spoon flies off. I surely stepped on the wire with my right foot. And as I moved my left foot forward, the grenade exploded. It couldn't have been any more than three or four inches in front of my leg whenever it went off, because it had that big a force, and the flash of it going off just cooked the front part of my left leg.

I even remember in the milliseconds dropping my weapon and throwing my right arm up in front of my face and turning away from the blast. The only time I don't remember was when I was up in the air—the concussion had knocked me out. This friend of mine, John McCombs, said years afterward, "You went way up in the air—probably fifteen feet." And I said, "I don't remember any of that."

I landed about ten or twelve feet from where I had been, and I'm still carrying all this load of stuff. I regained full consciousness when I hit the ground and woke up in excruciating pain. The best way I could describe it is about five or six men hitting my shinbone with twelve-pound sledgehammers all at once. As if nobody had known, I called back, and I said, "Hey, I tripped a booby trap."

The guys were coming up, and I could see blood running off my arm and feel it running across my face and see it running off my glasses, and I thought I was hit in the head, and I was hoping that it wasn't bad. It ended up that my head wasn't that bad—just pieces of shrapnel in and around my face, burning. But I had caught big huge chunks in and around my right elbow, where I'd gotten that arm in front of my face.

They gave me a shot of morphine for the pain. But your body itself does some wonderful things in terms of numbing itself if you've got severe injuries. And lower-leg wounds are like that. Of course, it still hurts like crazy, but the blood flow stops to your extremities. That's one reason that you go into shock—your blood pools into your main body cavity.

The gear that I had was all twisted and wrapped up around me to where I could hardly breathe. And I didn't realize I had a big chunk of metal stuck in the side of my chest either.

So they're cutting stuff away and getting it off of me—two or three claymore mines, lots of ammo. About this time my leg hurt so bad I said, "My leg's blown off." The top part of me was stretched back into a shallow ditch, so I couldn't see my legs. They said, "Take a look." I raised up a little bit and looked down. They had my left boot off—all they had to do was cut about one or two strings—and I could see my leg. Most of my pant leg was blown off, or burnt into the front of my leg. Plus, having just been in the water up to my waist, my pants were steaming from all the metal that went through them.

They said, "Your leg's bad, but it's not blown off."

They called the chopper back that had taken the first point man out; it wasn't even out of sight yet, so it just turned right around. I'm bleeding like a stuck hog everywhere, and the medic, besides trying to get a splint on my leg, is trying to get a bandage unwrapped to put around my arm. And I felt sorry for him, because his hands were shaking to where he couldn't get the bandage out. I was even talking with him. I said, "Doc, don't be so nervous. You can't get that thing open shaking like that." By that time the tab of morphine was starting to kick in. I hurt, but the sharp, extreme pain was being numbed.

He finally gets a bandage on my arm. My chest was bleeding bad—he put a bandage there. They stabilized my leg and put me on a litter. And while they're still working on me, the chopper landed.

They're loading me up on the chopper, and I was talking to McCombs—I said, "Be careful out here." And I looked up, and I could see Lieutenant White with his helmet off, just standing there, as white as a ghost. And he was shaking his head. So I raised up my left arm—my left arm was the only thing that didn't get any metal in it—and gave him a big peace sign, and he waved at me, and they put me on the chopper. The peace sign was to tell him, "It's gonna be okay. I'll be okay." I could tell that he didn't feel good about the whole situation. He was the one that had told me to walk point, and then I went twenty feet and tripped the booby trap. So I was wanting to make him feel a little bit more at ease.

They landed the chopper carrying me and this other fella at the helipad of the Third Field Hospital in Saigon. They put us on an ambulance to take us in, and I could see him. I thought, "Hell, I hope I'm not as bad as he is."

When you're wounded, the medic attaches a little tag to the back of your shirt to tell what's wrong with you. The reason it's in back is so you can't read it.

They opened the doors on the ambulance, and I see they're gonna take him out—they're reading his tag. Behind me I got somebody reading my tag, and he says, "No. Leave him there. Take this other guy. He's worse." Hell, they're talking about me! I'm going, "That's not real encouraging."

At the Third Field Hospital there was a big breezeway where they prep guys coming in from the field—cutting off what jungle fatigues you had left on you, trying to stabilize you. I had this one guy that kept asking me my serial number. And I'd go through it: "It's US55949237." He kept asking me and kept asking me. After about fifteen or twenty minutes, I said, "Why do you keep asking me my serial number? Don't you have it written down enough yet?" And he goes, "No. I just wanted to make sure you're still with us."

All the time I got people working on me. And someone said, "Where have you been?"

I said, "I've been out in the field."

"When was the last time you had a bath?"

"I don't know. I don't remember." We'd been about three or four weeks without any type of shower, and I really stunk.

"We have to give you a shower before we can even take you into the operating room."

So they run me through the shower, and then they take me into the operating room. By this time they give me another morphine dose—it's my third, including one they gave me on the chopper. And I've got, like, six doctors working on me. They've got my legs all propped up in a big metal frame, covered by a sheet so I can't see them. My legs are numb now, but I can feel them pulling metal out with tweezers—in addition to my left leg, I had shrapnel all up the back of me and in my butt and the side of my right leg.

I had two doctors working on my right arm. One was from Indianapolis, and I was carrying on a conversation with him. And I could hear remotely the doctors working down at my feet talking about taking the foot off this guy that's out in the hallway. Well, they were trying to disguise the fact they were contemplating whether to leave my leg on or not. I was conscious enough; I knew there wasn't anybody back in the hallway—I had just come from there.

I got ahold of the doctor that was working on my arm, and I said, "You tell those doctors down there"—and by this time I had a bad attitude about the Vietnamese and wasn't thinking real straight—"you tell those doctors down there to leave my leg on. I don't want any damn gooks eating my leg."

And I told him, "I know your name. I know where you're at. You'd better talk to them about leaving that leg on. Leave it on till I get back to the States anyway. Don't be cutting it off here."

So they did. After that they heavily sedated me so I could get some rest and stabilize—I had lost a good bit of blood. I slept most of the next day, that being March the thirtieth. The evening of the thirtieth, or maybe it was the thirty-first, some officers came by and made a presentation of my Purple Heart—I remember receiving that, but I was pretty incoherent. Then, on April first, one of the nurses on the ward said, "We're shipping you out of here."

I said, "Don't be telling me that. You're just pulling an April Fool on me."

"It's no April Fool. You're leaving."

They loaded me up on the transport. I'm wrapped from my hand to my shoulder on my right arm; it's immobilized totally. My left leg is in a cast from my groin down. They had my right leg wrapped up, too—from my knee down, clear to my toes—because that was also full of holes. I pretty well looked like a mummy.

I went from the Third Field Hospital to the 249th General Hospital in Tokyo, Japan. The evening I got there, there were lady nurses, and they were wanting to know what they could do. Well, nobody had ever washed my hair. And one of the biggest treats for me was for this one lady to wash my hair. It was almost like I was washing off Vietnam. That was symbolic to me, as I look back on it now, a cleansing.

I was in this one ward for about two or three days, and they hadn't done much. And my cast was all bloody and was starting to turn green. I called the doctor or nurse over, and I said, "I don't know if it's the guy next to me or if it's me, but one of us is stinking pretty bad. I think you need to take a look at this."

I went in for another operation. They opened it and did a debridement, but gas gangrene had started in that leg. So they put me on heavy medication and took me to another ward. It was probably forty or forty-five guys in that ward, and me and this one other fella were the only ones that had all of our limbs left on us. The rest of them had single or double or multiple amputations.

After a few days, they were taking pricks in my fingers like crazy, and I couldn't figure out why they were taking so much blood from me. I said, "Hey, I bled a good bit. I don't have a whole lot of that left." Trying to make light and trying to figure out what they're doing.

They said, "We think that you have malaria." And I thought, "Oh, great." And then the fever started. I was getting all kinds of fevers, up to like 106 degrees, and then getting chills. And then I started to have nightmares where I would relive getting hit. And guys on the ward were screaming out in pain and yelling, "Incoming!"—for incoming rounds—all through the night. That ward was a constant hellhole.

They were continuing the debridement. They would have fine mesh gauze that they would have over the open wounds, and twice a day, in the morning and the evening, they'd come and change those dressings. You'd have to wrap up a towel and bite into it, because they'd peel all of that gauze off, and you had raw nerve endings that were exposed. It was excruciating, and that's even after they gave you shots of painkiller. I bit chunks out of those towels.

But then you learn to take the pain a little bit better.

I decided, "I have to call Mom and Dad."

In the bouts in and out of consciousness from the malaria, and the bells ringing in my head and the hallucinations, I had one thing to think about: "If it is this time here, what time is it back in Indiana?" So I did some figuring. I knew that Mom and Dad would be getting ready for sunrise services on Easter, and that's when I made the call—it was like six in the evening in Japan.

Knowing I had the malaria real bad, not only was I wanting Mom and Dad to know what had happened, but I also wanted some divine intervention to make sure that I could get back to see them. I definitely needed their thoughts and prayers, so I wanted to make sure that I got ahold of them. And it worked.

When I called home on that Sunday morning, Mom answered the phone. She was all happy and was telling Dad, "Mikey's on the phone." She thought that I'd made it back into Saigon to call them on Easter morning and how nice that was. I said, "Mom, I'm not in Saigon. I'm in Tokyo, Japan." And she dropped the phone.

I heard her say, "John, Michael is in Japan." They knew that the only way you got out of Vietnam if you were in the infantry was by being either wounded or killed. Dad picked the phone up. I told him I tripped a booby trap and I was wounded. I said, "I don't know how bad it is, but it isn't very good. One of my legs is all torn up, but I still got all my limbs."

Growing up, to make sure we were telling him the truth, he'd go, "You're not storying to me now, are you?" And that's what he said now, thinking that I might not tell him everything. "You're not storying to Daddy, are you?" My legs were so bad, he wanted to know if I'd had them blown off. I said, "I still have 'em."

At this time I knew I was hurt badly, but with the fever and all, I didn't completely understand that my leg was half blown off. I had this fear that they were going to send me back to Vietnam, because we'd had guys that got recuperated in Japan, and hell, they'd send 'em back to the field—loading them into the cannon again. I said to Dad, "I think I'm bad enough I'm coming home. I don't have to go back there."

* * *

Before we left Japan, they give us a choice of hospitals where we could go to. I said, "Put me back down in Fort Campbell, Kentucky, where I started out."

Fort Campbell was probably the main orthopedic hospital during that time frame for all Army personnel with major combat wounds—Fort Campbell and then Walter Reed. But Walter Reed was mostly for amputees.

At Fort Campbell one doctor, Dr. Hunt, said, "I think we can do something with it," because the rest were all ready to send me to Walter Reed for amputation below the knee. He said, "It'll be a long way. Some stuff will be experimental."

I said, "I ain't got nothing to lose. I can't use it this way."

I was in the hospital for twenty-two months. I had a total of seven major surgeries and fifty-some-odd different casts on my leg. I had close to seven inches of the midshaft of the tibia, right in the middle of my lower left leg, blown away, so the main objective of the treatment was to replace that seven inches of bone. What things I had going for me were, first, the fact that the fibula, on the outside of my leg, wasn't even cracked; it was in place and was in good shape. Plus, the circulation was good and the nerves were all good. One operation was to take freeze-dried bone from someone's amputated leg and put quarter-inch bone pegs out to the fibula from the top of my tibia, at the knee, and from the bottom of my tibia, at the ankle, to stabilize what was left of the tibia. In another operation they chipped six inches of bone off my left hip and used that to fill in portions of where the leg bone was missing. And they did huge skin grafts to cover the raw muscle and all. They also put quarter-inch-diameter stainless-steel screws, one in my knee and one in my ankle, to stabilize the fibula to those joints. Those screws are still there. The lower one limits movement in my ankle somewhat.

When I first got to Fort Campbell, they said it would be two years before I could walk, and it was about that much time before I was able to start. Even at that I had a long leg brace that I walked with. I had been in long leg casts for so many months I had to have major physical therapy just to get my knee to bend and function again.

It hurts every day. It hurts right now. I hobble around. It takes me about ten, fifteen minutes every morning to get from stumbling around to having things working. And if I walk a lot, I tend to favor the left leg some. It's about an inch and a half shorter than my right.

I don't use a lift in my shoe. So to compensate for the difference in length, I shift my hip. Well, you do that for so long, you'll start noticing a limp, because it throws your back out. So I have a chiropractor appointment that I go to every month to get back adjustments. I've been doing that for the last twenty years, at least.

I used to take all kinds of pain medication, even to the point of abusing it. The major operations were real painful, and they'd give me Demerol and morphine. I'd be addicted to these for a couple, three weeks after each surgery.

I also took pills on a steady basis for about fifteen, sixteen years, till the mid-eighties. Pain medication is easy to abuse if you don't watch it. I kept having to get a higher dose, and stronger medication, to get to where I didn't have any pain. The first one was Darvon, sixty-five-milligram; the next one was Darvocet N-100; and then it was Tylenol-3, with codeine. Those pills make you very moody, sometimes unpredictable.

The next step up, pillwise, would have been Demerol. And I thought, "I can't keep going like this." So I decided, "I'll just tough it out, make the best of it."

I take aspirin now.

Before the war I was planning on coming back and going into farming with Dad. But in the hospital I come to the realization, I don't think I'll be able to do the heavy work on the farm. I enjoyed farming, but I didn't have the love of the farm in me like my brother did. I realized I had to do something with my head.

I had this goal that I set in the hospital: I wanted to get a master's degree. I didn't care what it was in, I just wanted that milestone in my life of having a master's degree from college, because not everybody has that, even nowadays. Master's degrees are a rare commodity, when you take the whole population.

I went to Indiana State University through a vocational-rehabilitation program from the Veterans Administration. I drove thirty-five miles each way, every day for five years. The first couple of years were pretty tough, but I got my degrees.

My baccalaureate degree is in two majors: school health education and community health education. And then I professionalized my teaching degree by getting a master's in one year. That year I was assistant to three professors and also taught a sophomore-level class.

It's a good thing I didn't go into teaching, because I probably would have been tossed out for being too strict. Being under the constant threat of being killed twenty-four hours a day makes you serious about life, because you know it can be gone real quick. I wouldn't have been able to tolerate kids and their tomfoolery. My wife still tells me I take things too seriously.

So I started with Great Dane Trailers in 1977 as a buyer in the purchasing department. I've been there twenty-five years now.

It was hard being a veteran when I came home, especially while the war was still going on—I'm talking '71, '72, '73. I got spit on. Had that happen at Indiana State University, in Terre Haute, Indiana.

Vietnam veterans would band together, because we were shunned and ostracized on campus. We were on a street corner one day, and this one guy passing by realized that we were vets—we all had our field jackets on—and spit on us. It wasn't like he spit in my face—most of the saliva landed on the sidewalk, a bit landed on my jacket. But he got his point across. I thought I did well in controlling myself and not choking that individual, because when you get spit on for being a veteran, you have a lot of rage that you have to contain.

When I started at ISU, I'd bring up the fact that I was a veteran. And I got looks like, "Oh, you're one of them." This was after the My Lai massacre, and the news media was picking up on it, so the Vietnam veterans became the villain. And that's not to sing a sad song. That was factual. That happened. A lot of people don't remember that now, but that's exactly what happened.

It was demoralizing. We did what we were asked to do. And then to get spit on for it—that was really a heartbreaker. It got to where at school I wouldn't admit to being a Vietnam veteran.

Hollywood moviemakers didn't help us out by any means. The persona of Vietnam veterans was, first of all, we were dope addicts. Then we were baby killers. And no-goods. And, oh, by the way, we lost the war. We just didn't do a very good job over there, and we got it shoved in our face all the time.

That even flowed through the VFW. When we first came back, there were World War II vets in there that said, "You guys aren't worth a damn. We won ours, we won the big one. What the hell happened to you guys?" Said it to me and some other fellas. You can go in to a VFW hall now, and you'll find Vietnam veterans running the show. But back then the VFW and the American Legion both had a problem accepting any Vietnam veterans. That's one of the reasons Vietnam Veterans of America was formed.

It was not much of a welcome home. They didn't need to have all kinds of parades and streamers. But to throw it in our face that we didn't win?

When I dwell on it and I bring up old feelings, I get intense. But I do a pretty good job of keeping the lid on and not saying too much.

I never opened up much to Dad. And this is nothing personal against Dad, but he never liked to hear any bellyaching or complaining or bitching or moaning about situations. So it's better for me not to say anything. I don't want him to have the perception that I'm a complainer or crybaby. He probably wouldn't think so, but I'm not going to take a chance.

I think about what he went through, and I don't think mine was as bad. First of all, I hate snow. I am so glad that I live in the South now, where it doesn't snow. And all the snow that Dad was in—I wrote in one of the Veterans Day cards that I give him, "I can't imagine how you endured what you did."

Not a day goes by but I don't think of the war. Not that I want to, but it's hard to remove it. For one thing, my leg hurts. And I've accepted that—when you can't do anything about something, you just well accept it.

I find solace in the fact that I don't know if I killed anyone. Like when I told the sergeant, "I'll kill the gooks, but I'm not counting 'em for you. I don't want that image in my head." I've got enough nightmares now. I'm glad I don't have nightmares with dead bodies of people I may have killed.

The nightmare I get the most is when we were pinned down by those snipers and they were shooting so close to us it was knocking dirt in my face, knocking branches off the limbs from over us. Some nights I'll spend all night long in a firefight, and I'll wake up the next morning, and I'm totally exhausted. I've even had people at work say, "You look like you're tired. Did you sleep at all last night?" And I'm thinking, "Man, it must be pretty obvious."

I feel real satisfied about Vietnam. I think the Vietnam War helped lead to the fall of Communism. When the Berlin Wall came down, I called a Vietnam veteran friend of mine and I said, "We scored a victory today."

He goes, "Mace, victory?"

"We had another positive thing happen because of Vietnam."

"What are you talking about?"

"Haven't you heard they tore the Wall down?"

"Yeah."

"Well, we spent the lives and energy and money to let the Communists know: Your way of life doesn't work. We won't accept it."

Even though we decided not to fight the war anymore, I don't accept the fact that we lost. And if anybody tells me we lost the war, I correct them real quick. We didn't lose the war. We just decided to stop the casualties.

That's how I now view our role in Vietnam. Maybe it's idealistic, maybe it's a rationalization, maybe it's a warped way of thinking. But I try to convey it to other Vietnam vets. In Vietnam we showed the Communists that democracy and our way of life are worth expending the lives of our people over—first of all to protect this country; but then also to offer that freedom to other people. We've seen the fruits of our labor in the fact that, even though Vietnam is still Communist, the world system of Communism has broken down.

Seeing that happen gave me a really good feeling—something we'd lived with all of our lives was now no longer a threat. But now this damn terrorism has replaced Communism. There are soldiers in the field, young men, and that bothers me. I know what they're going through, I know how they feel. The nightmares have been more frequent because of the military campaign; that happened during the Gulf War in '91, too.

It's all very unsettling, but we'll prevail. The American people never cease to amaze me as far as their ability to survive and overcome any adversity.

I have no doubt about it.

VIII

"It's not a movie."

FIRST BLOOD

For all the combat that soldiers, sailors, airmen, and Marines simulate in training, for all the combat they have read about, heard about, or seen on film, their first taste of it still shocks them. The death that pervades combat—that is the entire point of combat—is distant from the sad but sanitized version we are likely to encounter in our civilian lives. How can anyone understand death as it occurs in combat—its suddenness, its messiness, its stench—secondhand?

In his poem "The Death-Bed," Siegfried Sassoon, one of the British "war poets" of World War I, describes a death that occurs not during combat but just after. A wounded soldier lies in a field hospital; as a vigil gathers around, there is still hope.

Speak to him; rouse him; you may save him yet.
He's young; he hated War; how should he die
When cruel old campaigners win safe through?

But death replied: 'I choose him.' So he went. . . .

How can a noncombatant appreciate the randomness of death in combat, its flagrant unfairness?

JOHN HOWE

ALBANY, NEW YORK
STAFF SERGEANT, UNITED STATES ARMY, VIETNAM

On January 30, 1968, as the Vietnamese celebration of the lunar New Year—Tet—was beginning, Vietcong and NVA forces launched an offensive across South Vietnam. By the end of the following day, over one hundred cities had come under attack. Communist military planners intended the campaign to spark a broad popular uprising that would topple the U.S.-supported Saigon regime.

In a purely military sense, the Tet Offensive ended in unequivocal failure—no uprising took place, and American and South Vietnamese forces beat back the attacks, killing nearly sixty thousand Communist troops in the process. But if the Communists lost the battle, the Tet Offensive nonetheless brought them closer to winning the war. The American public had been assured that there was "light at the end of the tunnel" in this long, hard fight. But the stories and images sent home during Tet—most jarringly, those showing the presence, if only for a few hours, of a handful of Vietcong within the walls of the American embassy compound in Saigon—seemed to belie that promise.

News anchor Walter Cronkite symbolized American reaction to the Tet Offensive. Formerly a supporter of the American effort in Vietnam, "the most trusted man in America" returned from a post-Tet visit there to pronounce the war a stalemate that could be resolved only at the negotiating table. Lyndon Johnson lamented that if he'd lost Cronkite, he'd lost the nation.

And he had. On March 31 he surprised his fellow Americans by announcing that he would not seek another term as president. The following January, Vietnam would become Richard Nixon's war.

John served as leader of a mortar section in the 25th Infantry Division.

I got to Vietnam during Tet, in '68, and soon they put us up into a place that was called the Pineapples, because that's what grew there. It was just outside of Saigon, and VC were dug in all over there. We got involved in many firefights in the Pineapples. It was unreal. I don't know if you've ever seen a pineapple growing, but there's a stalk. Then the pineapple grows on top of the stalk like a ball that sits off the ground maybe six, eight, ten inches. So you try to move around in the Pineapples in hundred-degree heat and get in a firefight, and the bullets start flying, and this sweet pineapple juice and meat gets splattered all over you. And then every bee, every mosquito, every fly within fifteen miles is after you. And while the VC are shooting at you, you're trying to get these bugs off you that are biting the shit out of you. Those bees in Vietnam, they had a hate for Americans almost as bad as the VC had.

I saw people get killed almost as soon as I landed in Vietnam. But I didn't see it close up; I didn't look at somebody and watch him die. When one of our guys got it, it was like he was there one second, you turn away, you fire, you turn back, and he's hit. And he screams to get your attention.

The first time I watched a man die, it was a North Vietnamese. A guy named Elbert R. Perry, from Tennessee, shot him on the top of the head—blew the whole top of his head off. The guy's brain fell out. And he was still there, just like before he was shot, on the ground, crawling toward us—still coming at us, still coming at us. He was still going like that for a few seconds, I guess.

Oh, it was gut-wrenching. But what was more gut-wrenching was a conversation afterward. Now, this guy Perry was probably one of the best soldiers in terms of field craft that I'd ever seen. And he always had been very quiet. But after this guy was killed, he went to the command post to get a Spark Plug—a Spark Plug is a chaw of tobacco that's about the size of an audiocassette—and found out that we were still waiting to have our sundries flown in that night. So he stood there with his weapon locked and loaded, and he said, "I want that Spark Plug when it comes. No shit. If I don't get that Spark Plug, I'm going to feel like doing to somebody like I did to that gook today. You hear me, Howie? He was just crawling trying to get to me, but I shot this son of a bitch, didn't I? If I don't get that Spark Plug, I'm gonna be one upset motherfucker." He wasn't threatening me—he was just saying that out loud with me there.

PERRY POLLINS

LEXINGTON, MASSACHUSETTS
CORPORAL, UNITED STATES MARINE CORPS, WORLD WAR II

For American servicemen the most consistently brutal combat of World War II took place on islands scattered throughout the western Pacific Ocean. Beginning in August 1942 with Guadalcanal, over three thousand miles from Japan's home islands, members of the United States Marine Corps made amphibious landings at one island after another, each often no more than a few square miles of rock, jungle, and sand. With every conquest, American forces moved one step closer to Japan, gaining valuable real estate for the establishment of U.S. ground, naval, and air bases. In April 1945, when the Marines invaded their last island, Okinawa, less than four hundred miles of ocean separated them from their enemy's home.

The Marine assault on the island of Peleliu, which began on September 15, 1944, was designed to facilitate the U.S. Army's reconquest of the Philippines, which would begin five weeks later when American soldiers and their commander, Douglas MacArthur, waded ashore at Leyte Island.

MacArthur was a triple-faced idiot. I mean, the man was out of his mind. In 1932, when the Bonus Army marched on Washington, he had his troops attack them. He then attempted to disband the Marine Corps.

And he made a promise to the Philippines: "I shall return." Nimitz and some of the Navy commanders wanted to go to Formosa first, to get a base to attack Japan. But he had to return. The

First Marine Division landed at Peleliu—we were going to wipe out the airfields in that area and neutralize his right flank.

To satisfy his ego, a lot of lives were lost. I saw these lives lost. My second and third days in Peleliu were heartbreaking. I never saw so many corpses lying on the beach, so many people in battalion evacuation stations, so many people bleeding, so many people with arms missing and legs missing. We experienced sixty-five hundred casualties out of a landing force of twenty-eight thousand—to satisfy his ego.

It took us two weeks on the USS *Leedstown* to get to Peleliu from the island of Pavuvu, which was our staging area. They didn't announce where we were going until we were already afloat. The guys said, "We're gonna help that shithead?" We used to sing a song:

They called for the Army to come to Tulagi,
But General MacArthur said no.
He gave as his reason this isn't the season,
Besides, there is no USO.

I won't repeat the rest, because it's so foul.

My outfit was part of the floating reserve. They called us in on the first day because they were taking some terrible hits on the beach, but they couldn't muster enough amphibious tractors to get us ashore.

At six the next morning, we boarded our landing craft, LCVPs—landing craft, vehicle and personnel. Peleliu was an atoll; it was surrounded by a coral reef. So when we came up to the reef, we had to go from the landing craft into the amphtrac, because the amphtrac could grind over the reef.

So we're in the tractor, and we're heading toward the beach. There's shells exploding all around us, and we can hear machine-gun fire on the beach. We get hung up on another coral head about thirty, forty yards out, so we have to ditch and roll over the side, with rifles and radios and flamethrowers. Johnny Vecho goes over in front of me, and we land on top of two dead Marines floating in the surf. Right on top of them.

That immediately triggered something in my mind that said, "This is war. This is the actual thing that I'm seeing right now. It's not a movie. It's happening to me."

They don't train you for that. But they do train you. They train you that you do it, you do it, you do it. And that's what we did. We pushed them gently aside, and we waded in to the beach. There was stuff exploding around us like there was no tomorrow.

That's the initiation, when you're in that terrible area between leaving your amphtrac and getting ashore, because you're vulnerable. The artillery from shore, the machine-gun fire as you come up the beach—you can get yourself killed, for the love of Pete.

When we got ashore, Johnny went over to where they were digging in the radios and bazookas and stuff like that, and I went down the beach looking for the lieutenant. And I'm crouched down, and all of a sudden, I feel something rubbing against my backside, and I turn around. It's a big white dog. Honest. A big white dog, and bleeding—you could see blood all over him. He probably took a hit. And every time there was an explosion, he was trying to get under me.

I chased him away, and he disappeared somewhere. The poor animal probably bled to death. I gave up looking for the lieutenant, and when I got back to where we were digging in the stuff, they saw the blood on my clothes and were gonna call the corpsman for me. And I said, "No, it's a fucking dog."

We held three hundred yards of beach for about five days.

As the battle went on, the stench from that island was overpowering, because the Japanese didn't bury their dead. The odor almost brought tears to your eyes, it was so pungent. But then you got used to it. You saw decomposing bodies lying around, body parts all over the place. The island was only six miles long and two miles wide, mostly coral. There was some jungle on it. It was just a terrible, terrible place.

PAUL KEITH

Plymouth, Massachusetts

Specialist Fourth Class, United States Army, Vietnam

I landed at Tan Son Nhut 11 April 1968, and then they trucked us just down the road to a replacement depot at Bien Hoa. There you were given an in-country orientation. One of the first things we were told was, "Forget any crap that you heard in the States about being here to save democracy." This is coming from one of the NCOs who was doing the orientation. "You're here to stay alive, keep your buddy alive, and get the hell home." This is day one.

That was part of the waking-up process for me intellectually, as far as what the war was about and what was really going on, when I started to look beyond my own issues to a wider view of it.

All the Army NCOs I had met over in the States filled you with the normal military loyalty and code of conduct, that type of thing. And here's an NCO, in-country, telling me, "Forget all that crap. You're here to stay alive, keep your buddy alive, and get out of here." In my mind that boils down the essence of exactly what was going on there.

It's too bad to find out when you're in the middle of it that there really is no good purpose. But then shame on me for not having thought it out before I got there.

So I did my time.

MIKE PERKINS

Tremonton, Utah

Captain, United States Army, Vietnam

Elements of the Army's Special Forces—known as the Green Berets for their distinctive headgear—served in Vietnam as early as 1957, with their first mission to train fifty-eight South Vietnamese soldiers in techniques of unconventional warfare. In 1961, Special Forces began working with Montagnards, the indigenous people of South Vietnam's Central Highlands; this effort soon led to the formation of the Civilian Irregular Defense Group. Over the next several years, the training and advising of CIDG units would form the heart of the mission of Special Forces in Vietnam.

CIDG detachments were composed mostly of Montagnards, but included other ethnic minorities—Cambodians, ethnic Chinese known as Nung—and some ethnic Vietnamese as well. By 1965, more than eighty fortified CIDG camps had been built around South Vietnam to provide local security and to extend the Saigon government's authority to the country's more remote regions. At the program's high point, the CIDG's ranks numbered forty-five thousand.

The number of Special Forces personnel in Vietnam peaked in 1968 at 3,542.

After attending infantry Officer Candidate School, Mike Perkins was commissioned a second lieutenant in 1964, and then spent a year at Fort Hood, Texas, with the Second Armored Division.

"I'd been applying for Vietnam since about a week after I got out of OCS—because that's where the action was at. I was a naive young man. Finally, in November of '65, I got orders to go to Special Forces. I went to Special Forces school, and in July '66, I finally arrived in Vietnam."

I've studied the military for all my life, so I knew exactly what Special Forces was. I had known people who'd been in Special Forces, and they always would go back to it, because it's exciting. It's not your regular, run-of-the-mill line unit. It's dangerous, but it's exciting.

You're in small detachments—twelve-, thirteen-man detachments—called A Teams. And you're out training the indigenous people—what we called the "indidge"—leading them on operations. It's a small unit, and it's an elite unit. And it takes on all these tough missions that have to be done.

It's an NCO-oriented organization. The NCOs run it. The officers take responsibility, the officers make sure things are done. But the NCOs do it all. It's just a wonderful place to be.

I was initially assigned to an A Team at Ba To, a little tiny village up in Quang Ngai Province.

In about three days, I was out on my first operation. I went out with an American staff sergeant, Sergeant Woods—he's the boss, and I'm his assistant. This is how Special Forces works. It was two Americans on patrol with thirty Vietnamese LLDB—Luc Luong Dac Biet. That's the Vietnamese Special Forces. Americans are the de facto leaders of the operation, but officially we're advisers and a good LLDB sergeant—in three days there, I know he's one of the best—is leading the patrol.

We went down this valley, and sure enough, we got caught in a little ambush, and they nailed this LLDB sergeant. I went running to put down a base of fire for him, protecting him, while Sergeant Woods ran up and tried to save his life. After the bad guys went away, I remember squatting next to this LLDB sergeant as he said, "*Met qua, met qua,*" which means "I'm very, very tired." And I looked in his eyes. He'd taken a round in the gut, and he was bleeding to death. I've found that most people who bleed to death don't know they're bleeding to death. They just say, "I'm so tired," and that's because they're losing all their blood. It looked like he'd lost a gallon of blood; it was just sitting in a big pool. Woods tried to stop the bleeding, but the man fell asleep, and that was the end of it—he died not long after that.

We trussed him up in a poncho and strung him to a bamboo pole, like you would a tiger, and we hauled him out of there. For most of the three or four miles to base camp, I carried the back end and someone else carried the front end.

It was my first experience in how nasty war can be, because every time we'd walk uphill, his blood would spout at the back and it would all splash out. I was drenched in his blood. We got ambushed again along the way, and the terrain was difficult—rice paddies and creeks and bamboo and mountainsides—so it took us five hours to get him back. He was stinking bad. When we finally unwrapped him, he'd already bloated up because of the heat. And I'm going, "This is my first experience in combat. It isn't a very good one."

That day was an eye-opener for me—from just reading about combat, I didn't know how confused it is. In combat no one knows what's going on, and you're trying to sort things out and put people where they have to go. Woods, he's telling me, "Get over here, Lieutenant," "Get up there," while we're trying to put down a base of fire and get the Vietnamese moving and get 'em firing.

When it was over, I thought, "Boy, if it's all gonna be like this, this is pretty inconclusive. Who won this one?"

We're sitting around the patio a day or two later, and I asked one American, "Is this typical?"

"Yeah. Usually they kill one of us, we kill one of them."

I said, "We're not gonna win the war this way."

And everybody said, "Win the war? We're not gonna win this war."

"Well, what are you guys all doing here?"

They said, "This is the only war we got. Let's enjoy it." This is the Special Forces mentality—Marines, Special Forces, SEALs—"If there's a war, let's go to it."

It never was quite my mentality—I'm not a mercenary—but you fall into that way of thinking. My mentality at first was, I want to find out if I'm really what I think I am. That's what it was all about. I just wanted to see if I was soldier material.

MAX HUTCHINS

RETIRED EXECUTIVE, TRUCKING INDUSTRY
CONCORD, NORTH CAROLINA
FIRE CONTROLMAN FIRST CLASS, UNITED STATES NAVY,
WORLD WAR II

On the day we know as "D-Day"—after the military designation for any day on which a military operation begins—over 155,000 soldiers of the United States, Great Britain, and Canada landed in Normandy to finally breach Hitler's Fortress Europe. Eleven thousand Allied aircraft—fighters, bombers, troop carriers, reconnaissance planes—took part in the operation, as did some seven thousand naval vessels—troop transports, landing craft, minesweepers.

Twenty-three thousand of the invaders entered France from the air, descending to earth via parachute or glider. The rest came from the sea, divided among five sectors of shoreline. British and Canadian forces landed with little trouble at Gold, Sword, and Juno Beaches. American troops who landed at Utah Beach also faced weaker opposition than anticipated, but at Omaha Beach a last-minute reinforcement by Germany's crack 352nd Infantry Division inflicted such losses on the American invaders that their commander, Omar Bradley, considered withdrawing all forces from Omaha and rerouting them to Utah. But American infantrymen and tankers fought on, supported by punishing naval gunfire directed at German positions in the cliffs above the beach. Over a hundred warships—battleships, cruisers, destroyers—were anchored offshore to fire their massive guns in support of their Army comrades. Max C. Hutchins, a twenty-year-old native of Winston-Salem, North Carolina, helped operate the guns on one of those ships.

By day's end twenty-five hundred Americans lay dead on the shore and in the water, but the invaders had established a beachhead at Omaha, even throwing German defenders off their clifftop positions.

The drive to liberate Western Europe had begun.

The USS *Carmick* was a 1,630-ton destroyer, one of the oldest ones they had. I think they felt it was dispensable, because on D-Day, and also at the landing in southern France two months later, we were a thousand yards from shore, in the first line of the ships firing onto the beach in support of the landing.

While we were at Plymouth before the invasion, everyone was expecting something but didn't have any idea what. D-Day was one of the best-kept secrets.

The night before, the skipper spoke to the crew. I think he did mention the word "invasion," but the way he talked about it, it was more of a mission than it was an invasion. He said we were going on a mission different from anything we'd been exposed to. He didn't try to inspire us, other than to say that we'd been well trained for what we were getting into and all we had to do was do our job. I believed him.

We had orders to sail the next morning. Like I say, we felt like we were trained to do what needed to be done, but we didn't know what to expect, and we were scared. I had no idea, and don't think anybody else had any idea, about the size of the operation. Even after we got into it, it was hard to realize that you were sitting there in this mass of ships. The English Channel is not that big, and with thousands of ships, it felt like you could almost walk from ship to ship.

At four o'clock in the morning, we moved out to take our place in the Channel. We got in position by around five-thirty or six, I guess. Everything was eerie. Then the word came down to commence firing. Our targets were up in the cliffs above the beach; that's where the Germans were. According to what everybody said, and what they still say today, it was supposed to have been a surprise to the Germans—they thought we would be coming in at Calais. But if it was a surprise, they were pretty well settled in, because they had a lot of armament up there, had a lot of planes. If it hadn't been a surprise, I don't know what we would have done. They put up a pretty good fight.

The thing I remember most of all was the USS *Texas,* a battleship that was right behind us. They were firing over us with fourteen-inch guns, and our ship was bouncing out of the water. Of course, a lot of the others were, too. Then you get all the smoke and the fire—it's more than you can imagine. The noise was just out of this world. I've got an ear problem now; I credit it to that. I never did go to sick bay or anything. I don't know that that's what caused my loss of hearing, but I feel like it was.

We couldn't see that much of the landing. We could see some of the landing craft being hit and see the fires coming from that. We knew we were losing a lot of people but didn't have time to really understand how many. We didn't have time to sightsee.

We were under fire from planes and from the gun emplacements that they had up in the cliffs. The Germans had eighty-eight-millimeter guns. Those were extremely accurate guns with good-size shells—over three inches in diameter. The range wasn't enough to hit where we were, but you could see the shells ricocheting on the water out there.

At about nine or nine-thirty in the morning, the ship to our right got sunk—it was a destroyer also. There were quite a few got killed. We were able to pick up part of their survivors. That ship was awful close to us, and it could have been us. You have a feeling for them and, mostly, for their families. But that was something nobody could do anything about. It was too late at that time.

It was probably four o'clock in the afternoon before we decided that we could pull back. And then is when you start trembling. I think, being as young as I was, I had felt like nothing could happen to me. But then, after it's over with, you think, "Well, it could happen to me as well."

We talked about it after we'd pulled away. Most of the time it was a lighthearted talk and kidding—about what I was doing and what you were doing and all this kind of thing. But there was a lot of serious talk, too—about the loss of the soldiers in the landing craft that were hit and also about the ship beside us that was hit.

All the sailors mentioned that they were more nervous after it happened than while it was going on. While it was going on, you were doing what you had been trained to do. You didn't have time to think about your feelings, I guess. The real heavy part of the shelling probably didn't last more than a few hours. But after it was all over with, you started thinking about what you had seen—just the sound and the enormity of the whole thing. I kind of went into shock. I didn't feel like myself. I felt numb, completely out of it. I don't know exactly how to explain it, but I didn't have any real feeling for anything. That lasted for several days. In fact, it lasted probably until after I got out of the Navy, and some time even after that.

I've tried to forget the whole situation. It's just something I didn't want to bring up in my mind. Because I knew that if I didn't get it out of my mind, it was gonna haunt me for some time to come. I know a lot of people had nightmares and this kind of stuff—I never had that. And I think the big reason is that I did try to put it out of my mind.

But . . .

I still think about it. So when it does pop into my mind, I try to erase it as soon as I can, and I do that by thinking about something I've read in the Bible. I read the Bible quite a bit.

The Bible was a help to me during the war, it certainly was. I felt like all along that God was in control and that He would lead me where He wanted me to be; that my life was in His hands. And I really never felt like that I wouldn't come back; I felt like that I would come back. I'm sure there were people who didn't have the faith that I had, but without my faith I don't believe I could have gotten through it.

When Mickey was in Vietnam, I prayed for him on a daily basis. I prayed for his safety, I prayed that God would be with him. I think prayers certainly make a difference, and I think—well, I know—that they're answered, maybe not always the way we want them to be answered, but they are always answered. In this case I think our prayers were answered the way we wanted them to be answered. We knew there were other people just like us who had sons and relatives over there that they were praying for, and we prayed for them as well.

Having seen a lot of people who didn't come back, there was always the possibility in the back of my mind that Mickey might not come back. But I felt like all along that Mickey *would* come back, and it was all because of my faith. And I felt like if he didn't, he would be taken care of by God.

MICKEY HUTCHINS

Concord, North Carolina
First Lieutenant, United States Army, Vietnam

After attending infantry Officer Candidate School, Mickey was trained to join one of the Mobile Advisory Teams fielded by MACV (Military Assistance Command Vietnam) to assist the South Vietnamese troops known to Americans as "Ruff Puffs"—members of the Regional Forces and Popular Forces. "They were sort of the equivalent of our Army Reserve or Army National Guard except they were on active duty."

MACV had begun to organize the teams in 1967, but their importance increased dramatically after Richard Nixon took office and announced the policy that would be dubbed "Vietnamization": the gradual transfer of the war's conduct from American forces to their South Vietnamese allies.

Upon arrival in Vietnam on March 13, 1970, Mickey was sent to Di An base camp for in-country orientation. MACV shared the camp with the Eleventh Armored Cavalry Regiment.

About two nights into this thing, they announced that there was gonna be a party at the officers' club. Officers' club out here in the middle of a base camp? We walked in, and the first thing that immediately impressed me was that the crowd was segregated between the black hats—the Eleventh Armored Cav guys wearing their black Stetsons—and the MACV guys, just wearing our fatigue caps. It was a cordial crowd nonetheless. Then in comes the battalion staff, and several of these guys had American dates, and I was just floored. I could not imagine a female in this part of the world, let alone an American female in this part of the world. And then in comes the band—they had imported a rock 'n' roll band from the Philippines, part of the USO tour.

I guess it must have been about nine-thirty, ten o'clock, the band took their break, and this captain got up. He was obviously drunk out of his mind. This was his last night in Vietnam, and he was making his farewell address to his buddies in the Eleventh Armored Cav. I don't recall what he had to say, but it was a hilarious speech. At the end his final parting remark to his friends was, "I just want you guys to remember, anybody who can't tap-dance is a"—and I'll leave out the expletive, but it cast aspersions on their heritage. At that point every one of the guys in that place who was wearing a black Stetson got on top of the tables and started tap-dancing. In combat boots.

I was just completely blown away. I said, "What am I in?"

After orientation Mickey got orders assigning him to a team of advisers in Ben Luc district, Long An province.

I guess it was probably about three or four weeks later, I ended up going on my first ambush patrol with a South Vietnamese company. Typically, when the advisers went out with a South Vietnamese unit, we would go with one American officer and one American NCO—the NCO would carry the radio.

On this first ambush mission, however, the captain of the team, Don Cake, decided to go and take me with him, so I effectively operated as the NCO and carried the radio. We took twenty-two men out, and we set up in a triangle configuration. There were a couple of hamlets out there, and we put a seven-man ambush outside each of those two hamlets. The rest of us stayed back as the command element and the reserve element. It was night; we were looking for VC.

The plan was that if either one of the two forward units made contact, we in the reserve would come in to reinforce them. About eleven-thirty, I'd say, the ambush on the right made contact, and that was the beginning of all hell breaking loose. One of the things that Don told me was, "If anything goes wrong, here are the coordinates, call for gunships." I said, "Roger that." When the stuff started getting thick down there, I called for gunships. I also called for illumination support, because we knew there would be a delay from the time that we called for gunships till they would actually be on station, and we needed to do something to stabilize the situation immediately. We found ourselves assaulting across about two hundred yards of open rice paddy to reinforce these guys. Of course, the illumination was highlighting us out there in this wide-open rice paddy, and we could see the bullets kicking up around us, but we managed to make it all the way across and get in behind them.

At this point, however, we got word that the other ambush had been hit. There was no way to reinforce them now that our group was committed, so Don asked me to organize the withdrawal of all our units, and we started pulling the people back out.

This was the first time I was under fire. One of the things I think is a natural part of growing up as a young man is that you wonder, if you're going to be in that situation, how you will perform. The greatest anxiety is not that there will be danger but that you won't be able to handle it. And the thing that I came out of it all with was, I was absolutely amazed at how the training I'd had to that point had worked. It had gone like clockwork; it had been exactly what we had been taught to expect. As a result of that experience, I had very little doubt that, from that point on, I'd be able to handle it.

I also say that, given my time in college and my earlier time in the Army, it had been seven or eight years since I had attended a church with any kind of regularity. Although I still considered myself Christian, I certainly wouldn't have been called a practicing Christian. But as soon as that gunfire started, and I started seeing those bullets kicking up around me, I started doing some serious praying. For quite some time thereafter, I thought that it actually had been my prayers that had been answered. It was only after I got home that I learned that that really wasn't true. Vietnam was probably a lot tougher on my family than it was on me. After I got home, I found out that both my parents and my grandparents had been praying for me on a daily basis.

Prior to going to Vietnam, I probably would have sloughed that off and not paid a whole lot of attention to it. But after having gone through Vietnam, there is little doubt in my mind that the prayers that were answered that night were not mine but were those of the folks back home. It was largely their faith, I think, that ended up getting me through.

IX

"It was just like flying into a black cloud."

DOING BATTLE

After undergoing their baptism by fire, combat personnel must adapt to their circumstances. They must somehow come to terms with the terrible realization that they and their enemy are engaged in a prolonged struggle to kill one another—and then go on about their business. Whether they follow orders or give them, they must find a way to do their jobs, to earn their salary as we all do, whether we are stockbrokers, schoolteachers, or mechanics.

Living and working under extreme conditions, combatants must render the extraordinary routine, the monstrous tolerable, the unthinkable second nature. "Courage," wrote Mark Twain, "is resistance to fear, mastery of fear—not absence of fear."

BILL PERKINS

SPOKANE, WASHINGTON

CAPTAIN, UNITED STATES ARMY AIR FORCES, WORLD WAR II

Trained to pilot a C-47 transport plane, Bill served with the 315th Troop Carrier Group, based in the English Midlands. "There must have been a thousand air bases scattered all around England—from the air, everywhere you looked you could see them. The island was like a big, stabilized aircraft carrier."

During the course of the war, Bill made fifteen to twenty drops of paratroopers on the European Continent.

In combat all units are programmed to hit the drop zone at a given time. About two to three minutes prior to hitting it, you flick on the red warning light. At that the paratroopers get up and hook their static line to the cable that runs from the front to the back of the aircraft. Over the drop zone, you turn on the green light, and they jump. You're only given a minute or minute and a half to get them all out.

On March 24, 1945, we made a drop across the Rhine River. It was our very last mission, and it was the worst drop we ever made, because we lost a lot of aircraft.

The Germans had concentrated their forces on the eastern side of the Rhine, and as we crossed the river, the flak got so thick it was just like flying into a black cloud. I couldn't see another plane in the sky, not even my flight leader. I thought to myself, "My God, I'm the only one left."

I had to fly on instruments and time myself for the drop zone. Usually they have pathfinder aircraft to go in ahead, and they drop these colored flares on the drop zone. But you couldn't see anything, there was so much firing and flak. So I turned on the red light. And then, about three minutes later, I turned on the green light. I gave them about two minutes to jump, then started to make the turn to come out of the drop zone. But my crew chief came up and said, "We didn't get 'em out."

I thought, "Hell, I'm practically dead already. Why go around and get killed again?"

He said, "A shell burst in the door when the first man went to bail out, and it blew him back in the cabin." The tactic of the Germans, when they would see these aircraft coming over the drop zone, was to fire at your door. They'd hit the first man and blow him back in. That disrupts the whole jump, because if the first man hits the floor or is killed, he's still hooked to that cable and the others can't get by.

So I said, "Are any injured?"

"I don't know. Two of them are lying on the floor."

"Well, we're gonna have to go around again." And so I started to circle around, and I told him, "When we get back around, you kick 'em all out of the door. Those on the floor, pick 'em up and throw 'em out. The people on the ground can take care of them better than we can in the air, if they're alive. If they're dead, it doesn't make any difference."

Our orders were, you don't bring any of them back. You drop them. No matter if it's not on the drop zone, you drop them.

So I went around. And between the crew chief and the radio operator, I guess, they picked those two up and threw them out, and then got the others out.

When we got back to Spanhoe, I inspected the plane and found a number of shrapnel tears and bullet holes in the fuselage. One bullet hole was on the left side of the nose. Before we'd left on this mission, there happened to be an extra flak pad lying around, and so I put two flak pads under my seat. This bullet went through the first pad; we found it embedded in the second.

I still have that bullet.

MIKE PERKINS

TREMONTON, UTAH

CAPTAIN, UNITED STATES ARMY, VIETNAM

I love these NCOs. Sergeant Talamine was the team sergeant down at Ba To. Sergeant Talamine had made two combat jumps in World War II and fought through the Bulge. He made two combat jumps in Korea. And then he had been in Operation White Star, a clandestine operation in Laos.

I got to know the guy real well. He was another one of those guys I idolized. A great, big, tall guy. I guess at one point he was probably a good-looking guy, but now he's your idea of Sergeant Rock—you know, that old comic book, *Sgt. Rock.* He's muscular—has about a twenty-eight-inch waist and a fifty-inch chest. He's a heavy drinker. But you love this guy. He was the epitome of a soldier.

I remember the old man was out of the camp one night on an operation, and I was in charge. I'd been there about three or four weeks. And we began taking mortar rounds and small-arms into the camp. And I'm running around going, "Okay, let's go red alert."

Sergeant Talamine says, "Lieutenant, settle down. Come on over here, lad." That's what he used to call me. "Come on over here, lad. Let's sit here on the rock and watch this."

"Top, we're gonna get our ass blasted."

"No, no, no, no. Look where they're firing. They're firing blind. Let's watch this for a minute and figure this out."

Now he says, "Let's aim our four-deuce right there." So I went down and got it lined up. And he said, "Okay, let 'em fire. Put four rounds out there."

He knew what it was to be calm and collected. He'd seen so much combat he just knew everything there was to know about it. He was my ideal, old Sergeant Talamine.

He told me once, "Whatever happens in combat, never get excited. The more excited you get, the less thinking you do. Whatever's going on, pop in some gum. Chew some gum; then you can start making decisions. Until then don't make a decision."

Another thing he'd do: We'd be sitting around camp, and we'd get mortared, and guys would get pretty uptight. He'd say, "Okay, you three start panicking. The other two come with me—let's get something done." He was a funny guy.

My first half dozen missions, at the end of them these good sergeants would say, "Next time you ought to think about doing this." "Now if you hadn't done that, you'd have been . . ." These were good NCOs that were trying to take care of me.

After that they weren't telling me much. They're like the varsity team, and you're a freshman player. And when these guys are no longer giving you advice, you realize now you are a varsity player. But every day of my life in Vietnam, which was a thousand-something days, I was scared to death.

I was at Ba To for about three, four months, and then the XO up at the A Team in Khe Sanh got wounded, so they assigned me there. By then I guess my reputation was already nailed, or they wouldn't have sent me to replace that guy.

Soon Project Delta came in to Khe Sanh, and our A team got attached to it. Delta was the long-range recon unit for MACV. They'd put out recon teams, and then they had a reaction force, which was a Vietnamese ranger battalion. I was with that reaction force.

A recon team would be two or three Americans and two or three Nungs. These recon teams would go out looking for NVA movement, NVA trails, NVA whatever-they're-looking-for. And if they found it, then they'd call in air strikes and they'd report back the intel.

If they found something that needed people on the ground—like, if they found a base camp and wanted to go and see what was in there—then they'd call in the reaction force. And we'd go in and exploit it—blow things up, kill people.

One night all of us sat there on a little hill. And we saw all these Marine and Navy fighters bombing—it was an overcast sky, so they weren't bombing by sight, they were bombing by radar, on grid coordinates called in to an air-control center. And we sat there on that hill, just dumbstruck, because you could watch not hundreds but thousands of flashlights moving down these trails towards us. And we're going, "There's fifteen Americans and two hundred Vietnamese rangers here to fight these guys off."

You could hear the bombs whistle. You never saw the bombs, but you'd see these flashlights tumbling up in the air, maybe attached to people; it was dark so we couldn't tell.

Thousands of flashlights. We all just sat around: "You're kidding me." They were only like a mile away.

We began digging in, because we said, "We don't know what these guys are. Infantry? Or are they carrying heavy loads?" We kept asking, "Why are they carrying flashlights?" Well, because there's an overcast sky. They know that the airplanes can't see them.

The next morning we were waiting to be engaged with these people, but they went on down another road. We never did find them.

That left such an impression on me. These guys have only got to travel fifteen, twenty miles to get here, and we traveled ten thousand miles. They've got us outnumbered. No matter how many people we put in South Vietnam, they can match it and triple it, because they just move across the DMZ and they're here.

I'll tell you what, I've never forgotten that night. "They move this many people every night? We'll never match these people. Never."

TONY RIVAS SR.

San Antonio, Texas

Seaman First Class, United States Navy, World War II

As the Marines island-hopped their way ever closer to Japan, their landings were supported by fire from ships anchored offshore. The Indianapolis, *a heavy cruiser commissioned in 1932, supported Marine invasions across the South Pacific—at Peleliu, Iwo Jima, and Okinawa, among many others. For nearly three years, beginning in mid-1942, Tony Rivas served among its crew of twelve hundred.*

Tony's first stop with the Indianapolis, *however, was the far North Pacific. Japan had captured two of the Aleutian Islands, Kiska and Attu, in June 1942. While the remote, icy islands were of limited tactical use, their propaganda value was not lost on leaders of either side. The Japanese had occupied other American possessions—Guam, the Philippines—but the empire's establishment of these outposts just off the North American mainland represented an encroachment on America's home. The big guns of the* Indianapolis *kept pressure on the Japanese detachment in the Aleutians for almost a year, before American forces finally retook the islands in the middle of 1943.*

I went to a lot of battles. After maybe two or three battles, we would go back to Pearl Harbor for an overhaul. We were there three or four times.

Once we were on shore leave in Honolulu, and there was a lot of girls hollering at the guys. "Do you want to take a picture, soldier? Do you want to take a picture, soldier?" I was mad at my girlfriend. I knew that she was having a lot of good times with some other guys, because they used to write to me. She sent me letters: "I want you to have a good time over there where you're at." I wrote back, "I don't have no place for having a good time. All we do is fighting."

So now I took a picture with this girl hugging me, and I sent it to my girlfriend: "I'm having a good time, too."

That was the end of the romance.

I know she cried a lot afterwards, showing the picture around. She'd go to the priest and show him the picture.

I feel bad about it, but what else should I do? Always I feel bad for everything I do.

My ship stayed in the Aleutians for about a year. Then we went to the Central Pacific.

One morning I woke up and I said to myself, "What the hell is going on? Look at that, a lot of ships." American ships, and flattops with a lot of airplanes. Then we hit Tarawa.

At Tarawa, and then later at Iwo Jima, I saw a lot of dead people in the ocean. When we got too close to them, you could smell it. It smelled awful. Terrible, like a dead dog. If you looked slowly, you could see bodies all over the water. American people, Japanese, natives, whatever.

I'll tell you one thing: The Navy guys, they would take a hook and pick up the helmets off the dead Japanese. You could smell that, because part of the head was in the top of the hat—you could see the hair in it, even some brains. I don't know why they do it. They're crazy guys. I say, "What the hell you bring that stuff that smell like hell?" They say, "Don't worry about it, this is souvenirs." I didn't do that, not me. I'm crazy, but not that crazy.

The water had a lot of little fishes. When you would have swimming call, they used to bother us, all those little fish. At Tarawa and Iwo Jima, I saw the little fish eating the dead bodies. That's the reason why I hate fish.

I used to like to eat fish. I used to go to the market here—you could smell it when they were cooking. Beautiful smell. My wife loves fish. She says, "Oh, I love fish, oysters." But I remember that thing in my mind, and it keeps on coming up. So, ever since then, I don't eat fish.

When the Marines secured an island, they would announce through the speaker, "Old Glory is going up." And everybody looked at it. You could look through the telescope and see the guys raising the flag. When the flag went up at Tarawa, everybody was happy about it, cheering, "Yea! We made it! We made it!"

Then we said, "Get ready for the next island."

Although Tony Rivas Sr. never ate fish after the war, his aversion remained a secret to the family with which he shared a table. "My dad never talked about the war," says Tony Jr., who served aboard a cargo ship in Vietnam. "Maybe it's a bad thing, but we were brought up keeping everything to ourselves. Machismo—my dad feels that men shouldn't cry, and we never saw him cry.

"I've known for a long time about his ex-girlfriend and the picture from Hawaii. And I bring it up once in a while so my mom can get angry. But until we sat down to talk for this book, I didn't know that Dad didn't like fish. I always thought he ate it. But,

come to think about it, I never did see him eat fish. He had to keep it a secret all this long. Here I am, fifty-four years old, and I don't know my dad."

GREG CAMP
COLUMBUS, GEORGIA
CAPTAIN, UNITED STATES ARMY, VIETNAM

Greg's first job in Vietnam was as leader of a rifle platoon in the First Cavalry Division.

Some of the scariest things in Vietnam were nonevents, where in your mind you were in imminent danger, and yet when all was settled, there was nobody there. Nothing happened. You weren't in any danger at all. You just didn't know you weren't in any danger.

I can't tell how many nights I'd be lying in an ambush in the middle of the jungle during the monsoon season. If you've made contact earlier that day, you know you're in the vicinity of the enemy, and you know there's a high likelihood that somebody is going to approach you. And then you hear all these sounds—it sounds like soldiers marching and crawling at you from all angles.

It's rain. It's just rain. There are monkeys that go from tree to tree. But you're sitting there listening to it, and it sounds like a person's out there crawling from tree to tree to get a better shot at you. I think that the way we fought that war, at least where I was, I had more fear of things that turned out to be nothing than of things that turned out to be something.

When you're actually in a firefight and you're actually shooting at somebody and you're actually maneuvering, your heart is pumping pretty hard, too. But at least your mind isn't playing games with you. You know what you're up against—a sniper, a small patrol. But you're not conjuring up in your mind that it's a huge force.

We had contact one day, and we set up a night defensive position. And every time you set up a defensive position, you have listening posts well out in front of you, on all four sides, the idea being that if anybody's coming, the listening posts will warn you.

Everybody was a little bit touchy because of the earlier contact—a .51-caliber had taken a couple of our guys out. And the guys who were on one listening post said, "They're coming. There's a little stream in front of us, and I can hear 'em coming across the stream." They became panic-stricken.

I went out to the listening post, and I was hearing what they were hearing. And I was believing what they were believing. It sounded like platoon after platoon after platoon was coming across this little stream. And it was scaring us to death. So I called in artillery. I mean, I called it in all night long.

We got up the next morning and went out there. And there was a little beaver dam. And there was bamboo that was coming down and hitting this little beaver dam, and it was making the noise we heard. And I sat there, and I felt ridiculous.

WALTER KRAUS

RETIRED CAREER MILITARY OFFICER; PERSONAL-HISTORY INTERVIEWER, INSURANCE INDUSTRY
CRESCENT SPRINGS, KENTUCKY
CHIEF MACHINIST'S MATE, UNITED STATES NAVY, WORLD WAR II
LIEUTENANT COMMANDER, UNITED STATES NAVY, VIETNAM

Born in Germany in 1921, Walter S. Kraus emigrated with his family to the Cincinnati area in 1926. "My parents left Germany because of the financial conditions, with the great inflation. After Hitler came in, we got letters from relatives saying how well off they were. Of course, it was all because he was building a heck of a war machine. I remember receiving a letter that my father was angry about. It was from one of my uncles and included a picture of him dressed up in a Nazi uniform. He would start his letters with 'Heil Hitler.'

"In 1937, a man from the German consulate in Columbus came to our home and offered us passage back to Germany. I wouldn't say my father threw him out, but he wasn't very kind."

Soon after he joined the Navy in 1938 Walter became a submariner. During the war he would serve in the Pacific as part of the submarine fleet's effort to sink the shipping needed to support Japan's farflung empire.

Walter began the war aboard a boat called simply the S-36. *When that vessel was disabled, he was transferred to the* Snapper.

In a submarine, we didn't have face-to-face contact with our enemy—our enemy was an unknown. Our targets were ships. That's the way it is in the submarine force.

We didn't get to see the results of what we were doing. Sometimes you heard an explosion. But when your target is an escorted craft, you can't stay up there and watch the results—you'll get worked over by depth charges. So you have to get down.

You can actually hear the detonator of the depth charge before it explodes—sound travels fast in water, several times faster than in air. And then all at once you get the concussion, and the lights burst and things fall off the bulkhead. Anything that's not fastened down is gonna break. And then you're waiting for the next one to drop. You just stand and wait and pray.

When it's all over, you're a nervous wreck. You're tense and you have bad dreams—you're going through a depth-charge attack, and the water's rushing in, and you're sinking, and you're sinking, and you don't know what to do anymore. And you wake up and hit the bunk above you, because the bunks are very small. And you get up and you walk around. You don't sleep more than two or three hours at a time.

I came back to the States in March of 1945, before the war

ended. The reason I was rotated back home was that I didn't pass my physical at Pearl Harbor. My nerves were shot, which was not uncommon. I'd made eleven war patrols; most guys only made seven. So the doctor decided I needed a break.

It took a long time, till a couple of years after the war, before I settled down. Time is a great healer.

The big thing in my dreams was when I was in the *S-36* and it was hit. Being waist-deep in water with an up angle, and hearing the hull creaking and seeing the water come in through the rivets—that was the worst time.

I still dream of that sometimes. I dream about drowning. I always wake up just before I'm gasping for my last breath.

It doesn't happen very often. It might happen tonight after I'm discussing it.

STEVE KRAUS

Construction Superintendent
Woodbridge, Virginia
Sergeant, United States Marine Corps, Vietnam

For the United States Marines stationed in the northernmost reaches of South Vietnam after 1966, the Demilitarized Zone—the strip of land separating North from South Vietnam along the 17th latitudinal parallel—could not have been more inaccurately named. That year, as the number of American military personnel in Vietnam surpassed two hundred thousand, large concentrations of North Vietnamese moved across the North-South border to take up positions in the DMZ's southern half and, from those locations, send artillery shells, rockets, and ground troops south.

Rolling Thunder, the American campaign of bombing against North Vietnam, had begun in March 1965 and would last until October 1968. But Lyndon Johnson feared a repeat of 1950, when American and other forces of the United Nations crossed another parallel—the 38th—separating a Western-oriented south and a Communist north, and provoked Chinese intervention in the Korean War. Therefore, American military planners did not respond to North Vietnam's cross-border escalation in kind. Aside from occasional covert raids conducted in small numbers, the ground war, unlike the war in the air, would not be brought home to the enemy.

Instead, seeking to check the North Vietnamese Army's southward movement, the Americans established a series of firebases just below the DMZ and populated them with the men of the Third Marine Division. And in May 1967 U.S. military planners yielded to facts on the ground and permitted American forces to conduct operations in the zone's southern half.

No servicemen in Vietnam saw more unceasing or more intense combat than did the Marines who occupied the bleak outposts along this supposedly combat-free zone.

After arriving in Vietnam in the spring of 1967, nineteen-year-old Steven T. Kraus was sent to the DMZ to join Delta Company of the First Battalion of the Fourth Marine Regiment, then engaged in Operation Firebreak. "We were security for the Seabees, who were setting up a strip of just nothing, like six hundred yards wide, from the ocean to the mountains. Completely barren, so nobody could sneak through from the North."

After a month, Delta Company was sent to Con Thien, also on the DMZ.

We were running platoon-sized ambushes—just out making sure they weren't building up around us. But it didn't work evidently, because on the night of May the eighth, we were hit by a reinforced regiment from the 324B Division of the NVA. Delta Company had just two platoons when they came at us—Second Platoon was out on ambush—and Alpha Company was there, too, plus a few Special Forces and some others. So it was twelve-hundred-and-some of them to like two hundred of us.

They snuck up on our listening posts and slit everyone's throats, then they started mortaring the hell out of us. I was one of the first ones to see them. I started firing, throwing grenades.

We had a couple tanks, but they took the tanks out right away, *bam!* I was on the machine gun with my buddy Earl. He opened up the gun, and I don't think it was five seconds, the gun was blown, *boom!* He was blinded—temporarily, it turned out—and I was blown out of the hole. They had everything figured out and they just zeroed in. They knew where every gun was. They knew where the tanks were. I imagine for a week or two they had been probing our lines. They had everything we had—binoculars, telescopes. It only takes one guy sitting in a tree five hundred yards away to tell where everything is.

Earl kept saying, "Don't leave me, don't leave me, I can't see." So I stayed with him, but not inside the bunker. I stayed up on top, just behind the bunker, where I could see more of what was going on. I was throwing grenades and shooting these guys as fast as I could.

I did what I was supposed to do: hold my position in hell or high water. And make those guys die for their country. They say, "Yours is do and die for your country." Our DI used to tell us, "No, no, no. Your job is to make the other guy die for *his.*" Sounds better to me.

They were coming up and running over me. I was shooting as they came towards me, then turning around and shooting them as they ran to the rear of me. They were jumping over me—I have never figured that out.

I thought I was gonna die. I'm sure everybody did. The only thing I kept saying to myself was, "Yeah, I'm gonna die tonight. But tomorrow, B-52s will be knocking these bastards off of here." It's funny. When you know you're gonna die, there's a calmness comes over you. You think clearer. I guess if you feel there's nothing you can do about it, what the hell?

Puff came up for a while—the DC-3 with the Gatling guns and

flares. But they only stayed a couple minutes and left. I think they had to get back because Dong Ha was getting hit, and they had to protect the bigger base more than they were gonna protect us. Second Platoon couldn't make it through to come back. There was no artillery; everybody was too far away. They tried to bring reinforcements up to us; I saw them the next morning. The NVA had an RPG and a flamethrower, and our guys were just burnt crisp.

We were still fighting when the sun came up. We were looking for rounds in the dirt to put in our rifles.

You're just crawling through guts and brains and smoke. People talk about the smell of combat. When you know what somebody's insides smell like and feel like it does something to you.

The smell is a mixture of burnt powder and raw flesh and bowel and intestine. When you watch war on TV, you're only hit by a couple of senses; if you read about it, you're only hit by a couple of senses. Man, when you're in it, you find senses you never knew you had.

Some helicopters came in the morning; we were still shooting, throwing grenades. The enemy was still shooting at us, too, but they were retreating. We had fought 'em off. They didn't take the place.

ED JACKSON

Tipp City, Ohio

Staff Sergeant, United States Army Air Forces,
World War II

The strategic bombing campaign launched against the Third Reich was divided into two distinct components: British heavy bombers would attack by night, seeking to terrorize the German population by destroying entire German cities. The American side of the Combined Bomber Offensive involved daylight "precision" bomb-

ing intended to cripple Germany's production of armaments. Initially bombing runs focused on German factories, particularly those producing ball bearings, which were components in a wide variety of armament, and those producing aircraft. Facing unexpectedly effective opposition from German fighter planes, however, this campaign succeeded only in bringing about unacceptable losses of Allied aircraft and crewmen—and not in halting production in the targeted industries.

In early 1944, however, the Combined Bomber Offensive shifted its attention to attacking German industry at its root: its system of transportation. Targets of choice would now be railroad marshaling yards and facilities producing oil.

Based in Italy with the Fifteenth Air Force, Ed left on his first mission as a B-24 gunner just as this change was being implemented. Of the fourteen missions he flew, all but one were aimed at railroads or at oil—oilfields, refineries, synthetic-oil plants. Aided by new fighter aircraft with the range to escort heavy bombers all the way to their targets, Allied bombers, by early 1945, brought about the essential collapse of the German war machine. Disruptions in German rail capabilities left the Wehrmacht unable to move men and matériel to where they were needed. And the interruption in the Third Reich's flow of oil meant that no matter how many tanks and planes the Reich's factories might produce, they could not be used in combat. (See Chapter XXI: In March 1945 Paul Walmsley, of Patton's Third Army, discovered a large field full of spanking-new German fighter planes. Oil had never even been run through their engines—because the Germans had none.)

I was the left waist gunner. There was a .50-caliber machine gun mounted in front of a big window—just an opening—in the side of the plane.

The plane wasn't pressurized, so you had to put oxygen masks on. The other waist gunner and I had to wear a flak suit, which was real heavy. It was a big apron that covered down almost to your knees in the front and back, and it had little snaps up at the shoulders so you could drop it off real fast if you had to bail out. You'd wear your parachute underneath of it.

And then you had a heated suit that you plugged in—like these heated blankets—and that was a good joke. Sometimes none of it worked, and other times parts of it would be real, real hot and burn you up, and other parts didn't work at all and you'd get frostbitten. The suits had boots that fit on your feet, so you'd take your GI shoes off and set them to the side.

On the way to the target, you'd worry yourself to death wondering whether you were gonna make it or not. After you got out over water, like the Adriatic Sea or the Mediterranean, you'd test-fire your guns and make sure everything was working properly. And then, if you wasn't anyplace where there was a chance of enemy planes, why, you could sit on the floor of the plane and concentrate on what you were getting into.

When you got in close to the target, naturally you had to be up and looking for enemy planes, because they could come in from anyplace. If you was going to the oil refinery in Ploesti, Romania, you'd see a whole lot of planes before you ever got to the target. But if you was going to some marshaling yard over in France, you might not see a plane at all.

Out of the fourteen missions that I flew, there may have been three or four where I didn't ever see a fighter plane. But the others well made up for that, where the antiaircraft fire was so heavy that you couldn't even see the target. It was just black flecks of smoke everywhere and enemy fighters everywhere.

There was a sickening sound to it. They'd come up in batches of three, so that if one hit below you and the other one hit above you, you could bet your boots the third one was gonna be right where you were at. That was always scary. It was a sickening thing when you'd go into a target and see all this black smoke—a constant smoke that was coming up, because there were planes as far as the eye could see.

Everybody is flying in a real tight formation. I don't know

how the pilots ever did it. There's planes above you and planes below you.

The pilots weren't allowed to take any evasive action, because it'd cause all kinds of havoc—there'd be planes crashing into each other. So you just have to keep going in formation, and you know that the antiaircraft fire's going on, and that scares you.

The waist window is just like a big TV screen—you can see everything going on. You can see fighter planes coming in at you with their guns going—the guns are in the wings, and the wings just look like they're on fire—and you know they're shooting right at you. And you can see planes getting hit with antiaircraft and blowing up. You can see people getting hit. You can see guys bailing out of planes, and they don't have their straps fastened, and their chute pops open, and they just fall out of it. You see people coming out with their parachute on fire. You just can't believe the things you see.

You see them things day and night after you're away from it. Even now there's times when I see that. I can't watch combat movies for nothing. It's terrible.

There's one time I was on a mission and my gun jammed on me, which was not unusual. I think it had too much oil on it. If the ground crew used too much oil when they were cleaning your guns, the oil would freeze at the high altitude and the gun would jam.

So I tore the dumb thing apart. And we're in combat—there's planes flying at us and flak and everything else. And I look over at the other waist position, and I see him firing away, and then I see an enemy fighter, an Me-109, coming in from that side. He's firing, and then he comes under us and goes up on my side. I thought, "Jiminy Christmas, I ain't even got a gun." So I took my .45 automatic, and I was firing at him. If it would've hit, it wouldn't have done any good, but you're just desperate. And the pilot turned his head, and I could see him as plain as day, smiling. I thought, "I'm gonna get it now. He knows I don't have a machine gun." He was close enough where I could almost reach out there and touch him.

He had shot at the plane on his way in, and he could've come back, but I guess he felt sorry for me, because he never came back.

He smiled and never came back. It's terrible.

MIKE JACKSON

RETIRED CAREER MILITARY OFFICER; EXECUTIVE DIRECTOR, AVIATION FOUNDATION

TIPP CITY, OHIO

CAPTAIN, UNITED STATES AIR FORCE, VIETNAM

Born in 1946, Michael E. Jackson enlisted in the Air Force after his graduation from Ohio University in 1968. Trained to fly the O-2, a light, propeller-driven observation plane, in Vietnam he would serve as a forward air controller, coordinating strikes by fighter-bomber aircraft.

Mike left for Vietnam at the end of June 1971.

"At that point, you don't know where the heck you're going. I knew two guys on the plane—we just happened to be on the same flight. Then I get to Cam Ranh Bay and they say, 'Okay, Jackson, you're going to the Twentieth Tactical Air Support Squadron at Da Nang.' The two guys I knew were going to this place or that place, so when I get to Da Nang, I don't know a soul. At Da Nang, they say I'm assigned to Camp Eagle, which is just outside Hue.

"You end up going over by yourself, and you come back by yourself. That's a real difference between Vietnam and World War II."

There were forward air controllers that were assigned all over the place. The reason for that was the rules of engagement, and it was probably good sense. You could not drop a bomb off any airplane in-country unless it was cleared by a FAC—a forward air controller—so there had to be a lot of FACs.

We trolled for targets—that was our job. If we could get somebody to shoot at us, we knew there was somebody down there, and we'd call in the fighters to come and get 'em. Mostly we were doing that over the A Shau Valley, which was a free-fire zone. There were no good guys over there. It was all bad guys.

Every once in a while, that role would get taken over by your role in support of the U.S. Army or ARVN. If they got into what was called a troops-in-contact situation, we would have to go in and sort out everything—where the good guys were, where the bad guys were, what the best run-in headings for the fighters would be. We had gone to fighter lead-in school, so we knew the best way to bring the fighters in, the best way to pull them off. Then, before each bomb was dropped, you would have to clear it individually. You used the term "cleared and hot." If the fighter rolled in and saw the target but we didn't say "cleared and hot," he couldn't drop the bomb.

We flew the same areas all the time. With a pair of binoculars, I could tell if a trail had been used overnight. I could tell if the grass had been bent down. I could see if the footprints were wet on one side of the river and not on the other side. And sometimes, if there was a clearing of some sort—either for a trail or where a bomb or some defoliant had been dropped—I could look down on an angle and see in among the trees.

That was the advantage of us. The fighters were jets; they might be coming in at twenty thousand feet. We'd be down at five hundred feet. And the difference in speed was remarkable, too. We'd run about 90 to 110 miles an hour. I've gone faster in a car.

When the Army called you for a troops-in-contact situation, they were really in trouble. They'd already exhausted everything they could do with artillery and helicopters, so you'd have to wheel off as fast as you could and fly to where they were.

Number one, you had to find 'em. You're talking about triple-canopy jungle with no street signs. I mean, you're reading contour lines in the middle of the jungle and in the middle of hills. And you've got to remember the clock's running, because these guys are getting shot at and overrun.

In the meantime you're coordinating on your other radios—you had four of them in the airplane—trying to get some air strikes. You ask what we called an AB triple-C—Airborne Command and Control Center, a plane in the air, usually a C-130, that had all kinds of communications equipment in it—if they had any airplanes in the air, what they had, and if they had the right kind of ordnance. If they came in and they had the wrong kind of ordnance, you could kill the good guys as easy as you could the bad guys. What you were hoping for was maybe CBUs, cluster bomb units, or five-hundred-pound bombs, or maybe some napalm. Twenty-millimeter guns were good. You had to try to match the armament of the fighters to what you were trying to do. It was almost like being a surgeon, because on the ground the two sides are close enough that they're shooting at each other. So you'd try to sort out where all the airplanes were, and then you would tell the ground unit to pop smoke.

They carried different-colored smoke grenades with them, and they would pop one, and you'd say, "I see red smoke" or "I see yellow smoke" or white smoke, and they would say, "Yeah, that's it." So, okay, you know where the good guys are—kind of, because by the time the smoke has come up through the trees, it's drifted through all the branches and leaves and vines. So the good guys' position might be off from the smoke a little bit.

You do a little more trying to figure out where everybody is, and the whole time you're going lower. You're trying to get down so you can look under the jungle and see what's there. That's not necessarily a good thing, because there are bad guys there, and they know that you haven't come to help them out. The minute they know an FAC's up there, the FAC becomes the target, because, as I said, no fighter can drop a bomb unless it's cleared, particularly in a troops-in-contact situation. So the North Vietnamese, having fought this battle for many, many years, know that if they shoot the FAC down, there could be three thousand airplanes in the air, but the air strike stops. Nobody can do anything until another FAC comes in. So everybody starts shooting at the FAC.

You're going lower and lower. You radio to the ground, "Okay, I see a river. Where are you at in relation to the river?" Or "I see this dirt road. Where are you at?"

You finally sort out where you think everybody's at, and then you mark it with a smoke rocket. The guy on the ground could give corrections from there: "Twenty meters to the north" or "Thirty meters to the south." By that time, hopefully, the fighters are above and they see the smoke rocket come up, and then you have to describe to the fighters the whole situation.

Once you've got the fighters briefed, you tell them what heading to fly and what weapon you want them to use first—let's start out with twenty-mike-mike, which is the twenty-millimeter Gatling gun; or nape, which is napalm; or Mark-82s, which are five-hundred-pound bombs. Then they come in, and they start their run. The first guy will say, "Lead's in hot," and then you look at him and have to really quick make an estimate on where he's gonna drop that bomb. You're watching the fighter come down, and you're trying to line up where the good guys and the bad guys are on the ground and trying to visualize where this bomb's gonna go when he lets go of it, and then, if you think it's gonna be a good bomb, you say, "Cleared and hot." And he drops the thing, and he's out.

Then the next guy comes in. And you just repeat that until you've expended all the ordnance. If everything works out good, you've done the work of a surgeon and removed the bad guys from the good guys.

I don't know how many troops-in-contact missions I had, but I had a bunch, and they were always frantic. I had a total of 210 missions over there. If the last one was a troops-in-contact, it was just as hectic and just as scary and just as busy as the first one was. I mean, I got a little better at it, but it was always still, "Don't let me kill the good guys."

It could take no more than ten minutes, but when you got done, you'd lost about five pounds of sweat. You had to pull off and go fly around for a while, because you were just drained. But you felt great, because you had just saved a platoon or bigger of our guys.

I like to say I saved more people than I killed. I think I did. The Distinguished Flying Cross I got was for saving friendly troops. I killed some bad guys in the process, but I saved our guys. I was good at troops-in-contact, but, boy, I tell you what, it scared me every time I did it. Because if the guy makes a mistake and drops napalm instead of a hard bomb, he could kill the good guys instead of the bad guys. If he hits the rudder pedal by accident as he lets go, the twenty-millimeter gun goes swinging off to the left and hits the good guys instead of the bad guys. There was always pressure, and we earned our pay.

Being an FAC was a dangerous job, no way around it, and I didn't care for getting shot at. I didn't like it at all. Luckily, you couldn't usually tell when they were shooting. You had an airplane with two engines that were droning. You had a helmet on with earphones on it. You had four radios blasting away. So you couldn't hear a lot of gunfire. But you knew you were getting shot at pretty much the whole time. Even if there's just one guy down there, it's not a very big airplane. One lucky shot would take you out.

CITATION TO ACCOMPANY THE AWARD OF THE DISTINGUISHED FLYING CROSS TO MICHAEL E. JACKSON

Captain Michael E. Jackson distinguished himself by extraordinary achievement while participating in aerial flight as a Forward Air Controller near Hue, Republic of Vietnam on 15 May 1972. On that date, Captain Jackson flew his lightly armed reconnaissance aircraft in support of a unit of the Army of the Republic of Vietnam, which was in violent conflict with a numerically superior hostile. Despite intense ground fire and marginal weather conditions, Captain Jackson directed tactical air strikes onto the hostile positions which broke the conflict and resulted in one heavy machine gun destroyed, one heavy machine gun damaged, fifteen rifles destroyed, and five large supply caches destroyed, producing one large secondary explosion, eight medium secondary explosions, and three small secondary explosions, with twenty-six hostile personnel killed by air. The professional competence, aerial skill, and devotion to duty displayed by Captain Jackson reflect great credit upon himself and the United States Air Force.

X

"He came to die with me."

COMRADES

In *Drum-Taps*, a collection of poems about the Civil War, Walt Whitman writes that

> affection shall solve the problems of freedom yet,
> Those who love each other shall become invincible,
> They shall yet make Columbia victorious.

Combat demands of its participants the "manly virtues," as they are traditionally called—courage, physical strength, stoic endurance of pain and discomfort. Yet combat's circumstances—the close living conditions, the shared enterprise, and, above all, the reliance upon one another in the constant struggle to resist death—may forge among men bonds that in less extreme circumstances they would think unmanly to share and even more so to admit.

The relationships formed among men at war may be as steadfast and as intimate as any that link one human being to another, save that between mother and child. When I was looking for veterans to interview at length for this book, I conducted brief phone conversations with many men whom, ultimately, I never got to meet. One was Alan Fischer, of Carlsbad, California, who flew A6 Navy fighter jets during Vietnam. He said, "I could call my friend Jack Keegan, a fellow A6 driver, ask him to drive fifty miles to put *a cup of coffee on my front porch at two o'clock in the morning, and he wouldn't ask why—he'd just do it. I told my wife I want to be buried with the guys. Not that I love her less. But I saw real, deep love, men for men.*

"I can depend on Jack and men like him for anything at any time. A word never has to be spoken, but that deep, valid respect is there and it's a wonderful feeling."

Comrades in arms, writes Whitman, are "[m]ore precious to each other than all the riches of the earth."

MIKE PERKINS

Tremonton, Utah

Captain, United States Army, Vietnam

After several months working out of Khe Sanh with Project Delta, Mike was assigned to a mobile strike force headquartered in Da Nang. "If Special Forces camps got in trouble anywhere in I Corps, we'd send in the Mike Force to help 'em—we'd parachute in, helicopter in, whatever. Or we'd go on reconnaissance missions. Anything they asked us to do, from picking up cigarette butts around the colonel's hooch to going after the bad guys, that's what we did."

I was with the Mike Force till July '67, and then I extended in Vietnam for a second tour, six months.

What would I go home to? Working basic training at Fort Dix? I mean, what was there to come home to if you're a professional soldier? I didn't have a family, just me. I had my mother and father and brother and sister—I came and visited them. It was great. But by that time my family was the Army. I'd found my place in life. I knew all these guys. Everywhere I went, I bumped into guys I knew.

In Vietnam, for all of its mess and horror, you had a challenge.

You had a purpose. When I went there, I wanted to get blooded, to learn about who I am, what I am. Well, after I'd been in Vietnam for six months, I knew I was a pretty good soldier. And, yeah, I have to go on operations and do what I'm told to do. But I'm there to keep American kids alive. That was my mission.

Mike spent his second tour with the 101st Airborne Division, first running resupply operations as a member of a support battalion and then as operations officer of a new long-range patrol company.

Shortly after the Tet Offensive, Mike was ordered home to take the officers' infantry advanced course at Fort Benning, Georgia.

I came out one of the top graduates. I could have gone anywhere I wanted. But I said, "I want to go back to Vietnam."

They said, "You're an idiot."

About half the guys went back to Vietnam. Other people went to Turkey and Germany and Fort Jackson. Who knows where they go? I went back, because that's what I do.

I had a rifle company down in the Ninth Division, which was in the Delta. I was in the Second Brigade, which was part of the riverine force. We lived on a Navy barracks ship, the USS *Benewah,* and went out on Navy landing craft—ATCs, armored troop carriers. We called them Tango boats—T for "troops." Most of them were converted World War II LCM-6s, and just like you see in the World War II movies, they had the ramp that dropped down.

I had an adventure a day with the riverines. It never ended, it never let up. Except when you were back on board ship, it did not let up. It would just wear on you, wear on you.

You'd go out for two or three days, come back in for a day and a half, out for two or three days, back in for a day and a half. Sometimes you'd be thoroughly briefed on what you were about to do, and sometimes you wouldn't. Even as a company commander, sometimes I only knew that we had to get the guys up. I'd ask, "What am I facing?"

"We don't know."

Sometimes you didn't even have maps for it.

Sometimes you'd land on a nice white sandy beach, and sometimes the ramp goes down, and when you get out, you're up to your chest in mud and you have to wade as much as fifty, sixty feet till you get to shore. We got to be experts in mud—there were five hundred different kinds of it. If the mud was watery, a lot of guys would just lay on their backs and swim to shore. That's just the way it was. Sometimes we'd be an hour, hour and a half, two hours, trying to move fifty feet. We lived in mud.

Sometimes, when the first three or four would get off the boat and I'd see that mud, we'd pull those guys back on board and I'd tell the coxswain, "Find a better beaching place." Then I'd catch hell over the radio: "You're supposed to beach here." And I'd have to explain about the mud. But sometimes we'd get an order: "You *will* beach here." If they order you to, you do it.

That was just the nature of the game. We're out there stomping the countryside looking for bad people. I guess if you use the proper military terminology, it would be called "reconnaissance in force." Looking for trouble.

Sometimes you'd walk for a mile and see nothing. Then you'd call the boats and agree to meet them a quarter mile down the canal.

Other times we might encounter bunker systems. I've been inside the bunkers. This guy there is standing in probably knee-deep water. He's been waiting for you. He's looking through the bunker aperture and he's seen you coming down the river. He knows. He's got you in his sights. And as soon as that ramp comes down, *bingo!*—in come their automatic weapons, their RPGs, cutting down the first four or five guys out of the boat. You've seen the movie *Saving Private Ryan*—not quite that bad, but pretty bad.

All the bunkers are covered with foliage. You're going, "I'm getting fire, but where is it coming from?" It's twenty or thirty feet in front of you, and you're looking. "Where is this fire coming from?"

So what you do is you just put down the heaviest fire you can. And the Navy was good about this. Along with these Tango boats going down the canals, you'd have gunboats, and they had fifty-seven-millimeter cannons on them or eighty-one-millimeter mortars on them. You had the Zippos. That's a big old Navy craft that had the flamethrower in the front of it—it would burn everything. It was quite a flotilla. And you had air strikes going, and Army and Navy helicopter gunships in there supporting us, too.

None of the Navy kids ever backed down. There were all these young seamen and I never saw anybody whimpering or crying. They were all putting out fire.

About every third operation in the riverines, when you came back in to the ship, there'd be an order waiting for you. You'd go over to the battalion command ship, and they'd give you a briefing: "We're gonna go on a night raid tonight." Then you'd go back, and you'd ask for eight or nine or ten volunteers to go with you. Night raids were not fun.

We'd gone on fourteen or fifteen night raids before this one I'll tell you about; some of them were dry holes, some of them we killed a few bad guys. This time we choppered in and I realized that I'd been in this same little hamlet about two weeks before, the exact same place.

There were ten of us, and we were going through hooches. As a standard procedure, we'd apprehend all military-age males, bind their hands, and take them back with us to interrogate. Here there weren't any. They were all old women, young wives and children, and a couple of real old men. "This is a dry hole," I said. "Let's get out of here." This is about 11:00 P.M.

I was wrong.

One of my sergeants came in. He said, "You gotta see this." So I went with him down to the paddy dike, and he took his finger and rolled a piece of this dike back with his finger, and it's on rails and ball bearings. I turned my flashlight on and shined it down the hole. It's reinforced concrete. Three, four feet down there's a firing step—a big steel plate for someone to stand on—with some casings laying on it and a ladder that goes into a tunnel. And this little thing on top has dirt on it and looks like it's part of a paddy dike, but it's a reinforced concrete lid—a little bigger than a manhole cover; it must have weighed a couple hundred pounds. And it rolls back and forth with the touch of a finger.

This is an ideal thing. Helicopters come by. A guy fires at them. He hits this lid with his finger, the thing rolls over him, the helicopter looks down, and there's nothing there.

Another guy down about fifty meters says, "Hey, I found another setup just like that one"—that meant the tunnel kept on going. I'd seen lots of holes dug in the ground, but never anything this exotic and sophisticated. This isn't your average communal-farmer job; they must have had Russian or Chinese engineers building these things. This is where somebody big lived.

So I immediately called our helicopters. There were five of them—two lift ships, two Cobra gunships, and the command bird—just orbiting up in the sky, waiting for us. I said, "We are in the middle of something, and we need to get out of here right now."

They said, "We'd like to come and get you, but we're out of fuel." So they fly away. Ten, twenty, thirty minutes later, they come back. We're in the middle of this paddy; they can't find us. They're lost. I turn on my strobe light. They see it. And as they're coming in, I can hear voices all around us.

I said, "Oh, my gosh. These are male voices, and they aren't old men and kids." So I told the gunships, "They're all around us. When you come in, lay down everything you got, because that's what it's gonna take."

When the two lift ships landed, the air was full of green tracers. We're firing. Everybody's firing. We get on, and the birds take off. When we get up in the air, we do a personnel check. Somebody didn't make it onto the second bird.

We had artillery flares going off in the air for illumination, so I looked down, and sure enough, there's one of our guys laying down in the ditch. So I told the other bird, "He's your guy. You go in and get him." Oh, boy, they didn't think much of that.

Well, that bird landed. We were flared up a hundred yards behind him, in case he crashed. At this point there was no enemy fire; apparently, when the helicopters took off before, all the bad guys thought, "We've missed those guys, let's go home." So the guy in the ditch just stood up and jumped in the helicopter. But somebody had jumped out the other side looking for *him.* The helicopter took off; we still had a guy on the ground. Murphy's Law.

I was leaning out the door of my helicopter, and the pilot—Warrant Officer Hunt—never said a word to me. But he looked at me like, "Should I?" And I gave him a look back like, "Get him." And we went on in to get him.

Not a round had been fired at the other helicopter, the one that had just taken off. But before we could land, they hit us. Man, they hit us with everything. And the whole front of the helicopter was on fire. So I jumped.

It must have been thirty feet to the ground, but fortunately it was the wet season and the paddies were flooded, and I landed in that paddy. And I went looking over my left shoulder for that helicopter, because I didn't want to get hit with the helicopter blade. And *boom!* The helicopter came down on its side, directly on top of me.

So now I'm underneath the helicopter, facedown, and I'm moving my head side to side trying to find a hole to breathe. And I hear all this screaming and yelling going on out there.

Pretty soon they rocked the helicopter off me. They pulled me out, but I still have my left arm stuck into the helicopter.

Ed Eaton, who was my sniper—a really good kid, nineteen years old—he's up on top of the helicopter by this time. And he's blazing away at everybody with his sniper weapon, which has got the stock broken off. Just about all the machine guns and guns in the helicopter are all bent and the barrels are twisted, but he has that sniper weapon. Then somebody hands him up a working M-16.

Ed gets shrapnel in the jaw but keeps firing. They finally get me out of the helicopter. The reason I hadn't been able to get my hand out was that I had it clasped tightly around my weapon. Finally I opened up my hand, and my arm slid right out. But I am going into shock, and I know I am.

I can't move, because everything on my left side has been broken: pelvis, leg, arm, ribs. But it's interesting to lay here and watch all this. The gunships are expending everything they've got, Ed's firing away. The bullets are impacting in the water.

Finally the gunships land; they're maybe twenty, thirty feet out. The pilots raise those canopies: "Come on! Come on!" The Cobras have these little wing stubs—the rocket pods and guns are mounted underneath them. Guys are hobbling out to get on these stubs.

The first bird, they get three or four guys sitting on the stubs. The gunner is holding on to them, and the bird takes off, it's gone.

The second one, he comes in right behind. You can see the green tracers going by. "Come on! Come on!" Somebody picked me up; I'm not sure who it was. And he says, "Come on, we can get on there." He got me to my feet, and I was so weak, from loss of blood and everything else, I could not do anything. I said, "Just put me down. I'm not gonna make it."

If I remember right, he sat me down and gave me a grenade. I just laid there and looked, and they all got on that helicopter, and I said, "That's it."

My only concern was, "I want to die quickly. I don't want to be tortured to death." When I was at Khe Sanh, some Marine came up missing on patrol, and we found him two days later. They had cut off his penis and put it in his mouth. And you could tell he was alive when all that was happening. These people enjoyed doing things like that. I didn't want to be captured.

That second helicopter was just about to leave, but then Ed Eaton jumped down off one of those little stubs and ran over and laid down next to me. And then Marty Green jumped off, and he came, too. The helicopter left, and there's me and Green and Ed

Eaton. The bones were sticking out of Green's elbow and out of his shoulder, and I remember looking at that and going, "My gosh, he's a mess."

Now it was all quiet, very, very quiet. And because of loss of blood, I'm going blind. But I can hear, and I hear two shots. *Bam! Bam!* Ed told me later he killed two VC that were walking up the trail, thirty, forty feet away.

I know I'm dying, and I know that all three of us are gonna die soon anyway, because I could hear Vietnamese voices out there. The next thing I hear is another helicopter coming in. This was Colonel Pete—my battalion commander, Pete Peterson—who was controlling all this in the C&C bird way up high.

He landed. There's a whole series of machine-gun fire, and then I'm grabbed by my feet—by Colonel Pete and his commo officer, I learned later, each holding one foot—and I'm dragged facedown, and I'm thrown in the helicopter. I hear it winding up, and away it goes.

I spent four weeks, five weeks with Green in the hospital. I said, "Green, why did you get off that helicopter and run back with Ed?"

He said, "I'd follow Ed anywhere. I didn't know what I was doing, but he jumped off the helicopter. He must've known something I didn't know."

In my civics class, they're always saying, "Tell us stories." And I'll have funny stories. I have stories about when I was a kid. I have this treasury of stories.

But I only tell a few war stories, because I don't like war stories per se. There has to be a point in them. I've told the Ed Eaton story a number of times, because I want kids to know that there are some fine people in this world.

I tell the kids, "There are wonderful people out there, ordinary people who do extraordinary things when called upon. That's almost everybody, and that's including you. One day you may be called upon to do an extraordinary and remarkable thing, even though you're just an ordinary person."

World War II is a good example of what ordinary kids did. They came off the farm or off the street and saved the world and then went back to the farm or the street, just like nothing had happened. These are all the old men that live around us now. Most of them don't think it was extraordinary. We do, but they don't.

What Ed Eaton did is remarkable because he didn't come to save me. He came to die with me.

PERRY POLLINS

LEXINGTON, MASSACHUSETTS

CORPORAL, UNITED STATES MARINE CORPS, WORLD WAR II

There were quite a few Jews in the Marine Corps during World War II. In the First Division, I would say there must've been maybe five, six hundred. They had Jewish chaplains who came from the Navy.

As a matter of fact, about D + 3 or 4 on Peleliu, I'm on the line. We still had only three hundred, four hundred yards of beach.

And this sergeant comes up. The name is Beck. German, blond, tough. And he says, "Hey, Polinsky"—that was my name in those days—"the lieutenant wants you to go back on the beach."

I said, "What's back on the beach?"

He says, "They're holding High Holiday services."

I said, "What?" This is coming from a guy of German descent.

He says, "Yeah." And then I head back to the beach, and he says, "Say a prayer for me."

I get down on the beach, and there's still live fire coming in—I mean, all over. There's mortar and artillery. And the chaplain is there, Rabbi Ed Siskin. He was a lieutenant commander in the Navy.

He has a *bimah*—which is like a lectern or reading table—set up with two or three fifty-five-gallon drums. I thought it was a *tallis* over it—a prayer shawl—but that might be my imagination; it was probably some cloth from a sandbag or something.

And he held High Holiday services. Rosh Hashanah. We all had prayer books; I carried one all the time in my jacket pocket. There were twenty-two, twenty-three of us there.

The beach was loaded with debris. There were still Japanese bodies floating around. There were amphtracs still burning.

The service lasted maybe for almost an hour. But it was interspersed with having to take cover, about ten times. We'd be hearing the service, and all of a sudden, we'd just part company and hit the ground.

Having that service on the beach was outstanding. I thought it was wonderful. And it went through my mind that my lieutenant thought to have me go to the service, and this German SOB came up and told me to get my ass down there. It made me feel that these people were all with me.

JIM COYNE SR.

RETIRED TELEPHONE TECHNICIAN
MANAHAWKIN, NEW JERSEY
TECHNICAL SERGEANT, UNITED STATES ARMY, WORLD WAR II

When Winston Churchill and Franklin Roosevelt met at Casablanca in January 1943, their most important order of business was the opening of a second front in Europe to ease the pressure on their Soviet ally. Aside from Anglo-American forces undertaking successful but small-scale operations in North Africa, Joseph Stalin's armies had been the only ground troops engaged with the forces of Nazi Germany for a year and a half—since Adolf Hitler's invasion of the Soviet Union on June 22, 1941—and Soviet losses numbered in the millions. But the tide in the east was turning, and on February 2, 1943, the battle for Stalingrad ended in abject defeat for the Germans, with one hundred fifty thousand Axis troops dead and another ninety thousand captured.

American military planners at Casablanca, led by Army Chief of Staff General George C. Marshall, argued for an invasion of northwest Europe, across the English Channel, in 1943. British generals, however, contended that the Western Allies needed more time to prepare for so momentous an undertaking. Caution won the day, and the invasion across the Channel would have to wait until 1944. Instead, Churchill and Roosevelt agreed, the Allies would build on their accomplishments in North Africa by invading Sicily and then, possibly, moving onto the Italian mainland, aiming for the surrender of Germany's junior partner in the Axis, the Italy of Benito Mussolini.

James J. Coyne Sr., a twenty-year-old signalman from Jersey City, New Jersey, landed at Sicily on the invasion's first day.

The first time in my life I was under gunfire, I didn't know what it was. It was July 10, 1943. We crossed from Africa to a town called Gela.

I will never forget it. I came over on an LST, a landing ship tank. I went ashore. All of a sudden, there were a lot of religious monuments and stuff like that. Hide behind them! There was gunfire all over the place. From the ships, from land. We were frightened. Frightened. I had a battalion commander, a colonel. He was a West Pointer; there were very few of them around. We were shouting, "Hey, where are we going? What are we doing?" He said, "Down. Down. Keep down." He kept his head about him, and that kept all our heads about us. He was a good man.

We got stuck for a couple of days at Gela, until finally enough Americans and British got ashore and we were able to break out. We drove along the southern coast of the island, then back along the northern coast toward Messina. That was a long struggle.

We'd almost come to Messina, and things were moving fairly well, we thought. Then the Germans attacked—the name of the town escapes me. Real fierce battle there. We took a real shellacking. Our colonel knew what the score was. The other officers weren't as experienced as he was. He got them together, then sent them out to tell the guys, "Hang in! No matter what! Don't step back!"

Sicily is very mountainous country. We got out on the plain, on the coast, and the Italian mainland was just over there, behind the Germans, ten miles across the strait. Behind us were mountains—you never saw them so big. There was no place for us to go. "Hang in there!" We did.

This was when my buddy was killed. Anthony.

He was from Jersey, too, from South Orange, a very nice town. My wife was Ethel, and his wife was Jean—they got together while we were away. We kept up with Jean for a while after the war, went out a few times, then we lost contact. South Orange to Jersey City was, for me, like New York to Boston.

There wasn't much to do when we weren't in action, so Anthony and I would hang around and talk. He was a baseball fan, and I was, too. He liked the Giants, and I liked the Giants—we used to talk about them a lot. And then for some reason we'd get around to the Yankees. We didn't think too much of them. And we didn't like the Dodgers either.

When Anthony was shot, I was close by. Somebody shouted, "Medics! Medics!" I didn't have time to stop and think about it, because the fighting was heavy. He got hit in the belly, his insides were spilled out.

Sicily was a stopping-off point between Africa and Italy. When the Americans entered Rome, I was riding in the third vehicle in the column. The streets were jammed with civilians and soldiers. They'd be shouting: "*Viva America!* Hey, Joe! Hey, Joe! Hey, Joe, I lived in Brooklyn once!" They were very grateful to see us.

We stayed in Rome a couple of days—it took that long to round up all the Americans. I didn't really take part in the fun. In the first place, there were too many Americans who could speak Italian. I couldn't give any Italian out. The Romans were very friendly at that time, and I'm thinking, "It feels so great, we've got to get out of here." Yeah, we got out of there all right. The next boat. Before we left, General Mark Clark paid us a visit: "Thank you, guys, for helping get this done." And he said, "We're gonna put you where you want to be. And where you want to be is Marseilles, in the south of France." It was a very, very serious time in our lives, and Clark knew that many of us would die in the landings there.

Many did. We didn't land in a wave of glory or anything like that; we got there in the darkness of night. The landing was hard. The Germans had heavy, heavy guns. Firing from ten, twelve miles inland. Our warships—American warships, British warships—were firing back at them. We just needed to get a foot ashore, get a shoe on the sand. Then we went inland. There was firing behind us and firing in front of us. Heavy artillery all day long. I knew they didn't need to waste that much ammunition, but they did.

We stayed in France a long while. At that time we weren't sure we would win at the end. I wasn't so sure that there would *be* an end. I really didn't think so. We kept building up Allied forces, building up and building up and building up. But there was no breakthrough. The Germans kept holding the line.

We thought, "Hey, this could go on forever."

XI

"They were so brave, those guys."

AL TARBELL

AL TARBELL

RETIRED CONSTRUCTION FOREMAN

SYRACUSE, NEW YORK

SERGEANT, UNITED STATES ARMY, WORLD WAR II

On September 17, 1944, with the Allies in control of most of France, Luxembourg, and Belgium, Anglo-American forces commanded by British Field Marshal Bernard Montgomery launched what remains the largest airborne operation in military history, Operation Market-Garden. Montgomery's brainchild, Market-Garden was intended as a bold stroke that would bring about the swift end of the war. American and British paratroopers would be dropped along a corridor leading from the Allied front lines at the Belgium-Netherlands frontier north toward Holland's border with Germany. The Americans, of the Eighty-second and 101st Airborne Divisions, were to capture a series of bridges over the Maas and Waal rivers and a number of canals. Once those objectives were taken, British infantry and armor could advance to Arnhem, where Britain's First Airborne Division was to seize a bridge over the Lower Rhine. By establishing this bridgehead over the Rhine, the Allies would be able to invade Germany without having to penetrate the Siegfried Line—known to Germans as the Westwall*—the column of fortifications* *that protected Germany's western border but did not reach this far north. Montgomery would thus lead the Allied juggernaut into the Ruhr, Germany's industrial heartland, and then, within weeks, to Berlin.*

Montgomery predicated his operation on the belief that German armor in the area to be contested was sparse and German troops there no more than teenagers and exhausted old men. In the days before the operation's commencement, however, intelligence reports indicated that German tanks were present in far greater numbers than expected. But these reports were almost willfully ignored, and the operation began as scheduled.

The plan's success depended on the timely taking of all objectives in order to establish an unobstructed pathway for British ground forces to quickly meet up with their compatriots dropped into Arnhem. The Americans, including Albert A. Tarbell of the Eighty-second Airborne's 504th Parachute Infantry Regiment, promptly seized their objectives, but the British troops at Arnhem, hampered by a near total breakdown of radio communication and facing a nimble and unexpectedly forceful German response, could not do the same. Nor did the British tankers of XXX Corps reach Arnhem to reinforce them. Of the nine thousand British troops dropped at Arnhem, over seven thousand were killed, wounded, or captured. Montgomery's spectacular plan ended in spectacular failure. The war would continue.

My two uncles, Joseph Tarbell and Peter Tarbell, were combat engineers in World War I. They didn't get into the heavy fighting, but they did a lot of work for the Army—building bridges and roads and stuff like that. They both talked a lot about their travels in different countries, France especially, and about going over the ocean.

It was instilled in us that what they did was patriotic. We had a sense of patriotism when World War II broke out, so everybody started enlisting.

My cousin joined the Marine Corps and was one of the first

men on Guadalcanal, where he was wounded. One of my friends was with him, too. There were no slackers. Everybody wanted to go in the service.

I don't know why the Mohawks all served. But I figured, if I'm gonna join the service, I want to be where the fighting is. I always wanted to do that. I wanted to be with the brave men.

I was born August 24, 1923, on the Saint Regis Mohawk Indian Reservation in northern New York. It's between the towns of Massena and Malone, right on the Canadian border.

I went to the Mohawk Indian School right there in Hogansburg, on the reservation, and then to public high school off the reservation.

My mother couldn't read or write, but she encouraged me to read. I had to buy the Syracuse paper every day and read it for her, one end to the other. So I was right up on the dates. I even followed the civil war in Spain. I still have clippings I kept from that war. I made a project of it.

We talked about the situation in Europe a lot.

Don't forget, we were on the Canadian border, and Canada went to war first. We saw a lot of soldiers.

I wanted to do my part for the war effort, so in the summer of '40 I dropped out of high school and went with one of my cousins to Cornwall, Ontario, to join the Third Battalion, Glengarry Highlanders. We thought we could go overseas, but we were both too young—I was sixteen going on seventeen. I ended up as a training instructor with the rank of corporal, which was a very good rank at that time.

After Pearl Harbor happened, I came home on leave to see my father and mother, and I had a bad cold. Then I came down with pneumonia, and my father says, "You have no business going back there if they can't take care of your health."

I was sick for quite a while. When I got better, I went to work in Massena as an apprentice lineman. That meant doing outside electrical work—painting and repairing electrical towers, power lines, stuff like that.

In January of '43 I got married—we had been going together, and we figured we should get married before I got called into the service. When I got married, I said, "I might as well wait for them to call." And they did, about a month later. In March we were shipped to Fort Niagara.

I spent my last night before leaving with my parents, my wife. My parents were very loving, very wonderful people. They told me to be good. Pray. See, I was brought up in a strict Catholic community. Praying was a habit I started as an altar boy, and I prayed when I was fighting, especially when I was scared—which was all the time.

We spent just a couple of days at Fort Niagara; then we were all shipped down south to Camp Swift, Texas. They assigned me to the Signal Corps because of my work experience. I didn't have much knowledge of communications and electricity, but the Army figured I did. And so I took my basic training in the American Army in the Signal Corps, the Ninety-seventh Infantry Division.

We finished basic around July. On my way home on leave, I saw this guy strutting up and down the train dressed in a paratrooper uniform. Everybody was eyeing him, and I got talking to him. He's wearing boots, and his pants are bloused up, and his overseas hat is at a cocky angle. He was really laying it on.

Boy, I bit right into it. I wanted to know if I could jump out of a plane like them other brave guys did. Airborne was very new at that time. I wanted to test myself, I wanted to see if I could do it. *And* there was an extra fifty dollars a month. I said, "That's for me." I got back to camp, I put in for my transfer.

One day we were having a meeting, and some guy comes in and says, "Tarbell, you got a message down in the office." That was August 13, out of Camp Swift, Texas, 1300 hours. There were thirteen of us there that got called to go to jump school, and I was the only one that finished the course. So I always considered thirteen to be my lucky number.

In the beginning of the training at Fort Benning, the paratroopers seemed to discourage you, like they were trying to make sure that you really wanted to belong. A lot of times, you'd get up in the morning and you'd end up taking a run instead of going to breakfast. A lot of guys dropped out the first day. They didn't want no part of it.

You never walked, you always double-timed. If you did something wrong—like your pants came unbloused—regardless of what time of the day or night it was, if an officer or sergeant caught you, he'd have you do twenty-five push-ups. Well, you're doing it too fast or too slow. So after that you'd do *fifty* push-ups.

In our spare time, we were doing push-ups, pumping away, getting used to it. We did a lot of running in training, too. I loved running—we used to dare our sergeants to outdo us. Nobody wanted to be a slacker. It was tough training, and it paid off later on.

Quitting was the furthest thing from my mind. I was gonna make it. My thing was, "How am I gonna get out of that plane door? How am I gonna do it? How the hell am I gonna do it?"

The very first thing was a 34-foot tower. They got you up there and strapped you into a harness. And the harness had a line attached to it that they hooked onto this cable that went from the tower down to the ground. You jumped out a door, like you were jumping out of a plane. You dropped a few feet, until the line to your harness snapped straight, and then you slid down to the ground. You would be amazed at the number of people that refused to jump from the 34-foot tower. I think most of the guys that washed out did it right there.

Then we did jumps from the 250-foot tower—they told us it was a copy of the parachute jump at Coney Island.

It was the fourth week that you packed your own chute to get ready to make your five qualifying jumps. I'd never been in an airplane before.

My first jump was supposed to be on a Monday morning—it was raining. It was raining Tuesday morning, so we waited. In the afternoon, around three o'clock, we did it.

We had all lined up to get on the plane, and I stood at the head of the line—I was gonna be the first one out that door. I wanted to get it over with, to see if I could do it. But since I boarded the plane first, I ended up in the back, right on the end of the line. I was the last man out, number twenty-four.

There's a cable that goes from one end of the plane to the other. When you get up, you hook your static line to that—the static line is what opens your chute after you jump—and then, as you walk, you're pulling your line along.

There's a jumpmaster that stands by the door there to make sure you get out, and you do. Right on top of the next guy. Go, go, go, go, go, and *pschew!* you're out the door.

That was quite a world of experience, that first time. Man, I thought that was the greatest thing that I ever did in my life—especially when that chute opened up.

After you leave the plane, you're waiting for that pop, that jerk—they call it prop blast. Then, when your chute opens up, you stop dead right there for a few seconds. Then you start oscillating—swinging back and forth—and you start coming down. That's where the nice feeling is, when you start coming down.

Then you wonder, "Anyone near me? Am I going to run into anybody?" And then you sweat out the landing.

I hit the ground and got ready and went up again that afternoon. Two jumps that day.

Once you'd made a jump, hey, you were on top of the world. You were really something.

After our five qualifying jumps, which made us paratroopers, we got fourteen-day furloughs to come home. My daughter was born while I was going through jump school, so I hadn't seen her yet. I saw her and my wife in Syracuse, and we went by bus up north to the Canadian border to see my father and mother.

Right after I got back to Fort Benning, we went to Fort Meade, Maryland. It had to be only about two or three weeks that we were there. Then, on January 15, 1944, we shipped out from Norfolk, Virginia—Hampton Roads, I guess they called it—on the *Thomas Hart Benton* Liberty ship.

There was 250 of us went out of there and we didn't know where we were going. We got out into the Atlantic in a big convoy. After about three days, the convoy went to England, and we headed, by ourselves, to North Africa.

It was eighteen days before we got to Casablanca. They put us in an American base there, tucked away up in the hills. We got passes to go into town, and I looked for that place where Humphrey Bogart and Ingrid Bergman were hanging out. I could never find it. All I found was some beat-up old bars. We would see the nomads coming in from the desert, in a caravan. You'd see the kids and the women in front and the old men riding donkeys in the back. That was quite a sight to see. We saw some of the Moroccan soldiers. They were good soldiers. They were rugged guys.

After a few days in Morocco, we went by train to Algeria. The landscape was so beautiful—green valleys, orchards, hills. When we stopped, they had tangerines for sale, and homemade wine. We didn't have no containers, so we just had them pour that wine in our helmets. Some of the guys got loaded. Oh, jeez. One of the guys fell off the train; it was about two or three days before he caught up to us. The Senegalese that were guarding all the passes, they picked him up, took him to the nearest railroad station, then eventually sent him to Algiers.

From Algiers we went across the Mediterranean by plane—C-47s. We ended up at a racetrack in Naples, and we were assigned from there to different areas. I got assigned to the 504th Parachute Infantry Regiment of the Eighty-second Airborne Division, and they took us by LSTs then DUKWs to Anzio as replacements. We were transported that night by truck to the front lines.

This was over a month after the landing at Anzio, but well before the breakout—the beachhead extended only three miles in, and there was still a lot of fighting. We were holding a defensive position along the Mussolini Canal. The Germans were on one side, we were on the other.

You couldn't move around during the day at Anzio, because the Jerries were looking right down on you from the hills, and they'd put the artillery on the least little movement you made. Every now and then, we got fire from what they called Anzio Annie—it was a big gun mounted on a railroad car. They'd bring it out of the tunnel, fire, then move it back in. It could shoot right into the bay.

During the day we stayed inside the buildings, out of sight. At night there were a lot of combat patrols—I went on quite a few. The patrol could be four men, it could be six men. Or it could be up to twenty.

This one night that we went out, one of our .50-caliber machine guns started firing at us. They didn't know that we were going to be out there in front. We hit the ground the minute that gun opened up. But we sent word back that we were on patrol, and our gun stopped. When the guys started to move out, everybody tapped the guy behind him. You would just say, "Let's go." You'd whisper.

So I was tapping the guy behind me, and he wouldn't move. Come to realize, this was a dead German I had laid next to. It probably took just a few seconds for me to figure this out—just enough for me to lose contact with the guys that had gone. So then this guy finally came up to me from behind. His name, I think, was Stewart. He says, "I'm Stewart, I'm Stewart. Who are you?"

I says, "I'm lost. Come on. Let's go."

Luck had it that we were able to follow the trail the others were taking—engineers would go just ahead of our patrols to check for mines, and they would tie ribbons to show where it was safe to walk. We followed those ribbons until we caught up with the rest. They knew that we had been lost.

We stayed at Anzio until the latter part of March, and then we were relieved. We came back to Naples. Then, on Easter Sunday, we got on the *Capetown Castle,* a British liner, and we went to England to rejoin the division.

See, we were with Mark Clark's Fifth Army in Italy. He'd asked to have us, so the Eighty-second had left us behind with the understanding that we were to go to England as soon as he could release us.

They didn't tell us why we were going to England, but I think we all knew we were going to the mainland for more combat. We sailed into Liverpool. One of my jobs was to stay behind and bus the baggage, so I didn't go into Leicester until a day later. That's where our base was, on a golf course.

We did a lot of problem jumping in training for the invasion—like, dispersal area, how big an area we'd take to land. Different problems with the terrains they thought we might encounter.

We figured that we were going to make the Normandy trip, but then it ended up they had two other outfits—the 507th and 508th—take our place. They claimed that the 504th was not up to par to make the invasion because we had so many replacements.

On D-Day I heard the planes when they went over our tents—they woke me up during the night. D+1, my company commander came up and says, "Tarbell, we volunteered. You and I are going to go to Normandy for resupply." He says, "*We* volunteered." I says, "Oh, that's good, sir."

But that didn't pan out. They lost quite a few of the planes on that resupply, so I'm kind of glad I didn't go.

We kept training in England.

Right after D-Day a few of us rode our bikes up a long hill—there was an English pub there that we went to. We were sitting having this warm beer, and there was a bunch of locals. They kept looking at us, eyeing us.

Finally one of them says, "How come you guys are here enjoying yourself? We got all these people there in France. They're sleeping on the cold ground, and they're not getting no beer. They're not enjoying themselves."

I told him, "Look, we saw action in Italy, and now we're trying to get enough men to go back into combat." I says, "Do you know this man sitting over here?" And I pointed to Rosy—his name was David Rosenkrantz; everyone just called him "Rosy." And Rosy's face starts getting all red. That's the kind of a guy he was—he started to blush.

I said, "He's a hero."

The guy says, "What do you mean?"

"He captured two hundred Italian prisoners." When he was in Sicily—before I joined the outfit—he got captured by the Italians. He ended up coming back to camp two weeks later with two hundred prisoners—they all surrendered to him. We used to laugh about that.

My God, once I told them about Rosy, we couldn't drink enough beer. They were giving their rations of liquor to us.

We left there, and we had to go down that steep hill on our bicycles. I don't know how we made that sharp turn.

Rosy was quite a guy. I really loved him. He was always kidding around. Rosy was a big, heavy man, and I understand that he was a very good shot. Sergeant Fuller told me one time that Rosy spotted some Germans and started picking 'em off. Every time they got up, he hit one man. He got seven shots off, and he killed seven guys.

Rosy was killed in the Den Heuvel Woods, in a German counterattack after we landed in Holland. We took a shellacking there. We had to move that night, so we weren't able to bring out his body. Then, when some guys went to locate the body, they couldn't find it.

In the summer of 2000, his brother's son called me. The nephew said that he had been trying for five years or so to locate people that knew his uncle. Before that they seemed to have never looked into the situation too much, because they felt so bad about Rosy getting killed. I was so happy to hear from him, because I had often wondered whatever became of the family.

At the beginning of Hanukkah this past year, I got a call from Rosy's sister. This was the first time she made contact. I never knew that she existed.

She was so happy. She was half crying. "I have to talk to somebody that knew my dear Rosy," she says. "He was so good to me." She was just overjoyed. We talked for the longest time.

She said that he was such a nice guy, and I told her that he was. Everybody loved him. Nobody ever had a bad word for him. He was a good soldier.

She says, "The only thing I can think is that he went straight to heaven. That's why they couldn't find his body."

I said, "He sure did. He sure did go to heaven."

We went to the airport to leave for a jump two or three times, but they would cancel it because the ground army was moving so fast. But then, on September 17, we got up and got ready to make our trip across the Channel. We were going about fifty miles behind the lines in Holland, as part of Operation Market-Garden. The drop zone for the Eighty-second was in and around Grave.

We went to church that morning before leaving. And we had a good breakfast, wonderful breakfast. They had pie—everything you could think of. This wasn't the normal breakfast. This was more like the last dinner.

But we were too busy to think about that. This is something real big coming up. First combat jump for me. We got ready, and we got on the plane. And then, next thing you know, when we did take off, my God, we were amazed at how many planes were in the air.

When we get over Holland, we see these guys jumping, and we're not at the DZ—the drop zone—yet. We say, "No, no, no."

One of our company's planes got hit. We started to count how many chutes got out, and then the plane started going down, and then it went out of sight. I think mostly everybody made it. One of my buddies was in that plane there. His name was Dick Reardon. He was captured, and I saw him thirty-four years later. He called me up one Father's Day to visit.

We got to the DZ. And as we were jumping, we could hear the flak from the twenty-millimeters. They were trying to catch us as we were coming out the door.

On the way down, the first sergeant hollered over, "Watch out for that guy behind the barn." I landed on a fruit tree, and my weight and all my equipment dropped me to the ground nice and easy. I got up, and I got out of my equipment. I cocked my tommy gun, and I went over to this guy that was standing there. He was just a young kid enjoying the sight of everybody jumping into his backyard. I understand that barn is there yet.

There was a wheelbarrow near there—I motioned to him to bring it over. We put our gear in, and he wheelbarrowed us up to the main road where the other guys were. The first person I saw there was a priest, so I went over to him and had him bless my rosary beads.

There was a bunch of the locals—the kids, the women, the men, everybody. Intelligence had told us that anybody with orange on would be your friend. Some of the women had orange ribbons in their hair, the men had them pinned to their lapels. They were all happy to see us—it was a bright, sunny Sunday afternoon. There were even people sitting on the roofs waving to us. It was quite a sight to see.

We started going into Grave.

I was in Third Battalion, H Company, and we weren't involved in the fighting for the bridge in Grave; we were just told to group up once we'd dropped and go wherever they needed us. Second Battalion fought for the bridge, and it was taken by about five o'clock that night.

The following day Lieutenant Megellas led a combat patrol, and I volunteered to go. It was a nice combat patrol—no combat. We went in this one town. They were so happy to see us. They had beer for us. The cans were starting to rust—they'd been hidden so long, waiting for this day, I guess. We got cars. We got trucks. We ended up with some of the Dutch underground. They took us on motorcycles, and we drove around. The people were very happy to see us.

Late in the afternoon of the nineteenth, we started moving north towards Nijmegen. That night we bivouacked south of Nijmegen; we walked into the town the next morning.

The natives were all lined up watching us. When we stopped for a break, this little girl was standing there, and she offered me an orange. I didn't know whether to accept it or not. I wanted her to eat it—I thought I was depriving her. This woman standing next to her says, "Take that from the little girl." Very good English. So I did. I never forgot that. I often wondered about that little girl. Just a little blond girl, probably about five or six years old.

We went up to the Waal River and settled in behind the dike—there was a ditch, like, where we could stay hidden from the Germans. And then we found out that we were going to make a crossing of the river by boat.

There were two bridges in Nijmegen, the railroad bridge and the traffic bridge. We needed the traffic bridge to get the tanks across, but we were taking the railroad bridge, too, and that was our first objective. The problem was, this bridge was so heavily guarded that it couldn't be taken with units only coming from the south side. So our leadership decided that the bridge had to be attacked from both ends, and that's why H Company, I Company, and some men from Headquarters Company would be going over on the boats.

We were all hanging around there and laying down and sleeping, and we kept waiting, waiting, waiting. It was late in the afternoon before the British lorries finally arrived, and they unloaded these boats. They were made out of canvas and were folded up like an accordion. They had these wooden slats that you turned, and those slats opened up the canvas and acted as stiffeners. That was their version of an assault boat. Oh, jeez, everybody was flabbergasted. What the heck kind of a boat is this here? A lot of them didn't even have paddles.

We were not happy. We'd heard that early in the morning one of the lieutenants had got shot in the head and killed while reconnoitering around there. So everybody figured that we were all going to be killed in these boats, or quite a few of us, because the Germans had us covered on three sides: on the bridge, which was to our right; forward, across the river; then further down the river, to our left.

We got in the boats, and we started to cross—twenty-six boats, with twelve, thirteen men in each one. We were sitting ducks. The machine-gun bullets were hitting—it was like rain was falling on the river there. Then, when we got in toward the middle of the river, they hit us with the heavy stuff—mortars, eighty-eights, whatever they could get their hands on.

In the boat I was in, we were going in one direction, then another. Some guys had paddles. I didn't. I just used my hands and the butt of my tommy gun. Finally I hollered, "I'm gonna call cadence. Let's go. Right, left, right, left. Together. Come on." The current was so swift.

I happened to look out, and I saw one of the guys in my company in the boat next to mine. He stood up, and he looked at me, and he shrugged, and the next thing he was gone. I think he was shot by the time I saw him. When he shrugged, it was as if he was saying, "What am I gonna do?" Corporal Louis Holt. I'd gotten to know him in England, knew him very well. He was with the mortar section. I think he was from Texas. I never forgot that look that he gave me.

They knocked out fifteen of the twenty-six boats. They got sunk or damaged so bad.

Pretty soon a bunch of us took off towards the railroad bridge where all the fighting was going on. We got onto the north end, the 505th was on the south end, and the Germans were in the middle, boxed in. They ran at us, and we started throwing C2 grenades at them—C2 was like an explosive putty you could mold—and these grenades were just blowing up all the Germans. They say a lot of them jumped over the side there and committed suicide. They had no place to go. They counted over two hundred bodies the next day. That's war.

That was a lot of fighting there. Oh, God, all kinds. I think anybody that survived it was really something. They were so brave, those guys. They were good fighters. Everybody dove right in and did his share.

It was getting towards dark when we went to the traffic bridge. There was a lot of fighting going on down there, too. When you're fighting like this, you're just wringing wet, the adrenaline rush is so bad. And then you get scared. There's not much to think about, just that it's either gonna be him or you.

We took the traffic bridge, and eventually we bedded down for the night. Then, the following day, we moved up to an area where we set up our CP in a house and tried to count heads. I had my radio there, and I was in contact with battalion every now and then. We also had set up field phones—we'd laid the wire—to communicate within the company. I was talking to the different platoon leaders, trying to get a breakdown on the casualties, and our company clerk, Harold Shelden, was writing the names down as I was getting them. The casualty list for our company was fifty-four—that was all the killed, wounded, and missing, including the planeload that was lost coming in.

We were on the ground floor, and we could hear the shelling—it was getting closer to us. The first sergeant, who was in the basement, thought the Germans might be zeroing in on my radio conversation with battalion, so he hollered up, "Tarbell, you better bring that radio down here."

We bent over to pick up the radio, Harold and I. We were right next to the window. A shell landed in the backyard behind us, and shrapnel came in and hit him right in the head and killed him. His head was right next to mine. I didn't get a scratch.

The first sergeant came and put Shelden's name on the bottom of the list, the fifty-fifth casualty. That bothered me. There was two of us making the casualty list out, and they ended up putting his name on it. That made it a hard day for me.

I got downstairs with the radio, and the company commander looked at me and he says, "The medic's got something for you." The medic gave me a shot, and I went to sleep. I slept the rest of the day underneath that stairway until the company commander woke me up towards evening. He says, "Come on. Get your tommy gun. Let's go check out the positions."

I have to tell you about a funny incident that happened in Holland. A day or two after we secured the bridges at Nijmegen, we went off the line briefly, to a rest area in the rear. And we used to get these attacks—mortars. They made a heck of a noise, and that's why we called them "screaming meemies." We could hear when they'd start coming, and we'd run like heck and jump down into the dugout. We had a nice dugout there—it was a good six foot deep, and we had logs over it, dirt. It was really safe. There would have to be a direct hit to really do any damage.

At mealtimes in this rest area, this little scrunchy tomcat came around and started befriending us. Oh, he was beat up. His ears were all chewed up and everything.

Pretty soon Clark Fuller says, "You know, Tarbell, every time the screaming meemies come in, that cat is in the dugout when we get there. Let's watch him."

So we watched him. All at once his tail straightened up, and his ears straightened up, and he made a beeline for our foxhole and jumped in there, and we followed. Sure enough, right after we were in there, the screaming meemies arrived. Boy, did we take care of that cat. Every time that cat would take off, we'd say, "Incoming mail. Let's go."

* * *

After we recouped, we went toward the Den Heuvel area, right back on line.

September 26, Beyer and Sergeant Rice were in this house, and a German patrol came by and started throwing hand grenades in. One got Rice—it blew up and killed him.

I was carrying the radio with the company commander, Captain Kappel, and when we heard about Rice, we went to that house. They'd laid him on a stretcher out back.

At the same time, a patrol was coming back, and they had captured a German officer. People thought that this officer was leading the patrol that had killed Sergeant Rice, but in fact—and I only found this out years later—he'd been taken in an area nowhere near where Rice was.

Rice was a well-liked guy, so the captain thought we'd better get this captive out of there fast and take him down to battalion, because our guys might kill him. So we took him to battalion, and they started interrogating him. But this German officer couldn't speak English. Finally Captain Kappel says, "We can't get nothing out of him. Let's go out and let the Indian knife him if he tries to make a move."

I was standing right there, and the captain turns to me and he says, "Tarbell, if he makes a move, get him in the guts." Speaking loudly. "Get him in the stomach. Do a good job." I says, "Yes sir." Boy, I was scared shitless. How am I gonna kill this guy? All at once that guy spoke English. Was I glad to hear that! I was very happy.

We stayed there in Holland for two months. We established defensive positions, and it became a stalemate.

Don't forget, when we took that last bridge in Nijmegen, the British tanks were supposed to go to Arnhem, where the British airborne division was being annihilated. They crossed that bridge the night we took it, September 20, but then they stayed there. There was a lot of excuses, and they never went. Our colonel even offered to have us go along with them to knock out the German gun positions. They wouldn't do it.

* * *

It was November 13 when we got relieved by the Canadians. We went to Sissonne, France.

We had Thanksgiving there. We were licking our wounds, getting some replacements.

After a month in France, I was pulling duty in Reims on chute patrol—to help keep our airborne guys from running afoul of the Army MPs. I think it was on the second night I was doing that, we found out that the MPs weren't putting these guys in jail at all; they were just putting them in trucks and taking them back to camp. I figured there was something wrong there.

That was when the Bulge started.

I think it was the night of December 18, I came in, and they said, "We're moving out in the morning." Over by the orderly room, I heard the first sergeant talking to some kids who'd come in as company replacements. I call them "kids" because they had just come into the service. And one says, "Jeez, Sergeant, I've never even fired a rifle." The sergeant says, "Don't worry. You'll learn."

The next morning, sure enough, right around eight o'clock, trucks started coming in. They were flattop trucks, no covers. They belonged to the Air Force. We loaded up and took off.

The first real good battle we had was in Monschau, Germany, just over the border past Cheneux, Belgium. The Germans had two twenty-millimeter flak wagons—vehicles with guns that could be used against aircraft or against ground troops—and we tried to get the Germans before they got onto them. But they got there before we could kill them, and they turned the guns on us. They just peppered that hillside where we were at. We had about two truckloads of wounded.

By the twenty-third, we'd moved to a line quite a ways out.

On Christmas Eve we pulled back to consolidate our positions. We walked all night. We could hear our engineers detonating the trees, blocking the roads behind us. We got to Bra, Belgium, and we set up defensive positions. We fought the next couple of days there; then we got hit pretty bad.

It was so damn cold. A lot of us just had our jump boots on. No warm clothes. Of course, the Germans were prepared. They had good uniforms on, white jackets. You're out there, you can't take a bath. You can't wash your feet. All you can do is change your socks and throw the old ones away. A lot of people got frost-bitten. I had a lot of problems with my feet, but I had to go back to the medics just once, that's all. My main concern was underclothes and socks.

Today I have a fetish for having pairs and pairs of socks. Oh, I have socks. Tons of socks. Maybe fifty, sixty pairs. That and flash-light batteries. I don't like the dark.

The United States Army took an awful beating in the Bulge. When we first got there, a lot of guys were walking the other way. We tried to talk to one of them—he just threw his hat on the ground and kept walking. The Germans did a job on us. A lot of the American troops did wonderful fighting—they made a valiant stand there in the beginning of the Bulge.

By late '44 a lot of people who weren't close to the front lines were saying that they could see the end of the war, but you're not aware of any overall picture when some guy's shooting right at you and it seems like he has an awful lot of ammunition.

One time there we got held up by a bunker with a machine gun. Finally they must have run out of ammunition. They started coming out of there, holding up their hands. And, boy, they were crying. These were old men—thirty years old, forty—not the young kids that we were used to. And, jeez, they were giving us their wedding rings and showing us pictures of their families. They must have thought we were going to kill them all. We didn't. We captured them. They put up a good fight for old guys.

The German soldier was my enemy. But I didn't have nothing against him. I just wanted to get home. I wanted to get the war over with and get home to my daughter and my wife. At the time I didn't see anything bigger. I was just trying to keep warm. I wanted a good night's sleep more than anything else. Just to be home and relax—lay back and turn the radio up, every now and then have a drink, listen to a ball game, nice and warm, nice and cozy, instead of being wet and hungry and freezing your can off.

It was tough being away from home. You'd get so lonesome. I used to dream of holding my daughter. I knew I was gonna wake up. I'd just hold tight, but I'd wake up and there'd be nobody there. You knew in your sleep that you were only dreaming, yet you wanted to make it true.

Sleeping was dangerous. When guys joined us as replacements, I told them, "If you start getting warm and cozy at night, don't go to sleep. You're gonna freeze."

One time, before we went up a hill for an attack, they made us leave all our personal equipment, like our sleeping bags, on the ground at the bottom of the hill. They said they'd bring it up to us.

So we went up there, and we must have gone behind the German lines, because we didn't get our gear. It got awful cold that night. And making that climb, we got all wet and sweaty from the adrenaline.

We only had one blanket. We had about six wounded guys, and we put them under there so they could rest and try to keep warm. That's how you slept, body heat—three or four guys could sleep together.

I found a little tree, and I put my hand on it, and I kept walking around that. Pretty soon there were two or three other guys with me there. We were walking around in our sleep to keep our feet from freezing. All night long like that, walking around and around. We'd just keep moving, doze off. You can walk and sleep. The next morning some of the other guys were walking on their knees. They had fallen asleep, and their feet had frozen.

We were one of the first outfits to attack across the Siegfried Line, which ran along the western edge of Germany. That was in February. There were obstacles on the ground for the tanks, and then they had pillboxes. They were great big, solid concrete abutments. Even shells couldn't hurt them.

We were fortunate that we had one guy, Fritz Toenjoest, from the intelligence section, that spoke German, and he talked the Germans into giving up. I don't know what he said. He probably told 'em that there was no sense fighting anymore. He passed away a long time ago. Good friend of mine.

We were supposed to make an assault landing across the Rur River, but we got relieved. We came back to Lyon, France, for R&R. We didn't know it at that time, but in later years we heard that we were supposed to be preparing for a parachute jump into Berlin.

We left Lyon after a couple of weeks, and we went to the Rhine River, just north of Cologne. We were in a holding position on the west side of the river to keep the Germans from coming over.

A few weeks later, we went by train to Hamburg—the Allies were really advancing by then. We went by truck down to the Elbe River and crossed it on a pontoon bridge.

It was getting towards the end of the war, and we were given a lot of prisoners—125,000 of them. It got so that we were riding in jeeps, trying to move them fast, real fast. Guys were just giving up.

That was quite a sight there to see, all those people surrendering. Cavalry surrendered to us. Guys on horses. They were beautiful horses.

These soldiers were running away from the Russians; they wanted to surrender to us. It was just about getting dark one day when this German staff car pulled up. There were four German officers in this car, and they were just dressed to kill. This one guy gets out, and he's got this long leather jacket on, boots. He says, "This is the commanding general in the car. We're looking for your general. Where's his headquarters?"

I says, "What do you want him for?"

"We're coming back here to regroup to fight the Russians, and we want to meet with your general."

"You just go right down that road there, and there's some MPs there. They'll direct you."

That was their idea, that we would all regroup and fight the Russians. We laughed. But they were serious. They were not like the troops that were walking down the road—tired, dragging, hungry, beat. These guys were spick-and-span. Top shelf. They probably were put right in prison, I don't know. I know that our general didn't have nothing to do with them.

We had a very bad experience right after that, just about on V-E Day. We went into a concentration camp just north of Ludwigslust. There were a lot of civilians—a lot of Dutch, some Russians, but mostly Polish, French. Different nationalities. I think they were political prisoners. The camp was Wöbbelin Concentration Camp.

This was not a killing camp, this was a starvation camp. They starved the people to death. There's nothing worse than that kind of starvation. They were just skin and bones. You couldn't tell the dead from the living. Some of them had fallen into the latrine pits—they couldn't get up. No energy.

There were a lot of bodies they hadn't gotten rid of by the time we got there. They were stacked up, about seven or eight high.

Seeing this had an effect on everybody. I wanted to stay drunk for the rest of my life. There was nothing that could make me forget it. You wonder how the hell can one human being do this to another human being? I could see a person shooting another man, but to starve him to death?

It was an awful sight to see. Some people were so sick, so far gone, that the minute they got anything in their stomach, they died. And the people in town said they didn't know nothing about it.

Our general, General Gavin, made all the people—everybody, that whole city—go through there and see what they did. All the corpses were taken right into the middle of the village, and General Gavin made the German civilians bury them there. The mayor killed his wife, his daughter, and then himself.

They had a lot of food rations there. They could've given them something. These people were not put into furnaces. There were no gas chambers there. These people were just deliberately starved to death; worked and starved to death. There were survivors there, and they told us a lot about it.

During the war you often wondered, "What the heck am I

doing out here? What am I fighting for?" When you saw what happened at that concentration camp, you knew that you were fighting for a cause. That had to be the cause. What if we hadn't fought?

For twenty-four, twenty-five years, I never told nobody about the war. Till Mike went in the service.

Just this one guy I'd served with, we would talk about it. We knew that people didn't believe what had happened. When I got home, I'd tell people about the concentration camp—nobody believed it. Nobody. So I said, "Oh, the heck with it. I'm not gonna tell them," and I just tried to block it out of me. The people all over the United States did not believe what had happened in the Holocaust until the Jews brought it all out. That's when people said, "So that really did happen?"

"We tried to tell you that."

It was tough carrying the war inside of me. I had a lot of drinking bouts trying to drown it. That's why, when Mike came home from Vietnam, I always got him on the side and pumped him for all the information I could. To get it out of him. And every time my family heard it—his aunt, his mother, his grandmother—they said, "Leave him alone. Don't be bringing that up." But that's the worst thing you can do, is hold it inside.

I had nobody to pump me for information, so I was always thinking about it. A lot of times, I'd be driving home from work. And I'd look at the hills, and I'd say, "What a fortification. They could have gun positions there, and I could be ambushed going down the road. I'm wide open here." For a long time that happened.

I used to have nightmares. I couldn't keep my hands under the covers. I always had to have my hands out.

I think what happened was that we got overrun one night there in the Den Heuvel Woods. I was sleeping in a sleeping bag—zippered up—and I couldn't get it open right away, and I was trying to claw my way out. I finally was able to loosen my arms. I was trapped in there for a minute, maybe not even that. That's a long time, though, when you want to get out quick.

I could never sleep with my arms under covers for many, many years. I would get nightmares, and my wife would have to wake me up and uncover my arms. Then I'd go back to sleep.

I had nightmares right up until my wife died. Then they did go away, finally. Somebody said sleep on the side that your wife slept on. I slept on that side, and I only got nightmares once or twice after that. To this day I don't know why. Maybe it's because I worried so much about her, what she went through while I was in the service.

After Mike finished high school, he and I we were doing a job in Ithaca, and we were exploring around to see what university he could get into. But then he decided to go into the service instead. He had a chance to try out for the major leagues, too—baseball. He didn't cotton to that. He liked it as a sport, I think, not as a livelihood.

He asked me what I thought about the service. I says, "Well, there's a chance to continue your education by getting into the Air Force or the Navy."

He says, "I want to go in the Airborne."

I says, "What the heck do you want to do that for?" In the Air Force or Navy, he could have gone to school—electronics, maybe. He had the IQ. What can you learn in the infantry? Just how to kill, how to fight, how to set up ambushes. I thought about the hardships that he would endure. At that time Vietnam was taking its toll of men, especially the Airborne.

So that's when I says, "I'll see what I can do." I got hold of some guys, and they told me to make sure that he tells the people there at Fort Benning that he's a second-generation paratrooper.

All he had to do was announce that he was a second-generation paratrooper. The Airborne took it right from there. And that's how he got an extra year of training, stateside. Instead of sending him right from jump school to Vietnam, he had a chance to learn. He went to Fort Bragg, and they taught him. He was a sergeant when he went over to Vietnam.

When Mike first came back from Vietnam and was living in Fayetteville, I knew that he was using the helicopters there at Fort Bragg as a security blanket. He'd wake up in the morning, and he could hear them overhead: "I'm secure. I'm safe. I've got protection." I tried to get him away from there for a lot of years. Finally, on his own, he came back one day and says, "I have to come back up here and see what I can do for myself. I've tried everything, and I can't feel better, so I'm gonna go to the VA clinic."

What helped *me* was going to the conventions and talking with my guys about it. I started to get together with the guys in my outfit when Mike was in the service. We would discuss the different incidents during the war, we'd ask questions. We'd get it out of our system. And we were getting mellower and mellower and mellower. We were not angry.

Had it not been for Mike's being in the Army, I would not have gone to look up my old buddies. I guess I wanted to be the closest I could get to him. There's a lot happened to me and my friends that he can relate to.

I think it's a great gift of God that we can share all this. How many people have a chance to do that? Not very many, especially as we're both paratroopers. God truly made that gift. A lot of guys from my outfit don't have sons to share their memories with. I have mine.

It makes me feel good to talk to him, because I know he understands. For a long time we couldn't do it. It was just one-sided. I was always trying to drag those experiences out of him, and he was not willing to give up as much as he does these days. But now I can relate to him as he can relate to me. We both went through combat, whereas you try to explain combat to a noncombatant, he's got that look that he just about half believes you. He don't know whether you're giving him a line or not.

We know that we both went through this stuff. We know that we can't BS each other.

There's a saying that there's nothing like a happy, alive ex–combat paratrooper.

A lot of times I see young kids and I think about my buddies. My buddies are still young. Here I am an old man, and they're still nineteen, twenty, twenty-one. They never got home. They never aged.

When it really comes back is when I go to Fort Bragg and I see some young kid come up to me and ask me questions and shaking my hand and so happy to see me. And I ask him, "What's your rank?" "Oh, I'm a company commander" or "I'm a platoon leader." He could be a captain. Yet to me he's a young kid.

Then I get thinking about my guys, my buddies. They're still kids.

It's hard. You wonder, "What could they have been?" They might've been executives. They might've been gangsters. Who knows? Some of 'em were crazy enough.

There was one kid. His name was Romero. He was such a nice kid. He'd see a dead body, be it German or American, he'd kneel down and say a prayer. When he got killed, it was so fast. He got hit in the jugular vein, I think it was, and he bled right to death. I don't know what that kid would've been. He could've been a priest. He was a very religious kid.

What would these guys have been? We lost the cream of the crop. They stayed back there, they never made it home. They're the ones who are the heroes. They're the ones who deserve the accolades.

They're the bravest men.

XII

"You listen to the night."

MIKE TARBELL

MIKE TARBELL

TEACHER
COBLESKILL, NEW YORK
STAFF SERGEANT, UNITED STATES ARMY, VIETNAM

During World War II airborne troops had pioneered a new means of rapidly transporting a fighting force to a distant scene of battle. Large drops of paratroopers made no sense in the dense terrain of Vietnam, however, and so U.S. military planners looked to a concept of warfare the Army had begun testing in 1955. "Airmobile" operations, as this logical successor to airborne combat had been named, would become the American military's most prominent tactical innovation in Vietnam.

By the time the First Cavalry Division (Airmobile) arrived in Vietnam in late 1965, its type of warmaking had already been tested in combat there: American helicopters were airlifting ARVN troops to battle and were performing in fire-support and reconnaissance capacities. However, the First Cav would be the only division organized strictly for airmobile operations until 1968, when the 101st Airborne Division was retooled and renamed the 101st Division (Airmobile). These two outfits relied on their own fleets of helicopters to ferry them about the countryside, but many other ground forces in Vietnam, including the 101st before its redesign, engaged in airmobile combat at one time or another through the use of helicopters belonging to separate aviation contingents.

The First Brigade of the 101st Airborne Division arrived in Vietnam in July 1965; the rest of the 101st, among them Albert M. "Mike" Tarbell, arrived in late 1967.

In three tours in Vietnam, Mike Tarbell served first as an infantry sergeant with the 101st, then with two Pathfinder units. During World War II, small numbers of airborne "pathfinders" were dropped ahead of the bulk of jumping troops in order to mark drop zones and conduct reconnaissance. Pathfinders in Vietnam filled a similar mission as they prepared landing zones for heliborne troops, provided ground-level intelligence to those troops and their pilots, and stayed ready to come to the aid of men whose chopper might be forced from the air.

At Mike's request, the men with whom he served, and the veterans he knew after Vietnam, are identified by pseudonyms. The two Pathfinder units in which Mike served are not named.

There was a trail that used to run along the creek next to the house where I grew up. I used to like to sleep on the porch and dream about long ago, when Iroquois warriors ran that trail. And in my dreams, up around the bend where the trail disappeared, one of them would wait for me to see if I was going to run with them. In history the Iroquois—the Mohawk are one of the six tribes in the Iroquois Confederacy—have always been known as great runners, because there were only two ways of getting to battle: running or canoeing. As a little boy, I used to run the trails here. Someday I was going to be a great warrior.

The other day my grandson was running. He says, "When I become a soldier, they won't get me, 'cause I can run." And that brought me back to Vietnam, when I thought that as long as I could run, they would never be able to get me.

Being Iroquois, it worked out quite a bit that it was my legs that got me out of certain situations. One time we got pinned down. The enemy was mortaring and machine-gunning the hell out of us. No one was making a move to get at them, because when the machine gun shut off and they had to reload, two guys with AK-47s would pop up to keep us down until the reloading was done. They had a mortar team set up well to the rear of the machine gun, and they were dancing the shells in on us, getting range. So the next time the machine gun stopped, I knew that if it got going again, we'd be finished, because they would have the mortars right on top of us.

So that's when I thought that I had to do something. I dropped all my web gear—field pack, ammo packs, canteen. I dropped my weapon. I dropped my steel pot. I dropped everything down, and all I carried was this claymore bag with baseball grenades in it—I could throw them a lot better than I could throw the regular grenades, so I used to carry a little claymore bag full of them. And I jumped up, and I started running at them. And I was doing the dodging stuff. And I was hurdling stumps. I got the whole crew, all four of 'em—the two guys on the machine gun and the two guys with the AKs. And it was enough initiative for the others to get up and get out of that predicament.

I don't remember doing it. I remember getting ready to do it; I don't remember actually doing it. It was afterwards, when it was over with, that Davis ran up to me, that big Texan. He grabbed me and was hugging me and everything. He says, "Oh, you were wonderful. You were great." He says, "I never saw anybody run like that." And I don't remember what I did.

When I was a junior in high school, I kept having a dream where I thought I was going to die. And then later on, in Vietnam, it happened to me: I was running, and the air was so thick with moisture it was hard to breathe. And I remembered that in my dream I was having a problem breathing because the air was so humid. Now I saw the hill I was supposed to run up—in my dream I was running up that hill, and I got hit, and the guys dragged me over to the tree line and covered me with leaves and said, "We'll be back for you later."

In the dream I couldn't see myself completely. All I could see was my legs when I was running, my arms. And I kept reaching up to my head—I couldn't figure out what that was until it happened in Vietnam, because that's what I was doing when I was running: I was trying to fix the bandanna on my head so it wouldn't come off.

Whether or not I died in the dream, I don't know—I always woke up. But when it started to take place in Vietnam, I went up that hill backwards, because I wanted to see it happen. I wasn't going to get hit in the back. The dream was coming true—except that I didn't get hit, and we got away.

See, when I was in the 'Nam, I was dreaming about being home. And when I got back here, I was dreaming about being there. At times I wasn't really sure. Even today, sometimes when I think about that time long ago, it's like a big, bad dream. Did it really happen? Sometimes when I'm walking down the road and somebody hollers my name, I think—I wish—and sometimes I even hope—that it would be my mother calling me to wake me up, that it's time to get ready to go to school. That it's been just a bad nightmare, just a long, awful night.

I was in high school when Vietnam first really struck me. Billy got hit. Billy Tarbell, a distant cousin.

We had played halfback on the football team—I was right halfback, he was left halfback. Then one day Billy didn't show up for school anymore. He came back about a year later wearing a khaki uniform and sporting the patch of the 173rd Airborne Brigade out of Okinawa. And he was talking about a place called Vietnam—they were getting ready to send him there. February of '66 was when he got killed. He had extended six weeks to get out early, and he got killed two weeks before he was supposed to come home.

So they brought him back, and it was a closed-casket-type

thing, with just a picture of him. For me that was the first sign of what this war was all about.

It seemed like, okay, this is my war now. Everyone in my family had their war. My mother's youngest brother was in Korea, and I remember going to see him in the hospital at Fort Devons, Massachusetts, when they brought him back—he had gotten hit pretty bad in the Chosin. I knew my dad was a great warrior. Now it was my turn to prove myself. This was my opportunity.

After high school, in the summer of '66, I was taking a course in English every Wednesday night at our community college, because I had a chance to go to Eastern Baptist College in Philadelphia on a baseball scholarship.

There were seventeen boys in my class, but one Wednesday, halfway through the semester, I was the only one left. They all had gotten drafted, because being a part-time student did not defer you. So the next morning, I went down and enlisted at the Chimes Building here in Syracuse.

I hadn't talked it over with my parents. I thought that my mother probably would have talked me out of it. My dad would have tried to reason with me. But I didn't want to be left behind.

In fact, I had asked the recruiter if I could leave right away. He says, "Tomorrow?" I says, "No. But when's the next—" He says, "Monday morning." "Okay. I'll have a weekend home with my family."

It's traditional for Mohawks to serve in the military. During the Revolutionary War, there were Mohawks on both sides. And even back, far before that: In 1710 the Mohawks were with the British up in Nova Scotia fighting the French and the Micmac. Louis Cook was at the Plains of Abraham in Quebec, in 1759, fighting with the French against the British in the French and Indian War. Later he is given a commission as a lieutenant colonel in the Continental Army during the Revolution. After the Revolution we're in a predicament where we're surrounded by the dominant culture—it's not like we could declare war against Syracuse or the state of New York. So, in order to remain warriors, Mohawks have participated in all of America's wars. Ely Parker, during the Civil War, was Grant's aide-de-camp. He was a Seneca chief.

Mohawks show up in the darnedest places through history. In 1884 Mohawks were in North Africa at the Battle of Khartoum. The British hired them as paddlers to take them up the Nile River, shooting the white-water rapids.

At the supper table that Thursday night, I told my parents that I had enlisted in the Army. My dad asked me which branch. I know he wanted me to do something else, but I was drawn toward the Infantry and the Airborne. Like he was.

I jumped into basic training with great zest and zeal. I really did. When they took us from the clothing issue and they put us on the bus, I was pumping myself up. I said, "I can do this." And so when I jumped off that bus, I grabbed my bag, I threw it up over my head, and I went charging into the company area. And one of the two platoon sergeants who had the training platoon, he grabbed me right away and said, "Okay. You're my platoon guide. We're going to give you acting sergeant stripes." I saw it as something good; I knew when I went in that I was going to be the best at what I did, and I excelled at everything.

Basic was at Fort Jackson, South Carolina. AIT was at Fort Gordon, Georgia. And then from there I went to Fort Benning, Georgia, for jump school.

Physical training one week, 34-foot tower the next week, 250-foot tower the following week, and then the five qualifying jumps the last week. And that's when my mom and dad showed up, for that last week.

Oh, it was great having them there. Graduating from jump school—whoa! I thought that was the cat's meow. And it was. It really was. It was the elite of the elite. You could wear the Cochran jump boots and the bloused pants and everything, and it really did look sharp. And I liked that. And I was proud of that. I was proud to wear my uniform. My dad pinned my jump wings on me.

He'd gotten me another year of training, and that's probably what saved my life. If I hadn't said anything about, okay, my dad was a paratrooper, I would have wound up with the rest of the guys—in the 173rd Airborne Brigade or the First Brigade of the 101st Airborne Division. Those guys went right to the 'Nam, but I was assigned to my dad's outfit, the Eighty-second Airborne, and stayed in the States. I had an opportunity to learn a little bit more.

I was promoted before everyone else was. They saw that I had potential as someone who could lead troops. Not as an officer, but still, I could take care of my men and do my job the way that it was supposed to be done. I made my rank the hard way. I didn't go to a shake-and-bake or anything like that. I was promoted by doing my work. And in Vietnam, at twenty years old, I was one of the youngest staff sergeants in the United States Army.

Actually, my first combat was in Detroit, during the riots in '67. The Eighty-second went in, and the 101st went in. I was in the first seat of the first bus that went downtown that evening. When we stepped out of that bus on Seven Mile Road, there were National Guard, Detroit police, state troopers—and a whole slew of reporters. There was only one telephone out there, and when the reporters saw our unit insignia, Eighty-second Airborne Division, you should've watched these guys fight to see who was gonna get to that phone first so they could phone it in to their paper. And the next morning what was it? "Paratroopers in Detroit."

I just couldn't believe what we were doing, that this was actually happening, here, in the United States; that I'm crawling down a street being shot at.

Later on I found myself sleeping in a storefront window on a burned-out block. It reminded me of the pictures that my dad had of Berlin after World War II.

Some of the things that happened there in Detroit, they still bother me today.

We were staying at this school, and the Detroit police came by one evening after we came off of patrol. A policeman came in and wanted to know if they could have some of the soldiers to go with them that night. And so my battalion commander looked at me and said, "How would you like to go on patrol with the police?" I said okay. He said, "All right. I'll get up with your company commander and tell him that you're going out with the Detroit Police Department."

There was six of us in that car; I was sitting in the front seat in the middle. On one of the streets we got ambushed—somebody was shooting at us with a .22. I got out of the car, and I took my M-16, and I fired. And I hit him, and he fell. I wanted to go over and see if I could help him, but they wouldn't let me. The policeman said, "Let somebody else find him."

So that was my initiation.

Afterwards I had a very deep sorrow. The policemen that I was with, not allowing me to go over and to see this individual—I needed to do that. And I was denied that, you see.

I was just protecting myself, it was just a response. I didn't want it to happen, but it did. I was just trying to create a diversion, more or less, so I could get into a safer place. And in the process of doing that, I hit him. It never left me that I did that. And then they wouldn't allow me to go over to see him. So it became something I had to slam down inside of me.

It was pretty much like the 'Nam. Everything happened so fast and so often over there that we never really had the time to store it away properly. We'd just slam it down. Then, later, when the shit piled high enough, it fell on us.

After we came home from an operation in Vieques, in the Caribbean, an announcement came down looking for volunteers to beef up the 101st Airborne Division in Vietnam. I volunteered, and I went. We left Fort Campbell, Kentucky, in C-141 Starlifters, sitting in the plane facing backwards.

My first tour was down in Phuoc Vinh, which is just east of the

Iron Triangle and a little ways from the river called the Song Dong Nai. I was a grunt like everybody else, but I was head of a squad.

My dad had never said much about what he did in the service, but there was one friend who would come by. There would be just a little bit of talk between them, and I could hear some of it. That's what gave me my image of warfare. It turned out to be entirely different for me—there was still killing, but where we were, the only front line that we had was right in front of us. There was no rear area per se, no safe area. It's not like, if you got scared, you could run. There was no place to go. You couldn't run to the back because there *was* no back.

I remember my first firefight. This was December '67. I'd been in-country a couple of weeks. We were on a patrol when we got hit, so it was just my platoon. We lost six guys, you see, and we had a bunch of wounded.

They were laying for us. As a matter of fact, I remember listening to Hanoi Hannah welcoming us to South Vietnam. It was supposed to be a secret move from Fort Campbell, Kentucky, but she knew all our company commanders, our battalion commander, brigade commander, command sergeant major. She gave everybody a personal welcome to South Vietnam.

It was a real quick fight. We were out doing our thing, kind of getting used to the countryside around us; they just hit us and went.

When it was over with, I wanted to turn around and tell everyone, "Okay, it's time to get up. Let's go back to camp." But the guys weren't getting up.

See, in a training exercise, somebody would come around and point at us, one after another: "Okay, you're wounded, you're dead, you're dead, you've been hit in the arm. And so you're in command now—what do you do?"

So I thought, "Everybody up, let's go back." That was my first firefight, and that's exactly how I felt.

But this wasn't training anymore; this was for real. That's the only thing I want to remember about that first time. That's the only thing I want to remember.

Even before I got to the 'Nam, they used to call me "Chief." "Okay, Chief. I know you can run. Make like the deer." Look at what they called it when we went out there in the bush, in the jungle. They'd say, "We're going out in Indian country."

I didn't like that. I flat-out said, "My name's not Chief, and I am not a chief. We don't care for that." But they did put me out on the point. There's that mystique: I'm an Indian, so I'm a great scout. Actually, getting out there, I felt very comfortable. And I never walked the company into any ambushes.

I realized after a while that, when you do it correctly, the point's probably one of the safest positions, because most of the time they never hit the point. They hit the main element. My job was, basically, to find them before they found us. I trained a lot of guys, but I lost quite a few guys, too.

One guy, Scott Reynolds, only lasted about twenty minutes on the point. He had just joined the company, and he kept asking the first sergeant if he could be a point man, because he heard something glamorous about it. So next thing I know, he's up on the point with me. I asked him, "How long have you been here?"

"Oh, three weeks."

"What do you know?"

"I'm here to learn."

"No. What do you know? What do you hear? Listen. Tell me what you hear."

He sat there for a moment, and he says, "I don't hear anything."

"You don't hear the company back there? You don't hear them throwing stuff around? I can hear it. It's about fifty yards back." I says, "If I can hear it, Charlie can hear it. Charlie's out there. So now my job is to find Charlie before he finds us."

So we moved out. I told him I'd be right behind him, and told him which way to go. And when we came to this hedgerow, I says, "Cut partway through, but don't cut all the way. You want to leave yourself concealed but still see beyond." I wanted him to be able to see beyond the hedgerow before we busted out.

So he cut through there—all the way to the other side. And they saw him coming. So they moved a big ChiCom claymore into position. When he busted out into the open, I was just bending down to follow him through the hole, and *wham!* I heard a big explosion. I remember standing back up, and I remember something flying past me. I think it was his legs.

When I came to, they were working on him, trying to tie up what was left of his legs and stuff like that. I'd been knocked unconscious—it was like everything was out there in the distance. Then all of a sudden it came in, real quick-like, and I was back in it again. They were firing over the top of me, protecting me.

We got Scott out, but he died that next day of postoperative shock. I remember I wrote a letter to my parents about it, that I'd lost a guy, Scott Reynolds. I don't know if I asked my mother to send flowers. I don't remember.

I came home from my first tour in late '68 for thirty days. But I was already on my way back. I had reenlisted before I even left the country.

I walked into the local tavern, and a couple of the guys came up. "Where you been? I haven't seen you in a while." I couldn't believe this. I said, "Jeez, I've been on the other side of the world." Some of the guys were still sitting in the same seats they'd been sitting in when I left. Some of them are still there now, if they're not dead. Some drank themselves to death, getting lost in the brown bottle. Later I got lost there, too.

It was good being in Syracuse—I never, ever thought I'd get home. But deep down inside, something was telling me that I didn't want to be here, that I wanted to be back over there. Even though I had wanted this. I had wanted to come home.

We have a term that we pass amongst the grunts: the queen of battle. Well, sometimes you get raped by the queen of battle, you see. So it is very hard to put that down. That's why a lot of guys went back for second and third tours, because they found something there—not just the camaraderie that we had for each other, something that was more powerful.

Sometimes combat seemed better than sex, and you get addicted to that. It's the adrenaline: You get pumped up so much that everything comes alive. You are probably the most alive that you've ever been. Even the weapon that you are holding, your firearm, becomes alive, and you're controlling it.

Another reason I went back was, I was getting into a different aspect of that war. Being the grunt, being the infantryman—I liked that. When you were a grunt, you were in the fight. But about halfway through my first tour, I had a chance to get into the Pathfinders, and I took it.

I had started getting into the unconventional side of warfare before that. There were a couple other native guys in a couple of other companies, and I remember one of them was a first sergeant—Lewis, from Oklahoma. He got us all together when the companies were on a stand-down. That's when I started getting into the traditional side of the warrior. The native warrior.

We had been sent to Vietnam for a purpose, and a lot of us believed in that at the beginning. But it started to fade. And so, getting into that traditional outlook gave me inner strength that I needed to get through. I realized, too, that large-unit tactics wasn't my cup of tea—it's pretty hard to move through the jungle with 143 guys.

In the air-mobile concept, the pilots want somebody on the ground to tell them what the condition is. This is where the Pathfinders came in. So for the last half of my first tour, and then for my second tour, I was ranking NCO with a Pathfinder detachment attached to a battalion that operated in II Corps. We went in by helicopter, ahead of the infantry unit, to find out what it was that was out there and to set up a landing zone. Most of the time they dropped us in at night, and we'd rappel down. I worked with three three-man teams. Sometimes I took the whole unit out, nine guys. Sometimes I took just one team, three guys. When I got into the Pathfinders, I was really in my element.

We worked with the Koreans, we worked with the South Vietnamese, we worked with the Montagnards. I learned a little bit of everyone's tactics.

My first tour, I had seen the Montagnards when I'd been up in the Highlands. And I always said I'd love to work with them. And then finally, one day in my second tour, my commander came to me and said, "You got your dream, man. We're gonna send you up there with the mountain people."

We did patrols out on the Cambodian border with them. They were excellent fighters, and the enemy feared them. As a matter of fact, the ARVNs feared them, too.

The mountain people took me in because I was one of them. When I first got my assignment to work with them, there was a Montagnard nurse who was also part French. When I was walking into the camp, she saw me, and she asked me, "Who are you?"

And I says, "I'm Sergeant Tarbell. With the Pathfinder detachment."

"No. Who are you?"

"Well, I'm going to be working with your scout team."

She looks at me, and she says, "No. *What* are you?" And she was gesturing at her face, at her cheekbones. Native people, we have high cheekbones. And so I was different from the others who had come.

And I says, "Well, I'm an American Indian."

"Ah, yes. An American aborigine."

"I'm Mohawk."

"Oh. Iroquois, upstate New York."

"Wait. How did you learn about the Native Americans?"

She says, "I took a class on the oppressed peoples of the world, and the American Indian was covered in that." She had been schooled in Paris. She had been learning to be a nurse, to come home to fight with her people. And she also had studied about the Iroquois.

Here I am, ten thousand miles away from home, out on the Cambodian border, and somebody is telling me more about my people than I knew myself. And they accepted me. They adopted me. They moved me into the village, and I had two bodyguards everywhere I went. When I was with them, no harm was gonna come to me.

I was living in a longhouse, like my ancestors used to live in, except this was up on stilts and had teak floors—the Iroquois longhouses had earthen floors. I spent almost six months with them. It was probably the most serene time of my life. In the middle of that war.

I was learning a lot from the mountain people—going with my gut feeling more instead of going with what we were taught. And basically that's what got me through. Becoming a part of that natural world, listening to it. And it would talk to me. That was the nativeness. I didn't try to push it away, I didn't try to conquer it.

After a while you knew the everyday jungle sounds. The animals will tell you, the birds will tell you—when you know how to hear them—that there's somebody out there. Somebody is breaking apart the stillness that's out there. When we went on patrols, we would break that stillness. Then, if we sat someplace for a little bit, if we listened to everything around us, all of a sudden the stillness returned. And at that moment you were accepted into it. So now you're waiting for something else to break that stillness.

That was my awakening. It was getting back into the nativeness. It was awakening to that ability within me. Listen. It's alive. It's all there. You just have to be aware to be able to pick it out.

One night on a listening post, something was different. You close your eyes, and you listen. And you've got it all pictured. You've got the whole scenery as it is right there in front of you, but you've got your eyes closed. And I felt something. I opened my eyes, and I looked across this clearing; I knew something was there, but I just couldn't see it.

I took out the Starlight scope—it's a device that magnifies faint light. And I was looking through it, and something moved. I put my Starlight down, and I closed my eyes. Then I opened my eyes and looked through the Starlight again. Something was moving through the shadows in the night. It moved out, and then it came out to the edge of the clearing, and it stopped. It was a tiger.

I don't think I was touching the ground. The two men with me were sleeping—I couldn't wake them up, because I knew the tiger would hear me. I knew he couldn't smell me—there was a breeze that was coming off of the river, and it was in my face.

He came out of the clearing, went to the riverbank, and got a drink of water. He's probably ninety feet away, and I'm standing and I'm watching. Then he lifted his head and turned, and I swear to God he was looking right at me. He got a little more water, and then he went the other way along the bank. And every once in a while, he'd think and he'd look back. And then he was gone out of sight. Inside, right now, I can still feel that moment.

I shook the guys awake, and I whispered, "You're not gonna believe what I just saw. I saw a tiger.

"Do you remember when we were talking about what happened to our dead and our wounded?" When you're in a firefight and you're moving and guys are badly hit, you want to remember where they are because you want to recover them when it's all over with. But sometimes when we went back, we couldn't find those guys. We couldn't figure out why. I says, "What do you think? Do you think the tigers could be getting them?" Nobody said anything. And it wasn't until, I don't know, ten years ago, in a TV documentary, that I heard it mentioned that there was a good possibility that a lot of our dead were taken by those tigers.

There's a lot that most people missed over there fighting that war. They never really saw anything. They never saw the land. They never saw the people.

But I was very much tied in to that. It changed my whole outlook on that war.

You listen to the night.

I spent two days one time, my men and me, with three North Vietnamese soldiers.

Five of us were on an operation. We were trail crossing—just seeing what trails were being used. And if somebody was using one, we waited to see who. Well, we were traveling along this ridgeline trying to come upon some new trails, and I got a whiff of something in the air. It was marijuana. And I turned around and looked to see if any of my men were smoking. Nobody was.

So we moved a little bit further, and I got another whiff. I says to Metzger, "Do you smell that?" He says, "Yeah." The breeze was coming out of the valley, just a slight breeze.

So we moved on into the valley. There was a stream down there and a little clearing. I saw something, so I had three guys go way down and cross the stream, then come back around on the other side. Then we closed in from two directions. And what it was, was three North Vietnamese soldiers. They were sitting by the stream. Had their weapons stacked up, and they were smoking marijuana.

I secured their weapons right there, and they looked at us. They couldn't do anything; they probably thought we were going to shoot them. Metzger could speak pretty good Vietnamese. And so I says, "Metzger, ask 'em if they want to share the wealth." And Metzger asked them. They looked at us and smiled. And so we sat down, and we spent two days together.

They were showing us pictures of their girlfriends, letters from home. Military philosophy is to dehumanize the enemy, make him lower than you. But they were human beings just like us, and they were young like we were. Their ideas of what they were doing were pretty much like the way we saw this whole thing. There was no need for us to have a firefight. There was no need for us to kill one another.

It was a good two days. Then they went one way, we went the

other. I always wonder about them, but I'll never know. Maybe one of them is telling a story, too, just like this.

Those two days made things a little bit different. They made things a little bit difficult. But it was still a war. So it's not like I didn't do my job. I did my job. I did it very well. My perspective on the war did change, but I still did my job.

After my second tour, they sent me up to Fort Lewis, Washington, to do in-service recruiting—recruiting guys already in the service—for the Eighty-second Airborne Division. I used to get letters from Fort Meade, Maryland, commending me on my ability to recruit. I met my quotas every month.

But after a while I realized what I was doing: I was recruiting a lot of native people from out west to go into the service—basically to go to Vietnam and maybe die. So I wanted to go back there again, to see what I could do to get some of those guys into my unit so that I could help them get back home.

I went to a Pathfinder unit in I Corps. This was November of '71. And I went around to the different units and found out where some of the guys were. And some of them found me. These were guys I had recruited. I got three of them into the Pathfinders.

One time we were choppered in to help out an American Ranger unit. They had AK-47s, and we had that ammo, and we were close. So they asked if we could go in with some ammo and give them some support to get them out of the situation. And I remember running down through there, and I dropped off four bandoliers of AK-47 ammo.

I ran into a guy many years later. I was doing a talk at the community college, and I told him what my handle was in the 'Nam. And he says, "You were the guys that they dropped on top of us to help out and bring us supplies."

I says, "Yeah."

"Do you remember what you said when you ran by me and you dropped off those belts?"

"No."

He says, "I never forgot it. As you ran by, you looked at me and smiled and said, 'Isn't this a lot of fun?' "

I didn't remember saying that.

When I look back at it now, I don't wish it on anyone. But at the time we *were* having a lot of fun. It *was* a game. At least some things I saw as a game.

After the war, as I got into studying and teaching Iroquois history, I'd be telling my students about a different type of warfare.

Warfare was a highly stylized game among the Iroquois. And the object was not to kill. The object was to basically beat the snot out of whoever it was but bring him back alive. And the utmost was to touch the enemy on the shoulder and in that way take his spirit.

Knowing this gave me a new understanding. It gave me something to believe in, it helped me when I couldn't find answers anywhere else. And it helps me today.

When I got to Vietnam the first time, half of the company were guys that I went through jump school with. It was like homecoming week. I thought that was nice until we started to lose some of them. It was like losing your brother, because I knew everybody. And after that is when I started having problems matching names and faces. I did not want to anymore. And so when new guys came in, I would not tie names to those faces. Because when I heard the name of someone that got killed, I didn't want to know who it was. It became very, very hard after a while to put names and faces together. Even today I still have the problem, so I don't even try.

It's all part of that long-ago.

I had one friend my first tour, Barker, a medic. He was a conscientious objector. I always told him to let me know when he was around me, so that I could protect him. Because he wouldn't carry a weapon, you see. But he and two other medics died one morning.

The enemy was waiting for us. They'd moved up in the middle of the night under a waist-high ground fog, and they knew we were there. And we didn't know they were. We started moving up, and then they opened up on us. We lost eighteen guys real quick.

Eighteen from my company, seven from my platoon. Three out of the eighteen were medics who were friends of mine, and one of them was Barker.

I went down to the Wall and just happened to come upon them. There they all were, all together: This is what died that day.

When you came off a battle, they usually gave you what they called a three-day stand-down—three days back at camp to basically get over what just happened: If you lost a friend, to grieve; if you wanted help, to seek it, whether from the chaplains or the other men. To get mail and write mail. To get drunk if you had to. Then you go back out again.

But it got to the point where there was so much trauma, we never had enough time to digest what had happened. So we slammed it down.

If you were a grunt and you did your tour and you're going home, within hours you're back on the city block. Within thirty-six to forty-eight hours, from the combat zone to the street. Like it never happened.

When we left the 'Nam, we hoped that we'd left all of the trauma there, too. But when you got weak enough and vulnerable enough, it started to come back in like gangbusters.

My room was right next door to my parents' when I was growing up, and I used to hear my dad's nightmares sometimes. So when it began happening to me, right after I got back, I just accepted that it was something I would have to bear for the rest of my life. There wasn't anyplace I could take that, you see, not until way later, because I wasn't diagnosed with severe PTSD until 1982. And still nothing was really being done about PTSD.

My unit was pulled out of Vietnam in February of '72. I left the service and went to live in Fayetteville, North Carolina, where Fort Bragg is located.

At that time—during the Vietnam War, just after the Vietnam War—the whole town of Fayetteville was suffering from post-traumatic stress. It was probably the same for any town around a large military post. People were watching those planes fly away with soldiers and then watching them bring soldiers back, some dead, some alive. So when I was living in Fayetteville, everybody down there was acting the same way. For me it was the norm.

I avoided talking about it. I thought I could handle it. But it ate a big hole in me. When I would think about what had happened, there was a great emptiness. It was a deep, deep hurt.

I got lost in the brown bottle for a couple, three years. There were some pretty bad moments, because I would get into a lot of fights, and I got scared because I thought I was going to hurt somebody. When I fight, it's not pattycakes. I'm gonna win. And I'm good at it: I'm gonna take you down and you're not gonna get up.

I can tell you exactly when it stopped. It was in May of '76.

I had run off my wife. Then I'd left Fayetteville and come back up to Syracuse.

One night I think I had beaten up everyone in the tavern. And I saw somebody who looked like he wanted to fight, too, so I was getting ready to do battle with him. And it turned out to be me. I was looking at myself in the mirror behind the bar, and I didn't even know myself. That's when I went and asked my mother if I could borrow fifty dollars so I could drive back to North Carolina.

At first she said, "Is this another fifty dollars to go get drunk some more?"

And I says, "No." I says, "I want to be with my wife and want to be with my kids." My wife, Sam, had always said, "You know where I'll be. And when you're ready, I'll be waiting for you." That was twenty-five years ago. It's been a hard road, but she's been with me all the way.

Sam worked at the Pancake House in Fayetteville. The state troopers used to come in there and have breakfast every morning, and one of the troopers happened to notice my wife's name. And he said, "Wow. I served with a Tarbell in the 'Nam."

And she says, "Oh, yeah? My husband was there."

"What unit was he in?"

"He was a Pathfinder."

"Not Mike?"

It was Lawson, my first commander in a Pathfinder detachment.

So I went to see him one morning at the restaurant, and we had a grand reunion there. And he says, "Bobby's home."

And I says, "Metzger?"

"Yeah. He's finally come home."

What Metzger did was, after Vietnam he went and did a tour in Korea. I don't know why. He stayed in Korea for a year, and he brought back a Korean wife.

I wanted to take Sam down to meet Bobby—I wanted her to know who he was. We drove up to his house, and when I pulled up, I could see him standing out in the back behind the house, and he was looking off into the pines.

I walked up to him. I knew what he was doing—the thousand-yard stare. I introduced him to Sam. I talked with Bobby for a moment, and I said, "We need to get together and talk about things. Talk about the 'Nam."

And he says, "Oh, yeah, yeah. We gotta do that."

And I says, "Bobby, I have to leave. I have to go on a trip." I was working for Purolator then, driving long-distance. "I'll see you when I get back."

When I got back at the end of the week, I went to pick my wife up at work—she'd just started a new job, at a law firm. And that's when my buddy, Russ Burton, a veteran who was her boss, came to me, and he says, "I got some bad news. Bobby killed himself a couple of days ago."

I felt so bad that we never had a chance to talk.

Driving long-distance was a way of hiding. I started having flashbacks out on the road.

I went to the VA hospital in Raleigh-Durham. There wasn't

much they could tell me. They just took statistics—When was I there? Where was I? They diagnosed me with severe post-traumatic stress, but they didn't have any programs there.

Then Russ Burton got involved with somebody who wanted to open a place where Vietnam veterans could go to get help. I started helping out there.

This one kid came traveling through, and we got to talking. He came from up here, and he says there's scuttlebutt that there is going to be a combat-stress clinic opening up in the Buffalo VA hospital. And I says, "Wow, that's great. When is it supposed to come about?"

He says, "It's in the talks now, but I don't know when it will open."

I says, "Well, they're not doing anything for me here."

About that time I had left Purolator, because they had closed down their transportation department. And that's when Vietnam came in like a storm trooper, because now I wasn't active. I'd take my wife to work, come home, do the dishes and do the laundry, make sure the kids got to school, and then pull the shades and sit in the dark. I knew I had to get some help.

That was 1984. We left Fayetteville to come back here, but the clinic didn't get started until '86. There was an outreach center in downtown Syracuse; it took me a year to get there.

This center took me in and confirmed the PTSD diagnosis that had been made in North Carolina. I was going there every day. It was a sanctuary. Then, when the clinic opened up in Buffalo, I said that I think I'm ready for it. The program was a three-month stay on the tenth floor of the hospital.

It was hard on my kids. We were living in the neighborhood where I'd grown up, and everyone knew everyone. My children were going to school with the children of people I went to school with. And when I was in the hospital, those kids would say to my kids, "How is your crazy dad doing?" But I explained it to them. I says, "No, I'm not crazy, I'm just having a problem. I'm having some bad dreams. I'm taking care of things. I'm not crazy."

The clinic was good, but it just scratched the surface. I came to accept it for what it was. I accepted that there wasn't some magical medicine out there somewhere that would take care of this. I knew I was in it for the duration, that I wasn't gonna be cured in a year or two years or three years. I accepted that. And so I'm still being helped.

That first weekend in the clinic, there was a lock-in where they had us seated with all of the clinicians. They started to ask us questions, and they asked each of us to reminisce on something that was troubling us.

No one was doing anything. I wanted to get this thing going, so I was the first one to talk.

What I talked about was, I was in this mode of washing my hands literally every few minutes. Whenever I went to pick something up, I went and I washed. Sometimes when I would wash my hands at night, I couldn't get them clean enough. It was like I almost washed all the tan off.

What I was doing was, I was washing the blood off my hands, you see. While I was in the 'Nam for my second tour, my interpreter got hit, and I couldn't do anything for him. He was dying there in front of me. I felt so inadequate. He had been hit very badly, and I was trying to stitch him up—because we didn't have a medic in the Pathfinder detachment, I'd learned to do suturing and stuff. But the sutures weren't working, and I couldn't stop the bleeding.

I held him and had his blood all over me. And when he looked at me, I could see the life leaving his eyes.

My mother always told me I was born three hundred years too late. Maybe she had something there.

In the fall of '88—just after my mother died—I began college. I got my associate's degree in humanities from Onondaga Community College. I always wanted to be a teacher, so I got a transfer and was accepted at Syracuse University as a full junior and majored in English and Textual Studies. I got my bachelor's in 1992.

With my electives I started getting into the history of native peoples—my people and other peoples. I had some really good professors, and they planted a seed—I just couldn't let it go; I had to nurture that seed. And so I started reading more books, and I started talking to more people. And I went to conferences at Cornell University to talk with native people from all over the North American continent. South America, too. I got into studying the written history and then the oral tradition. And I started seeing some good things in there. I could feel something welling up inside of me.

I associate myself with the natural world. The wintertime, I'm out there harvesting materials the way my ancestors did. I make things the way they made them and try to understand why they did things the way they did them. It all comes back to the same idea: They were living in balance and harmony with the natural world.

I try to incorporate this into my teaching of Iroquois history. I teach students from elementary school to college, and I take them out in the natural world. I explain how my ancestors saw that natural world, and how my people still see it. But I also explain to them that at one time their ancestors were the same as mine: people of the natural world.

It is Western man who removes himself from that natural world and tries to conquer it. And in this way he gives up his spirituality. Everything is alive, everything has a spirit and a soul. We're a part of that natural world. But not that important a part; it will survive without us.

Today we look at ourselves and we think that we've progressed a long ways. In reality it is only the technology that has progressed. There are still predators amongst us, and those predators hide amongst all our technology. You look at what my dad witnessed at the end of the Second World War, what one human being could do to another. Look at Bosnia, ethnic cleansing. How far have we progressed?

So I'll step back. The ancient time was a hard time, but it was a good time, too.

After I got out of the service, I started going to some of the conventions with my dad. And it felt really good. But I have yet to go to a convention where my guys are. I've felt a closer tie to my dad's friends than to my own, because I haven't been able to find Vietnam vets willing to talk about it.

It's only happening now. I have one friend, Don. I met him when I was doing a class in the Iroquois Indian museum in Howes Cave, New York. He had seen the sign for the class and had stopped in the museum.

I noticed him sticking around all day listening to me talk. And then he started to volunteer there, and we got to know each other better. I found out that he's a Vietnam vet, too, and that he was having problems. I've known him for about three years now. He's got ninety acres of land, forest land, and we share some of that forest. We have a little camp right in the middle of it, and once in a while we go down there, and we take our wives with us, and we sit and listen and talk. We listen to each other and listen to the natural world. We get away from everything.

There are many people today that come to the museum looking for some spiritual side to life. And I see myself as a stepping-stone along the way. Don is on a journey, and I'm a part of that journey. We're taking the same path together at the same time. But in time he will seek something else out. He'll go that way, and I'll continue on the path that I'm on.

This understanding has helped give me something to live for. I feel that I've become useful, not just that I've been used up and discarded, the way a lot of Vietnam vets have felt. I don't want it to end there. It's a promise I made to my mother, that someday I would be somebody important, if not to the majority of people, at least to a couple of people I can help along the way.

When I had a heart attack in 1992, my dad took me and my wife to the hospital. They ran some tests on me, and the doctor said that they had found damage to my heart from my first heart attack. I said I thought this was the first one. "Oh, no," he says. "You had one before." He drew me a diagram of it and everything. He says, "We lose a lot of the guys to what we call 'the silent one.' "

That first heart attack was in my sleep from a nightmare. And I never realized it, because when I woke up, it was like waking from any other nightmare that I would have: adrenaline pumping, legs hurting like I'd been running all night, arms hurting like I'd been carrying something very heavy for a long period of time, sweating, breathing hard. Except this one time when I woke up, I had these pains in my chest. I'd been dreaming about once when I was on a helicopter and took some rounds in my chest armor.

It was probably the only time that I wore my chest armor. Most of the time I sat on it in the helicopter, because I was vulnerable from the underside.

But the night before this mission, I was looking in the mirror, and I thought the mirror was bad, because my face kept fading out. I said, "What the heck?" I cleaned it and looked at it again—I was still fading. I took that as a premonition that something was going to happen to me the next day.

So when I got ready to go out that morning on an operation, I took my armored vest off of the seat, and I put it on. And during the mission I took three rounds right in the chest on this armor. And you feel that. It hurts.

So when I had the chest pain after the nightmare years later, I thought that it was just from the dream—that I was experiencing that pain again. But it was my first heart attack.

When they brought me in for the second, I was laying on the gurney, and I remember feeling like something had come down from the ceiling. You have high parts on your body when you are laying down, so I felt something hit the tip of my nose—it was like an invisible blanket, cool—and I could feel it settling on my body. And that's when I said to the nurse, "I think you'd better get my wife in here."

I was scared for the moment, because I just wanted someone to hold on to. That was one of my fears in the 'Nam: dying out there somewhere alone.

But I didn't fear dying itself. In our culture we don't believe that spirits and souls die. It is only the container that grows old, wears out, and dies. There are no good-byes, you see, because we will meet again, whether it is here or in what the native people call the "Land of the Strawberries." That's what we call our heaven, that's where the warriors go. It is the symbolism of a new beginning, because strawberries are the first-blooming fruit of the new year. That's why I love strawberries. In fact, in Mohawk we use the word *shohyakwenh* to say someone has died. And the literal translation is "He's gone to pick berries."

In 1994 a wellness group at Onondaga Reservation invited me to come out there with my dad. I thought they were just having a little get-together and that they wanted me to come and bring my dad because he wasn't feeling very good at the time. What it turned out to be was what we call a "cleansing." This is what long-ago warriors would go through when they returned from their world, which was the forest world, the masculine world, and before they could come back into the women's world, which was the clearing and where the gardens are. The men would stop at the edge of the forest, and they would hail the village, letting them know that they were there. And the women would come out, bringing to the men their best outfits. The men would change into those clothes, and then they would ask the Creator to forgive them for any and all wrongs that they'd done while out there. And that was so they could return to the women's world as what they were before they left: good partners in life.

The cleansing came as a surprise to me. I was getting ready to take my dad home when they said, "Oh, you need to sit down and stay." A real good friend of mine and my dad's, Tom Porter, who was the Mohawk Bear Clan chief, was there. They put me in a seat at the center of the floor. And they took my hair down, and they combed the snakes from my hair. And then they put a blanket on me. I knew right away what it was.

I felt really good at that moment, because now I knew that my people were behind me. I had thought that I was walking this path alone. But you never are really alone. And so I asked them if my dad could get under that blanket with me. That was a moment that assured me that I was on the right path again, that I needed to continue this searching into the nativeness.

I felt strong. That cleansing was what I needed, because afterward, when anything would pop up—any new nightmare, any new problem—I had the strength to deal with it. At one time I didn't care whether I lived or not. I never thought I would get old enough to see my grandchildren. The cleansing gave me a new hold on life, and I'm very happy to be here. And then, having my dad, too.

He's become my sounding board. There are times when something comes up that I find difficult to handle or that I need some reassurance on. So I'll talk to him about it.

I try to stay busy—in my work, in my research. In the night when I wake up, I try to keep my mind occupied. So I'll go down and I'll study something. In this way there is not a free moment when Vietnam can come back in. But it does. And when it does, I don't know what it's going to bring.

Anything can trigger it. It might be a song, it might be a smell.

I remember once four guys from another Pathfinder detachment came through, back from R&R, and they stopped into our base camp and stayed the night, and we partied. We'd never met the guys before, but, hey, everyone is welcome.

The next morning they hitched a ride on a Chinook helicopter flying up to Pleiku. And bad weather came in. We called Pleiku, and they never got there. Well, we thought maybe bad weather had held them off. Later on, Pleiku called and said they still hadn't gotten there. So we started to send out helicopters to search the area. There was a total of thirty-seven guys on that chopper, all killed. We weren't sure, but we thought they got hit by some kind of rocket, because the helicopter blew up at treetop level.

It took us a week to find them. And it all came back to me one evening a number of years ago, when we returned from the grocery store, my wife and I. We had bought a lot of chicken, and she was cutting it up and putting it in plastic bags to put in the freezer, and I was helping her. And all of a sudden it hit me that I did this once, but it was with human bodies. I was looking for the four guys that were partying with us the night before. We were putting bodies into body bags, but they were all pieces. And so we made sure that each body bag got a torso, two arms, two legs, and a head.

For a long time after Vietnam, I was having dreams of the guys who died. They would come visit me in my bedroom. And I would always see them as they had been; they hadn't grown any older. I was the only one who was growing older.

For a long time having these dreams was hard, but with the traditional understanding, I can accept it. Because they haven't died. They've gone to pick berries.

XIII

"An officer doesn't lie, cheat, or steal."

LEADERS AND FOLLOWERS

Greg Camp recalls that as a plebe at West Point, he was required to memorize, and repeat on the whim of any upperclassman, "Schofield's Definition of Discipline." From a speech delivered at West Point in 1887 by Major General John M. Schofield, the definition begins:

> *The discipline which makes the soldier of a free country reliable in battle is not to be gained by harsh or tyrannical treatment. On the contrary, such treatment is far more likely to destroy than to make an army. It is possible to impart instruction and give commands in such manner and in such tone of voice as to inspire in the soldier no feeling but an intense desire to obey, while the opposite manner and tone of voice can not fail to excite strong resentment and a desire to disobey.*

Officers in the U.S. armed forces face the dilemma of commanding warriors raised in a society that elevates individual free will over obedience to central authority. During World War II, officers of the Nazi army, who had to deal with no such contradiction, were incredulous that the American army's most brilliant general could find himself passed over for a command because he had slapped—

not shot, but slapped—two enlisted men who had been hospitalized for battle fatigue in Sicily. (And there were two men slapped, not one—despite what the movie Patton *depicts and Frank Recendez recalls.)*

BILL PERKINS

SPOKANE, WASHINGTON

CAPTAIN, UNITED STATES ARMY AIR FORCES, WORLD WAR II

In between combat drops, our biggest job was resupply. Patton was moving rapidly, and he'd run out of ammunition and fuel. So he'd call on what he called "my Troop Carrier boys" to resupply him. His people would pick out some little field, whether it was a damaged airfield or just an agricultural field, and set that up for us to land in. To him the Troop Carrier was a real workhorse.

A lot of times, Patton would come out and talk to us and thank us for getting that matériel to him. I never said anything to him, but I was face-to-face with the guy. He had those ivory-handled revolvers on two holsters, one on each side. He had his helmet on with his stars on it. He had a leather battle jacket.

We'd carry five or seven hundred gallons of gasoline in just these five-gallon jerry cans, and he'd come right out to the airplanes and stand there and tell his people where to take them. "I want this tank refueled. Move this stuff over there." He was right there with his people all the time.

I'd heard a lot about Patton being strict and everything, but he looked after his people. One time we landed at a strip out there where he'd spearheaded. And when we'd unloaded all the fuel, he said to one of his officers, "Lieutenant, you take two of these trucks and some of your men, and you go down to this warehouse, and you load up these trucks and bring 'em back and load these airplanes for these flyboys."

Well, they came back with cases of cognac. We flew them back to England, and I'll bet every club in England had cognac after that. I thought he was quite a character to do things like that.

FRANK RECENDEZ

RETIRED TRUCK DRIVER
HANFORD, CALIFORNIA
CORPORAL, UNITED STATES ARMY, WORLD WAR II

Twenty-four-year-old Frank R. Recendez was living in Corcoran, California, when he was drafted at the end of November 1941. He trained with an artillery outfit, then shipped out of New York Harbor in mid-1944.

"There were probably about four thousand or five thousand soldiers on that transport. We started moving out. And the Statue of Liberty—we seen all of it, then a little less, a little less, a little less, until we could see the tip of the torch. Then it was gone.

"I can remember some of the soldiers saluting and waving. I could hear some of them just bawl.

"We didn't know whether we'd see her again or not."

Frank got to France shortly after D-Day to join the 195th Field Artillery Group, which was soon assigned to George Patton's Third Army. Frank drove a messenger jeep, conveying information between the front and the rear.

Oh, my golly, golly, golly.

We went through St.-Lô and then to Paris. We kept on traveling. Old Patton, he wanted to move.

Three times that man came up to us. Of course, we were way back when we seen him. He came out—"Hello, how are you?" and this and that. We could see the two ivory-handled guns he had on. He thanked us for doing a good job. Said we gotta move.

I heard about it when he slapped that guy in the hospital.

In a way I was on his side, because there were a lot of gold-bricks. Two friends of mine, they didn't want to go forward. They got yellow. One, he started running back, and some of our men killed him. I didn't see it; we just heard about it. I don't know whether that was the right thing to do or not. But, hey, we were there for a purpose. Forward, forward, forward.

When Patton slapped that man, he wanted to show that no one else should be tempted to stay in the rear. You had to do your job and keep doing it. See what I mean?

Nowadays our society has gone to the dogs. When I was little, Dad had one of those razor strops. And, man, if you did something wrong, you got it. He was a man of the law.

To me Patton represented the guts of the Army. He represented the reason that we were there.

Wounded in early December, Frank spent ten days in a hospital, then returned to his outfit. After the Battle of the Bulge, he continued to advance toward Germany.

One thing I can't forget. We were waiting to cross the Rhine. The engineers were repairing the bridge to go over, because it was partly bombed out. And at the same time, they made pontoon bridges.

Good old Patton, he came in and he said, "Okay, boys, we're gonna go." And he got to the edge of the river, and he just pissed on it. He was showing us what he thought of the Germans. I was fifteen, twenty yards from him. They had a picture of it in the *Stars and Stripes.*

JOHN HOWE

Albany, New York
Staff Sergeant, United States Army, Vietnam

My biological father was unique because as an African American—or a Caribbean American, I guess we could say—he had blond hair and blue eyes. A very striking guy. Just look at me, how light I am.

And the first thing he said to me about the war was, "Son, I hope that you don't have to have the same experience that I did." And he was laughing.

I said, "What's that, Daddy Mel?"

He says, "Well, when I went in the Army, they sent me to Camp Claiborne, Louisiana. And when I got down there, they had me lined up, and I looked around: Everybody in the line was white." Remember, he had blond hair and blue eyes and light skin, like mine. "And I found a doctor, I says, 'Hey, Doc, you'd better send me over there where I belong, with the darkies.' " He said, "I laughed about it. But I was hurt inside, because I knew what would happen if I opened my mouth the wrong way in Louisiana. I would have been lynched; I'd have been strung up."

Harry Truman integrated the military by executive order in 1948. But I think that the professional officer corps of the Army, although they would march after receiving their orders, still had a long way to go in the fifties and early sixties. Vietnam fully integrated the military. That's what Vietnam did for America. Vietnam created a fully integrated military, vertically and horizontally.

I learned just how much the military had changed a few days before Christmas in 1967.

I was in the Sixth Battalion, Thirty-first Infantry, stationed up in Fort Lewis, Washington. We were getting ready for rotation overseas.

They told us we had sixty days' leave before we shipped. So I call back home, tell my mother to tell my wife, "Get the first thing smokin' and come on out here." I had found out about a wonderful trailer park, with this beautiful house trailer that was for rent for sixty days. It was on the Nisqually River, and I was learning to fly-cast then, so I'm saying, "Yeah, trout on the table. Steelhead. Salmon."

My wife arrives, and we pull up in front of the joint. The landlord looks at her, says, "We're sorry. You can't move in."

And I say, "Why is that?"

And he goes through this whole thing—you look different, we don't know how you people act, we don't know the things you do, and blah, blah, blah.

I say, "Why don't you just say what's on your mind?"

He says, "We don't allow no niggers in here."

Now, this is in the Northwest. This is outside of Seattle, Washington, on Puget Sound. This is the place where there's supposed to be no discrimination.

Up until then he only saw me. Suntan, short haircut—what we call "high and tight"— so you couldn't see the curl. Barrel-chested, with the militaryspeak: "My name is Staff Sergeant John Howe. Grr, grr. I'm here for the trailer rental." He didn't know who I was. He just saw another GI. "Combat infantryman." He took my money, no problem.

So I go back to the company, and I go to the first sergeant. And I say, "First Sergeant, I can't move into my house."

"What's the matter with you?"

"They looked at my wife, and they said they don't want no niggers."

"What?!"

So the first sergeant calls up the company commander: "Sir, we got a problem down here." The company commander comes down. I tell him. He says, "What the hell?!" And he calls the sergeant major. The sergeant major says, "What?!" And he calls the battalion commander.

So I got the first sergeant, the company commander, the sergeant major, the battalion commander, and then the post housing officer and the post deputy commander. This is when I knew the Army wasn't bullshitting about what they said on a policy level about the way they wanted their soldiers treated. So all of these guys pile in staff cars and jeeps and they go down to this place with me.

The battalion commander knocks on the door. "My name is Lieutenant Colonel Bielman. I want to know what's going on here."

The landlord says, "We have a military family that owns this trailer. They're in Alaska on duty, and they don't want anybody different in their trailer."

So the post housing officer issues an ultimatum: "Either you let this man move in or else."

The landlord chose the "or else." He didn't think there was going to be any consequence. But the post housing officer quoted Department of Defense policy and declared the housing development off-limits for anybody who received a military housing allowance. Everybody in there was soldiers or sailors or fly guys. So they moved all their asses out of there.

The point is that in the Army racism doesn't happen in the official capacity. There's always animosity by individuals. You learn to expect that. Because of the nature of the population that has chosen to become professional soldiers, the redneck is a mainstay of the military, particularly when you get into units like the infantry. Guys who have been in the infantry all their life, you take a look where they come from: Chitlin Switch, Arkansas; Mule Chew, Texas; Get-back-out-of-my-way-'fore-I-lynch-you, Mississippi. Look at the large infantry centers of the United States Army—Fort Bragg, North Carolina; Fort Benning, Georgia; Fort Hood, Texas. Where they at?

And whatever happens on a military installation, you're still subject to the pressure of the outside community. When you're on post at Fort Bragg, you're treated like a king. Go to Fayetteville, downtown. I was treated like a king on Fort Lewis. I was a soldier, an American fighting man, serving in the armed forces to defend my country and a way of life. When I went off base to rent a trailer, I was treated poorly.

The military was a place where I was probably treated more fairly than anywhere else in this country. You see, soldiers carry out their missions, and soldiers obey rules. And when I was told I couldn't live somewhere, soldiers looked out for me. They were obeying the rules. There are two components to being a leader in the Army. One is accomplishing your mission, the other is what they call care and feeding of the troops or the welfare of your men. That's the way you carry things out: Mission, welfare of your men. Mission, welfare of your men. What they were doing was, they were looking out for the welfare of one of their soldiers.

MICKEY HUTCHINS

CONCORD, NORTH CAROLINA
FIRST LIEUTENANT, UNITED STATES ARMY, VIETNAM

As advisers we went around to different Vietnamese units and inspected them. We went out on operations with many of them to see how they operated in the field. And then, every month, we had to create two reports: One was called a Territorial Forces Evaluation Survey, the other was the Hamlet Evaluation Survey. The Territorial Forces Evaluation Survey was our assessment of how we thought our units were doing in terms of training and proficiency for that month. The Hamlet Evaluation Survey was aimed at how we assessed the security of a particular hamlet for that month—the degree of infiltration of the VC and, conversely, the degree of control by the government forces. I got my first introduction to the politics of all of that with my very first set of reports, because I had to evaluate the two hamlets where I'd been involved in my first firefight. Just before I'd gotten to the district, an entire South Vietnamese platoon had been wiped out within a mile of these hamlets, and so I considered them not to be terribly secure. But when I looked at how they had been previously rated, they were showing as pretty secure. So I downgraded them a couple of notches.

Within a matter of days, I was summoned up to the district compound to meet with a couple of colonels from III Corps headquarters. The meeting was fairly tense. Basically, "Lieutenant, you're new here. Do you have a clue what you are doing?" They wanted to know the whole nine yards of why I had thought that it was necessary to downgrade the security of these hamlets, because this was definitely running counter to what it was that we were supposed to be reporting.

I'd been eyeball-to-eyeball with it. I'd been in the firefight and I didn't care what they had to say, I wasn't changing my report. It wasn't an easy thing to do, by any means, but one of the things that they had impressed on us throughout OCS was, an officer doesn't lie, cheat, or steal or tolerate those who do. I didn't think that this was a minor thing at all; I thought that the assessment of how secure these troops were keeping an area was something that we needed to be honest with ourselves about, and I thought that the actions that we had just seen should have raised at least reasonable doubt in anybody's mind as to whether this really was as safe a place this month as it was last month. I have very little doubt that my report got covered up. It was clear to me that a true picture of what was going on wasn't necessarily appreciated in III Corps headquarters.

This pretty well convinced me that this was not my father's war. This was not the way I had understood that war was to be fought and units were to be commanded. I guess this is when I started forming my first impressions about the distinction between the role and the performance of company-grade officers as opposed to senior field-grade officers. I shouldn't paint them all with the same brush, by any means. There were many, many senior field-grade officers who shared the risks of their troops and who shared the concepts of leadership that I had, but there were plenty of the politicos around, and the organization chart for MACV was top-heavy with brass. A lot of people were just looking to fill out reports, get their ticket punched, and go on to the next assignment.

MIKE PERKINS
TREMONTON, UTAH
CAPTAIN, UNITED STATES ARMY, VIETNAM

Bill Perkins: "Of course, I was real concerned that with the number of people being killed over there, Mike might be one of them. But you couldn't change his mind. In fact, when he kept returning to Vietnam, I wouldn't even know about it until right before he'd leave. He'd come to see us and he'd say, 'I'm going back.'

"I'd think, 'You're crazy, little boy.' One time I even told him, 'I think you're nuts for going to Vietnam when you don't have to.'

" 'Well, that's the way it is.'

"When Mike gets involved in something, he goes all out for it. He doesn't go halfway. He's dedicated to it."

I have a lot of friends who pulled one tour in 'Nam and that was it. Me, I had to go back. A lot of American kids came home because I was there. Maybe that's an exalted view. Maybe I'm not being humble enough.

I guess I'm on my soapbox. But there were too many officers who would do as little time as they could on the lines and then seek to get back to the rear somewhere. And they could do it. Some lieutenant or captain can worm his way back to working where there's no threat. The average private can't do that. So I went back to keep kids alive, because I knew how to do it.

For instance, I realized sometimes you have to amend or change orders.

In the Ninth Division, the kids in my rifle company would be worn out. They've been up all night—on all-night patrol, all-night security. The kids are just worn out. They're tired.

So the call would come in. "Are you in contact?"

I'd say, "Yeah, we got small contact going on here. I think we got a squad-size element." We're not in contact. I got kids sleeping because they've been up all night. If you don't let kids sleep, they get tired, and when they get tired, they get sloppy, and when they get sloppy, they get killed. So I'm letting my company sleep for three hours.

I'd phony it up. I'd lie. Didn't happen very often, but it happened often enough. I think the operations officer knew I was lying.

"Yeah, we got contact going on here. Let me give you coordinates."

"Do you need artillery?"

"No, I think we got this in hand. There's just three or four of these farmers out here. We'll let you know what happens."

Half an hour would go by, and they'd call again. "You still got contact?"

"Yeah. I think we got these guys moving. Give me another hour."

An hour would go by. By that time the kids had had a couple hours' rest, and I'd call in and say, "Contact ended. We got results here."

"What did you get?"

"We captured two grenades and one AK." It was all a lie.

"How many did you kill?"

"We don't know. We got blood trails heading west." A total lie.

So I compromised my own integrity. I did that to keep kids alive. Now the kids are rested. They've had their three hours. Now we'll go out, and we're on a real contact two hours later. Because the kids are rested, they can function.

Almost every company commander I knew in Vietnam did the same thing. So he could protect his troops. Otherwise the colonels and above would drive, drive, drive, drive these kids twenty-four hours a day.

We often wondered who was the worse enemy, the VC or our generals.

I never felt scared once people started shooting. It's usually before and after when you shake and you can't sleep for a couple of nights. Once you're actually in the middle of it, you're getting infantry moved up or "Get that gun over here, get that gun over here," and you're grabbing a guy: "See that?" You're pointing at things.

Bullets are going right by you, mortars are going off, grenades. But you're focused. "Now I gotta get down here." "Move over here, Brown. I need somebody right behind this tree." You're picking up shrapnel on your cheek. You're getting punched up. You're getting knocked down.

All the guys are the same way. Whether you're a private or whatever you are, you're putting out fire, you're thinking, "I can't move there, but I can move here." And then, when it's all over—you either knock them down the hill or it's two days later and somebody finally comes in and relieves you—you're sitting there on that tree stump thinking, "What am I gonna do now?" And you're tired. Then it starts to hit you. Maybe that's the worst part.

The fact that you came that close to dying, or you saw six men taken out at once, or Dugan will never be the same again because he took a round through his eye. Whatever it is. That's what hits you.

I've seen guys walking along almost totally asleep. Then a round goes off, and they're in a fight. They just do it all on automatic, they've done it so many times. And then an hour or two later, when it's over with, guys sit down and they're gone. They're totally, 100 percent wiped out. Other guys sit there and shake. Other guys start to bawl. Everybody takes it different.

But officers can't afford that. Neither can NCOs. You've got to be thinking about the next one. So officers and NCOs take the worst of it—especially NCOs, I think, because they're the closest to the men. They now have to start thinking, "I gotta resupply the ammo. I gotta get fresh batteries for my radio. I gotta get a second squad up here and get the first squad down the bottom of the hill and get canteens full." It never ends. Whereas if you're a private, you just do what you're told to do.

"We might get counterattacked. Well, if they're gonna counterattack, will they come up this ridge or that ridge? Okay. Put Miller in charge. He knows that stuff real well. Oh, Miller's been hit? Okay. Who's the next guy?"

Finally it's two o'clock in the morning. You're going, "I need a break here," and you nod off. And an hour later they start probing you. So you never get any sleep. Officers and NCOs, they're tired and worn out all the time. And I think that's why you lose so many of them. Because they get so tired they do stupid things that get themselves killed.

I can't speak for William Westmoreland. I think he tried to do what was right. But Westmoreland needed to be up on some of these recon patrols. I think it would have made a believer out of him.

Westmoreland was one of those guys who was everywhere. We were impressed by that. We were not impressed by what he said.

He'd come up with these rah-rah speeches. He's looking at ten or twelve Special Forces guys all dressed in tiger fatigues and haven't slept in three days. And he's going, "You men are the cornerstone of democracy."

"Yes, sir. Thank you." We all grinned for him, thinking, "When will this guy leave?"

I heard him get up and do these at least a dozen times when I was with the 101st and Special Forces; whether he had ten men there or a thousand, he'd get up on that jeeptop. I read the book *We Were Soldiers Once . . . and Young.* And he got up and gave a speech to the Second Battalion of the Seventh Cav after the battle at X-Ray. And they had the same opinion of him: Why doesn't he just shut up?

Vietnam wasn't like World War II: You take the hill or take the town and move on. Here the number-one thing was "Kill VC." The body count. If I heard it once, I heard it a thousand times: "Kill VC."

We killed 'em. So what? You kill 'em and the next day there's a bunch more guys who are madder than a snake. You killed their uncle; now they're gonna come and get you. It dawned on me about three or four months into Vietnam that we can kill all we want. But this is like stirring an anthill with a stick. That's all we're doing, is stirring the anthill.

Down there at rifle-company level, we all knew what was going on. The average GI knew we could kill these people in a firefight—we were killing 'em left and right. But we were not making any inroads. The average GI just wanted to go home. I knew that I had to do the best I could as an officer to keep my people alive. But it was a bottomless pit.

When the NVA finally took over in '75, the war stopped. And Vietnam hasn't taken over Thailand or Malaysia or anything else. It's one of the poorest countries on the face of the earth. They haven't got the manpower or the will to go out to Thailand or Malaysia. They just want to be one people, one Vietnamese people. Maybe I'm a traitor now, thirty years later, but I'm telling you that I saw no threat to the United States by these poor Vietnamese peasants.

I did see a threat to American boys. We were there to survive and help the other Americans survive, and try to do as much as we could to keep the enemy off center. You don't ever want to be on the defensive—you want to be on the offensive. That was my strategy anyway: always attack, never defend.

After a while you learn all the techniques and rules. And I think a lot of the old guys who came back for second or third tours, that's why they were there. There might have been a few ticket punchers, but most of the guys like me who kept going back were there because they wanted to bring as many Americans home as they could.

When I was with the riverine company, I got a first sergeant sent to me. This guy was about fifty, I guess, fifty-one, fifty-two. An old man. I said, "Tell me about yourself, Pop."

He said, "I was in World War II and Korea. I retired six or seven years ago. But they were asking for first sergeants, and I came back on active duty, and I wanted to be in a rifle company in Vietnam."

I said, "Here you are, Pop."

First Sergeant Jones was a good man with a lot of wisdom. Mostly I had him stay on board ship. I said, "You talk to these NCOs. I'll teach 'em how to be good warriors; you teach 'em how to be good NCOs." And he did.

He did go on one operation with me right after he got there. We came back in. And he said, "I gotta talk to you."

"What's up, Pop?"

He said, "I spent a year in New Guinea and the Philippines in '43–'44. I spent a year in Korea, '52. This is worse than those ever were."

I said, "Come on. All World War II veterans say this is a cakewalk."

"No. This is much worse than I ever saw in those places. In Korea you knew you were gonna get shelled by the Chinese artillery, so everybody was dug in underground. A few guys would get hit. In New Guinea and the Philippines, you'd get shot at. But it was on line. You could tell you had A Company on your right, B Company on your left, and you were moving up.

"Here, jeez, you'll walk through one paddy where somebody's shooting at you, and then you go across to the next paddy, there's somebody still shooting at you. There's no place where you can just say, 'They're over there.'

"They're not only in front of you. They're all around you. They're everywhere. It's a 360-degree war."

DAVE POLLINS

LEXINGTON, MASSACHUSETTS

LANCE CORPORAL, UNITED STATES MARINE CORPS, VIETNAM

The big thing over there was medals, especially for the lifers, the ones who were making a career out of it. They all want to be heroes.

Don't get me wrong about lifers; a lot of them were decent people. But there were always a couple of—excuse the expression—assholes. I was in-country maybe ten months and we had just finished a fifteen-day patrol. Everybody's tired, sweaty. It's 120 degrees in the shade. So we come back into a secured area, and as we're coming through the wire, here's this gunnery sergeant that's probably doing his second or third tour over there. He was out of the supply division—ammo, clothing, boots—and he's going, "Wash your trousers." "Shave." "I gotta put you guys on a work detail." He's grabbing all these grunts as they're coming in.

This gunny has two months left in-country and he hasn't been out in the bush. He's always been in the rear with the gear. He wants to get his Combat Action Ribbon, so he decides he's gonna go out on the next search-and-destroy. We stay at that firebase for a couple of days, and some of the grunts find out he's planning to go out on the op with us. So they write him a note, leave it on his rack: "Don't bother coming out, because if Charlie don't get you, one of us will."

The guy was a real jerk. He ignored the note and came on the patrol. About five days out, Charlie hit us. Everyone is capping off rounds. When it's over, they find the gunny dead. He had a bullet in the back of his head. We knew Charlie didn't get him. One of the grunts blew him away with an M-16.

Rounds are going all over the place. You got 150 Marines shooting. You got gooks shooting. It's not like they're gonna dig the bullet out of him and do a ballistics test and say, "Oh, this one's an M-16 round, not an AK-47." They tag him, bag him, call the chopper, and haul him out of there. "Stray round happened to get him. Killed in action."

Didn't bother many people. They used to have two sayings in 'Nam: "Payback's a motherfucker" and "Frags don't leave fingerprints."

XIV

"The soldier who died that night was about nineteen."

FIGHTING, KILLING, DYING

As integral as killing is to war, for American servicemen it did not occupy the same place in Vietnam that it did in World War II. In World War II, our soldiers were ordered to kill the enemy as a means to an end—so that they and their millions of comrades might take territory, and then take more territory, until they reached Tokyo or Berlin. In Vietnam, the means and the end were virtually one. Our soldiers were ordered to kill the enemy, so that eventually the enemy death toll would reach a level unacceptable to the enemy leadership, which would then agree to leave South Vietnam alone. This was the "war of attrition" pursued by William Westmoreland, the American commander in Vietnam from 1964 to 1968. In World War II, hundreds or thousands of miles, of land or ocean, lay between the act of killing and the final objective; in Vietnam, that distance measured only as far as the nearest tally sheet.

This fusion of front-line tactics with overall strategy may help explain the difficulty Vietnam veterans had in reintegrating into civilian society, and civilian society's difficulty in accepting them. In both World War II and Vietnam, we sent young men off to do our dirty work. When our soldiers won World War II, we saw past the dirty work and praised them for its end result; when Vietnam persisted for years without resolution, the dirty work became all that remained, and so we turned our backs on that work and the men who performed it. In describing his Iroquois ritual cleansing, Mike

Tarbell says, "And they took my hair down, and they combed the snakes from my hair."

Warriors do not return from war unburdened. These were our countrymen, sent far away to do our bidding, yet we never helped them comb the snakes from their hair. We Americans have a lot to answer for in our treatment of Vietnam veterans.

STEVE KEITH

LOCKSMITH
MILTON, MASSACHUSETTS
SERGEANT, UNITED STATES MARINE CORPS, VIETNAM

Like hundreds of thousands of other American service personnel, twenty-one-year-old William S. "Steve" Keith entered Vietnam through the huge American air base at Da Nang. Unlike most of them, however, he didn't have to go far to find his outfit. "I was with the Marines' First LAAM—Light Antiaircraft Missile—Battalion. I was right on the air base, in the Headquarters and Service Battery, which didn't have missiles; we were the command center for the three firing batteries.

"If enemy planes got beyond the Air Force jets or the Navy and Marine Corps jets, then our battalion was last resort. But it never happened while I was there, and it didn't happen before I got there either. They never engaged an enemy target and let the missile go."

Steve spent eleven months in Da Nang before the entire battalion was sent home during the summer of 1969.

There are two distinct smells I always remember from Vietnam. One was the nuoc mam sauce or the burning shit or whatever it was. You smelled it as soon as you got off the plane.

The second: We were by the main runway at Da Nang, and at the end of it was the morgue. So to drive around the runway you had to go past the morgue, and when you did that—I don't know what it was, formaldehyde or something, but you could smell the morgue. And you could see them stacking up the caskets, four one way, then four across the top of them, then four the first way, and so on—silver boxes, on a pallet. It was like sixteen in a stack.

It was a full-time job for some people, just picking them up on a forklift and driving them onto the planes, one load after another.

They're saying fifty-eight thousand died, right? How many is that a day?

PAUL KEITH

PLYMOUTH, MASSACHUSETTS
SPECIALIST FOURTH CLASS, UNITED STATES ARMY, VIETNAM

Although Paul was not a front-line combatant—he was assigned to elements that supported combat operations in the Twenty-fifth Infantry Division—he, like everyone else, was assigned a role in perimeter defense.

In July the base camp at Dau Tieng was attacked, and they cut it in half. The colonel had to call air support in. It was a pretty bad night.

As I understand it, the reason it happened was that the base was not properly defended. There were a number of infantry and mechanized outfits on that firebase, as well as some support units like us. But they had parceled out most of the gun units and armored units into various field operations, with no one—except the Vietcong—really paying attention to what was left on the base. So at the time of the attack, there were only about six hundred people left behind. The base just didn't have enough people to defend it, and we had virtually no heavy gun support. That's why they broke through.

They came right into the bunkers. There was no way out for us, because we had our own gunships firing down inside the lines; if you moved, you'd get hit by them. And so it became pretty uncertain which way to shoot, because fire was coming from all directions.

I remember Alpha Company, the One Fifth Mech, they came back before it was over. They had been mauled in the field and were just trying to get back in the base. You could see the bodies stacked on top of the personnel carriers, with blood on the side.

It made the *New York Times.* When I came back, I pulled it up on microfiche.

FOE INVADES G.I.S' BUNKERS AT BASE, BUT IS HURLED BACK.
By the Associated Press.

SAIGON, South Vietnam, Friday, July 5—American infantrymen, joined by cooks, clerks and drivers in close-quarters fighting, hurled back an attack on a major United States base camp yesterday, turning small arms and machine guns on enemy commandos who advanced into their bunkers.

The assault on the Twenty-fifth Infantry Division's base camp at Dau Tieng, about 40 miles northwest of Saigon, began with a 500-round barrage of mortars and rockets.

We used to count rockets and stuff when they'd come in at night; almost every night you'd get some rounds. Usually you'd get up to ten or fifteen. If it got up as high as twenty, you'd say, "Bad night." This was five hundred rounds. We knew we were fucked.

Daylight came, and the attack wound down. Several hours later they took the rifles of our dead and stuck them in the ground by the bayonets. They put the helmets on top of the butt and the boots in front. It was an eerie sight.

They played taps. I think the colonel said something. He was an idiot. He spent the whole thing up in the air in an observation helicopter. We heard later that he had his ass reamed. I don't know, maybe the colonel did what he did because a general somewhere told him to do it. But he was in command at that base. Those units weren't there.

The dead enemy soldiers found inside—there were ten—got scraped out and bulldozed somewhere. One image from that morning I remember: I was looking at a VC. He couldn't have been more than fifteen, sixteen years old. He was lying on his back in a drainage ditch, just wearing the black shorts and sandals. He didn't look like he had been wounded. He looked like a kid sleeping.

There was a bullet wound right in his thigh. It was probably a spent round because it didn't tear the flesh apart. It must've hit the femoral artery, and he just bled to death.

That was worse than the bodies that were blown apart. Because it was apparent he was just a kid. *We* were just kids.

The bodies that were blown apart didn't look real. You could look at those, and, as gruesome as they were, they didn't look real. They didn't look like people. But except for that one hole in his thigh, this kid was intact. He looked like a kid sleeping. This was the worst one, and it didn't matter that he was a VC.

The kid shouldn't have been dead. He was attacking us, and we had to defend ourselves. I can justify that. But my whole feeling about the war eventually came to, we shouldn't have been there, so he shouldn't have had to attack. And we shouldn't have had to kill him.

How do you kill a fifteen-year-old kid for your country? You might have to do it to defend yourself, but how do you do it for your country? And I'm assuming this kid was a combatant. He was inside our wire, he was a sapper.

I had no idea how many people I might've directly or indirectly killed. In that situation you just put up a wall of fire. And occasionally, in the flares being fired, you'd see someone drop. Did you hit him? Did the guy next to you hit him? You really didn't know.

One thing I used to do was go up to what we called the North Pole. That was the code name for the place in the Dau Tieng camp where we did the rearm and refuel for the choppers supporting the Twenty-fifth Division. During firefights the gunships would come in when they needed to be reloaded. We'd load them, they'd go back out.

Did I kill the people that those rockets were fired on? I didn't pull the trigger. It's the age-old question: Where do you stop the responsibility? Is it back in the munitions factory where it was made—in Kansas City or wherever? I think that seeing the effects of the weapons, even if you weren't the one to do the actual killing, makes you feel responsible in a way that you don't if you're apart from it.

Did I pull the trigger that killed this kid? Probably not. He was on another part of the wire. Did I feel later as I gnawed on it that I had some responsibility for it? Yeah, I did. Did I feel more that my government had responsibility for it, for setting this whole thing up and sending me there in the first place? Yeah, but I was stupid enough to volunteer. Where does the responsibility lie?

One thing that I don't do is say I had no responsibility. I won't do that. If our government and our military were wrong in Vietnam, I have to share that. I was there of my own free will. They'd given me orders to Germany.

So did I kill that kid? Yeah.

PERRY POLLINS

LEXINGTON, MASSACHUSETTS
CORPORAL, UNITED STATES MARINE CORPS, WORLD WAR II

The Japanese defenders of Peleliu did not end their resistance until November 25, 1944, more than two months after Marines first landed on the island's shores. Some ten thousand Japanese and two thousand Americans were killed in the fight for Peleliu.

When I first went overseas, I met guys who had been at Guadalcanal—the Marines had landed there on August 7, 1942. These were gutsy guys—top-rate, hardworking, diligent people—and they taught us to hate the Japs like there was no tomorrow. And when you went into action, the Japs were terrible people. They were absolutely terrible people. They mutilated our dead. People don't know. When we couldn't get to our dead, they frequently would cut off the penis of the dead man and stick it in his mouth.

The Japanese were savages. They were complete, utter savages. You meet them today and they're calm and they're collected and they're well educated and they're bright.

But back in those days, the soldiers in the field were monsters.

I didn't engage in actual hand-to-hand combat with them. The only time I got near a Jap was once when six or seven of them charged us on the beach at Peleliu. This was after we'd advanced inland. I just happened to be on the beach to pick up some water, because we were running out.

It turned into almost a brawl. And one Japanese soldier went by me, and he caught me in my ribs with the hilt of his bayonet, and he opened a gash, and I fell down. And then Freddie Cohen bashed this Jap's head in with the butt of his M-1.

In war, if you don't kill them, they're gonna kill you. So if someone's going to kill me or kill my friends, there's no doubt in my mind I'll kill them first. And I'm not a killer—I mean, I'm not an instinctive killer. I want to save my life, and I want to save the lives of my friends. The sanctity of life is based on protecting your own life. If you didn't, that would be suicide.

I put myself in the position I was in back then. That brawl on the beach was about survival, for the love of Pete.

These bastards are trying to kill us. Kill the bastards. Kill them.

ED JACKSON

Tipp City, Ohio

Staff Sergeant, United States Army Air Forces, World War II

I had three "probables"—German fighter planes I might've shot down. At the time you have no idea whether you really have shot that plane down or not. You can see your tracers going out there and looking like they're going right into the plane. But there's a whole bunch of guys shooting at the same plane you are. When you're in a bomber formation like that, with all that many planes around you and all that many guns shooting at people, the only way you could really tell if you shot one down is if he was coming right at you, and you was shooting at him, and he exploded. But even then there could be other guys shooting at him from some plane that you didn't even know about.

So there was three times that I thought I had shot down planes, but I never really knew for sure. And now that I'm older, I hope I didn't. I wouldn't want to kill nobody.

I like to think that I didn't. At the time you're just trying to protect your plane, your crew, and yourself—you know it's either you kill them or they kill you. And you're doing what you're trained to do. But years later you look back at it and you hope you didn't kill anyone, because most of them Germans were forced to do what they did. If they didn't serve in their military, the Nazis would have probably shot them.

I'm sure that everybody don't look at it that way. Some people probably enjoy killing. I never did.

MIKE JACKSON

Tipp City, Ohio

Captain, United States Air Force, Vietnam

A lot changed between the first person I killed and the second. To kill somebody is a pretty big step. It's what you're trained to do, but when you actually do it, it's something different. It was a hard thing to carry home. It never leaves your mind, ever. Ever.

After we'd do an air strike, we'd go in and we'd say this is the damage that was done. It's called bomb damage assessment—BDA. We'd say there were *x* number of people killed, *x* number of weapons destroyed, *x* number of secondary explosions. We had to count all that.

The first few air strikes, I never really saw anything. You get a report that there's something on the ground, and you bomb it, but you never really see anything in the jungle.

Then came a mission where I saw twenty to twenty-five guys on the ground hauling rockets and other supplies, and I called for air strikes. We went in and bombed 'em, and I killed one of 'em. I didn't drop the bomb, but I'm the one that said, "Get him." I'm the one that said, "Cleared and hot." It just tore me up.

To start with, there wasn't a whole body there. War is not nearly as neat as you see in the movies. When you shoot somebody, it doesn't make a nice little hole and they grab their chest and fall over. You shoot somebody and it can take their whole chest off, or their head, or their legs.

I saw what was left of this one guy, and I felt awful. I went to Vietnam a little Catholic altar boy. My understanding was, "If you leave me alone, I'll leave you alone. I just want to go home. That's all I want to do—in a year I want to go home." So I killed a guy. I couldn't sleep. I just felt terrible.

That lasted about a day. The next night we got rocketed, big time. I'm laying under the bed scared to death that I'm gonna get killed, and I say, "Okay, if that's the way it's gonna be, that's the way it's gonna be. You're gonna try to kill me, so it's fair for me to try to kill you." From that point on, it changed. If they hadn't rocketed me, I don't know if I would have ever shaken that off. I guess I would've, but the rocketing helped.

In hindsight it was probably a good thing to have happen, to know that somebody was trying to kill me, because up to that point I hadn't seen anybody shooting at me. I did later, but until now it was just, I see somebody and I bomb him. It took the reality of what the dead guy and his buddies were hauling—rockets, which is what they were now using against me—to change my state of mind.

After that I was okay. The next air strike, there were four or five bodies, and I didn't feel quite as bad. I don't know if that's a good thing or a bad thing, but it's a survivable thing. I don't wake up in the middle of the night screaming about it, because they'd just as soon have shot me as I would them.

Even the Catholic Church says in a war you're allowed to kill for your country and for your own survival. So from then on, I honestly did not have a problem with the morality of it. Sometimes I wonder. I've become much more pacifist as I've gotten older. I don't see a reason to kill people; I think there's got to be another way around it. But at the time I didn't have a problem with it.

It's a terrible thing, it really is, when you stop and think about it, that you can reduce a human life to me or him. To this day I probably don't value other people's lives as much as I should. Heaven help somebody who messes with my family or my friends, because I've killed 125 people. One more isn't gonna hurt. I think that's what some of the problems of Vietnam veterans relate to—you've done it once. It kind of takes the stigma away from it. Not that that's a good thing, but I think that's what happens.

A hundred and twenty-five is what I counted when I took all the BDAs that I had and added them up. It may have been more, it may have been less. Who knows how many bodies I didn't see? Who knows how many I counted that were dead before I had anything to do with them? I don't know, but that's what it added up to from the BDAs.

I don't have those sheets anymore. Decided I didn't want to know, so I threw them out.

Catholic altar boy.

DAVE POLLINS

LEXINGTON, MASSACHUSETTS

LANCE CORPORAL, UNITED STATES MARINE CORPS, VIETNAM

I have to admit, after some time in Vietnam, my attitude changed a little bit. I kept saying, "Why are we here?" My feeling was, they let the politicians and big business run that war; they should have left it up to the generals.

There was one hill there—Hill 102, 105, something like that; they numbered them for their elevation in meters. They told us we're going up there to get Charlie off, because Charlie's shooting rockets at us. Charlie's shooting RPGs. Charlie's shooting mortars.

We took it within a day. We lost—I want to say maybe twelve, fourteen guys. Probably we killed about thirty-five or forty of them. A lot of them got away, too.

We held it for two weeks. Then they said, "We don't need it anymore. Get off of it." Within days Charlie's doing the same thing again—shooting at us from that hill. Two months later they told us to go back and retake it.

I was always under the impression that in a war it takes men to occupy a space. You take land, you hold land. You go after the enemy. That goes back to Napoleon's time.

It should have been: You mass your troops, you keep bombing. Charlie could come down through the DMZ. He could come down through Laos and Cambodia on the Ho Chi Minh Trail and then into 'Nam, but we couldn't.

We'd send Special Ops into Laos and Cambodia and ambush the trail. But you want to play that game? Put a couple hundred thousand guys there. Go into North Vietnam. We were bombing the hell out of 'em; then we stopped the bombing. It's like Custer's last stand: "Custer, you're gonna sit down here in this little valley while all the Indians ride down upon you."

It's a war. People are dying. People are getting killed. For what?

I'd never get that question answered. Why did we take it, hold it, and then get off of it?

SONNY DUNBAR

ALBANY, NEW YORK
SERGEANT, UNITED STATES ARMY, WORLD WAR II

After training as a stevedore, Sonny shipped out from the West Coast. His first stop was New Guinea.

The place where we lived was in a jungle, and you'd slosh around in the mud because of all the rain.

That's where I unloaded the ship with the bodies.

They brought a ship into the dock that was torpedoed, and a lot of men were killed on the ship. We had to go unload the corpses that had been floating in the water in the hold. The bodies were in bags when I got on the scene, and we had to put them on the winches. What I remember is the smell of the decomposing bodies.

The way I saw combat was not as fully as my son saw it. I was in a port outfit. I didn't have a gun in my hand to shoot somebody or be confronted with somebody, but the point is, I was under fire, I experienced it.

Once, after my battalion was taken to the Philippines, they took us to unload ships in some islands that were close by. They had just invaded the day before, and we came to drop more ammunition and whatever needs that they had. This was a day trip to go to unload these ships and then go back. That was when I had my baptism by fire.

I was on this landing craft, and was coming out of one of the hatches, when a gun went off above me, the big gun. I said, "Damn! What is this about?" At that time a Japanese plane was coming down the beach strafing, and the people on board were firing at him. And I watched the plane come down the beach, and all these guns shooting at him—shooting, shooting, shooting. I said, "Damn, these cats can't shoot." They didn't catch the sucker until he banked up to make a return. *Bam!* That's when they got him.

You have your background, your experience, your family, what you've been taught, what you've learned—and then to be confronted with that type of violence, you never get over it.

It's very hard to talk about this to people who haven't experienced it. You can look at someone and see: If a person has felt it, then they understand what I'm talking about. And not particularly the words that I put out—they can feel the feeling and the energies that come out of me. But if I'm dealing with somebody else that has never experienced that kind of thing, I can't converse with you. You don't know what path I'm walking unless you walked that path.

JOHN HOWE

Albany, New York
Staff Sergeant, United States Army, Vietnam

My biological father went to Evander Childs High School, in the city, and then went off to war, a young man full of vim and vigor.

He and my mother were married in '41 or '42, but they separated in 1947 or so, when I was less than two years old. What happened was the war. War changes you, and based upon what I was told by my father and my mother and by those people who were around, it just made my father unbearable; the things he had seen had changed his personality so very much. He was just a kid.

He was in a number of Army units. The one that stands out is the 761st Tank Battalion, a black combat unit. He was what they call an armored infantryman, one of the guys assigned to secure the tanks.

He told me that two things most influenced him in the course of the war. One was the D-Day landing. This was before he joined the 761st; he was there with the Fourth Infantry Division in a noncombat capacity. He was in the second wave—he came ashore at seven, eight o'clock in the morning.

The other thing was the thrust that they made to free the people who were in the death camps.

He told me that war was something horrendous. He said that taking a human life was something not to be taken lightly. But he said that he would have rather seen a hundred Germans and GIs fighting than enter the camps. He said that that was the milestone that changed his life. He talked about the evidence of human depravity he saw—people who had uncontrollable outlet of their bowels, people who had no teeth, with bleeding gums, people so emaciated that they were just skeletons.

My aunt, his sister, told me how he cried about that when he came home. He just cried all the time. Just because of the sheer inhumanity and the brutality of what he saw. He was a very humane person. They called him Pinky when he was a kid. He was a comedian. He was the class clown. He was a guy that was full of life.

It wasn't battle fatigue that he had—he didn't suffer from that. No, he had what's called "the thousand-yard stare." You find that most guys who are in close combat end up with that at some point in time. In Vietnam we called it "the look." You can see it. You find guys who claimed they did certain things, and if you were in combat infantry, you can see if they got the look. If you don't see it, you can say, "He wasn't shit, he wasn't there." I know a guy named José Ramos, who is a combat medic from Vietnam. Combat medics in particular have the look—they have this propensity for absorbing the pain around them.

My father-in-law, William Walker Jr., fought at the Battle of the Bulge. He was a heck of a guy. A big strapping fellow. And one day we were sitting in his backyard. Now, you have got to understand, my wife's sisters are very strong-willed, and so they said, "What are you talking to Daddy about?"

I said, "None of your business."

"What are you talk—"

"We were talking about the war."

"No, Daddy never talks about the war. Daddy doesn't talk to anybody."

"Well, he talked to me."

You recognize that character, that quality, in someone who has been there and who has seen the shit. They've experienced that baptism of fire. And it doesn't necessarily have to be infantrymen; everybody got shelled in Vietnam, everybody got rocketed. Still, the experience was particularly powerful when it was up close and personal. Very rarely did you have somebody run up in your face with a hand grenade if you weren't in the infantry. I was in the infantry, and it was up close and personal.

War affects a family as a whole. It affects the children, it affects whoever you touch. My kids could tell you stories. I couldn't go to fireworks displays for years because of the sounds—or more so the smell. When the smoke comes down and the cordite settles, it smells just like an artillery duel. Particularly on a hot, muggy night—that's a throwback of memory. The one thing that's missing in all these movies that you see about war, regardless of how good the special effects are, is the smell.

Now, I had a habit of pissing people off, and I had a first sergeant that I pissed off real bad once. I love to take pictures, and so I always had a camera with me. One time we were getting the shit kicked out of us. And F-100 Super Sabres are coming right over our heads, dropping napalm, maybe two hundred meters in front of us. When napalm comes in, you lay on the ground and you feel the heat—it feels like a mini–atom bomb. So I pop up and see this big ball of flame, and I start clicking my camera. And my first sergeant says, "Oh, you wanna take pictures, huh? You and your other two buddies come on over here with me, young Sergeant." That's when I got my first experience with a grappling hook. There was a stack of bodies that had been wiped out by, I guess, Third Platoon. He gave me the grappling hook and says, "Okay, you bury 'em. Take pictures of that, motherfucker." He was a real prick.

That wasn't the last time I used a grappling hook. After a battle we'd throw the grappling hook out and drag the bodies, because 90 percent of the time you had fear of a booby trap—a grenade planted underneath a body, or a trip wire. These were mostly dead enemy soldiers, but if a GI was left out there, we'd have to do the same thing.

My stepdad unloaded bodies off a ship. My biological father pulled bodies out of the water on D-Day. And through my experience of seeing four hundred or five hundred human bodies in a heap, with lines thrown over them and with them decomposing in 120-degree sun, I could imagine: What would it have been like to go into those concentration camps?

The smell of dead bodies is a sweet, putrid stench. It's full of urine, ammonia, crap—it's all blended together. And as the little animals come by and the sun heats up and the humidity rises, the bodies burst. And the bodies make sounds—gases are escaping, methane.

And the agonizing look on people's faces in terms of their last living memory. Their faces freeze in a contortion. You look at something like that and it stays with you.

You always go through the pockets of the dead—that's how you gather intelligence. You look at the pictures of them with their girlfriends, and letters from their family. Wallets. Money. I'd imagine that somebody someday would be going through *my* pockets. Finding a picture of *my* family. Taking *my* money. It was a fucking horrible experience.

GREG CAMP

Columbus, Georgia
Captain, United States Army, Vietnam

Beginning on April 30, 1970, fifty thousand ARVN troops joined thirty thousand Americans in an invasion of Cambodia. Aimed primarily at NVA/Vietcong sanctuaries in that country, the operation was limited in scope: It focused on only two areas of Cambodia, the Parrot's Beak and the Fishhook; ARVN troops were restricted to only sixty kilometers inside the border, Americans to thirty; the American part in the operation would end on June 30.

U.S. and ARVN troops in Cambodia captured ten times more Communist matériel than they'd taken within the borders of Vietnam the previous year. And, if official totals can be believed, they killed over eleven thousand enemy soldiers at a cost of fewer than one thousand of their own.

No American outfit played a more active role in the invasion of Cambodia than the First Cavalry Division. Greg, by this time, served as one of its company commanders.

Probably two or three days before I left to come home, we found a huge cache of rice in Cambodia—literally tons of it. We carved out a little landing zone to haul the rice out and send it back to the South Vietnamese.

Another company used the landing zone to come in and then went on down into the jungle a bit. And they hadn't gotten very far from us at all when we heard an explosion—the NVA had set off a claymore mine. We were in radio contact with this company. The mine wounded a couple of guys, one seriously.

He was hit right after it got dark, seven or eight o'clock at night, and by this time a monsoon had come up. They were in deep, deep canopy jungle, so they couldn't get a helicopter in there to medevac this guy. It was just pouring down rain.

Where I was, inside our defensive perimeter, we had a little headquarters, like a little hooch—we had big bags of rice all around us like sandbags. I had the medic with me and the radio telephone operator, and so I called to have the wounded man brought over to us. We had our LZ there—just a little hole in the triple-canopy jungle—and I called for a medevac helicopter.

The other company's commander was a classmate of mine, Doug McKenna, and he sent a small patrol out to carry the wounded soldier to our position. Even though we were only a couple hundred yards away, it took them two or three hours to reach us, because they got completely and totally lost. It was so dark, and conditions were so bad, I violated everything I ever learned about security to try to guide the patrol to us. We started out by firing rounds in the air so they could home in on us, but they couldn't hear them through the rain. So we started popping flares so they could try to see us. These are all things that you don't want to do, because you don't want to give your position away. As they got closer, we banged steel pots together.

When they finally reached us, the wounded man was unconscious. He was pockmarked from head to toe. No big gouges, just pockmarked from head to toe. I was on the radio trying to guide the helicopter in.

I think the pilot came there thinking he would land, but by the time he got on station, he realized there was no way he'd be able to negotiate this little landing zone. And that's when we went to the idea, "Let's try a jungle penetrator."

A jungle penetrator was a type of litter that would be dropped down from a hovering helicopter—you would put somebody in it, and they'd pull him back up. But this was one of the worst storms I saw the whole time I was there. It was really, really windy, rainy, stormy, and the helicopter was just bouncing around in the air. The pilot was almost in tears that he couldn't stabilize the helicopter enough to be able to let down the jungle penetrator. He made a valiant, valiant effort; he tried and he tried.

Finally he left, and we sat there and watched the life ooze out of this poor young soldier, little pockmark by little pockmark by little pockmark. He lay in my lap until he died, at two or three A.M.

When they'd brought him to us, he had lost enough blood that he was unconscious, but he was alive. Nobody thought he was gonna die. There was no reason for him to die. All he needed was blood. But our medic had only a little medic bag, with a little bit of plasma, and this young soldier was oozing blood faster than the plasma kit could supply it. And we could not get a helicopter in there.

When the doc said he was gone, we put a poncho over him. I

kept him in my lap until the next morning, when they took him away.

I never knew the young man. I never saw him until he showed up in my lap the night that he died. He wasn't in my company, he was in Doug's company. Doug and I, we relive this story every five years when we go back to a reunion. Invariably it'll come up in some conversation we'll have, and we'll lament on how badly we feel that we lost this young soldier. Doug wasn't with us when he died. He'd stayed with the rest of his company while the small patrol carried the guy to me. I think it weighs heavily on his mind that the young soldier died and he wasn't there. But I don't think there's anything else that either one of us could've done.

This soldier's death comes back to me from time to time. I wonder what he would have done, I wonder what he would have made of his life. I didn't know him, but you just wonder, "Would he have gotten married? Would he have had kids?"

I don't know what his parents know about how he died. He didn't die in agony; he was unconscious, so he just slipped away. But if I were a parent and knew that the only reason he died is circumstances . . . That kind of an injury was 99 percent "You're gonna live through this."

In fact, I had a guy six months earlier who had the exact same thing happen—the exact same thing, looked exactly like him. A platoon sergeant. Got hit with a claymore mine. We put him on a helicopter, sent him back. They pumped him full of blood, let all his wounds heal, and he was back in the field within a month. He's probably still got shrapnel coming out of the pores of his skin, but it was not really a serious injury.

The soldier who died that night was about nineteen. I knew his name for a long time. I don't anymore.

XV

"They had plenty of courage."

ENEMIES AND ALLIES

While postwar revelations of genocide have cast the Nazi regime as more malevolent than its Japanese Axis partner—although forces of the Japanese Empire certainly committed their own atrocities, especially in China—during the war Americans serving in the Pacific harbored a contempt for the average Japanese soldier far more visceral than the feeling most of their counterparts in Europe held for the men wearing the uniform of the Third Reich. This is not to minimize the bitterness of the contest in Western Europe—men were, after all, trying to kill one another. But it's hard to imagine battle-weary GIs in France imparting to newly arrived comrades a lesson like the one Perry Pollins and his friends, upon their arrival in the Pacific, learned from combat-scarred Marines: "[T]hey taught us to hate the Japs like there was no tomorrow." Likewise, it was the rare island-hopping Marine who viewed his enemy as charitably as Al Tarbell looked upon his: "The German soldier was my enemy. But I didn't have nothing against him."

American fighting men in Vietnam bore little love toward the men they were charged with killing—engaged in combat, few found time to look at a dead Vietcong or NVA soldier and say, as Whitman did, "[A] man divine as myself is dead." But Americans respected the resourcefulness and courage of an enemy fighting a technologically superior foe.

Indeed, many, if not most, Americans fighting in Vietnam held greater respect for their enemy than for their allies, the troops of the Saigon government. Where the enemy was brave, the ally was timid; the enemy relentless, the ally lazy; the enemy selfless, the ally corrupt. American GIs in Europe often derided the caution—and the tea-drinking—of their British allies, but rarely with the scorn many veterans of Southeast Asia still reveal when speaking of the South Vietnamese. Mickey Hutchins, on the other hand, who for a year fought side by side with South Vietnamese soldiers, found that they "demonstrated exactly the same range of competence, proficiency, and commitment in their ranks that we exhibited in our own."

In the Vietnam War, the United States had chosen to ally itself with a government struggling to establish its legitimacy and exert its authority, whereas in World War II, America's two main allies were well-established nation-states. But in that conflict America made common cause as well with people throughout occupied Europe—with organized partisans who resisted Nazi rule by force of arms, and with brave citizens whose potent weapon may have been a radio tuned to the BBC.

ED JACKSON

Tipp City, Ohio
Staff Sergeant, United States Army Air Forces,
World War II

On July 12, 1944, on a mission over a marshaling yard in France, Ed was wounded. "A piece of flak went through the plane and it cut the hose to the other waist gunner's oxygen mask, then it went through my upper left arm. It tore out a lot of muscle."

Ed spent more than two weeks in the hospital recuperating.

It wasn't that long after I got out of the hospital when I started flying again. I still had the bandage on my arm on August 7, when we were going up to Blechhammer, Germany, to hit the synthetic oil plant there.

Just as we was about ready to go to the target, we got hit with flak, and it knocked one of the engines out. We went ahead and dropped our bombs and started back, but we couldn't keep up with the formation. So we were left by ourselves back there, and when you're a straggler like that, that's when all the German planes come in after you and put their guns on you, which is what they did.

I got hit with probably a twenty-millimeter shell. It hit the ship and made a big hole in it close to where I was standing, and the shrapnel went into my right arm.

The bombardier come back and gave me first aid. I begged him not to give me any morphine, but he did anyways because of the pain. I was bleeding like a stuck pig, so he put a tourniquet on me.

The pilot, Donald Amann, wanted everybody except me to go up into the forward part of the plane to start jettisoning stuff. But they left the other waist gunner and the ball-turret gunner back there to look out for me.

These two guys started acting suspicious; I didn't know what the heck was going on. The plane was losing altitude fast, like it was gonna crash. We were too far back in the plane to see the flight deck, and the intercom wasn't working, so they assumed that everyone up front had bailed out. They figured that the alarm bell had been rung but that we hadn't heard it, because it was broken, too. Finally they came over to me and told me the plane was crashing, and they wanted to know if I could pull that rip cord. I said, "Yep, if you put my hand on it, I can pull it."

When I went through gunnery school, I was trained that if you ever had to bail out of a plane, you took your GI shoes with you. I bet there wasn't one in a hundred that did that, but it was just automatic for me. So I grabbed them GI shoes with my left hand, and they put my right hand on the rip cord, and I bailed out the escape hatch. We were always taught that when you bailed out, you ought to count to ten before you pull the rip cord, so that you don't get snagged on the plane. But I don't remember ever counting to ten. I just bailed out, and I guess God took care of it from there.

Anyways, my chute opened and I went down fast, and I seen all these people that had formed a big circle. It looked like there was maybe fifty or sixty of 'em—men and women and old people and children and everything. And they all had some kind of a gun, and the guns were pointed at me.

When I landed, the chute was dragging me on the ground, and these people were running along with the chute. And I'm yelling, "*Americano! Americano!*" I didn't know whether they knew what I meant or not.

Finally they helped get the chute under control. They tore a piece of it out, made me a sling, put me up on an old mule, and took me into a town. I didn't know where the other guys were—because of the clouds, I never saw them bail out. When I got into this little town, I heard somebody yell, "Hey, Jackson!" Who in the heck?

Well, it was the ball-turret gunner, a guy by the name of Hiram Whitener—we called him Whitey. He's still alive, lives out in Wheeler, Texas. They had him locked up in a second-floor storeroom. They didn't know who we were or why we were there. They took me and put me up there with Whitey. I said to him, "Where in the heck are we?"

He said, "I don't know. There's supposed to be an interrogator to come and talk to us sometime tonight."

Later that night an interrogator did come in, and he talked to us—he could speak English—and told us that we were in Yugoslavia, and that we were with Marshal Tito's underground.

We felt pretty good about not being captured. I found out after I got back to the States that the plane had crash-landed—the reason they didn't just bail out is that they didn't think I'd be able to pull my rip cord. After they landed, they destroyed the plane with their flare guns. The Germans saw the fire and captured them, and they were prisoners until the war ended.

Anyways, they picked up the other waist gunner, Willie Hunt, about a day later, and then they put the three of us on mules and moved us out of there. Eventually we ended up at a camp where there was an American captain, who was a liaison officer, and an English radio operator. They was over there to help them get supplies, number one, and, number two, to help get airmen that was there out of the country.

Willie Hunt was the oldest person on the crew—maybe twenty-six, twenty-seven years old. He was from up in New England somewhere, and he was a real chain-smoker. You know how dangerous it is to be smoking around oxygen. Well, when we was flying combat, he'd light a cigarette and take his oxygen mask off and take a puff. And just keep doing that. The guy just smoked constantly. He like to went nuts over there when he was missing in action, because he didn't have any cigarettes. And neither of those guys had their GI shoes with them.

That got to be a joke after we got back to the States and met years later. The wives got a big kick out of that. I'm the guy that only had one good hand, and I came down with my GI shoes in one hand and the rip cord in the other. They had to walk in their heated shoes.

While I was with the partisans, I was more concerned with my wound than anything else. I kept thinking I was gonna lose my arm or get gangrene and die because my arm swelled up and it hurt so bad, and I wasn't getting any first aid.

As far as conditions, there wasn't anything to eat. It was occupied territory, and the Germans took everything. All there was to eat was stuff that the Germans didn't want—maybe a sheep or a goat that had some kind of a disease. They could kill that and make a soup out of it. Well, it was August, and it was real hot, and the flies was like our horseflies over here—great big flies, and they would land in that soup. By the time they brought you a bowl of the stuff, it would be cold, and you'd have to pick the flies off and eat it.

I couldn't eat hardly anything for at least a week because my mouth was sore—when I bailed out, I hit it on the side of the escape hatch. But then eventually I got so I could eat, and I'd even try to con the other guys out of their food, saying, "You ain't gonna eat that. It's a dead animal, and it's got flies in it." And they give you a piece of hard black bread—it was so daggone hard it would last you all day.

We were missing in action about six weeks. One day there was some C-47s that landed in a cornfield pretty close to where we were. We raced down there and got in; they took a bunch of wounded partisans on the planes also. We went to Bari, Italy, and then they put me in an ambulance and took me to the hospital there. I was in the hospital for just one night. They said that there was no point in trying to get the shrapnel out of my arm. It had healed over by that time and there were so many little pieces that they just left everything like it was. And if I ever had any trouble with it, well, they could take it out somewhere down the line.

I still got about twenty-two pieces in that arm. The only piece that ever really bothered me was the piece in my wrist—you can see it move when I open and close my hand. When I'd work at little things like just to trim around the sidewalks with these little hand trimmers, it felt funny in there. But the doctors said that if they did anything, there was a possibility that I'd have stiff fingers, and I thought, "No way. I'm not gonna have them do anything if it'll make me so I can't use my hand."

Another thing in Yugoslavia, we got ate up with lice and bugs and everything else. So when we got back to Italy, all of us had to be deloused. We had to take all our clothes off, and they burned them up. Then they sprayed us with some kind of a delousing chemical, and you had to stand there for, like, ten minutes with it, and it just burned like fire. Then you could go in and shower it off and put on clean clothes. It was a mess.

GENE CAMP
San Antonio, Texas
Captain, United States Army, World War II
Major, United States Army, Vietnam

After World War II, Gene stayed in the Army, moving from artillery to infantry. In 1958, after assignments in Texas, Europe, and Kansas, he received orders for Vietnam. It was, in military parlance, a "hardship tour"—an overseas assignment, unaccompanied by family.

At that time Vietnam was unknown to most people. When I got these orders, people were saying, "You're going to Vietnam? Where is Vietnam?"

And I'd say, "Have you heard of French Indochina?"

"I think so."

"Well, that's Vietnam."

I was an adviser there to the Vietnamese army's command and general staff college in Saigon. Most of my advice to them was in how to set up lesson plans and classrooms—the logistics of running the thing, not the curriculum content.

Saigon was a big, beautiful city. The French were all gone, and we had not yet displaced them. We lived in a hotel that had been converted to a faculty-officer quarters. You could go to town in Saigon and walk around and go to a bar and never see another American.

Things were very peaceful. I drove in a jeep one time all over the Michelin plantation and down to the Cao Dai Temple, by myself, unarmed. No problem at all. Later some of the biggest battles of the war were fought in there. Went duck hunting on the Saigon River. It wasn't a bad year, except for missing my family. The kids were in formative stages—our daughter was going to her first prom, Greg was playing Little League.

There were only six hundred or so American advisers in the

whole country, and most of those were logistics or technical types—how to make uniforms, how to run a supply depot, how to maintain vehicles, how to keep records. It was not an emphasis on combat, although we did have some advisers with combat units.

To get a little pin money, I taught English two or three nights a week down at the Vietnamese-American Association, which was actually run by USIS, the United States Information Service. I had the advanced students, and I was teaching English grammar. I was usually just about one chapter ahead of them, because our grammar is not easy.

I made one very good friend, a Vietnamese officer, Colonel Lam Ngoc Huan. In my spare time, I taught his wife English. He wanted to pay me, and I wouldn't let him. She would fix a different kind of tea every time I'd come to teach her.

Colonel Huan kidded me two or three times, saying, "Your son, he'll be over here someday helping us." But he didn't mean in the role that Greg ended up playing over there. It was that they would have American advisers and they would hack this on their own. And they fully intended to. They didn't want us or feel that they needed us. And I think if we had kept our noses out of there, they might not have.

They had several problems while I was there—insurrections or terrorists. And when they had a problem someplace, they would seal the area off and their troops would go in and take care of it. Our advisers were never permitted to go with them. I don't know what they did; they may have gone in and slaughtered some people. But once they withdrew, there were no more problems in that area. Of course, our State Department was horrified as to what might or might not have happened when they would use their strong-arm tactics. If we'd let them run the show, I think they might have been able to pull it off.

Colonel Huan had two beautiful daughters, and they both married Vietnamese officers. They were involved in an unsuccessful coup, and although my friend was not involved, they ushered him out of the army on family association alone. He ended up as the manager of the Caravelle Hotel when it first opened. That's where all the foreign newsmen stayed.

Sometime during the sixties, I found out that he had been assassinated. I felt terrible. He was such a fine, intelligent man, with a lovely wife and family. And he was pro-West, of course. I have no idea why he was assassinated, but he was.

Got home in '59, and spent four glorious years at Fort Riley, Kansas, with the First Infantry Division, the Big Red One. And then in '63 I went to Washington, to the Pentagon, where I would stay four years in the office of the deputy chief of staff for personnel.

The war was escalating rapidly, and at the Pentagon we were doing everything we could to support the effort.

I don't recall many people there at that time saying we ought to get out or that we can't win. But I did hear "If we do it my way" or "This is wrong" or "We're getting too much guidance from the White House." A lot of frustration. On the other hand, there were a lot of people in the Pentagon who just couldn't wait to get to Vietnam to get their ticket punched, so that they could say, "I served in Vietnam."

While I was there, you could see the antiwar, antimilitary stuff building up. We said, "Look, we're in this thing, and we've got to support it, and we've got to do our best." It was tormenting to hear everybody getting on their stump and damning this and damning that. I thought, "What's it doing to our soldiers over there? Instead of being privileged like I was to have the whole nation behind me a hundred percent, here these fellas are over there fighting, they're dying, and the people back here are protesting and making speeches and running to Canada." We weren't getting a fair shake from the media either, which were almost all against us. To us who were involved in the military, it was, to say the least, disgusting.

When Greg was in Vietnam, we worried terribly about him. Knowing how gung ho and conscientious he is, I knew he would never shirk anything. If he thought it was his responsibility—his men out there and something he needed to do—he would do it, regardless of his personal safety.

At the same time Greg was there, my son-in-law and a nephew were also there, so you can imagine my reaction to all the liberals barking and carrying on. If you're not gonna support the thing, then let's declare defeat and pull out. Let's don't keep having our men slaughtered while we're arguing about it.

GREG CAMP

COLUMBUS, GEORGIA
CAPTAIN, UNITED STATES ARMY, VIETNAM

Five days before the fall of Saigon in 1975, an American colonel, Harry G. Summers, said to a North Vietnamese colonel, "You know you never defeated us on the battlefield."

The North Vietnamese colonel thought for a moment, then answered, "That may be so, but it is also irrelevant."

When I was in Vietnam, I believed I was doing something that was noble. And I still believed we could win the war. Of course, I was a pretty low-level guy there. But we never lost a fight. I either wasn't old enough or hadn't read enough to realize that that wasn't important, that there was a much more strategic-level battle being fought there, and that we were losing it.

I was not involved in any big, knock-down, drag-out fights. All of my contacts, by almost any standard, were small and of short duration. They were scary nevertheless. But the big battles, like LZ X-Ray, had all come and gone by the time I got there. By then I think the North Vietnamese had realized that when they did an LZ X-Ray, they'd lose a thousand soldiers. But they could have a thousand battles with guys like me, losing a soldier here and a soldier there, and sustain the war for another year with minimal casualties.

The thought of the North Vietnamese was "The American people won't put up with this forever. All I have to do is hang on. I don't have to win a single battle, don't have to win a single skirmish, don't have to win anything. I just have to not give up. If I don't give up, they will." And in essence that's what happened. They didn't give up, and we did.

MICKEY HUTCHINS

CONCORD, NORTH CAROLINA
FIRST LIEUTENANT, UNITED STATES ARMY, VIETNAM

At Special Warfare school in Fort Bragg, about 50 percent of our time was spent in language class. At Fort Bliss we were in language class eight hours a day, five days a week.

I was able to communicate over there reasonably well, but I still needed an interpreter. Ho Van Tu was his name, a Vietnamese corporal. He was a super guy. Loved to play cards, had no poker face whatsoever. Couldn't hide his hand to save him. He saved *me* at least once that I know of. We were out in the paddies, and I was about ready to step on a dike when he grabbed me and pulled me back and said, "Don't go up there."

And I said, "Why not?"

"Look, there's grass."

"Well, it's a paddy dike—there's grass."

"No, look at the other paddy dikes." And I looked at the others, and sure enough, there was no grass on them. "The locals know that that one's booby-trapped, and they don't walk on it, and you don't walk on it either." So I hung in there with him. He kept an eye out for me.

One of my biggest regrets of Vietnam is that I was never able to find what happened to him afterward. In the early eighties, I organized a committee in my church to conduct a refugee-resettlement program. I was trying to resettle Vietnamese, but I ended up resettling an entire extended family of Laotians. I knew that Tu had a wife and a child in Saigon. I would have loved to have gotten them all back to the States. I have no idea how he fared in the fall of Saigon.

I still think about him. During one joint Vietnamese-American mission, we set up a box. We had four companies involved—two American and two Vietnamese—one on each of the box's four sides, all moving toward the center. And there comes a point where these units come together, and when they do, somebody's got to stop, or people are gonna step in front of somebody else's line of fire. I was with the Vietnamese and was on the radio with headquarters reporting our position as we moved along and getting updates on the American position—we couldn't see them yet, but we knew that they were there. We came to a point where our flanks were about to touch. And so I told Tu to tell the Vietnamese captain that we needed to stop, and the captain turned around to Tu and said, "No, we go."

And I said, "No, we stop."

The captain then told Tu that the district chief had told him to keep on going. I felt that we were all in danger at that point, so this captain and I got into a real pissing contest right there on the spot. Tu, of course, was caught in the middle of all this. He was faced with trying to faithfully convey what I was saying to this captain and at the same time be aware of his own rank and station in life. He was having a heck of a time; it was getting pretty heated. We practically came to blows on this thing. I radioed to my folks and told 'em what the situation was, and finally at that level they got things squared away and got it back down through the radio to the Vietnamese captain. At that point he relented and said, "Okay, we'll back off," so we backed off. I walked over and I sat down on the paddy dike, and Tu came over and sat down beside me. And he took his hat off and threw it down and said, "Fuck me, why do I have to be an interpreter?" He said it in English—in American—and that just tickled the fool out of me. He was quite a character.

* * *

Shortly after I got to Vietnam, I got a call on the radio early one morning from one of our Vietnamese company commanders, Lieutenant Lua. They had had an ambush the night before, and they'd killed a VC, and he wanted me to come see. And so we showed up there about eight o'clock in the morning, and I still hadn't had breakfast. I don't think I'd even had coffee. I walked out, and there was this body lying on the road, and he had obviously been hit several times. His entire knee had been laid open—it looked like a grenade had hit him there. The body was in pretty bad condition, and this was the first time that I had ever seen a dead body outside a casket. Especially at that hour of the morning, it was more than I could comprehend. But the more I looked at it, the more I just sort of marveled. The overwhelming sense that I had was, "Gee, this is just a pile of flesh and bone. What's different between this and a living man?" And it was that there was no spirit there. I guess it was then that I started to gain some appreciation for what makes us human, for the spirit within that makes us more than just a pile of flesh and bone. We went back and had some strong French coffee. It was a heck of a way to start the day.

WALTER KRAUS

CRESCENT SPRINGS, KENTUCKY

CHIEF MACHINIST'S MATE, UNITED STATES NAVY, WORLD WAR II

LIEUTENANT COMMANDER, UNITED STATES NAVY, VIETNAM

Our submarine had two banks of batteries—the forward battery and the after-battery—and four diesel engines. A diesel engine needs air, so when we were submerged, the batteries powered the ship. Then every night we had to surface so the diesel engines could charge the batteries.

When we'd surface after dark, we'd listen to the radio. And what we always wanted to listen to was Tokyo Rose. She had the best program of anybody. We had other programs like the *Voice of*

America, but they were boring—all talk and news. Tokyo Rose was entertaining. She was the best morale booster we had.

Remember, we grew up in the thirties, the majority of us. And she would play us all those old songs—"Goodnight, Sweetheart," "Goody-Goody" ("Goody Goody! for him, Goody Goody! for me"), "The Glory of Love." All those things that we grew up with. And they'd bring back memories.

The guys would say, "Man, I remember dancing to that with my wife." "I was with my first girlfriend when I heard that tune." And we would sing along with her. But then she would say, "Now you boys on the *Seadragon*"—or "you boys on the *Snapper*"—"what do you think your girlfriend is doing right now at home? Don't worry. You're not long for this world, anyway." And she would name names of people on submarines. You might even hear your name. I don't know how the Japanese got the names, but they got 'em somehow.

I guess they thought that she was spreading a lot of propaganda and would break our morale. But we all laughed about the things she said.

She was tried as a traitor after the war. Then, Gerald Ford finally pardoned her when he got so many letters from the submarine people. I signed a petition.

Look, she was an American citizen. She went to Japan before the war to visit her relatives, and when the war started, she couldn't get back. So the Japanese used her. What choice did she have? At least she made us a good program.

We really looked forward to listening to her at night.

In the middle of 1943, the *Snapper* came into the shipyard at San Francisco for repairs. We stayed eighty days. Right in the middle of that, I came home on leave for a month.

People were so receptive to you. If you came home in uniform during World War II you were treated like a king.

For example, since everything was rationed, our neighbors gave my mother their meat coupons so my mother could get steak for me. Gas was rationed, so I had several people loan me their cars. I never had a driver's license, I just drove all around. I was a hero.

From Cincinnati, I went back to San Francisco. And, man, that was great. I dated a nurse from the Marine hospital there up by the Presidio. We went to different nightclubs in San Francisco and always got a good seat. You were treated well as a serviceman.

Following the war, Walter remained in the Navy. In March 1967, he went to Vietnam for a yearlong tour on the staff of the naval commander there.

I was in Vietnam in May when my mother died. They didn't bury her. They kept her body on ice till I came back seven days later.

When I got in to Travis Air Force Base, I was told to change out of my uniform. They said the Berkeley students were demonstrating and I would have rocks thrown at me. So I came home without my uniform to bury my mother.

I thought it was terrible, but I didn't want to get hit by a rock. There were demonstrations outside of Travis, and at the airport in San Francisco, too, where I went to get on a plane going east. The climate was altogether different from what it was in World War II. Even here in Cincinnati. I was reading the editorials—it was not a popular war.

At home, everybody wanted to know, "Walter, where's your uniform?"

I stayed four days, then went back to Vietnam.

MIKE JACKSON

TIPP CITY, OHIO

CAPTAIN, UNITED STATES AIR FORCE, VIETNAM

A recent Department of Defense dictionary gives the following definition for "rules of engagement": "Directives issued by competent military authority which delineate the circumstances and limitations under which United States forces will initiate and/or continue combat engagement with other forces encountered."

As forward air controllers, we were the referees for the war. We had to take rules-of-engagement tests every thirty days.

Rules of engagement were strictly political. This was the most insane war you could have ever fought. It was fought in Washington, D.C., by people that didn't have a clue. This gets me off a little bit. These people didn't have a clue. They didn't have the right. They didn't have the skills. They didn't have the intelligence. They didn't have the background to be doing what the heck they did. Bunch of rich, pampered draft dodgers that were sitting in Washington, D.C.

I'm talking about old draft dodgers. I'm talking about everyone from the president on down telling us what we can bomb and cannot bomb from eight thousand miles away. We had the most insane rules you could ever have.

We lost American lives based on stupid rules. We lost American lives because we decided to recognize Christian holidays in a country that wasn't Christian. Why? Why would we do that? All it did was give them the chance to rearm.

I can give you a perfect example. This sums up the whole Vietnam experience. I was flying over a road that we called the Green Alpine Highway. That road became very active—there were a lot of troops and a lot of weapons being hauled along there that resulted in a lot of lives being lost.

I forget what the cease-fire was; it may have been a Christian holiday, it may have been a Vietnamese holiday. We were told that we would have a cease-fire until six o'clock at night. So I'm up at five-thirty, and we're gonna show them that we're back at six o'clock. This is the politicians: "We're gonna show 'em we're back."

I'm in the DMZ, as far north as you can go without being in North Vietnam, and I've got four sets of fighter jets out there ready to fight. I'm looking down at this road, and there are troops carrying supplies south out of North Vietnam into South Vietnam. They know I'm there. They know what a forward controller is. They would have to have been blind not to see the smoke from the F-4s above me. And they waved at me.

At about ten till six, one of them, who I assume was an officer because he had a watch, looked at his watch, flipped me the bird—he was Americanized enough to do that—and then they all disappeared. At six o'clock all I could do was start puking bombs all over the jungle. They were in there, but I had no idea where. With any luck I got some of them, but who knows?

Insane, totally insane. I don't know how you justify it. I don't know how those people could sleep, McNamara and his bunch.

We could've won Vietnam. We could've won it in months instead of staying over there for ten, twelve, thirteen years and losing as many lives as we did. We could've won that thing easy. We had the airpower. We had the ground power. We could have had the support of the people if we hadn't puked it away. We could've won it militarily. We never lost a battle.

We'd have had to fight to win, and that wouldn't have been pretty. We could have hit the dikes up in North Vietnam and flooded the entire north, hit their population centers, hit their military, hit their industrial centers. But we didn't do it.

If you're gonna fight a war, you fight it. If you're not gonna fight it, don't fight it. You can't say this is off-limits and this is in-limits because what they do is—and we've seen this in Iraq and Afghanistan—they move their missile sites or their barracks close to a school or a hospital or a mosque. You either fight the war or you don't fight the war.

We were dealing with the masters. They'd been fighting forever, and they knew they could outlast us. The American public didn't have the stomach to stick it out for that long, and rightfully so, rightfully so. We should've cut our losses and left a long time before we did. Declared peace and walked away.

That's what we wound up doing anyway. We just waited for somebody to sign the sheet.

JIM COYNE SR.

MANAHAWKIN, NEW JERSEY
TECHNICAL SERGEANT, UNITED STATES ARMY, WORLD WAR II

The Germans were a very shrewd enemy. They didn't just go where you thought they'd go—they were all over the place. They never gave us a day off from the fighting. And they had plenty of courage, plenty of courage. Certainly people hated them.

I didn't hate them, but I didn't like them either. The reason at first I didn't like them was that there I was in the Army and they were trying to kill me. But the more I saw of the German army, the more I disliked them—what they did, who they persecuted. They did to the civilian population what they wanted to do to them. God.

When we drove on into Germany, I met some of the German people. These weren't soldiers, these were fathers and mothers with a son in the army someplace. So I didn't hate the Germans, and I don't now. I suppose I would, though, if I was Jewish.

I think the American people had a great deal of hatred for the Japanese, much more than for the Germans. That was because of the color of their skin, the shape of their face; of course, that was made up into cartoons. I think that we were fed a bunch of propaganda. Europe and the Pacific—to me they were two different wars. You take the American soldier, the ordinary American soldier, put a uniform on him, march him off. When he got to France, there wasn't so much difference. The color of their skin was white. Their eyes were blue. Churches were there. But the American soldiers against the Japanese? An entirely different race of people. Entirely. I don't think that the Americans have ever made it up to the Japanese.

PERRY POLLINS

LEXINGTON, MASSACHUSETTS

CORPORAL, UNITED STATES MARINE CORPS, WORLD WAR II

On April 1, 1945, Perry landed in the third wave of Marines at Okinawa. The fight for the island would last three months.

I was still in Okinawa when the atomic bomb was dropped on Japan. We were preparing for an invasion of Japan in March of the following year, 1946. Our division and the Sixth and Fourth Divisions and a number of Army divisions were supposed to land in and around Tokyo.

We figured that when we landed, the whole country would be armed, and the civilians would be as dangerous as the soldiers. So it would be necessary to kill civilians, which at that stage of the game really didn't make a hill of beans to most of us. I'd been overseas almost two years. The war had to end, and there was no one to blame for its still going on but the effing Japanese.

If the A-bomb hadn't been dropped, we would've landed there. And I'm sure we would've defeated them. But the word was out that there would've been millions of casualties. The war had to be stopped immediately to prevent that.

We were very happy when the bomb was dropped. Being as candid as I possibly can, we gave no thought to the civilians that lost their lives. Sure, we thought about it later on, and it was tough. It was terrible.

But I'm sorry. It was they who started the war and they who had to take the punishment.

They dropped one A-bomb on Hiroshima first. And seventy-two hours went by, and they dropped a second one. Why? Because the bastards didn't surrender. The people in the First Marine Division didn't expect that they would surrender after the first bomb: "They're that kind of people."

But when they dropped the second one, we said, "See ya later."

MAS TAKAHASHI
TORRANCE, CALIFORNIA
TECHNICAL SERGEANT, UNITED STATES ARMY, WORLD WAR II

I had no relatives in Japan. The only person I knew with any relatives was a guy that used to run around with my older brother. He had at least one brother in Japan.

The way I look at it, they shouldn't have dropped the atom bomb on civilians. You're not hitting military targets. So in later years, I figured that wasn't the right thing to do. They didn't have to drop the bomb, because the U.S. was winning the war hands down. The only thing it did was shorten it.

What army did the Japanese have left? What navy did they have left? They didn't have anything left. The Americans were gonna invade Japan, but they didn't need to invade, because if they blockaded them, they were gonna surrender, right? Nothing would get through. The people would be starving. What were they gonna do?

We'll never know what would have happened if they didn't drop it. They say it saved a lot of lives, ended the war. But that's not real warfare. You could do that to any country: kill all the people, and you've won the war. But the innocent people aren't military.

So I don't know. You got pro and con there. It shortened the war. But we had it won anyway, the way I look at it.

RICHARD RECENDEZ
RETIRED SMALL BUSINESS OWNER
HANFORD, CALIFORNIA
SPECIALIST FOURTH CLASS, UNITED STATES ARMY, VIETNAM

Born in Corcoran, California, in 1946, Richard Reyes Recendez was drafted in November 1965.

"What's interesting is that all the training they gave us was for

conventional-type warfare. We were doing maneuvers like we were in Europe. Even the weapons we used: We used the M-14. I never seen an M-16 until I got to Vietnam. I didn't know how to use it. Had to learn.

"In AIT, they mentioned punji stakes and booby traps, but never trained us in them. We learned all that in 'Nam. OJT—on-the-job training. We had to adapt to the Vietcong way of battle."

Arriving in Vietnam in January 1967, Richard served with the 101st Airborne Division, first in the Mekong Delta, then in the area American GIs called the Iron Triangle. Less than twenty miles northwest of Saigon, the Iron Triangle served as a base area for the Vietcong, who had fortified it with an extensive network of tunnels.

In April a squad went out of their sector. They got lost, and we lost contact with them.

We found them a couple of days later.

Their necks were cut. Their ears were cut. And then part of their body was skinned. So you didn't see any skin in that area, you just saw this blob, and the skin kind of flopped over. I thought, "My God, what kind of war is this? I've seen people get blown up, but I've never seen a person tortured and skinned like that." They were all dead; I don't know if they were dead at the time they were skinned. Their nails were gone. They had gashes about an inch long, like they were stuck with a bayonet. Their hands were tied above their heads to a rope slung over a tree; their feet were just barely touching the ground. They were stripped of everything. Nothing was on them, no clothes. There were no weapons in the area, no uniforms. Everything was gone. Just these six bodies hanging from these trees. There was eight in the squad; we couldn't find the other two.

We looked at them, the medics examined them. I says, "I don't know what we're fighting here. We didn't never do that to them." We had codes, right? But these NVA, when they came down, they were like machines.

In training they told us the reason we were going was to stop the spread of Communism. But as I stayed in 'Nam, my purpose was to go home. To stay alive to go home. What happened after that, I didn't care. You can have your stinking country.

And yet when I saw what happened to the lost squad, my feelings turned more into rage, like, "Now I have a reason to be here: to kill as many as I can." I think a lot of us felt that way, because after that we didn't take many prisoners anymore. Guys lost it.

You go to their level in order to survive that kind of warfare. You've got to become like them. And that was weird. I wanted to go home, sure. But now I was angry.

A couple of days later, we found a tunnel by one of the villages. They'd have different networks. I wouldn't go in, but we had these tunnel rats, and they'd go down and recon them. If they spotted any activity, they'd come back out and report it.

Before we found the lost squad, we would wait until the enemy came out of a tunnel and then capture them. But after that we just started chucking grenades in there. There was no more waiting for them to come out. Sometimes, after the grenades, we'd shoot a flamethrower into the hole. That would kill anything several feet in or starve the oxygen out of it.

Then we'd pull out everybody that was in there—90 percent of the time, they'd be dead; if they were alive, we made sure they weren't gonna live long. That would increase our body count. It was a numbers game.

That lost squad changed the makeup of the war for me. When you think, "How much worse can it get?" and you see that, it's amazing how much worse it can get. It was done to strike fear in us, to scare the hell out of us. They were giving us a message: "This can happen to you." And it was a strong one.

A little while later, I seen a stake put in one of Charlie's heads with our unit patch on it. I thought, "Okay. They know we're here, and we're gonna stay."

ARTHUR WAY

RETIRED CLIMATE CONTROL OPERATOR, UNITED STATES ARMY CIVIL SERVICE
HAVRE DE GRACE, MARYLAND
CORPORAL, UNITED STATES ARMY, WORLD WAR II

A native of Baltimore who moved to Havre de Grace as a child, twenty-two-year-old infantryman Arthur H. Way sailed overseas in June 1943. "The most difficult part was leaving my wife. She was pregnant and I didn't know if I would ever see my first child."

The following month Arthur landed with the Forty-fifth Division in Sicily and then in September on the Italian mainland. When the Italian campaign stalled, Arthur was among the Allied troops who were taken by sea up the Adriatic coast to Anzio, behind German lines. The landing took the Germans by surprise, but a day later they began pouring in reinforcements. Allied forces would not break out of the Anzio beachhead until May.

I wasn't in the initial invasion of Anzio. We came in as reinforcements two days later, on January the twenty-fourth, 1944. There was no opposition; we just walked off the ship with our rifles slung on our shoulders.

We were assigned a defensive position, and for my unit things were more or less quiet until February the seventeenth, when we got hit by the German counterattack.

We took a defensive position on the Dead End Road. It was called the Dead End Road because it was a piece of road that was under construction. Actually it was a big, wide ditch, with piles of gravel and sand along it. German tanks penetrated our left flank, and then our Third Battalion, on our right, withdrew. That left us hanging out in the open.

They had a lot of irrigation ditches in that particular area, and I tried to kneel down in one. The next thing I knew, I looked up and there was a German tank, with the commander out of the turret holding a machine gun on me. I don't speak German, but I understood "*Raus!*"

I thought he was gonna kill me, because it was the understanding that tanks, especially, didn't take prisoners. They'd break through and destroy whatever came in front of them, and then infantry would follow the tank and actually occupy the territory. But I found out later that a lot of times they would take prisoners, particularly on an initial assault, in order to get as much information as they could. Luckily for me, they were just regulars, not SS, because the SS had a habit of just mowing you down.

When he didn't shoot me, I kind of calmed down about it. I got up on the road, and there were other prisoners in a big line—it looked to me like about two platoons at least. We marched down this road and back up to a factory the Germans had fortified.

We were there only a few hours. Then we were taken to what used to be a motion-picture studio outside of Rome. I was at that studio as a prisoner for my twenty-third birthday, February the twenty-second.

We didn't get much in the way of food or water, but we weren't mistreated in any way. We were interrogated, but there wasn't no brutality in the interrogation. What they wanted to know is what outfit you were from. That's all they were interested in at that time, to find out what they were really facing. I told them what company and battalion I was in. They didn't ask too much besides that.

We were sent to another camp in Italy for a while; then in May we left Italy by train.

We were on one of those forty-and-eight boxcars—it would hold forty men or eight horses. We had fifty men in our boxcar. We had a big bucket in there to take care of our sanitary conditions; before we got to our destination, that bucket had reached its capacity. Needless to say, it was a stinking mess.

After three or four days on the train, we arrived at a place called Moosburg, which is near Munich. It was a large camp, Stalag

VII-A, and had different nationalities in there. There were Yugoslavs—they were more or less taking care of the kitchen. And there were British and French and what have you. A big camp.

I wasn't there long. From VII-A, I was taken to VII-B in Memmingen, Germany, and there they broke us up into what they called *Arbeitkommandos*—work groups. Twelve, fifteen men went to Immenstaad, Germany, a small town. We were in a small building—there were guards on the first floor, and we were on the second floor. There was equipment that you would use if you were on a crew for a department of public works.

One of the things we did was clean up rubble from American bombing. They said, "Your air force did it, so you're gonna clean it up." Usually we'd take the bricks and knock off all the mortar, then we'd stack those bricks so they could use them again.

To eat, they gave us what we called "air-raid soup" because it was "all clear." They had blood sausage and horse meat, but not on a regular basis—the only reason I knew it was horse meat was because I helped unload it from the truck. And they had what they called *ersatz* bread. It was about 20 or 25 percent sawdust in order to hold it together. You would get a half a loaf for two days. And if you didn't eat that bread in one day, it would be hard as a rock.

When you got your Red Cross parcel, you had a can of powdered milk, and then you'd sometimes soak that bread in that milk. The parcel had crackers that we could soak in the milk, too. We'd get a twenty-pound parcel for two people, but we didn't get it regularly because of the transportation situation in Germany. Twenty pounds sounds a lot, but it wasn't. That includes the cans and all the packaging.

After a while you get used to hunger.

Sometimes when we got those Red Cross parcels, the Germans would trade with us. There was a carton of cigarettes in each pack. I never smoked, so I used all my cigarettes for bartering. American cigarettes were like gold. You could get somebody killed for a pack of cigarettes.

One time we were working on some bricks, and there was a bakery right there. We had already bribed the guard—he'd get cigarettes on a regular basis. So what we did, we would stack up the cigarettes, and maybe a candy bar, on top of these bricks so this person working in the bakery could see them. He sent out his daughter to bargain with us, because she spoke fairly good English. She was attractive—I won't say she was any beauty, but we didn't have much contact with women. We got some baked goods, mostly buns.

During the harvest season, we worked on farms. A guard would bring us out in the morning, we'd stay there just about all day, then the guard would come before dark and pick us up. At that time the German army was in such sad shape they would come and confiscate the horses to pull their artillery—they were getting low on fuel, and their factories that built trucks were bombed. So you had to do the work on the farm by manual labor.

I was lucky. The family that had the farm that I worked on, they let me eat at their table. Some guys worked on the farm further down, and they told me that the farmer would just give 'em a plate of food and make 'em sit outside. But I was sitting right there, and I was talking to the father and his wife, and they had two daughters. I ingratiated myself with the family because of the Red Cross parcels. The family had *ersatz* coffee; I don't know what it was, but it was terrible. But I got Nescafé instant coffee, and I would give it to the wife. Also sugar cubes. Sugar was rationed in the United States; you could imagine what it was in Germany. She would make little cakes and give them to me. She would say, "Don't tell Papa."

He asked me, "Why are you here?" He wanted to know why as an American I was over there fighting. I guess he figured that it was a European problem. I quoted to him what Hitler said: "Today Germany, tomorrow the world." Well, he said he didn't think that was true. But at that period of time, I think they were kind of disillusioned with Hitler, because he used to kid me. My name is Arthur, and he used to called me Adolf. When the meal was over, he'd say, "*Adolf, arbeiten!*" and we'd go out in the field. Sometimes we'd put hay in the barn up in the loft. The old man would throw the hay up, and the girls and I would distribute it in the barn.

The prisoners would joke with each other. We weren't walking around with gloomy faces and heads down. We had a good spirit. Most felt the Allies were gonna win this war. We'd always talk about what we were gonna do when we got home—we didn't say, "I'm not gonna get home." We'd talk about the kind of food that we liked to eat. Things like that. I'd think about desserts—ice cream, primarily—because we didn't have any dessert at all, except in the Red Cross parcel there would be a candy bar.

And, of course, I had a daughter at home.

We received some news by the underground. There were Hungarians in the town, a man and wife. We'd be out on the street, and they would come by and drop a rolled-up piece of paper on the ground. One of us would pretend to tie our shoe, and we'd pick up that paper and drop it in our shoe. The guards were perfunctory when they checked us—they just patted us down. We knew when the second front occurred—of course, that was June the sixth. We found out when the Allies penetrated Germany. We knew the Russians were heading for Berlin. This couple had a radio and got the information from the BBC.

Because we knew from these Hungarians that it was getting near the end of the war, we didn't try to escape. We said, "This is gonna be over soon anyway. Why take a risk? When you go out there, you might even be shot by your own troops." So we laid low.

Near the end, aerial activity got a little more frequent—we could see big bomber formations going over.

May 1, things got a little hot, and we went into an air-raid shelter inside the town. There were Germans there also. And then the French came in, from the Second French Armored Division, and roused everybody out with their guns. I couldn't speak French, and nobody could speak French, so they thought we were all

Germans. They separated out the women, and the men they put out in a field with a machine gun guarding us. One of the fellows tried to explain to them, but they wouldn't listen. They pointed a gun, made him get back.

We did have one man that could speak French, but that day he was on the other side of town with a different work detail. It wasn't too long before this jeep drove up, and it was a French officer with the fella that could speak French. And the French officer said to release us. He gave each of us a hug and a pat on the back, and he kissed us on both cheeks.

Some members of an airborne outfit—I'm not sure if it was the 101st or the Eighty-second—came and picked us up and took us to their area. Then, the next day, we went back to Camp VII-B, because all the released prisoners were sent back to that camp. That's where I saw the Stars and Stripes for the first time since I was captured.

I don't know why I still break up when I talk about that. After all these years.

We flew out of the Munich airport in a C-47, and we arrived at a hospital near Reims. That was the first time I rode in an airplane.

After I was released, the very first meal I had was pancakes. Well, I threw up, because my system wasn't used to that rich food—they're fried, and they have a lot of butter. But in the hospital they'd give you more bland food, so I was eating regular.

I was suffering from malnutrition. I also had sinus trouble so bad that my left eye was swollen shut. And I didn't have too many teeth left. When I got back to the States, I had one lieutenant chew me out because my teeth were in such sad shape. He called the colonel over to take a look at 'em. I said, "Colonel, the Germans did not issue their prisoners of war toothpaste and toothbrushes."

In Reims they gave me a lot of penicillin—that was primarily to get that sinus cleared up. They gave it practically around the clock, and my swelling gradually went down.

I stayed there ten days. Then we went by train to the 196th General Hospital in Cherbourg. And on the way we got ice cream. It was delicious.

I believe it was the thirtieth of May, I was put on the USS *Mariposa.* We went from Cherbourg to Le Havre and picked up some more troops, then we left Le Havre on June the third and arrived at Boston on June the eighth.

They put me on a hospital train going south. I didn't know where we were going until I heard a couple of the southerners saying, "Guess what? We're going to Alabama."

I said, "Kiss my ass."

That's because I knew we were gonna go right through Baltimore, where my wife and child were living. These guys were all happy to be going to Alabama.

After we got there, I tried to get a transfer to a camp maybe in Virginia, somewhere near my home. I was able to talk to the major, and he told me any camps up near Maryland or Virginia are special ones—for your amputees or something like that.

So in my frustration, I wrote to my father. My father was in World War I, and his company commander was Millard Tydings, who by this time was a senator from Maryland. My father wrote to Senator Tydings—I didn't ask him to and had no idea what he was doing. The next thing I know, this major comes into my room. Of course, I snapped to attention. He had a piece of paper in his hand. He called me a smart-ass son of a bitch. I didn't know what he was talking about. He chewed me out and threw the piece of paper on my bunk and walked out. It was a letter from the surgeon general of the Army, a three-star general, to transfer me to a hospital in Staunton, Virginia.

I didn't have too many teeth left, and they were in sad shape. So at Staunton they said, "We're gonna have to take 'em all out." I've had dentures ever since. It wasn't too long after I was in Staunton that I was given a ninety-day convalescent furlough. I came home.

First time I saw my daughter, I scared her half to death. I had a little satchel, and I walked in the front door, and my wife was right there. I dropped that satchel on the floor, and it made a noise. And then I grabbed my wife, picked her up off her feet. The next thing I know, I hear crying. My daughter was apparently right in back of my wife when I came in and she come running to her mother. For a couple days, she wouldn't have nothing to do with me.

But that didn't last, because she had seen my picture. She would look at the picture and call me "Daddy."

It was fantastic to be home. I can tell you how fantastic it was: I was on a ninety-day leave, and when I went back, my wife was three months pregnant.

VINCE WAY

FEDERAL INVESTIGATOR
HAVRE DE GRACE, MARYLAND
SERGEANT, UNITED STATES ARMY, VIETNAM

Consider the chronology of 1968. On January 30, the Tet Offensive began. On February 27, Walter Cronkite announced his disenchantment with the war. On March 12, Eugene McCarthy, an obscure senator running on an antiwar platform, humbled Lyndon Johnson in the New Hampshire primary. On March 16, Robert Kennedy entered the race, also in opposition to LBJ's war. On March 31, Johnson announced he would not run for reelection. On April 4, Martin Luther King Jr. was killed in Memphis; civil disturbances broke out in cities across the nation, including its capital. Just after midnight on June 5, after accepting victory in the California primary, Robert F. Kennedy was shot at the Ambassador Hotel in Los Angeles. He died a day later.

And on August 26–29, at the Democratic convention in Chicago, supporters of McCarthy and the fallen Kennedy refused to cooperate in the nomination of Lyndon Johnson's vice president, Hubert Humphrey, as their party's standard-bearer. Americans watched in amazement and horror as anarchy filled the hall, and violence, between young antiwar demonstrators and Chicago police officers, surrounded it. A man addressing the convention—a United States senator!—spoke of "gestapo tactics in the streets of Chicago."

Something had gone terribly awry in America.

Vincent L. Way was born in 1947. Facing the draft, he enlisted for four years in the Army on July 31, 1967, and trained as a specialist in military intelligence. Working in communications security, he served two tours in Vietnam: his mandatory year-long tour, then, after thirty days' leave at home, a voluntary tour of six months.

I arrived in 'Nam at the beginning of June '68, wanting idealistically to bring democracy to these people. We'd just seen Martin Luther King assassinated; Bobby Kennedy was assassinated just after I got there. In August they held the Democratic convention in Chicago. Guys would get newspapers from home, and I was reading the accounts and seeing the pictures of the police clubbing the antiwar demonstrators on the head.

One thing my parents did instill in me was, if you have a thought on a subject and it's not going to hurt somebody else, you're entitled to speak that opinion as long as you do it respectfully. And these were people who were trying to make a point about the war. Being in the military, I may not have totally agreed with their point, because I'm sitting out here with a rifle in the middle of East Jesus. But I valued their right to express their opinion. People against the war—people my age—were being beaten down by their own police, and I'm supposedly over here saying to this little nation of yellow people, "You need to have all the rights of freedom that we have in the United States, where you can speak your mind."

It didn't make a whole lot of sense.

When I came back from my second tour, in early 1970, the movement against the war was much more organized than when I left. I still had fifteen months to do in the Army, and I spent it assigned to the Fourth Army detachment in San Antonio, Texas. Once I went to pick up a friend of mine at the airport, and I was in uniform. I was approached by people who were against the war; they were handing out pamphlets.

I stopped, and I took the pamphlet, and I was reading it, and I was having a discussion with these people. The guy I was picking up was a career soldier, and he got on my butt pretty hard about that. I said, "Well, they may have a point. Shouldn't we hear what they have to say?"

"You don't wanna get caught doing that. There might be somebody watching those people. You could be called into question as to what you were doing with them."

The Hare Krishnas are in another corner. If I take one of their pamphlets, am I "called into question"?

Vietnam—that era—was the closest this country came to civil war since 1865. That war tore this country apart, damn near destroyed it. Thank goodness it didn't.

And in a way it changed the country for the better. We came of age, we grew out of our innocent idealism. We now question the government. We're not so trusting.

XVI

"There's always been wars."

GENE SWANSON

GENE SWANSON

RETIRED MACHINERY MECHANIC, AEROSPACE INDUSTRY

EDGEWOOD, WASHINGTON

PRIVATE FIRST CLASS, UNITED STATES MARINE CORPS, WORLD WAR II

Before the battle for Iwo Jima was a week old, it had taken root as a symbol of the courage and resolve of the American fighting man after the Associated Press published Joe Rosenthal's photograph of six Marines raising the flag on Mount Suribachi. Fifty-six years later, a photograph of New York City firefighters raising the flag over the ashes of the World Trade Center instantly drew comparisons to the earlier picture and the earlier heroism.

But the battle for Iwo Jima was no symbol for the men of the Third, Fourth, and Fifth Marine Divisions, who spent more than a month during February and March 1945 grimly annihilating the island's well-prepared defenders cave by cave, tunnel by tunnel, bunker by bunker. Nearly seven thousand Americans died and nineteen thousand were wounded in the taking of this minuscule piece of volcanic rock set in the Pacific Ocean some seven hundred miles south of Tokyo. The island's strategic value lay in its airfields: the Japanese fighter base that the American invasion neutralized; the landing strip the Americans built to accommodate aircraft in distress—mostly B-29 bombers unable to reach home base after dropping their payloads on Japanese cities. By war's end, more than twenty-five thousand American airmen had landed safely on Iwo in crippled planes.

As they plotted the Pacific war's endgame, American military planners saw in the battle for Iwo the seeds of a nightmare. Casualties among the attacking Americans had been heavy, but those among the island's defenders had been preposterous: Of twenty-three thousand Japanese occupying Iwo Jima when the Marines landed, only 216—less than 1 percent!—were left alive when the shooting stopped. Then, as the Marines on Iwo Jima were mopping up, their brethren invaded Okinawa—an operation that cost the lives of another twelve thousand American servicemen and brought the spectacle of thousands of Japanese soldiers and Okinawan civilians jumping off steep cliffs to their deaths rather than fall into enemy hands.

Here was a people, American commanders feared, who would not submit, no matter how desperate their circumstances might become. Only a massive invasion of Japan's home islands could secure the Allies' objective: the empire's unconditional surrender. But as they began planning for Operation Olympic, a landing on the island of Kyushu set for November, and Operation Coronet, on Honshu several months later, military leaders were faced with estimates of unthinkable costs—one recent history reports the prediction of as many as half a million U.S. casualties, although a million is the figure commonly heard. Two million Japanese soldiers were stationed on the home islands; fighting alongside them would be an equally fanatical civilian population, urged by their government to wield pitchforks and sharpened sticks of bamboo as they took part in "The Glorious Death of One Hundred Million."

But on July 16, a plutonium device called Fat Man was detonated in the New Mexican desert. Harry Truman had the tool he needed to cancel the invasion.

* * *

Prior to the battle of Iwo Jima, Eugene P. Swanson, of the Third Marine Division, tasted combat on Guam, where he arrived two months after the first wave of Marines had landed. At Iwo he landed with his regiment, the Twenty-first Marines, on D+2, February 21.

I had more friends that were IV-F than went into the military. Most of us from our neighborhood in Superior, Wisconsin, were real skinny. During the big Depression, sometimes we didn't have anything to eat in our home, not even a crust of bread.

My dad had a friend whose wife ran a whorehouse, and she would bring food over to us. She'd bring a great big kettle of chow mein or chop suey, whatever it's called. To us everything was chop suey. It would sit on the back of the coal-burning stove and stay hot all the time. We'd go grab a bowl anytime we wanted and eat some of that.

People went back to work slowly. My dad finally got on the WPA as a blacksmith.

In 1940, when I was fifteen, I joined the merchant marine and sailed the Great Lakes. I went because I was a very poor student. I was a good seaman, poor student.

I never saw money like that before. I was making as much as a grown man would make. I liked that. I always carried four hundred dollars around in my boot.

In wintertime the lakes froze up, and so I'd have a nice long vacation, three or four months. As soon as I was off work in late '43, I said, "I'll get a job at the shipyard." But at the shipyard they said, "Just a minute. We'll check up on you." They got on the phone and called my draft board and found out that I was gonna be drafted with the next bunch going out.

I said, "I'm not gonna be drafted. I'm gonna join." So I went up to the draft board and volunteered for induction into the Marine Corps. Basically I was drafted, but this gave me my choice of where I went.

I wanted the Marines because my oldest brother was a prisoner of the Japanese—he was taken shortly after Pearl Harbor—and joining the Marines was the only way I was assured of going to the Pacific. I could've gone into the Navy and never left the United States, or that's what they told me. But I wanted to get my brother away from the Japs. So that was the reasoning of an eighteen-year-old.

I wanted to do my part to get him back home, and I did. Definitely, yes. And he's still alive. In fact, at one time he says, "I'll give you half of what I got," because he got all that back pay. I forget how much it was—it didn't matter to me. But he was willing to give me half of that because he says, "You saved me."

To him I'm a hero.

The draft board gave me so much time to get all my affairs in order and what have you, which I didn't have to. I didn't have anything to put in order. I got on the train in Superior and went down to San Diego in January of '44.

It was a regular passenger train, so it would have been about thirty-six, forty hours. I'd been on a train to go catch my ships and that when I was sailing, so the train wasn't new to me. But eating dinner on the train—now, that was an experience. I'd seen it in the movies, and it looked so elegant. And it was just that, elegant, even for a boot going to boot camp. I got the same treatment as everybody else, and Uncle Sam paid for it. I felt real classy.

But then I got to San Diego, and I was shocked. Because those people didn't even know me, and they're hollering at me. I didn't think people'd holler at you for no reason at all. You had to have done something wrong to be hollered at. Well, I was hollered at just about all the way through boot camp. And I never could take that. To this day somebody hollers at me, I'm very angry.

I could see it for the other guys my age, but I couldn't see it for me. I'd shipped out at fifteen. I'd already had three years of being a grown man. I never got hollered at when I was sailing, and here they were hollering at me for trivial things. And this is why I thought it was stupid. In fact, I still do. I don't think the troops have to be harassed as much as they are.

You lit your cigarette before they said the smoking lamp is lit. You knew he was gonna say it. But maybe you happened to be a few seconds ahead of him. Well, I'd do that, and I'd get dressed up and down. It was that quick.

I enjoyed close-order drill. I loved it. That to me is the way a person gets disciplined. I thought it was amazing what we could do together, how we could be synchronized in our movements. The forward march, the rear march, oblique march, all that stuff, and then going through the manual of arms with the rifle. I guess that's what they call it. Throwing the rifle around anyhow. I thought I got pretty good at that.

I'd say the Marines could've done the very same thing as far as preparing people to fight and only used one thing, and that's close-order drill. They would have had to train them longer. Make 'em march and give 'em orders and give 'em orders. The fancier the better. Have them get to where they do what they're told automatically.

But they hollered at everybody, from the first time we got off the train and stood there at attention, which I wasn't sure what attention was. They wanted to show us who was boss. In fact, one of the first things they said was, "Give your heart to God, 'cause your ass belongs to me." They meant it. That's the attitude they had all the way through boot camp.

"Get your fucking ass going." "Get outta here, you buncha girls." "Get your ass in there." "Suck in your gut, you sonsa bitches." I guess they wanted to make us mad. Well, they got this Swede mad. And a few times I got into trouble with the drill instructor. He was a corporal.

I stepped out of line one time when we were in close-order drill, and I swung at him. Of course, I missed. I'm glad I did—I was small, and still am really, except for my gut.

One time at rifle range, we had already sighted in our rifles. And he wanted us to crawl underneath our hut from one end to the other.

Well, our huts were about three feet off the ground at one end and about eighteen inches at the other. And I just refused to crawl underneath that hut with my rifle because, I says, "I spend all this time sighting in my rifle, and now I should go underneath there and knock the sights off?" And Mack, our sergeant—McBride was his name—he was quite a guy. He never swore. Always used real good language, and he did not scream or holler. And he came up and grabbed this corporal and spun him 'round. "What's going on here?"

The corporal told McBride I disobeyed a direct order. McBride didn't raise his voice to him; he could chew your ass out, and you'd say thank you. And so he chewed out the corporal, and he said, "Now, you leave this little Swede alone. He's trying his damnedest to be a good Marine. You leave him alone."

I thought about that for many years, and it didn't come to me till I was out of the Marine Corps a long time that it could've been because I was the last son at home. My two brothers, one was a prisoner of war and one was up in the Aleutians. I figure they were protecting me, because I did get a few privileges along the way. I still got a lot of hollering at and a lot of ass chewing, though. I guess I was a real fuck-up.

After boot camp I had to pull thirty days of mess duty. Then I went home on leave for about a week and a half. I was with my girlfriend—which is my wife now—just as much as I could be.

I guess I did quite a bit of drinking, not a heckuva lot of thinking. I never felt morbid about being in the Marine Corps and knowing that I'd be going overseas soon. I always figured that I had my peace with the Lord, so I had nothing to worry about. If I got killed, I got killed; if I didn't, praise the Lord. That was my attitude all the way through.

On the line, though, when you're being fired at, you're scared. But you'll revert back to the training you had, and everything is automatic. I was a machine-gunner overseas. In a machine-gun squad, you have a number-one gunner; he carried the tripod. Number-two gunner; he carried the gun itself. And then the other six or eight people in the squad, me being one of them, carried ammunition. You had your duty to do, and you knew where to be and how far you should be away from the machine gun. You don't want to be close to that machine gun—the enemy wants to knock it out.

You know what has to be done, and you do it. You don't have time to question anything; you just do what you were taught. I guess that was the difference between a lot of the Army units and the Marine Corps units: the discipline that they had during the firefight.

Of course, we didn't call them firefights. I got that from Gary here.

Got on a small ship. Of course, I volunteered for mess duty—I always wanted to be close to that chow. It took us seven days to get to the Hawaiian Islands. I spent my nineteenth birthday there, August first of '44.

In Hawaii we got on the *Sloter Dijk,* a Dutch ship, to go to Guam. On the way over there, we stopped at Eniwetok and we had a few days of R&R. They gave us four warm beers and took us in to the beach. There wasn't anything there; it was just a big sand spit. There were still dead Japs floating in the water around the island. That was R&R.

Seeing my first dead Jap was scary. I bet you I jumped six feet when I saw him. Nobody else saw—I got off the landing craft on the port side, and the rest of the Marines got off on the starboard side. There he was. His eyes were closed, but he was faceup.

Guam was secured before we arrived, although we killed plenty of Japs after the island was secured. The reason for that is, when is an island secured? They call it secured when there is no more organized resistance. There were still a lot of Japs, though, in small groups.

There was no fighting going on at the harbor when we landed. In fact, on our march all the way up to where we were going to bivouac, there wasn't any shooting. Then there was sporadic shooting at night.

The first action I saw was past two weeks after we landed, and we were on a push. We were going to sweep the island and get all the stragglers picked up. We ran across some.

They had a little bivouac going. The clearing wouldn't have been more than forty feet in diameter. There were about five to eight people, and they were cooking rats over an open fire. We surprised them. Imagine you have a bunch of people pounding through the jungle and you could sneak up on somebody. Well, we did. From where I was, I couldn't see an awful lot. But I know they went into the jungle and then fired back at us.

I never shot a round—I was in the middle of the column, and when there's somebody ahead of you, you don't draw down on anything. We called up a BAR—a Browning automatic rifle. He had a lot of firepower, and *bang*, just like that, he killed them.

Now, you realize I was nineteen years old. I was just a kid. And I'd seen an awful lot of dead already on Guam, on our way through where the Marines had made the main drive to secure the island. Any Marines that got shot, they were hauled off right away. But the dead Japs were left lying around, and there were maybe a hundred I saw. In fact, I sat on a dead Jap and ate my lunch one day.

I guess it was just to say I did it. We came up, and we were all taking a break. It was swampy, and this Jap's body is up there high and dry. So I sat on his belly and ate my lunch. That's the only reason I can give for it now. A cocky kid.

The Japanese weren't human to us. I don't think I could have shot anybody if I'd been over in Europe, because they looked like me. But a Jap was completely different. They smelled different, looked different. They ate different. And I couldn't understand what they were saying. They weren't human, that was the thought. It's like we were out deer hunting, really.

There was no reasoning that, hey, they bleed red, too, or they're children of God. That never entered into it. It was, "They're different. They're the enemy. They're to be killed." It wasn't a personal thing. Individually, you can't hate them unless you know them. It was just, "Hate the Japanese. Every Japanese is bad. Every Japanese should be killed."

Some of the guys got so inhuman—I can't think of another word—that they were taking the teeth out of the dead Japs' mouths to get at the gold fillings. I even remember that at the same time I was sitting on the Jap's belly eating, this one friend of mine knocked the tooth out of a dead Jap's jaw, and he missed it, and it went down the throat. Well, he just reached out and cut this man's head off and got the tooth out of his throat.

I was appalled. That's my word now. I don't know what word I used then. That was being a butcher, and there was no way I would want to be classified as a butcher.

We all saw it, and afterward we talked about it: "Oh, my God, how could you do that?" That was about it. Nobody dressed him down for it, nobody chewed on him for it.

As I say, we weren't human. We ourselves weren't human to be able to do something like that.

Now, remember, I'm putting myself back in the days of the war. I couldn't go do now what I did then. They're children of God, too. We all are.

It changed for me after the war—when I was in China, in fact. We were repatriating the Japanese who'd fought there and occupied it, shipping them home. I was working in the mess, and Japanese prisoners would be brought in to wash down the windows and the walls, sweep the compound outside. Well, I would pidgin-talk to them. Neither one of us could understood each other's words, but, doing sign language and the like of that, we could communicate.

That was when I got the different feeling, that, hey, they're human. I don't think I had any love for them, but I no longer hated them or thought of them as an enemy.

During the war we weren't very nice. I could try to justify why we were that way, but I'm not going to. There's always been wars.

* * *

We loaded onto a Navy troop carrier to go from Guam to Iwo Jima. Again I volunteered for mess duty. It was very stormy. Of course, we could hear them talking to the radar people about suicide airplanes—kamikazes. When we got there, it was like the Fourth of July you never saw before, all the big guns going and plastering Iwo Jima. It's not a very big island—about eight square miles.

I wanted to land in the first wave—gung ho. But they held me back and put me to loading the landing craft that were taking our ammunition in. Again I think they were protecting me. I did that the whole first day. The second day I got off and ran to find my outfit. I got lost.

The Fourth Marine Artillery was supposedly laying down a barrage in front of us for our advance. But many times the shells were short and laid right into us. One shell blew me right into a pile of shit. Of course, everyone shit in the same area. The other fellas in our squad saw me go through the air and thought I was dead, so they took off without even looking for me. And here I am trying to throw sand on me and get the stuff off. I had two canteens of water, and I wasn't about to use that to wash it off. I got most of it off with sand.

It must have been right on the edge of the sulfur field, because I got lost in the fumes coming up off of the sulfur. And you know what burning sulfur fumes smell like. It's like a guy that drank a lot of beer and ate hard-boiled eggs.

I was going through there, and all of a sudden, here's an airplane on the ground about ten feet in front of me. I got that close to it before I could see it. It was a Zero. They had parked it in the sulfur fumes to hide it. Did a good job, too. So I knew my guys weren't there. I just kept going and had to keep asking questions, and I finally found them.

The terrain on Iwo? I'd like to say there was none. There was nothing growing, no vegetation whatsoever. There were a few pieces of tree limb and stuff like that. It was a volcanic island, and so we used to heat our rations by putting them about two inches below the top of the soil. And then you had to make sure you didn't leave them in there over ten minutes.

On Iwo Jima it was like a game of cops and robbers, of cowboys and Indians. We'd hide behind *here* and shoot at that guy over *there.* Of course, being an ammunition carrier on a machine-gun squad, I didn't personally take my rifle—I carried a carbine—and shoot. Unless there was a bunch of 'em coming at us, like a banzai charge. That was different.

I think it was my second day on the line, we lost everyone in Third Platoon, all at one time. There was a big long draw that went through, between two rocky walls that were on a small slant. And Third Platoon was in the draw when the Japs shot a great big garbage can full of explosives that landed right in there. The concussion exploded every round they had on their belts. All of the hand grenades exploded. Everything that could explode exploded. That was a helluva sight, because the guys were killed with their own ammunition. That's all it was, just a concussion. No one in Third Platoon survived—I'd say maybe thirty-five or forty people were killed.

Iwo Jima was not the best place to fire an automatic weapon, because there was too much rock, too much ricochet. You didn't know which way the rounds were gonna go. Yet we fired our machine guns and wore out every one of them.

They burned up; the barrels were ruined. We knew there was no water on the island, so we couldn't take our heavy water-cooled machine guns. All we had were those heavy air-cooled ones, iron barrels about two inches thick and two feet long. This was a .30-caliber machine gun.

Shooting at night, it was beautiful. You never knew what direction your projectile would go; you'd see tracers going all over. We knew there was no sense in firing those guns.

So then I became a litter bearer. I never actually went into the field to get the wounded, but I'd meet a stretcher partway and grab hold and help carry it out. That's one of the most dangerous jobs, because you're completely exposed. You're walking through rocks or open spaces—you can't be crawling. Your rifle has to be slung.

One of the first guys I helped carry out was a sergeant. We got him to some motor transportation, but he died before he ever got to the aid station. It's heart-sickening, figuring what we went through to get him as far as we did and then he didn't make it.

I saw a lot of dead, Americans and Japanese. But the particular circumstances made a difference in how I was affected.

The thing that bothered me the most happened a few days after I came ashore, when I saw just a finger with a ring on it. It was just laying there on the path we were taking, just the one finger—it wasn't a hand—and in the dust you could see the ring on it.

A ring is a symbol of somebody else in his life. I don't even know if it had a stone in it or what type of ring it was; it would've been bigger than a wedding band. It was just a ring.

To this day I still see it.

There were some Japs that surrendered, but most of the time Marines didn't let 'em surrender. They'd take enough for interrogation. That'd be about it, because when you're trying to take somebody on and take him back, you're gonna get killed. See, on these islands a lot of times there was no front. You can't say, "I'm going up on the line now." It's all around you. And if you're taking a Jap back, there's going to be a sniper up on a rock somewhere. He's gonna kill you and let that man free. I never had anything to do with prisoners.

Sometimes Japs would come in to surrender, three of them. And the guy in the middle would have a machine gun strapped to his back. He would fall to the ground, and the other two would feed the belt through the machine gun, and they'd mow you down if you weren't fast enough. That happened on both Guam and Iwo Jima. I didn't see it on Guam; I saw it on Iwo.

We got a newspaper on Iwo every day. One of the ships must've printed it out and made copies, I imagine by mimeograph. It was one sheet of paper, and it always had a picture of the island and would have the numbers of the different outfits at their positions. That's the only way we knew where we were, by getting that slip of paper. That came out real early in the fight for Iwo.

We landed on the southern end of the island. I remember when we got to the northern end, which is all caves. I was shooting with my little carbine into the caves, because that's where the Japs were all holed up. I didn't know at that time that tanks had flamethrowers on them. And this tank came up and came to a stop. Then it swung around to point into the cave, and a great big shot of flame went out from it. That was something.

What you heard then was a bunch of screaming and then *pop, pop, pop*—however many were in there, blowing their guts out with grenades.

They were disemboweling themselves. They carried a grenade about the size of an evaporated-milk can. It had a little piece sticking up from it, and that's your igniting point, your cap. So they'd pull the pin, hit the cap on their helmets to activate it, then hold it to their bodies. It'd just scoop their guts right out. Most beautiful gutting job you ever saw. We remarked that we never cleaned a deer that good.

Apparently our flamethrower didn't get them; they killed themselves. For them to surrender—that was the worst thing they could do. Killing themselves was no problem. It was their way of life, their belief.

I'm not sure where I heard about this or where I was taught it. I imagine it was during boot camp. If they got killed in battle, they were sure that they would go to their ancestors. I don't know where they'd go if they didn't. That's what was told us anyhow, that they were fanatical because it was glorious to die for the emperor.

I was in one banzai charge that came through the lines. You heard them coming for miles, because they were drunk up on sake, and they were having a great time: They're gonna get killed. They came through the lines firing and hollering. A lot of 'em were out of ammunition—they had hatchets and knives, anything that they could carry.

It was utter chaos. I just laid down in my foxhole and let 'em come, and *bang*, anything that came over the top of me I shot at, straight up. I had one that fell fairly close by. And after it was done, I snuck over there and field-dressed him, and that's where I got my Japanese flag.

I don't think it lasted ten minutes, but it seemed like forever. I think I can tell you, I shit my pants. It wasn't that I had diarrhea either. I was just scared. And I didn't even know I'd crapped my pants until it was all over.

There were a lot of things that went on in Iwo Jima that I can vouch for that were not kosher to a war. Two lieutenants in charge of our platoon were killed, and they weren't killed by the Japs. You can't have an officer leading you, and who can press charges on you later, who sets you up in the wrong place. You're not going to do it. You're going to kill him first and then go set up where you want to set up. Because if you don't place your people right, you're dead.

The first one that got shot was a college kid. It's about the only way I can describe him—he was a cocky college kid: "Boy, you better do what I say."

We had stopped to set up our FPL—final protective line. Our perimeter. And the lieutenant said to our squad, "You set up there." And then he went to place the other squads. He came back, and my squad leader, a corporal, says, "Sir, do you really want me to do it there? You know that we'll draw fire the first time we open up."

He says, "Yeah, I told you. Right there. That's a direct order."

I was close enough to hear that. And the corporal says, "Okay." The lieutenant walked away, and the corporal unslung his carbine and *bang*. At thirty feet, pretty hard to miss. Shot him in the head.

I wanted to run. Whether I was scared or what, I don't know. All I knew, I had the feeling I wanted to get away from there, and I knew I couldn't.

I was a peon. I didn't know all about placing men in line, so I didn't know if he was placing us right or wrong. I was just an ammo carrier. When we finally set up our perimeter, the squad leader came over and explained to us if we would've set up over there, we wouldn't be alive now, because the Japs are looking right down on that spot. All they'd need to see would be one burst of our automatic fire, and they'd zero in on us.

That's all it took to explain it to me. It was something that had to happen; otherwise I'd be dead instead of him. War does not give anybody a right to do things, but they take the right. Which does not make it right.

Actually, I think I looked up to the corporal more after that. That he had the guts to do it. It's better the lieutenant's life than—how many in the squad? Eight? Ten? Rather his than ten other people's. He was going to have his way. And if you disobey a direct order under fire, that's mutiny. Death.

Of course, killing him's mutiny, too, but I think the corporal knew that he was pretty safe, because nobody liked the lieutenant. Nobody said a word, and there was no inquest. You're not gonna go around and look at each and every dead person in the middle of a war and see what they were shot with.

The second time a lieutenant was shot, it was for the same reason. A ninety-day wonder who didn't know what he was doing and wouldn't listen. Different guy did the shooting—our sergeant.

Like I said, we weren't human.

I didn't see the flag when it went up on Mount Suribachi. Now, maybe at one time or another I saw it, but I heard about it long before I saw it, because the news spread real fast. When we heard about it, we were extremely happy, happy enough to holler. The flag's always been special. "Old Glory's up there. We've got it now." Not necessarily that the fighting was all over.

We were mopping up on the north end of the island when we were relieved from the fighting. Then we all went back to where we'd landed, and the guys cut pieces of the lava to make headstones: "In remembrance of . . ." Down near the water was where they had buried everybody.

By the time we left, there were crosses on every grave, plus these stones that the guys had personally made for their buddies. They were so light that a block as big as a kitchen chair you could pick up with one hand. It was all full of air. In fact, if you threw it out into the ocean, it'd float.

When we left Iwo on the twenty-ninth of March, I didn't give any thought whatsoever to those graves. The only thing I thought about is, "Boy, I'll be glad to get back to Guam, where I can get some cold beer." That was my only thought, to be honest with you. Or, "Boy, I get aboard the ship, I can get some good, fresh bread. We get fresh bread every night."

When we got close to Guam, it was a beautiful day out, and I could smell something awful strange. It was the grass growing and the trees growing on Guam. I didn't know you could smell something like that. There was nothing on Iwo Jima to smell except shit.

I left Guam the day after Christmas of '45 and went to China. I volunteered for mess duty. I didn't want to do anything else—I did mine, I thought. All I wanted to do was just stay there until my number was up, go on home.

My brother who was a prisoner wasn't liberated until the end of the war, but he beat me home. He met me down in San Diego, at the Marine recruit depot down there. And that's where I saw four recruits standing in the hot sun with galvanized buckets over their heads, on a platform about four or five foot high, counting cadence and marching in place. In the hot sun with a galvanized bucket on their heads. Now, what is that gonna prove to a person? I don't want to be there, that's what it proved to me.

But anyhow, we went out and drank a few. It was April of '46, and I had my greens on. It was pretty warm, so I took off my jacket. We're sitting in a booth at a bar, talking over old times. We go to leave, and standing right outside is an MP. This MP grabs me and throws me up against the building and says, "Marine, you're outta uniform."

He didn't have to be mean to me. All he had to do was tell me. I noticed he had the Third Divvy patch. Well, that's the division I went through the war with. I pushed him back. I said, "You're chickenshit. You come from my outfit." He grabbed me, and he pushed me up against the building again, only this time he kept me pushed up. He said, "You're under arrest." Threw me in the brig. My brother kept saying, "Aw, come on. He just got back from overseas. He's going home for discharge." I was afraid of wrecking my record and I wouldn't get out.

They put me behind bars, took my belt off, took my shoelaces. I got back just in time for muster.

From then on I said, "Yes, sir. Where you want me to sit?" And if I was anyplace off of a troop train, I made sure that my necktie was tied, my jacket was buttoned, my belt was buckled. Oh, yeah. I didn't wanna give nobody no problems. All I wanted was o-u-t. And I got it.

They discharged me a corporal at Great Lakes, Illinois. I never got one day's pay as a corporal—I was a corporal and I was out the door. They wanted me to sign up again. Of course, they'd already screwed that up for me. I couldn't stomach their type of discipline. Discipline's what made the Marine Corps different.

Went from Great Lakes over to Rockford, Illinois, and I picked up my beloved, and we went home. There's no words for what it was like to see her again. Absolutely none. I could've died right then and I'd have been happy.

I had a rough time squeezing out even "I love you." In fact, I don't think I told her I loved her until we were married. But she knew I loved her. I never even proposed to her. Isn't that horrible? In fact, my oldest brother bought her a wedding ring. I didn't have any money.

I was home anyhow.

* * *

When Vietnam got going, I said, "Son of a bitch, we don't need any more recruits for the VFW."

Mom and I both did a lot of soul-searching in those days. Didn't stop me from drinking, though, I hate to say. I cried an awful lot when Gary went overseas. Mom and I cried our hearts out.

I counseled him to stay out of the Marine Corps. Nobody has to be hollered at like that, stand there and count cadence with a galvanized bucket on your head in the sun. You can make a man a soldier without that.

I never counseled him to avoid the military. I thought, and still do think, it's a duty of the people. Right or wrong, it's our country. I think that says it. Right or wrong, it's our country.

When he was gone, I was awful lonesome. I used to go out in the side yard in the sun and talk to him on the tape recorder, making a cassette to send. That was hard. "Oh, there goes a truck down there. Did you hear the rattle? I bet there's something loose." You had to make up something to say. I had no words of wisdom, nothing profound.

When he came home, it was, let's have a party. That was a very, very joyous thing.

My daughter had had a baby while he was gone, so we had a banner on the side of the house that said, "Welcome Home, Uncle Sergeant Gary." The kids had gone up on a ladder to put it up, and somehow they got it upside down. I wasn't about to go up there and change it.

He didn't tell us exactly when he'd be home. I saw this airplane fly over, and it flew this kind of strange approach to McChord for a civilian airplane. I said, "I betcha Gary's on that." I guess I'd had about three or four drinks in my belt, so I sat around and waited and waited and waited, but no phone call. So I says, "I guess I was wrong. I'm gonna lay down on the couch."

Well, a few drinks and you lay down, you go to sleep. The next thing I know, my wife is screaming, "Gary! Gary! Gary!" And there he was, big as life, with a nice clean-shaven face.

When he got to Fort Lewis, they made him shave off his beautiful mustache. They could've handed him his papers in less than two minutes. He would have been outside of the office and a free person. But the captain had to take and prove what, I don't know. As far as I'm concerned, all he proved was that he was a jackass.

Those first couple weeks I wouldn't let him out of my sight. Awful hard to believe that my boy was home. I shouldn't say "boy." My young man was home.

I'm proud to have been a Marine. And, to be truthful, I'm not ashamed for anything I did or didn't do. I'm really not ashamed. If I wouldn't have went and fought along with the rest of the people, we would be under the rule of either the Japanese or the Germans. And that I didn't want. I was fighting for the freedom to be able to live and believe the way I want to, instead of living according to somebody else's whim.

After the war I loved harder. I've always loved people. Well, dogs, too—everything's included, everything living. I like to hug, touch. I guess I was that way before I went in, and I'm still that way. But I think I loved better after the war. And I don't mean sex. I think I am more tender.

I find it much easier to say "I love you" to my wife and my family. And I'm talking about extended family. I'm associated with a church, and perhaps 125, 130 people go there. I can walk up to any one of them and hug 'em and tell 'em "I love you" and mean it.

I couldn't have done that before. I hope if the war did anything to me, that's what it did. Of course, age has a lot to do with that, too.

Life itself is so precious. We don't know when we're gonna die or get killed. We don't know when the Lord is gonna take us home. So we'd better be ready now. I want to tell people I love them now, because maybe tomorrow I won't be able to.

XVII

"Not my kids."

GARY SWANSON

GARY SWANSON

MACHINIST, AEROSPACE INDUSTRY
DES MOINES, WASHINGTON
SERGEANT, UNITED STATES ARMY, VIETNAM

In 1960, John Kennedy ran for president on the slogan "Let's Get This Country Moving Again." The United States had hardly come to a standstill in the 1950s. By decade's end, television had taken its place in American living rooms, rock 'n' roll had been born, and the modern civil rights movement had had its baptism in Montgomery, Alabama, with the bus boycott set off by Rosa Parks and led by a twenty-six-year-old preacher named Martin Luther King Jr.

But many Americans did perceive, rightly or wrongly, that for eight years Dwight Eisenhower had presided passively over a nation whose progress had stalled. Joseph McCarthy's career as the nation's most truculent anticommunist had ended with his censure by the Senate in 1954, but McCarthyism had outlasted its namesake, still confining respectable political dissent to narrow boundaries. Eisenhower had sent troops to Little Rock, Arkansas, to enforce court-ordered school desegregation, but he otherwise called for black Americans to have "patience" in their struggle for equal-

ity. Rosie the Riveter had relinquished her place on the assembly line to the returning GI and gone back to tend home and family.

America's pent-up political, sexual, and social energy exploded during the 1960s. Early in the decade, civil rights organizers launched a series of campaigns deep in the land of Jim Crow. Watching on TV as peaceful protesters were set upon by police dogs and water cannons, average American citizens were confronted with blunt evidence that the laws and customs of their country did not always accord with its promise of liberty and justice for all. In 1960, the birth-control pill appeared; over the next decade it would help spark a revolution in relations between men and women—both in bed and everywhere else.

Starting in 1965, this ferment helped feed—and was fed by—the antiwar movement. Using the successes of civil rights activists as a model, young people opposed to the nascent escalation in Vietnam wasted no time before taking to the streets, and in April, fifteen to twenty-five thousand antiwar demonstrators marched in Washington, D.C. As American involvement in Vietnam swelled over the next several years, so did the antiwar movement grow larger and more visible. Not all involved were college students; however, they formed its core and supplied its energy.

Meanwhile, African Americans in urban ghettos erupted over their poverty of resources and hope. Riots ravaged Los Angeles in 1965; Newark and Detroit in 1967.

Then, in 1968, all hell broke loose, and at its center was Vietnam.

Most military personnel in Vietnam were contemporaries of the protesting college kids, whose studies—those of the male students, that is—were made possible by the college draft deferment not done away with until 1971. Some in Vietnam were affected by the maelstrom at home; others paid it little heed.

Gary J. Swanson went to Vietnam in 1969, shortly after the inauguration of Richard Nixon had given the antiwar movement a new villain on whom to focus its anger. Gary served in II Corps with the Fourth Infantry Division.

Do you know about the way they used to train dogs? I'm not so sure it's even true, but it certainly brings my point across about the way the military trains soldiers. A dog trainer would put a hangman's noose or a choke collar on a dog and then hang him to a tree. And the dog would fight the choking from the noose or collar. Fight it and fight it and fight it. And then finally realize that fighting it is only making things worse, because the noose or collar's getting tighter. So the dog just gives up fighting it. At that point the handler will let the dog down. He's broken its spirit. Now he can train it, easily and quickly.

If the dog fought until it died, well, so be it. You didn't lose anything—it's not trainable.

I liken that to the way the military brainwashes their inductees. And I don't like that. They take away your dignity. It's not right, and I agree with my dad that it's totally uncalled for. They don't need to beat you over the head to get an idea across.

If I were my dad, knowing what I know now, I would have told my son—me—"Go to Canada." In fact, when my sons were growing up, I said that if a draft was instituted and they came of age, I'd move to Australia. The wife and I looked into jobs in Australia, the airfare to Australia. We ordered newspapers, found who was hiring machinists. What the housing cost was. How you go about giving up your American citizenship and becoming a citizen of Australia. I looked into that. You bet. If I'd been forced to, I would have even tried to do it illegally, like the Mexicans do here.

Everybody has an obligation to their country—I agree with my dad on that. However, not my kids. I hate to say that. I know it sounds like a double standard. But I've seen what they do.

The infantry's the backbone of the military. I won't say they do all of the killing, because you've got the fighter pilots that kill, and you've got the submarines that kill, the gunners on board ships that kill. But, for the most part, they don't get shot back at like the infantry does.

You have to have a special type of person for that. Perhaps that's the purpose of the training: to make that type of person out of anybody. Maybe the Army and the Marines need to do a better job of selecting who they put in the infantry. There's people out there that love to kill. Right here in Seattle, you got all kinds of murders going on. Grab those people and put 'em in the military, for Christ's sake. Let 'em kill legally. You don't need to *train* somebody to do that. You got lots of people who already *want* to do that.

All right, maybe there aren't enough criminals out there to fill up an army. I don't know what the answer is. But it certainly isn't beating some guy over the head with a hammer to turn him into a mad dog.

What's the answer? I don't know. My kid's not the answer.

Let the neighbor's kid go.

My senior year in high school, we started having recruiters coming around to the school telling us that if you wait to be drafted, you're gonna end up infantry in Vietnam. You're better to join now, and we'll promise you a desk job in Maryland somewhere—whatever, Germany. Someplace where they're not fighting.

After I graduated—in 1966—I thought I'd go to college and get a II-S deferment. I went to Tacoma Community College, where I couldn't get into studying. Just couldn't get into it. Flunked out in the first quarter.

While I admired my dad and wanted to serve my country, I didn't want to die in Vietnam. It was like a pendulum hanging over your head, swinging ever lower and lower. At that time, since Boeing was a government contractor, I thought I could get a deferment for being an apprentice there.

So I went to work for Boeing, got into an apprenticeship. I was there almost a year, and I got my draft notice.

I went to the company. I said, "Hey, you gotta get hold of my draft board and tell 'em that they can't draft me because I'm an apprentice for you." The company said, "Sorry, we can't help you. You need to go talk to the union."

So I went to talk to the union. They said, "No, you gotta go talk to the company."

I went to my draft board—"Sorry. We gotcha." To this day I do not know why I didn't get that exemption. I've heard there was a minimum number of hours in the apprenticeship needed to qualify; maybe I wasn't there long enough. I was only there to get out of the draft. I didn't care about the job.

I had, if I remember right, three weeks to report to my induction center. I gave Boeing two weeks' notice.

The day that I brought my toolbox home, I opened up the mailbox and there was a postponement letter there. I had already quit my job. Now what do I do?

I talked it over with my dad. He told me, "Don't join the Marines." He said that my chances of dying would be greater with them. "Go down and talk to the Army recruiter. See what he can do."

The recruiter says, "Oh, you bet. Sign right here." I signed. I ended up RA—Regular Army—and I was in the military in two weeks.

I took it because of that pendulum hanging over my head. I wanted to be able to determine my own future. I didn't want to have to sit there and wait; I wanted to get it over with.

At that time you could enlist as RA and still only have to be in for two years—it was a program the Army had for only six months. By having an RA in front of my serial number instead of a US—what draftees had—I thought I'd have an advantage over everybody else. I could still serve my country, just not have to go die in Vietnam. The recruiter never exactly promised me I wouldn't go to Vietnam. But he said being RA would "make all the difference in the world."

I got fucked. Which was the case with everybody who went in the military, RA or US. It didn't matter.

* * *

My dad drove me up to the induction center on the waterfront in downtown Seattle. It was hard on me, boy. He had an old pickup truck. You don't want to get out of the old pickup truck crying—not a good sign. So I swallowed the tears.

He said, "Well, bye, son," shook my hand. I said, "Bye, Dad." I got out and closed the door. The window was down, and I was going to say good-bye one more time. But he moved on.

They took us into the induction center, where we're all still in long hair—those who had it—and civilian clothes, and we stood in a room, probably fifty of us. An American flag and the military flags were all there, with a big strapping drill sergeant in front giving us the old gung-ho talk. Raise your right hand and swear to God.

They loaded everybody onto olive-drab buses to go down to Fort Lewis. The drill sergeant on the bus was a nice guy. Told us what to expect, that they were gonna be hollering at us.

The bus stopped in the middle of nowhere. We got off, and there was a fella there in a drill sergeant's hat hollering at us, just like my dad says. Hollering up a storm.

We pretty much all snapped to, tried to do what he said. But we had no idea what "dress right" meant or "attention" or "at ease." We were just civilians. Hollering right in your face.

There was this one guy with long hair, and one of the drill sergeants was calling him "Suzy." Then this sergeant took out a marker and pulled this guy's hair back and wrote "Suzy" in his scalp underneath his hair. And when we all went in for haircuts, this guy came out and he had "Suzy" written right across the top of his head. I can remember being surprised at the quality of the penmanship. The sergeant had used permanent marker—it was there for weeks. That poor guy got harassed like crazy. He didn't last very long. They just had a way of doing it, hanging you by that choke collar. Either you give up or you die. After a month of basic, they got him out on a Section 8. That means you're nuts.

When we were raising our kids, I didn't holler at them unless they deserved it. In the Army it didn't matter. You got abused for doing nothing. That's what I couldn't see my kids having to go through.

There was some rule in there where the drill sergeants couldn't hit you. They couldn't "destroy government property," was the way they put it, and you are now government property. That was if they had witnesses. Guys would come back all beat up and say, "My drill sergeant just beat the shit outta me." And there was nothing they could do, because there were no witnesses. For all anybody knew, it could've been the guy sleeping in the bunk next to him. Happened all the time. Choking you with the choke collar.

I have to tell you, once I got in, I was gung ho. My dad mentioned how he really liked the cadence. Well, I did, too. I enjoyed that marching, everybody together, the teamwork. Take care of the guy behind you or the guy in front of you, and he'll take care of you. That was kind of nice.

But if somebody wasn't toeing the line, the whole company would be punished. Well, you let that happen two or three times, and pretty quick the company's beating the guy up. The Army doesn't have to do it. We'd have "blanket parties"—throw a blanket over his head, beat him to a pulp. The blanket is so that he can't tell who's doing it.

We had two or three blanket parties in basic, if I remember correctly, maybe more. And I took part. You have to realize, the way I feel now is a lot different than then. I felt I was doing the right thing by being there. I was being forced to do it, but, by golly, I was gonna make the best of it. And I wanted to get rank. I wanted to be a sergeant. I wanted to be somebody that everybody else looked up to.

Well, in order to do that, you have to follow the rules. You don't want to be a red light among a bunch of white lights. If you weren't part of the blanket party, pretty quick the blanket was over *your* head. So you take part.

I was gung ho. That was the way they wanted you to be, and that's the way I was.

I was gung ho all the way up until I stepped off the airplane in Vietnam.

* * *

We had two guys commit suicide in basic. And in my opinion both of them were due to harassment or abuse, whatever you want to call it. The guys just cracked, is what I think.

One fella, his father was a military chaplain. We were on the hand-grenade range. The drill sergeant walks you through everything, step by step by step, and it's very accurately done. You pull the pin. You still have hold of the spoon of the grenade, the handle—it's spring-loaded. Then you open your hand and that spoon—*ping*—pops off, and you got four seconds before the grenade explodes. So you throw it out towards this stack of old tires—you're supposed to think it's a person out there.

We couldn't see what happened to this kid; we were behind a berm in a prone position, facedown. The sergeant related the story later. What the kid did is, he pulled the pin, and he looked at the sergeant, and he popped open his hand and just stood there with it. That sergeant had four seconds to get the hell outta there, because it was obvious the kid wasn't gonna throw it. The sergeant jumped behind a little ridge, and the grenade went off and killed the guy. It was a definite suicide.

Well, they stopped training immediately, made us all get back on the bus and go back to our barracks. We knew immediately that somebody had died on the hand-grenade range, but we didn't know it was a suicide until they posted it in the dayroom at the company quarters a week or two later, after they had investigated it.

We were all shook up. It made the whole purpose of the military clear: death and dying. That's what the Army does. And this was my first experience with violent death, even though I didn't see it.

The second suicide was only about a week after the first. A fella jumped out of a second-story window with one end of a rope tied to his bunk and the other around his neck. Right in our company.

I tried to do my best in basic, and I finished third in the company. I figured that if they thought I was a good guy and was really earnest about doing all right, I wouldn't end up in the infantry, and I could go somewhere else, anywhere else.

Well, the last day of basic training, I got my papers telling me that I was infantry. That means you're going to Vietnam. You're not going to Germany, you're going to Vietnam.

All I knew about Vietnam was what I'd seen and heard on TV. They gave casualty reports, and the reports were always positive. We never lost any fights. We always kicked ass. I thought it was all right. And on the news it looked pretty interesting. Kinda scary, certainly an adventure. Always been kind of an adventurous guy. I didn't see anything wrong with it. Even after I got my papers, I was still gung ho.

My dad was pretty patriotic. I certainly didn't want to disgrace my parents by being kicked out of the Army for whatever reason. Going where I was called was the right thing to do. Until I stepped off that airplane in Vietnam.

My country needed me. I didn't know why. Never gave it a second thought. There were people protesting it and people going to Canada. They were the druggies that did that, right? Not me. Certainly my government wouldn't lie to me. I followed it blindly. What a mistake.

I took my advanced training at Fort Lewis also, right across the parade field from where I had done my basic training. Then I came home on leave, drunk for a month.

Got introduced to drugs during that month, too—marijuana and speed. The guys that I'd gone to high school with who didn't go into the military, that's what they were doing. Yeah, fine. Doesn't matter. I'm gonna die anyway, so let's do it.

I didn't want that scene of saying good-bye to my dad at the airport. This one was going to be worse than when he dropped me off to report for induction, because I might not be coming back. So I said good-bye to my parents at the house and had a good friend of mine drive me to Sea-Tac. I flew to Travis, near Oakland, got on a civilian airplane.

After we're on this plane for twenty-four hours, they come over the intercom and warn us that they have to make a rapid descent into the airport at Tan Son Nhut. They don't do a long glide path because of the danger of being shot down.

So the airplane noses down. I'm looking out the window to try to see the ground, but it's overcast and we're weaving in and out of clouds.

Pretty quick, here comes the ground. All I see are woods, jungle. The wheels hit, and we come to a stop. The pilot comes over the intercom and tells us what the temperature is outside, and welcome to Vietnam.

This is the part I keep referring to: when I stepped off the airplane.

My first whiff of Vietnam was burning shit. I'd never smelled burning shit before. That's how they'd get rid of it. The whole country smelled like that. What an ungodly smell. And right then, that instant, I knew: "I've made a mistake. This is wrong. I can't live like this for a year." That smell changed my life.

I had this ready-to-go attitude, this picture in my head that when I step off the airplane, there'll be a jeep or a bus that we'll get on, and we'll get our weapons and get into the war.

Instead I got this terrible smell and a blast furnace in the face. I was prepared for heat. I wasn't prepared for the combination of heat and that smell. I've never smelled it since. Only in Vietnam have I smelled that. And my heart sank in horror right there.

The smell was overwhelming. I had been trained for combat—I knew how to camouflage my face, I knew how to load ammunition into an M-16, I knew where the trigger was—but I was not trained for that smell.

After a two-week orientation, I went right up to my company in the field—that would have been March 19, 1969. I was a replacement; I went in alone. My company had just had a big firefight, which killed and wounded a lot of people, so there were several of us new guys out in the field. The old hands didn't like to see new guys—"FNGs," they called us, fucking new guys—because we were green, didn't know what to expect. Of course, we were scared to death.

We went into the Chu Pa Mountains. The whole battalion was set up on mountaintops around a valley, because it was suspected that in the valley was a North Vietnamese military R&R center. And the Air Force was running Arc Lights—B-52 raids—on this valley. Thousand-pounders from thirty thousand feet. They were so high up we couldn't even see the airplanes.

We were a mile away. You couldn't see the bombs dropping, but you could hear them. Kind of a *zhoop-zhoop* sound. When they hit, there was a big flash of light, and then a ripple would go out through the jungle—the ground would shake, and all the trees would just fall over. And when the smoke cleared, there was a hole in the ground from each bomb that was huge—I'd say fifty feet in diameter and probably twenty feet deep. This went on for probably a whole hour—they were just walking the explosions right up the valley floor.

The only way out of the valley was to come up over the hills, where we were. So we ended up in a lot of firefights. Our first night in the mountains, they sent my company down a ridgeline to another ridgeline, where there was a gap in our lines.

The enemy saw us walking down that ridgeline, so they started dropping mortars in on us. I was brand-new in-country, and I thought I was in pretty good shape, but I wasn't. I couldn't make it back up to the top, so I just kinda sat down and figured, "If that mortar's gonna get me, it's gonna get me." But it didn't. Close call. From that point on, I tried to cut down on my cigarette smoking.

We had artillery set up not too far away, and they would drop big four-deuce mortar rounds and 105 howitzer rounds around our position to deter the enemy from sneaking up on us. One of the rounds they dropped was a Willie Pete round, white phosphorous, and it landed in some dried bamboo, which started a fire that burned right up our side of the hill, right over the top, and down the other side. There was nothing we could do except get down in our bunkers and pray that we didn't get burned. A couple people did get burned, but for the most part, all it burned was our sandbags.

It burned right over the top of us. I hadn't been in Vietnam more than a month. What a christening. I thought, "What the hell have I gotten myself into here? And I've still got a year to go."

18 March 69
Tuesday

Dear Mom,

I'm going to give it to you straight. Tomorrow morning I'm leaving for the boonies (jungle) at 0700. The company I'm going to has got only 70 men in it. Last week they had heavy contact with the NVA and had 9 killed & 21 wounded. I am definitely scared.

We're leaving here on a convoy, going to a landing zone, then to our company by helicopter. I don't know how often I'm going to be able to write so don't get worried if you don't get a letter for a couple of weeks. The army will let you know right away if anything happens to me. . . .

My mustache is really getting long. I have enclosed only one of my hairs so be careful when you open it. . . .

Better go now, so I'll write later. Say hi to Duff & Marsh [Gary's brother and sister-in-law] for me would you please. I don't think I'll write them cause I don't have much to say.

Love,
Gary

I've got some more time to write so I guess I'll try to think of something to say.

I'm finding it easier to make friends—it seems like everyone over here has one thing in common, survival!

I'm really going out there, into the jungle. My rucksack is all packed and I'm ready to go in the morning, but not looking forward to it.

I've got three canteens on my pack, and from what I've been

told I'll need more. Water is supposed to be hard to get hold of out there. I won't have that problem much longer, cause the monsoons are supposed to start in about 40 days.

Oh I wish I was home. . . .

There were 3 trucks full of bodies at the dispensary today—it's unbelievable over here, something I'll never forget. You've probably already been through all of this, Dad. How did you feel the day before you went out into the field? Everyone says it's normal to be scared. I hope so.

There's a monkey in our living quarters right now—it's the cutest thing you've ever seen.

Guess I'd better go now. I'll see you in 354 days.

With lots of love & thought,
Gary

I started out as a regular old grunt, private first class. Those of us that were nobodies and nothings took our turn at walking point, digging the bunkers, doing the grunt work. As I was there longer and longer, I realized what the good jobs were. First off, being a sergeant was a good job. You could always assign somebody else to walk point. But even better than that was being an RTO, a radio telephone operator. At three or four months into my tour, I saw an opportunity and volunteered.

As RTO you had information. You knew where you were gonna go and how long you were gonna be there. You got to carry the map. You knew which way to go if you were separated. You went with an officer, usually, and officers weren't going to put themselves in any more danger than they had to. And the higher you went in rank as an RTO, the easier you had it. I eventually worked my way up to a sergeant at the company level, so for the last two months of my tour I was with the captain, and I very seldom left the perimeter.

Being with the captain, I could see that we had bad management. And it wasn't just the captain. All of the officers.

In one particular case, we were walking single file up to the top of a hill. It was triple-canopy jungle—you couldn't see four feet off the trail. And we walked into an ambush. The gooks liked to ambush in the center of a column of guys. Split you into two—half up the hill and half down the hill. But in this case they only got the lead element.

We had a scout dog with us that smelled out the ambush. He alerted—pointed, whatever dogs do—and apparently the dinks saw that and sprang the ambush. The dog was killed. We didn't have any people killed during the ambush; some were wounded. We fell back into a defensive perimeter, and we spent the night there licking our wounds.

The next day the captain made a decision that we're gonna go after these guys. But rather than continuing up the trail where we were ambushed and then walking along the ridgeline that connected the hills, he had us go down into the valley, then up the next hill back up to the ridgeline. And on top of that hill was a whole company of NVA.

We got our asses kicked because this guy was stupid. You want to maintain the high ground, so you don't purposely go downhill. You don't do that. Either he wasn't listening in class or he had a better idea. We ended up with two dead and one missing, who is still missing. Dennis Lee Gauthier, nicknamed Sharkey because he liked to play cards. Never found him. Not even a piece of him.

This captain got shot by one of our own bullets. It was a machine-gun bullet, a 7.62-millimeter round. The same bullet is shot by both the M-60 machine gun and the M-14 rifle, and we didn't have M-14s. So either the enemy had an M-14, or an M-60 machine-gunner shot him, which is my guess. It hit him right in the stomach. Lost a lot of blood, but he lived through it. The way it was officially explained is, it was a ricochet. In triple-canopy jungle, where are you gonna get a ricochet?

That ambush was a bad deal. Nasty fight. Bullets zinging everywhere, hand grenades going off. You just go numb in that situation.

Another time we were in a small firefight. A bullet hit a guy's helmet. It went in one side, then went around the back and hit the metal hinge that the strap connects to, and a piece of the bullet went right into his temple. Later we saw he had a crease all the way around the inside of his helmet.

He went berserk. Of course, in a firefight, we're all keeping down. And you hear this guy screaming for his mom. Eventually died. We couldn't get any help to him. Hollered for his mom for probably a good fifteen, twenty minutes. That's how it was. It was never Dad.

Sometimes when it got really rough, I'd think about playing rummy with my mom. She and I always played rummy in the kitchen. She probably doesn't know how much that meant.

For the most part, I shut the bad stuff out when I think of Vietnam, and I try to remember the good things, the fun times. A lot of drugs in Vietnam.

Mostly marijuana and opium. There was some acid. But marijuana was the most prevalent. I smoked pot quite a bit. For the most part, everybody did. Certainly infantry.

It grew wild. Every now and then, you'd go into town and buy it—you could get a grocery sackful for five bucks. But if it had seeds in it, the tradition was, wherever the seed came out, rather than putting it in your pipe, you'd put it in the ground and let it germinate and grow. In fact, there were a couple times when we came back to an area where we had been earlier, and sure enough, plants were growing. It was everywhere. If you plucked some of it out of the ground, you had to dry it. So you just wrapped a wet towel around the roots and hung it upside down out of your helmet and backpack. The wet towel supposedly helped the resins—the good shit—make their way to the leaves; when the towel was dry, the leaves were ready to smoke. One thing I tell everybody is, the next time you see a photograph or newsreel footage of Vietnam and the infantrymen are wearing camouflage, take a close look at the camouflage. It's probably a marijuana plant.

I don't want to make excuses for everybody else, I'll just tell you why I did it. The pressure of combat is terrific. Smoking pot was a release. It was a way to relax. It put a different light on your situation. Worked great.

You'd light up before you went to bed and really sleep good. If you didn't, you'd be laying there and every little twig that would crack, every leaf that would fall, would wake you up. Any sound out of the ordinary. But, boy, if you were stoned, you slept real well, no matter how many leaves fell.

Most of the lieutenants smoked, some of the captains. You've got to realize, there was a lot of stress.

I want to emphasize, not all of the officers did it. More so it was the enlisted men that did the drugs. And sometimes we had a captain who was real strict on not smoking; then we were more careful. But you got to know who you could trust and who you couldn't trust. It was pretty much tolerated.

You could take practically everybody in our company and divide them into two groups. You had the heads, who smoked, and you had the juicers, who drank. You also had some people who did both. Not too many people who didn't do one or the other. Everybody knew who the other guy was, and you could pretty much tell by how they dressed and what they wore. The heads always wore the beads and had the peace symbol on—the upside-down bird's foot.

I still have my beads. They were made by a Montagnard village. They were carved out of wood, with a big wooden peace symbol in the middle.

Wearing the peace symbol was a way of protesting the war, saying you're against it, you shouldn't be here, didn't want to be here. A political stance.

We knew about the protesters at home, and I was for 'em. I wanted to be at home doing it, and I did after I got out. I liked the whole idea of it. Peace and love; drugs, sex, and rock 'n' roll. I saw that as the way out, not fighting in Vietnam.

The hand peace sign—the V—was big, too. We'd use it all the time. Instead of hello or good-bye, you'd give the peace sign. Or anytime you would wave at somebody, you'd wave with the peace sign. That's the way it was. It's one of the reasons why I was interested in the peace movement after I came home. But my interest had started the moment I stepped off that airplane at Tan Son Nhut.

There were soldiers in Vietnam who were angry that the people back home weren't behind what we were doing in Vietnam. In my view our government's supposed to be for the people. And if the people don't want us here, why are we here?

I still have that question. I just chose a side, and mine was the peace-love-and-tranquillity side.

However, I was stuck in Vietnam.

[c. August 1969]

Dear Mom,

I don't know what I'm gonna tell you for a whole hour. It's thirty minutes on each side. I guess I'll just record one side, and then you can send me back one.

I bought this recorder for fifty bucks. It's a thirty-five-dollar recorder. I gave the guy an extra fifteen dollars for batteries and tapes.

It's about—what time is it, Pete? It's about four twenty-five in the afternoon. We're about fifty meters from three or four barrels where they burn the excretion. Smells, the flies are all over it. The flies aren't as bad as they were when we first got here. They were really bad when we first got here, no kidding. . . .

Had LP last night. Really a hassle, it rained. No hooch. I'm soaking wet, cold. It's muddy. Got mud about two inches thick on the bottom of my feet. Might as well make that all around on my feet, on the tops, too. It's really—it's miserable, is what it is, Mom. . . .

Okay, I'm gonna play this back, see if it works.

[break]

Been having a little trouble with this tape recorder again. Can't figure it out. Seems to be working okay now.
Last time I was telling you about the flies around here. Doc [Hooks, the company medic] says the reason we got so many flies is 'cause there's so many gooks buried only six inches under the ground instead of six feet. And I told Doc he's crazy, because it ain't the gooks that's bringing the flies, it's Doc's—excuse the expression—shitters. Yeah, they just ain't worth shit. I guess they're okay in emergencies, like if you're gonna dirty your pants. But that's about it. I think I enjoy relieving my bowels out in the boonies better than I like relieving my bowels on Doc's shitters.
Dear Mom, gotta close for a minute, got some work to do. Be back as soon as possible. Got KP today, see you tomorrow.
[break]
Day is over. It's getting late, sun's down. I'm off KP. I had KP all day today. They're fixing to fire some LAWs over on the other side of the perimeter. LAW stands for light antitank weapon. M-72 LAW. It's kinda like a bazooka, only it's a single shot. Once you fire it, you gotta throw the tube away. You can probably hear 'em when they shoot 'em. Not too long from now.
[sound of fire]

Keep in mind, all of us out there were draftees. We didn't want to be there. We wanted to come home, and we were saving our own butts, whatever way we could. We didn't care about the missions, and we certainly didn't cooperate with our officers. That's probably a big reason why we lost the war.

The way we normally operated is, we'd send out two kinds of patrols. Ambush patrols consisted usually of seven people who would choose a trail and set up alongside it. Anything that came by, human or animal, was fair game. SRRPs—short-range recon patrols—would be two or three guys going out not to engage the enemy but just to see what's out there. As many as two or three different ambush patrols would be out at one time, and maybe two or three recon patrols.

Well, we didn't like to be out there in such small groups. We'd all leave the perimeter the way we were ordered to, so that the officers would see us going in the proper direction. But once we got out of sight, we'd circle around, meet up at a prearranged location, and then go together to a spot where we'd all set up. So now, instead of having four small groups of people, we have one large group. Safety in numbers.

At night the command post inside the perimeter would ask for sitreps—situation reports—from all the patrols. And since we were all there, we only needed to have one person awake, and he would send situation reports for everybody.

When you were out in the bush like that, you didn't talk, you'd "break squelch" on the radio by pressing then releasing the talk button on the handset—when you released the button, a scratchy white noise would be transmitted for a fraction of a second. You break squelch two times and everything is fine. If you only break squelch once, that means there's a problem.

All the patrols would operate on the same frequency, so every hour a radio operator in the perimeter would call for a sitrep from a patrol led by, say, the squad leader from Second Platoon, First Squad. "Two-one, two-one, send sitrep." Then to the patrol led by the leader of Third Platoon, Second Squad. "Three-two, three-two, send sitrep." Each time he'd get the sitrep, but from only one location instead of four. We'd just lie to him, break squelch twice: "Yeah, everything's fine." It worked out really slick, and nobody was the wiser.

Well, one particular night this group of sixteen or eighteen of us were probably a klick away from the perimeter when there was a ground attack back there.

They told us over the radio that we had three KIAs, but they wouldn't say who—we didn't know until we got back the next morning. Of course, before we got to the perimeter, we split up again and came in from our different angles. And then they told us all about what had happened, where the attack came from, and that Dieter Willert took a B-40 rocket hit to the head and died right away. I didn't see him; they'd already medevacked him by the time we got back into the perimeter.

Dieter was probably my closest friend that was killed over there. We played cards a lot, joked, talked about home. He was from Chicago. Everybody liked Dieter. Always happy, almost always stoned.

I have a lot of guilt over the fact that we were cheating that night. Had we done our job right, had we been out there doing the reconnaissance we were supposed to do, we probably would have been able to warn the perimeter that there was an attack coming. But as it was, the enemy surprised them and overran the positions.

> *We're on kind of a little hill. We can see—oh, wow—twenty miles it looks like in all directions, except for in front of our bunker, and we can only see maybe a hundred meters. So if we get a ground attack, it'll be from our side of the perimeter. No sweat, though.*
>
> *In that ground attack we had that last place we were at, a good, close friend of mine was killed. Dieter. I wrote you a letter, but I don't think I said anything about it. He was really a good guy—kinda ugly, but a good guy. He was from Chicago.*
>
> *Dieter had about six, seven months in-country, so he was getting pretty short. Not short, but he was getting down to be short. You probably remember me talking about Jones—he's home now. He was from Chicago, and Dieter was from Chicago. And when Dieter got out, he was supposed to look up Jones. Now somebody's gotta write to Jones and tell him Dieter won't be coming home.*
>
> *I was out on a SRRP, nine hundred meters from the perimeter, when the ground attack happened. I heard over the*

> *radio that three guys had been killed,* beaucoup *wounded. We didn't find out who had gotten killed, because they can't say that over the radio, until we got back to the perimeter. I asked my platoon sergeant who it was. Just came right out and said it: Dieter was killed. It just hit me like somebody hit me right in the head with a hammer. I ain't kidding. Really something.*

You've seen those movies where the infantry company would go out in the jungle for three days, *bang, bang, bang,* kill a bunch of people, and then go back into base camp until the next mission? We didn't do that. We were in the jungle for twelve months. We came into base camp three times in the year I was there. Those were called stand-downs. The reason we got to come in was to get new canteens, new boots, shave, get a shower, that kind of stuff.

There was a rule for us: You could have your sleeves rolled up during the day, but at six o'clock every night, your sleeves had to be down, no matter how hot it was, and you had to have the top button of your shirt buttoned because of the mosquitoes and the threat of malaria.

Resupply was terrible. We were supposed to get one hot meal a day, C rations for the other two. We perhaps got one hot meal a month. My Christmas Day in Vietnam—or maybe it was Thanksgiving—we had turkey out of a C-ration can (although we did have three beers each). Come to find out later, the food had been waylaid somewhere. Somebody stole it, took it to *their* troops.

As far as the weather goes, when it rained, you got wet. You can only get so wet, so the rain was no big deal—unless you were cold. Most everybody believes that Vietnam's always a tropical, warm place, even when it rains, but that's not true everywhere. We were in one place you could see your breath in the air, it was so wet and cold. Just miserable.

I still suffer with bad feet from jungle rot. When your feet are wet all the time, that's just what happens. My kids used to come up and try to tickle me on the bottom of my feet. I'm one of those guys, I'm just not ticklish on the bottom of my feet. But my feet are all scarred up, so I'd tell them, "The reason I'm not laughing is because my feet are dead." They believed it up until just a couple of years ago.

The rain was noisy. You get a big, heavy downpour, it's deafening. If it's at night, you can have an enemy walk right up to your face. You can't see him, you can't hear him, can't smell him, can't do anything. Totally defenseless. A miserable existence, just totally miserable.

During the dry season, water was a big issue. When you shaved, it was with cold water out of your helmet. For the most part, we all had beards in Vietnam. Didn't want to waste the water. We had some captains who were assholes. They tried to make us use our drinking water to shave.

One time we went three days without water. We ran out, but they couldn't resupply us because of weather conditions. We were drinking water out of bamboo. Bamboo comes in sections, and each section will harbor some water in there to feed the plant. We were taking our P38s—our can openers—and carving little holes in the bottom of the bamboo, and then we'd drain the water out into an empty C-ration can. It was coming out black and had bugs in it. And guys were fighting over that water.

That's the thirstiest I've ever been. When we finally got resupplied was the only time I've ever had water taste like silver. When you're thirsty, water's the best thing there is, even over beer, as hard as that is to believe.

That wasn't the only time we ran out of water either. The Fourth Division was terrible at resupply, just terrible. They didn't care. The people running the Fourth Division were in base camp, enjoying the good life. Probably had a map sitting in front of them: "Oh, this looks like a good place to go." And they would just negligently send the troops out there, not considering whether they had enough water or clean socks or the right shoes.

It seemed like the people in the rear just didn't give a shit, didn't care. Consequently, we didn't care either. The hell with 'em. But we were at their mercy. There was nothing we could do.

There were a lot of funny things.

When I made sergeant, the first job the captain gave me was to build a shitter. This was in a small firebase called the Punch Bowl.

So I got together three or four guys. We took some empty ammo crates apart, and we built him a shitter out of these wooden cases. We left the open side of it towards this hill, so he'd be a perfect target. Dug the hole nice and deep, and we built up sandbags to sit on, a crack in between. It was comfortable. We all sat on it and worked it down so it had a nice little round spot for his ass. It was a good one; I have pictures of it.

There was a type of telephone called a landline, which has a wire running from one radio to another so it's not using airwaves. And to call the radio that you're connected to, you turn this crank on it, and that sends an electrical signal through the wire and rings the bell on the other end.

We took the wire attached to one radio, and we snaked it through the sandbags on his shitter, and then buried the wire so you couldn't see it. And we told the captain, "Okay, Captain, your shitter is ready to go."

He didn't have to take a shit at that moment. But we waited and waited until he did. And we gave him a couple of minutes to really get a good turd hanging out of his ass, and we rang that telephone. *Rrrrring!* We sent electricity right to his ass.

He came outta there trailing shit behind him. He went to the medic with his ass bared.

We didn't get caught. He thought he'd been bit by a snake.

* * *

Before I got to Vietnam, I spent days and days training with a bayonet on the end of an M-14 rifle, sticking it into a dummy, hollering, "Kill! Kill! Kill!" I was ready to kill.

In talking with people, I've been asked that question a lot: "Did you kill anybody?" That's an important question. And I have a standard answer: "I don't know." Whenever I was shooting, I wasn't looking where I was shooting. I had the rifle over my head and my head stuck two feet down in the dirt. Don't know if I hit anybody. I was RTO and called in a lot of artillery, so indirectly, sure, I've killed people. But I didn't see anybody I shot at die. No blood on my hands. Clear conscience.

I've heard interviews of fighter pilots who say the same thing. Their job was to drop bombs. They didn't think beyond that. "What about when that bomb hit the ground and blew up little babies?" Well, that's not their job. Their job is to drop the bomb. Same with me. I didn't see anybody I killed.

Sure, we'd go and count bodies after a good barrage that I called in. But I didn't pull the trigger. I think that's why, in a firing squad, they have more than one person and somebody has a blank.

I have no qualms about what I did. In the training they make sure you understand that that's your job. There's nothing personal in it. You're not going out to kill an innocent person. If you kill somebody, they deserve to be killed—either you kill them or they'll kill you.

That's the reality, and that's a fact. If you're in a showdown, muzzle to muzzle, the first person to pull the trigger wins. You can't think twice about it. You can't stop and think, "Has this guy got a pretty wife? Maybe I shouldn't kill him." You can't do that. Immediately, he's got to go. It has to be second nature. That's the purpose of the training. I just don't agree with the training. Has to be a better way.

I hated the Vietnamese. They didn't like me, and I didn't like them. And it wasn't just the enemy either. It was all Vietnamese, even the South Vietnamese.

A good example of that: Every now and then we'd get to go on a convoy. And these convoys would be two, three miles long, hundreds of trucks carrying supplies, carrying infantrymen, going up through Mang Yang Pass between An Khe and Pleiku. And these convoys would go through little villages.

Well, the Vietnamese kids would line up alongside the roads, and the GIs in the back of the trucks would be tossing candy over the side for them. Feeling sorry for them.

My group always liked to be in the last truck—you could smoke dope. And while all these kids would be scrambling for candy that the other guys were throwing out, we'd be back there throwing full C-ration cans at 'em—*plop*—watching them go head over teakettle and laughing about it.

I'm not proud of that.

It wasn't directed at the kids, just the situation. Bad deal. We were all drafted. We didn't want to be there. A lot of hostility. A bad time for everybody.

No wonder they didn't like us.

Dec. 19, 1969

Dear Mom & Dad & Rick,

I'm really getting short—just now I have realized that coming home isn't as impossible as once I believed. A lot of my buddies have DEROS'd—and all of 'em one at a time. . . .

Remember now, when I come home I want to forget about Vietnam. Wait, I remember hearing myself say once that if I do make it home I'll never be sorry that I came over here—that <u>might</u> be true, I'll have to wait & see, I'm not home yet—about 77 days left. . . .

All my love & miss you much,
Sgt. Gary

Left out of Cam Ranh Bay, 213 guys on a civilian airplane with stewardesses, real round-eyed women. It was quiet when we got on the airplane. And as it took off, you could hear the wheels hitting the tarmac—*be-dump, be-dump, be-dump,* getting faster. And the minute it lifted off the ground, applause broke out. It was a happy moment.

Landed at McChord. I just had to go across the freeway to Fort Lewis to process out. And since I lived only ten miles from the base, I was basically already home.

I had grown quite a mustache while I was over there. Kind of a handlebar type. From my nose out, it was three inches, so a total six-inch mustache.

I had gotten a haircut and a shave in Vietnam. So here I am, all showered up, clean-shaven, except for my mustache. And the captain at Fort Lewis would not sign my discharge papers until I shaved off my mustache. Kept saying the rule is no hair past the corner of the mouth and below the lip. I'd rather have no mustache than a small mustache. So I shaved it off.

It meant more for me to get out of the military than it did to have a mustache. I wasn't nice to this captain. But you can't be too bad, or they'll throw you in the stockade and won't let you out of the service. They got you. You're stuck right to the last second. Nothing you can do.

Mustaches were a big thing in Vietnam, the big handlebar mustaches. They're nonmilitary, so everybody who had the nonmilitary frame of mind grew one. Again, if you see newsreel footage or photos of Vietnam, pay attention to the mustaches. There were some big ones over there, the bigger the better.

After they got me to shave it off, I immediately grew it back again. And I still have it. It's a statement about Vietnam, about the military in general. It says they didn't break me.

I took a taxi from Fort Lewis to my house. It was a ten-dollar ride, and I gave the cab driver fifty bucks. It was that important of a ride.

I didn't leave the house for two weeks. And then I started to come out of what little shell I was in, and I'd go around to the taverns and meet my friends. Kind of ashamed of the short hair that I had. My mustache was growing back. Drunk a lot of the time.

I didn't get a haircut or a shave for a year after I came home. I had sideburns so long I could tie 'em under my chin and a big old mustache. And the long hair. I was quite a sight.

At that time—spring of '71—a friend of mine was stationed at Walter Reed Army Medical Center in Washington, D.C. He was just getting out of the military, and he invited me to fly out there and stay with him while he did his outprocessing and then drive with him back across country.

When I got there, it was in the middle of some antiwar protests in Washington.

We took in a couple of protests, just to see what it was all about. While I was certainly against the war and everything it stood for, I was kind of numb. I didn't actively participate.

Glenn went to one of the rallies in uniform. He was still in the military at this point—I thought, "Boy, this guy's got big *cojones.*"

There were a lot of people protesting. And all the hippies and all the girls with no bras. It was great. I don't know how many times I fell in love. Those were good times, just one big party. And it was for a good cause. I'll join in on the party, but you guys go tell them what you think, I'm not stepping up.

I did have my own way of protesting. When I got out of the military, my status was inactive reserve—everybody had a six-year obligation. And so I would have to update my status every now and then. Did I get married? Did I change address? Did I lose any fingers?

The reserve board or whoever it was would send me this piece of paper that I had to fill out. I'd write "Fuck you" right across the front of it, sign it, and mail it back. And they'd immediately send me another one. "Fuck you. This is garbage. Don't send me this shit anymore. I've done my time." And send it back to them. What are they gonna do? Draft me and put me in the military? They can't do that—I've already been there.

I stopped writing "Fuck you" on the face of these forms when they sent one registered mail. Okay. I filled that one out and mailed it in. But that's what it took. They had to send one registered mail.

So you can see my protests were limited. There was a line there, and I didn't cross it. Didn't wanna do anything illegal. Didn't wanna end up in jail.

It took Glenn and me three months to drive to the West Coast. We ended up staying around Los Angeles with some friends he'd been in the service with back in D.C. It was great. Ten of us in a two-bedroom apartment, right on the beach, Marine Avenue and the Strand, in Manhattan Beach.

Those were the good days. Good time of the year, great weather, girls walking right by your front door all day long. And we're all ex–military guys, all wearing our love beads. We were hippies on the beach. Good stuff. Again, nobody really did any big protesting. We just didn't conform to what a good upstanding American would do. Drugs, sex, and rock 'n' roll. Not necessarily in that order.

Stayed there for a month or so. I came back up here, lived with my parents for a couple months till I found a job. And the drugs, sex, and rock 'n' roll lasted another, I don't know, five to ten years. I got married, and it didn't work out. Too much drugs, sex, and rock 'n' roll. Then I met the wife I have now, who straightened my ass right out.

My big problem was drinking. This started right after I came home. A six-pack of beer for breakfast, a six-pack for lunch, and a case for dinner. For at least ten years. Every night was Saturday night, and Saturday night was New Year's Eve. I never went to any AA meetings. Didn't think I needed to. I knew why I was drinking: Vietnam. No question about it. The military. Being mentally fucked over.

Maybe that's an excuse. The problems I had with Vietnam haven't gone away, but the alcohol has. Now I can have a couple of beers and not think another thing of it. So maybe it's not Vietnam; maybe it's just my personality. I don't like to blame things on Vietnam. But certainly Vietnam's at fault.

There was one incident that made me take a second look at my drinking. My twin daughters were just babies at the time. I was working swing shift, and I came home one night stumbling all over. I tripped and fell right between them.

They were both lying on the living room floor, under blankets, sleeping. Had I fallen a foot on either side, I would have probably killed one of them.

The wife said, "If you wanna stick around here, you're gonna quit that drinking." Well, I did. I won't say instantly, but I certainly tapered off. I'm an asshole when I get drunk. So I don't do that anymore.

When I was getting ready to come home from Vietnam, I left my phone number with the close friends I left behind. I told them that if they ever came through McChord, they should give me a phone call, and I'd get them drunk or buy 'em dinner or drugs or whatever they needed. Really only two people did it.

One was Henry Hooks, our company medic. He had just finished his tour in Vietnam and was on his way home to Atlanta. He called, and I went down to the base to pick him up. I brought him to my parents' house, and we had a big steak dinner. He was very appreciative, and my parents loved the guy. He was still kinda stung from his tour.

After dinner I took him up to Sea-Tac, and when we got there, two MPs started giving Henry a hard time because he didn't have the top button buttoned on his uniform.

I lit into these MPs for what they were doing to poor Henry. He'd been home less than twenty-four hours from Vietnam, and they're giving him a ration of shit about his top button not being buttoned.

I'd been home for three or four weeks, and although I hadn't shaved, my hair was still fairly short. So of course they wanted to know if I was still in the military, and they wanted to see my driver's license or my military ID or my separation papers. And a crowd started to form. I was yelling at them, and they were yelling back. And the next thing I know, I look around, and Henry's gone. He took off. I haven't seen him since.

You hear a lot of people talking about the hippies who spit on them, called them baby killers. The harassment that I got was from our own military.

When I got out of the Army, they would give you a psychological evaluation. And this captain I talked to said one of the things that would help me the best, being a combat veteran, was to talk about it. "Don't hold it in," he says. "It'll blow up on you. Go talk about it."

I took that advice, and I think it was a healthy thing. My friends will say that if you get me into a conversation about Vietnam, you'd better be prepared to sit down. I'm gonna talk your ear off.

My dad and I compared experiences when I got out, and we still do it today. We agree that the big difference between the Marines and the Army is the training, the abuse that they give to people. The Marines are much harder. That saying "Once a Marine, always a Marine"? Well, there's a reason why they say that. It's because the brainwashing goes so much deeper that you can't shake it. Choking you with the choke collar—the Marines hang on to you a little longer. The Army doesn't brainwash you so deep that you can't recover from it. You don't recover from the Marines.

I've got to give it to the Marines. It's a tough group. It takes a special person to be a Marine. My dad is a tough guy.

He and I talk about triggers, things that bring you back to the fight. Dad brings up sounds. Helicopters were the most prevalent sound in Vietnam. Even today, when I hear a helicopter, it immediately brings me back to Vietnam. For him the sound is sharp, loud noises.

Smells are another big thing. The burning shit. I've never smelled anything like that here, but you walk by an outhouse, that's close. That'll bring back Vietnam.

My dad had smells, too. One discussion we had was about the

smell of dead bodies, and we both know what that smells like. There aren't a lot of people who do. Or the difference between a burned body and somebody who was shot and killed in a road and has been lying there for a month. The burnt flesh has its own smell. He says now that Iwo Jima smelled like shit. But when we've talked about it in the past, he's said it smelled like burning flesh.

You become numb. There's no remorse; you just become numb. You see a dead body, you don't think about that person having a wife or kids. It's just a dead body, nothing to it.

That was the purpose of the training, and certainly you can understand why. They grab some kid off the street and train him to kill. You want to make him numb. Otherwise he'll turn into a basket case.

I was raised religiously—"Thou shalt not kill," which meant you don't step on an ant, you don't squash a fly. But it's okay to go to Vietnam and kill somebody. Pretty warped, isn't it?

I lost my religion in Vietnam. If there's a real God out there, how could He allow that to happen? I haven't found a religion yet that says that's the way to go. Can't be. I'm sure we were spawned by some alien. Where life began, I have no idea, but it wasn't from a God. Or if there is a God, it's not a good God.

And I'm not talking about what happened to me. I'm talking about the poor Vietnamese people. I still don't have a lot of love for them, but they suffered terribly. Terribly. In fear all the time. If not from us, from the VC or the NVA.

I saw what we did to them. I feel responsible, and I feel guilty. We would do what they called "cordon and search" of villages. We would walk at night to get in position to surround a village. And then a group of other military people would go in and search the village.

Well, they find that some poor guy's stuffed a rifle into his bunk, so now we say the village harbors VC, and we burn it down. That's not right. Poor guy just wanted a rifle to defend himself, probably. It's not proof that the villagers are VC. Or we burn their crop so they can't feed the VC. But then what do these villagers eat? They starve.

We didn't do right by them. They really had a right to dislike us. I'm surprised any of them wanted to come live over here.

I didn't have to go in the military. I could've gone to Canada, Australia. But I felt it was my duty. I needed to save my country. Save it from what, for crying out loud?

This Internet group that I belong to, they don't like to hear that stuff. They're, "We had a duty to do." What duty? Why were we there? I still don't know, other than my government told me I had to be there.

I've heard a lot of people try to answer that question. Just so many words. Doesn't mean anything to me. I do not know why I was there, why I had to go through that. My kids won't.

I'm proud of the service that I did in Vietnam. I look back on it with great pain and indignity, but it built me into what I am. I'm certainly a wiser person now. I certainly don't trust my government now like I used to, and I think that's healthy.

I hope I've brought this point across to my kids: "Question everything the government tells you."

I wouldn't change what I've done. Because I can pass it on, warn somebody else to go through life with their eyes open. In fact, grow another set behind your head. Don't just let things happen; take control. I didn't take control, and what happened to me could happen to anybody. I'm glad I went, so that I can let other parents know what could happen to their kids.

I survived, but it was traumatic. It was just a horrific experience.

XVIII

“It’s got to change you.”

LIFE AFTER WAR

The Artilleryman's Vision," by Whitman, begins:

While my wife at my side lies slumbering, and the wars are over long,
And my head on the pillow rests at home, and the vacant midnight passes,
And through the stillness, through the dark, I hear, just hear, the breath of my infant,
There in the room as I wake from sleep this vision presses upon me;
The engagement opens there and then in fantasy unreal,
The skirmishers begin . . .

As the vision deepens, the artilleryman hears "the sounds of the different missiles" and sees "the shells exploding." Then: "All the scenes at the batteries rise in detail before me again."

Veterans do not leave their wars behind them. In years following, their experience in war makes them quicker to anger or quicker to love. It colors how they drive a car, what they do for a living, even the foods they eat. After war, a veteran must find a way to live in two worlds, one present, one past, because the past world, the world of war, will always live within him.

JIM COYNE SR.

MANAHAWKIN, NEW JERSEY
TECHNICAL SERGEANT, UNITED STATES ARMY, WORLD WAR II

I left Europe just after V-E Day. I was one of the first to go, and it was all right with me. At that point the war against Japan hadn't yet been terminated. When we first got on that ship, we thought, "Hey, they're gonna take us out west. They're gonna land us over there at the Pacific Ocean, and then they'll ship us along toward Japan." But it turned out they didn't. It was a wonderful feeling when they told us we were going home.

Coming up to New York Harbor, Jersey City was right there. You couldn't miss it. They had a sign: "Welcome to Jersey City." I thought there was no place like it. And there wasn't.

MAS TAKAHASHI

TORRANCE, CALIFORNIA
TECHNICAL SERGEANT, UNITED STATES ARMY, WORLD WAR II

Mas fought in Italy with the 442nd Regimental Combat Team. He was near Milan when the war ended.

It was more fun after the war than during the war.

We moved up to a place called Lecco. We had pup tents, and we just rested and played ball and stuff like that. After that we moved to a place called Ghedi, and we started processing German prisoners that were gonna be sent back to Germany. They were coming any way they could—motorcycle and ambulance and whatever.

We'd have to search them for weapons—just like what happened to us before camp. Everybody was looking for souvenirs; I couldn't find anything.

We moved back down south again, near Livorno, and we were in a compound guarding German prisoners from an engineer group. So now the irony is, *we're* in the towers, and we're watching the Germans down there.

We got to go places. A Switzerland trip came up, so I took it. A couple of weeks later, there was one going to Nice, so I took that. A couple of weeks after Nice, there was one to Rome—I took that. I figured, "I may not come back this way again. I might as well take advantage of all these passes we're getting."

The Italians, they treated us good, because, after all, they got things from us. If we had extra rations, we gave them rations. They did our laundry, and we paid for it—with lire, or with chocolate or cigarettes. One time we were on a pass to Milan, and a couple of us guys jumped on the streetcar. We went, "Jeez, do we have to pay for this?" And some Italian guy—he spoke good English, so he must've spent time in the States—he said, "Nah, you guys don't have to pay. You won the war."

HOWARD L. BAUGH SR.

MIDLOTHIAN, VIRGINIA
CAPTAIN, UNITED STATES ARMY AIR FORCES, WORLD WAR II

When Howard arrived in Sicily in July 1943 to join the Ninety-ninth Fighter Squadron, the outfit, part of the Twelfth Air Force, flew tactical missions in support of ground operations. Early the next year, however, the Ninety-ninth joined the newly formed 332nd Fighter Group, also all-black, which was assigned to the Fifteenth Air Force and charged with the escort of heavy bombers.

"We were the only group over there that didn't lose any bombers to enemy fighters. We flew over two hundred escort missions and, all told, about fifteen thousand sorties.

"At first the bomber pilots didn't believe that blacks were in

those airplanes. Of course, they couldn't tell because with the oxygen mask on, your face is covered—that plus the distance between their airplanes and ours. But each of the fighter groups had their tail assembly painted a different color so that the bomber crews could look out and identify them. Word got around that blacks were flying those red-tail airplanes."

Howard flew 135 missions before being sent home in October 1944.

We were over there fighting for freedom and democracy. Came back to find that over *here* nothing had changed.

In my hometown in Virginia you still rode the back of the bus. The theaters and the restaurants were still segregated. The schools were still segregated.

I didn't expect it to change. A lot of people in the 332nd Fighter Group did expect it, but I didn't. I had grown up with segregation, and I just accepted things as they were. Maybe I shouldn't have, but that was my nature, I suppose.

The Army established a system of points for separation from service; I had more than enough points to get out. My wife wanted me to. She said, "Everybody else is going. Why aren't we going?"

I said, "Going where? What am I gonna do in civilian life?"

I would have gone to the airlines if they were hiring black pilots at the time, but I knew that they weren't. They didn't start until the mid-1960s, and they had to be sued to do that. The airlines thought that passengers wouldn't ride with a black pilot.

The military integrated long before that. During the war the military services were the most segregated segment of our society. Today they are the most integrated segment of our society. That's how much has changed.

GREG CAMP
COLUMBUS, GEORGIA
CAPTAIN, UNITED STATES ARMY, VIETNAM

About two days after the young soldier died in my arms, I got on the last helicopter out of that rice cache; we took some fire as we were leaving. I went back to the firebase, picked up my stuff, went to Saigon, outprocessed, and left.

I landed in San Francisco. They showered us, they sprayed us, they got us a brand-new khaki uniform. Then I was gonna go to San Diego to see my grandmother—Dad's mother. In those days you had to wear a uniform if you wanted to fly military space-available on a commercial flight, which was like half price. I was certainly gonna do that; I wasn't making any money.

So I got on this plane to fly from San Francisco down to San Diego, and I sat down. It was a little plane, just two seats on each side of the aisle; I was next to the window. And this young girl—she couldn't have been more than sixteen—comes and looks down. She sees that I'm in the seat next to where she's gonna be, and she turns pale white. I mean, pale white. She walks over to the stewardess and says, "My dad paid full fare for me to take this plane down to San Diego, and my seat's next to a soldier."

The stewardess was just as apologetic as she could be, like I was a leper. She said, "I am so sorry. I had no idea you'd have to sit next to a soldier. Let me see what I can do for you." And so she went and found some businessman who was willing to swap seats with this girl. He didn't say a word to me the whole flight.

That was the attitude. You were coming back as a pariah, as a second-class citizen.

I wasn't so much mad at the time as I was thinking, "She doesn't even know me. I'm not a bad guy. I went to West Point. I'm a college graduate." I wasn't thinking I was a war hero, because I certainly never felt then or now that I'm a war hero by any stretch of the imagination. It just shocked me that somebody would be that judgmental of me simply because of the uniform I was wearing.

STEVE KRAUS
Woodbridge, Virginia
Corporal, United States Marine Corps, Vietnam

I don't know what we were doing in Vietnam. I mean, at the time I had to have a reason. It was because I was ordered to. I was an American. I did what I thought was right. But now, I don't know what the reason was.

I don't know really whose war it was. Why were we there? Those people I saw working in the fields out there—they didn't care, I don't think, whether the Americans controlled them, the North Vietnamese, the South Vietnamese. They wanted their bowl of rice and some fish every day. That's all they wanted.

After I got home, I'd watch the news and read the papers: This is falling; they've taken that. I said, "Jesus Christ, we were in that same place two years ago. So-and-so died, and we took it. Now it's gone? What are we doing? What the hell are we doing?"

It was a real waste. There could have been a better way, whatever conflict was going on there. There must be a different way.

Mostly your kids, eighteen to twenty-two years old, were the combat guys. When I look at the guys my daughters are dating, shit, I wouldn't hardly let some of them walk across the street by themselves, let alone fight a war.

I'd hate to see it happen to them. It's not only the guys that died. Amputees, I see them in the hospitals. And there's a lot of things that happened to guys after they came back. Lives were destroyed. Plus I don't know why. Why? I don't think anybody's ever told me, really.

We were over there evidently for a treaty that we signed in 1954 to help the Vietnamese. It's been years since I read that stuff.

We were supposed to be there because of this and that and the other.

I don't know why we were there. They used to tell me in the sixties, and maybe even the seventies, but I don't think anybody can tell me now. Money? That treaty? I haven't the vaguest idea. I haven't the vaguest idea anymore.

MIKE JACKSON

TIPP CITY, OHIO

CAPTAIN, UNITED STATES AIR FORCE, VIETNAM

I'm angrier than I used to be. As far as being on medication or in a straitjacket, no. But war does change you, there's no doubt about it. Now, I'm not talking about being a clerk or a cook. I'm talking about people who are being shot at or are shooting at things on a daily basis, which is what I did and a lot of people did. It's got to change you. It's got to.

I don't share my war experiences with anybody. I share a lot of stories. People love my stories—but they're all funny. I've got great Vietnam funny stories, and that's all anybody ever hears.

Nobody cares, for one thing. Who wants to sit and listen to this stuff? I think it makes a good story for a book. But for me to sit down with friends and talk about it? This isn't the Mike Jackson they know.

Nope, I don't tell anybody about it. Not my wife, not my kids, not nobody. I just don't see the reason to do that. And I sure don't want to talk about it to my dad—I'd have a hard time keeping my emotions in check.

I'm sure for my dad's generation, and probably for mine, we didn't have this need for bonding that people have today. He was just my dad. Sitting down to understand him was never something I gave much thought to. Which is a shame, because there may be some day I'll wish I had done that, and it will be too late.

We do have a common bond, having been to war, but it's understood, not spoken. He's never sat down and told me his whole story, but I knew early on that he'd been shot down, and so I'd ask questions, and I pulled it out of him in bits and pieces. I love to hear about what he did, because it's a great story. But it's a different story. He saw airplanes and he shot at them. I saw people and I killed them. If he hit one, it went down. I had to go count feet and divide by two. That's how we did it.

There wasn't much left. Count feet or legs. Count and divide by two.

Here's one of my funny stories:

When I was living at Camp Eagle, there had been trouble with people trying to get through the wire, and there were stories about how they would come through and slit your throat in the middle of the night. I don't know if it ever happened or not, but that was the story, that the North Vietnamese guys would come through and would slit your throat and leave an entire hooch full of dead people. Being a new guy, I believed that was entirely possible.

In our Air Force hooch, each guy had his own room. It was nothing more than a plywood wall and a plywood door. All I had in the room was my bed, a light hanging over my bed with a little string that you turn it on and off with, and an AK-47 that was set on full automatic and cocked right next to the bed. Everyone had guns in their room, and you knew that it was unsafe to go into another guy's room at night, because he wouldn't know who it was. You didn't pull tricks on anybody at night.

One night I was asleep. In the middle of the night, I woke up, and I thought I felt somebody rubbing his hand across my head. And I thought, "I'm dreaming. It can't be," because nobody would come into my room. You just don't do that. I got an AK-47 sitting right next to the bed.

As I got more awake, I realized that the rubbing was not stopping. And the rumor had always been that what they do is they wake you up before they slit your throat, so they can see the look in your eyes as they kill you.

So I'm convinced there's somebody in the hooch, and probably everybody else in the entire place is dead, and I'm about to be the next one.

My bed is up against the wall. I'm laying there trying to decide what to do, trying not to open my eyes or act like I know that there's somebody there rubbing my head. So I finally decided that what I would do was, I would roll out of bed as fast as I could towards the open side of the room and try to knock him over before he could slice me up with the knife. And as I did that, I would grab the lightbulb and pull the string—trying to blind the attacker—then grab the gun if it was still there, and pull the trigger and spray it around the room, knowing full well that the bullets would go through all the walls in the entire hooch and shoot everybody else that was living there. But I figured they were all dead anyway.

I'm laying there, and I can still feel somebody rubbing my head.

So, in an act of desperation, I rolled out of bed as fast as I could, pulled the light switch, and grabbed the gun, which was still there. And just as I'm starting to swing around and squeeze the trigger, I look on my bed, and there's the world's biggest rat. It had to be as big as a cat. And what it had been doing was walking back and forth on top of my pillow, rubbing its body against my head.

That rat was the last thing in the world I expected to see. I threw the gun up in the air. Why it didn't go off when it came down, I don't know. And I ran out of that place as fast as I could.

I was pulling the trigger when I saw the rat. The first round would've gone through the living-room wall, where I don't think anybody was. But how many other rounds would've gone off would've depended on how fast I turned—I was gonna just pull the trigger and spin around.

But I saw the rat in time, and I stopped myself.

After I got outside, I thought, "Man, everything over here is supposed to have rabies." So I grabbed a .38 pistol out of a little living-room thing there—there were guns all over the place—went over to the mirror to see if there was any blood on my head, and thought I've got to go kill the rat so they can inspect it, because otherwise I'm gonna have to get rabies shots.

So I go back into the room, and just as I'm getting ready to shoot the rat, it goes out through a hole in the bottom of my floor.

I decided I didn't have any bites. But the rest of the week, I couldn't go to sleep. I'd get in bed, and I'd lay down, and I'd feel things crawling up and down my body, things walking on my head.

If I'd seen a person, I'd have been all right, but I saw this humongous rat. It had teeth about eight inches long. I've never seen a rat that big. Biggest scare I ever had, and it was a rat. Closest I ever came to hand-to-hand combat.

That's it. That's my funny story. That's my rat story.

ARTHUR WAY

Havre de Grace, Maryland
Corporal, United States Army, World War II

Before I left for the Army, I had been working in the small-arms firing range at Aberdeen Proving Ground; I went back to work almost immediately. I had a wife and two children to provide for.

Right after the war, I had some bad dreams. I remember one time particularly. I was wearing my watch to bed—why, I don't know. I jumped out of bed, and I was screaming, "Let me out of here!" and banging with my hands against the closet door. Broke the watch crystal, cut my wrist. It scared my wife to death.

We were living with my parents at that time, and my father came into the room, and he shouted in a loud voice, "Attention!" He figured that would stop me—and it did. I just stopped, and I stood at attention. Just the reaction when you hear that word.

Another time I had a nightmare in bed, and I was actually straddling my wife and choking her. My father came in that time, too, and stopped me.

I don't recall these things happening—I was told later. I don't even know what I was dreaming about.

But the nightmares didn't last too long. We moved out of my parents' home, and I got in a routine of going to work.

When the children were young, I didn't tell them about what I had done in the Army. We were at peace, and I didn't want them to know about the horror of the war. I didn't even tell my wife too much about it at that time.

I've talked more these last few years. The older I get, the more I want to leave some kind of legacy for my children. So they will remember me.

When it comes time, what eulogy I'd like to have at my funeral is to say that I loved my family and my country. That'd be all I'd need.

VINCE WAY

Havre de Grace, Maryland

Sergeant, United States Army, Vietnam

When I came back from Vietnam the second time, the roof on my parents' garage was leaking. I had a month's leave before going to Texas to finish up my enlistment, and my father said, "While you're on leave, we'll put some new paper on that roof."

I was feeling all uptight and sorry for myself: "Oh, goodness, I've just been through this horrible experience." I figured I'd go up there and open up to him a little bit, talk to him about what I'd just done. And he wound up telling me a few things that he did in prison camp. Some of the stories, like the people passing notes to him, humbled me very quickly. Made me realize my experience was nothing compared to his.

I was in Texas till July of '71, and then I relocated back home.

Over the course of the next two to three years, our conversations evolved more and more to where he had a comfort level to speak about what he went through. We sat and we talked. And I gained such an appreciation for what he did and what he went through. I was in Vietnam seventeen, eighteen months—he was a prisoner of war almost that long and was in the war twice that long.

We have a common bond. I wasn't a grunt, I wasn't a combat soldier. But we've been through some similar experiences. Those experiences change a person very much. We understand each other.

As little kids we knew you don't go over and touch Dad if he's sleeping. What we used to do was take the newspaper and fold it up like you'd be delivering it to a porch, chuck it at him, and yell, "Hey, Dad," because otherwise you could get hit by him. It wasn't intentional, but he would flail his arms and legs.

My understanding was, the German guards, if you were sleeping in the morning and you didn't get up when they called you, would come in and smack you on the foot with a rifle butt to encourage you.

He helped me when I came back. I was a little spooked after a year and a half over there, and I was home within thirty-six hours of leaving the combat zone. Sudden noises or movements made me a little edgy. He used to come up and throw things at me. He'd say, "You're a little edgy, ain't you?" Poke at me, slam doors behind me, trying to get me to get over that. Not a kind way to do it, but it was thoughtful.

And it worked. Because once the noise was made and I reacted to it, I realized I was not in a combat situation anymore. He was trying to drum it into my head: "You're home. You don't have to do that anymore."

Last summer Dad and I took a five-day road trip to Andersonville, Georgia, to the Prisoner of War Museum, which they just opened. It was time that he and I had alone without my mother listening to everything, because she doesn't like to hear it.

Talking has helped him a great deal. I think that my father's problem initially was that being taken prisoner was something less than glorious, and he was ashamed that he'd been captured. If you're staring at a German machine gun and all you've got is an M-1, there's not a whole lot of choice in the situation, but I think he had a lower opinion of himself and his service because he had been taken prisoner. Through time and through discussion, that's changed. Plus receiving the Prisoner of War Medal.

A lot of men felt that their service was demeaned by having been taken prisoner, so in 1985 Congress authorized this medal, and the military did ceremonies around the United States. I talked to the commanding general of Aberdeen Proving Ground, and he set up a ceremony. There were about thirty-five men who came there, and he pinned their medals on them. And it was good.

That took my father from where he felt bad to a newer level of pride in what he did. It gave him a reason not to feel ashamed.

For ten years beginning in 1961, the American military sprayed a variety of herbicides over South Vietnam to rob the enemy of forest cover and food.

Code names for the defoliants were derived from the colored bands around the fifty-five-gallon drums containing them. Between 1962 and 1964, Agents Pink, Green, and Purple accounted for most of the chemicals applied; in 1965, the spraying changed to Blue, White, and Orange, with Blue preferred for crops and Orange and White for forests. Orange proved the most useful of the compounds because it was oil-soluble—not water-soluble, like Blue and White—and thus effective in clearing out large patches of wet jungle. Of the almost nineteen million gallons of defoliant sprayed on South Vietnam from 1961 to 1971, 60 percent consisted of Agent Orange.

In 1970, the military ceased using Agent Orange because of concern over the toxicity of one of its ingredients, dioxin, a component also of Pink, Green, and Purple.

The U.S. Department of Veterans Affairs maintains a list of diseases whose cause among Vietnam veterans is presumed, for the purpose of granting service-related benefits, to be Agent Orange or similar herbicides. The most recent addition to the list is chronic lymphocytic leukemia.

* * *

At the time we didn't have any understanding of Agent Orange. Usually you were out at a camp or a firebase somewhere. And in order for the enemy not to sneak up on you, they would clear back maybe two hundred yards of all the brush and shrubbery so you had a clear field to fire at them.

A big plane would fly three or four concentric circles around your camp and spray something. Two days later all the vegetation was dead. And in a matter of a couple of weeks, you could go out and kick tree stumps over. You had a clear field of fire without a lot of effort on your part.

No one ever told us, "Don't stand outside when these planes are coming" or "Cover your drinking water." Whatever they sprayed got all over your clothes, got all over everything. Our drinking water came from sources locally. We showered in water that usually was stored in a tower, and the tower was open on top.

Nobody said anything. It was just "Oh, here come the planes." And after you saw them the first time, you hardly even noticed them. Nobody gave it a thought. Nobody ever told us that these chemicals that were sprayed on us could cause any problem.

I took an Agent Orange physical through the VA in the early 1980s. I gave them a list of where I had been in II Corps and when. They said that I was significantly exposed to Agent Orange by virtue of being in those areas and that it might have health effects later on, which is why they were doing the screening physicals.

In September of '98, after taking the routine physical I have every year on my birthday, I was diagnosed with chronic lymphocytic leukemia, CLL. Happy birthday to me. It's a slow-growing form of leukemia, and it's treatable. I know several veterans who had other forms of cancer, and the doctors weren't able to do anything for them. They went quickly.

In May of 2001, I began four months of chemo, and at the end of that, I was told that the cancer's in remission. They'll be checking me every ninety days, but hopefully it'll stay gone for a lot of years—we're hoping eight to ten, at least.

I'm optimistic now. I count myself very, very fortunate.

RICHARD RECENDEZ
HANFORD, CALIFORNIA
SPECIALIST FOURTH CLASS, UNITED STATES ARMY, VIETNAM

The morning of May 15, 1967, Richard was among a group of men sent by helicopter to rescue a reconnaissance platoon that had run into an NVA ambush. For his part in the rescue, Richard would be awarded the Bronze Star for heroism.

When most of the trapped, wounded men had been dragged to safety, Richard was hit. "The round went in through the back of my arm; they later took the bullet out from the left side of my chest." A sizable chunk is missing from the upper portion of Richard's left arm.

Richard spent the next six months recuperating in military hospitals before finishing his enlistment at Fort Ord, California, where for two months he trained soldiers in the use of the M-60 machine gun.

"There I was, training what I was a year and a half earlier. My first drill sergeant used to tell me, 'You'd better listen well, and learn, because most of you guys are going to Vietnam.' I said the same thing."

Came back to Corcoran. I was unstable, rebellious. I'd get in jail because of fights.

I was out of control for a couple of years. I was heavy into pot and drinking. I didn't want people close to me. My wife tried to figure out what was wrong—I just didn't care. I had a lot of guilt. I still have a lot of guilt—why I made it and my buddies didn't.

Richard sought treatment for combat trauma in 1978 and 1992 but found little relief until 1999, when he enrolled in a program of counseling and medication at the Veterans Administration hospital in Menlo Park, California.

He remains in treatment.

I go to a vets' center, and we'll share how we feel. A lot of us who have experienced combat have a tendency to deaden our feelings. So when people ask, "How do you feel?" there's just a numbness. Do you feel hate? Do you feel joy? Do you feel happiness? A lot of those feelings were taken away—and at a very young age. I was twenty. I was still a kid.

The numbness lets you survive. That's something I learned when I first got to 'Nam and started seeing this stuff, scared as hell. It became a way of life to see a buddy get killed. We had this saying: "It don't mean nothin'." You're still alive.

It sounds cold, but that was out of protection, my protection, dealing with the everyday life of the grunts that we were.

So you put up this wall. I don't let many people in, if any.

My dad—that's been his way of life. He's got that wall. And that's why it's hard for him to recognize what PTSD is. The way he sees it is that I'm physically okay. He doesn't realize that it's a mental condition. My mom's the same way. "What's wrong with you? Why do you take these pills?"

"I need to take them to keep me stable."

"Well, I don't see nothing wrong." My mom's seventy-eight and he's eighty-four. They can't relate, and I don't have the patience to explain it.

I know for a fact that a lot of the World War II veterans have PTSD. When you're faced with life or death on a daily basis, it messes up your normal way of thinking.

When he was younger, my dad was constantly nervous, jumpy, short on patience. In 'Nam I felt like, when you're in combat, you can't overconcern yourself with people, because it'll get you killed. That leaves an impression in civilian life. Now I realize that Dad didn't want to become vulnerable. He used to drink quite a bit. That was probably his way of dealing with feelings. Drinking or dope or whatever, it numbs your feelings. That's what I did.

He moved a lot. We really didn't have roots. My mom and dad split up when I was about eight years old, so Dad was gone a lot. We stayed with my aunt and uncle. And when I was raising my kids, we were always on the move, too. I can't recall how many times I moved my family. And, much like my dad, I've had all kinds of different jobs.

One thing I've learned through programs, the soldier in us—the soldier that we were—dominates our life. Until we recognize that soldier and shrink that soldier, our life is gonna be like a soldier's. Always on the move. Securing the perimeter. The soldier has to keep moving to stay alive. If you didn't, Charlie would peg you, and you'd get wasted. You had to be hypervigilant. So now I don't like crowds. If I go shopping, it'll be late at night, and only if I absolutely need something. There's a lack of trust in people.

You don't want to deal with feelings. You don't want to feel the roller coaster, the ups and the downs of life, the crawling back into ruminating about the war and the people you lost—not only in the war, but here, too. I know it's part of life, but it seems like I've had a lot of close friends die through the years, and I'm not that old. Neither were they.

I got out of high school in June of '65, got married in September. My father-in-law had six gas stations, and I was running one. He only had two girls—I was like the son that he never had.

My life was pretty well set: "I know what I'm gonna do. I'm gonna run gas stations." And that was a good thing back then in Corcoran because the only other thing was to work out in the fields, and I didn't want to do that.

All that changed when I got drafted.

I'm aware that some people don't believe in PTSD. But I know that before I went to war, I wasn't the way I am now. I had a joy of life. I had a lot of things ahead of me. But that was all gone. That was taken away from me.

My joy of life is gradually coming back. I don't think of suicide or homicide or anything like that now. I used to, periodically.

Time to time I still think, "Why can't this feeling just go away?" But it won't. It's a matter of coping, just like when I was in 'Nam. Then it was being able to adapt to a situation. I guess life is pretty much the same way today.

I'm proud of my service there. But I'm not proud of the fact I took some lives out. When you take somebody's life, it's nothing to be proud of. I regret that. And I can't justify it. I can say, "Sure, that's war. Better him than me. Sorry about that." But deep down inside it's not right. War is so unnatural.

I was trained to be a soldier, to do the job. That wasn't in my plan when I was growing up. I was satisfied playing cowboys and Indians. Vietnam made me grow in a different way than I'd planned to.

So here I am.

SCOTT TAKAHASHI

Radiologic Technologist
Gardena, California
Sergeant, United States Army, Vietnam

The Army drafted Lawrence Scott Takahashi shortly before his twentieth birthday in 1968.

"There were people doing everything they could to get out of the service. I wasn't going to enlist. I wasn't particularly enthused about going to war. But avoiding the draft was never anything I thought about, either. If you were called to duty, there was no question.

"I may feel more strongly about it now than I did then. Living in America is not a right, it's a privilege, and serving your country is something that goes with living here. The fact of the internment never diminished that feeling.

"In fact, I got that feeling from my father. I remember hearing from his mouth those very words—that service goes with the privilege of being an American—not long before I went into the service."

Scott spent his year in Vietnam on the crew, or "section," that manned a 155-millimeter self-propelled howitzer in the Thirty-fifth Artillery Regiment.

We didn't accomplish anything that I'm aware of in Vietnam. I don't think we did any good. Sometimes I think that we went to this country and all we did was blow it up. A lot of Vietnam is really green, and I got the impression that some of the places we saw were really green at one time, but we had killed the vegetation, defoliated.

In my unit we did a lot of shooting. The thing is, we never saw what we were shooting at. In the artillery we were always shooting in the distance.

Targets could be anywhere from five to nine miles away. We'd get reports—"There's a bunch of trucks going down the road." But, really, we didn't know what we were shooting at.

I can remember thinking when I came home that as far as I knew, I never killed anyone. I didn't think about it while I was doing it; you're just shooting in a particular direction. Which was probably good for me. I know there are a lot of infantry who went out on patrols, and those are the people who came home with problems. Their friends would die in their arms. Or they would see who they were shooting at. We had the luxury of never knowing exactly what we were hitting.

Thinking I didn't kill anyone eased my conscience; in my mind it lessened my involvement in the destruction. I mean, it's bad enough that we were over there, and we were blowing up the countryside. But to think that I killed someone?

I can still truthfully say that I'm not aware that I killed anyone. But it's highly probable that I did.

I was a lot younger then. I didn't know what I was doing and why I was doing it. Now it's just something I accept. It's part of my history. I can't change the past, and I'm not going to change the way I feel about myself. At the time you did what you had to do.

When I got drafted, I really had no direction. But after Vietnam I couldn't just go through life and exist. I had been part of enough destruction. I needed to do something where I felt I was helping people, which is how I ended up working in a hospital.

There are days when I feel like what I ended up doing wasn't enough. But there are days I feel good about what I've done.

PAUL KEITH

Plymouth, Massachusetts
Specialist Fourth Class, United States Army, Vietnam

After returning from Vietnam, Paul spent the remainder of his enlistment in Texas, at Fort Sam Houston and Fort Hood, then went back to Massachusetts to attend Gordon College, graduating in 1975 with a degree in theology. "It was on my mind that I might have a calling to go into the ministry, but my wing of the Christian Church—Protestant Evangelicalism—had an even stronger policy against gays than the military did.

"I made an assessment of what I knew how to do: not much. So I went back on active duty."

The second time I went on active, I stayed for four years, and at that point I had had at least some thought in my own mind of staying for the full twenty.

But I got tired of hiding. It got harder and harder as I moved up in the ranks to lie to myself and to make sure that the military didn't come down on me with both feet. They lose a lot of good soldiers that way.

There were always rumors of witch-hunts at this base or that base. If you read any of the underground papers, you would read about things like that.

In my own experience, it was more like "don't ask, don't tell." Just don't bring it up. I know there were clubs in Killeen, Texas, that were clearly off-limits and known to be patrolled by the Army. Texas in the military in 1970? Not the place to be. The atmosphere in Hawaii, where I was stationed 1975–77, was more like, "Just be cool—and things will be cool." But even in Hawaii, there were a couple of clubs where friends strongly advised, "Don't go, because that nice guy you meet is bound to be undercover."

Still, you could connect. The first gay-themed book that I ever read in my life was at the post library at Schofield Barracks, Hawaii. *The Best Little Boy in the World,* by John Reid—which was a pseudonym, because back then you didn't dare publish a book like that under your own name. I had half an assumption that the Army had put that book in there just to see who signed it out so they could run them down. No way I was gonna check that book out and put my name on the card. That was one you read in the stacks. I could see others had gone in to read chapters—it was a well-thumbed book.

If you went through history, I think you would find that gay troops have been among the best the Army has had. José Zuñiga, soldier of the year. Canned because he's gay. It goes on. Margarethe Cammermeyer, a highly decorated nurse who became a colonel. A waste. Almost all Western European countries have scrapped this nonsense by now.

All of my feelings about what the government did in Vietnam and all that insane bullshit have nothing to do with my feelings about the military per se. I'm not an antimilitary person. Now, some of the people in the gay community would be appalled at that; that's not the good PC position. But, historically and traditionally, there has been a strong and positive representation by gays in the military, and I think I was one of those.

In fact, I think gays serve in the military in disproportionate numbers. If 4 to 10 percent of the general population, depending on which study you want to read, is gay, my own guess is in the military it's 10 to 15 percent. I don't know. The longer I was in the military, the more I learned, the more open I was, the more I ran into an awful lot of gays. And more so than on the streets.

Part of what drove me to join the military was the fascination with history I had as a kid—Alexander, Caesar. And the Sacred Band of Thebes. There's a concept that really got me going: the army of lovers out on the fields. There are a lot of people who feel that way. But the military says, "No, we can't deal with it."

As a Vietnam vet and a gay vet, I feel double-dissed. I mean, it's bad enough the way that our leaders conducted the Vietnam War. Fifty-eight thousand guys died for nothing, not to mention the ones who died on the other side. And then the leaders we have today—even Colin Powell, and I have a great deal of respect for Colin Powell—aren't willing to look at the individuals they have ridden out and say, "But this is a good soldier."

I don't feel good about it. I don't think it's right. And I think they're making a big mistake with a lot of good people.

MIKE PERKINS

TREMONTON, UTAH
CAPTAIN, UNITED STATES ARMY, VIETNAM

In November 1971, Mike arrived in Vietnam for his fourth and final tour of duty. He spent the tour's first six months with a series of Vietnamese ranger battalions, then moved for the last six months to the Son Hoa district, where he was the sole American adviser among as many as twenty thousand Vietnamese.

"That last tour, I'm not keeping young Americans alive, I'm keeping myself alive. And I'm keeping Vietnamese alive, because I had a high opinion of most of the Vietnamese that I worked with—officers, NCOs, civilians. These were good people.

*"They had a good ARVN major—*thieu ta*—I worked with, a super guy. I trusted him with my life. He and I were friends."*

* * *

Vietnam has some of the most beautiful country in the world. Where I was in Son Hoa was good cattle country. Me and the *thieu ta* used to sit at night and talk about building a cattle ranch out there. We were almost serious.

We thought about it. I guess if things had gone right, I might have gone back to look at that. Oh, man. Just a beautiful country. Beautiful beaches. But it got all chewed apart.

When I was up at Khe Sanh before the Marines came in, we used to go on tiger hunts. We used to go fishing. Elephants were there. Vietnam back then looked like a set from *King Kong.* Remember the old Fay Wray movie? You'd go back looking for King Kong, and there were these waterfalls. Well, that's what Vietnam looked like back in those mountains—big, beautiful waterfalls, and these mahogany trees growing two hundred feet tall. I don't know how much is left now, after all the B-52 raids. I can't tell you. I haven't been there in thirty years.

When I left in November '72, they were still finagling over the peace treaty. It wasn't signed until January of '73, but they had already made all these arrangements. They went around, and everywhere there was a red flag, that was gonna be Communist; where there was a yellow flag, that was gonna be ARVN.

Well, once they put up the flags, there'd be these night raids, with guys stealing yellow flags and guys stealing red flags. You'd fly over in a helicopter down by Tuy Hoa and you'd see all these red flags and you'd see a few yellow flags. The next day there'd be a whole bunch of yellow flags and a few red ones. We knew that there was not gonna be any peaceful resolution of this thing, none whatsoever.

The treaty didn't last. I wasn't there by that time, but the *thieu ta* used to write me every month or two. The NVA never quit probing. The war ground down a little bit, it was a little bit less hectic, but, he said, not much had changed. They killed the *thieu ta* in '75 when they attacked and took over. They disemboweled him, so his wife told me.

We always figured the takeover would happen a lot earlier than it did. It should have happened ten years earlier. It would have saved a lot of American lives.

We should have let them be.

I retired from the Army in '85.

Now I teach civics and geography and English, eighth and ninth grade.

I'll tell you, I have a seventy- to eighty-hour week. It never stops. I get up at six in the morning and usually go to bed eleven at night. I have responsible church positions. I'm gone all the time on community projects. I'm involved with scouting—that takes a lot of my time. And just school itself.

My life's fine. I enjoy teaching. The kids are great.

But every day I miss the action. As I drive my car, I wonder if the place I'm passing through would make a good landing zone for bringing in a company. I'm always checking the perimeter to see where I could put in a defensive position.

It's just one of those things. I did that every day for twenty-five years in the Army. I still do it all day long. Every day. There are mountains right behind where I live, and they look like the mountains in Afghanistan. Not quite as high, but they're out there. I look at them, and I wish I were twenty years younger so I could be in the action. I feel left out. A lot of old soldiers are that way. It's tough to be an old man.

XIX

"For those who were left behind."

REMEMBERING AND FORGETTING

On each end of Washington, D.C.'s new World War II Memorial, to be dedicated Memorial Day weekend 2004, will stand an arch forty-three-feet high—the one on the north end to represent the war in the Pacific theater, the one on the south end the war in the Atlantic theater. Inside each arch, four bronze columns will be topped by four American eagles that will together support a victory laurel; inlayed in the floor of each arch will be the words "Victory on Land," "Victory at Sea," and "Victory in the Air." Twenty-eight granite pillars, each with its own laurel, will form a semicircle around each arch. The fifty-six pillars—one for each state of the union at the time of the war, plus territories and the District of Columbia—will, according to the American Battle Monuments Commission, "celebrate the unprecedented unity of the nation during WWII." The already existing Rainbow Pool and its waterworks will be restored to "contribute to the celebratory nature of the memorial"; additional fountains will "complement the waterworks in the Rainbow Pool." On the western side of the memorial a "commemorative area" will recognize "the sacrifice of America's WWII generation, the contribution of our allies, and the suffering of all humankind." Within that area, the "Freedom Wall" will display four thousand gold stars—"[d]uring WWII, the gold star became the symbol of family sacrifice"—one for every hundred Americans who perished in the war.

The World War II Memorial will stand at the east end of the Reflecting Pool that extends from the front of the Lincoln Memorial. About two hundred yards north of the pool's west end lies the Vietnam Veterans Memorial. This structure celebrates nothing—not victory, not unity. No words appear aside from fifty-eight thousand names—those of the American men and women who died in Vietnam. Nothing rises from the ground—no arches, no pillars, no waterworks. Instead, from each end of "The Wall," as Vietnam veterans simply call the memorial, the visitor walks down into the earth, as into a mass grave. At the center of the crevice, where the two halves of the Wall meet, the war's last victims, in panel 1West, abut the first, in panel 1East. No "commemorative area" recognizes sacrifice or suffering; the entire edifice is devoted to the remembering of those who died. Even the names of the two memorials are instructive: The World War II Memorial commemorates an event; as part of that commemoration—not an insignificant part, but not a dominant part either—it makes reference to the people who perished in that event. The Vietnam Veterans Memorial commemorates no event, only people. The Vietnam Wall is not a "Freedom Wall." It is a wall signifying lost lives and lost futures. It makes no reference to what those lives and futures were lost for.

There is only silence, eloquent and deafening.

VINCE WAY

HAVRE DE GRACE, MARYLAND

SERGEANT, UNITED STATES ARMY, VIETNAM

My daughter always kids me. On Saturdays I run around and do my little chores. But I always stop and get a can of Coca-Cola and a Mounds bar, because that's what I got when I came home.

Coca-Cola with bubbles in it is an erotic experience when all the Coke you've seen for the past six months has been flat. Coming home for good, the first thing I did when I got to the San Francisco airport was walk over to the soda machine and put some change in there. And I got me a cup of Coca-Cola, and it had bubbles in it. There were a bunch of us coming back from Vietnam, and we're all standing around staring into the cup, and we're just fascinated. The girl at the Avis counter started laughing at us. Then she walked from behind the counter, and I found out what a miniskirt was. I was fascinated by that, too.

And chocolate candy. Chocolate doesn't do well in hundred-degree heat. In Vietnam what you'd get was a disk wrapped in aluminum foil. You couldn't really bite the damn thing, you had to let it melt in your mouth, but it was too huge to put in your mouth. So at the airport I got a Mounds bar, and I love a Mounds bar. I get one every week.

My father has pancakes every Saturday. Come hell or high water, he has his Saturday pancakes, because that was his first meal after liberation. It's a ritual; we all have little things that we remember and like. Mine's a Mounds bar and a Coca-Cola.

I was a kid in Vietnam—I turned twenty-one and twenty-two there. I think that Vietnam's major impact on me is that I appreciate the small things in life. To me enjoyment is a hot shower and a roof over my head. I'm not worried about having a Jaguar or a large boat. I have a modest house. I'm not worried about keeping up with the Joneses. I'm not worried about impressing anybody. I have a wife and two good kids, and I take very good care of them.

I do what I like to do because I like to do it. Being a volunteer in the EMS—I started that in 1972 because I like helping people.

It's the small things. Taking care of somebody who has broken their leg. Going home and just having an ice cream out of the freezer. I didn't see ice cream for a long, long time. I like ice cream. Ice cream's a joy. Probably eat too much of it. Having a hot shower when you haven't had a hot shower in about three weeks is a damn nice experience. When you haven't seen a flushing toilet in a year, it's a nice thing to have.

I know what's important to me, and that's my wife, my kids,

my parents, my brother, and my sister. War makes you aware of how fragile life is.

My parents are eighty years old. My father's health is deteriorating. I'm going to lose him here someday. I hope not too soon; I'll do the best I can to keep him going. But rule number one is: Everybody dies. Rule number two is: I can't change rule number one. And they're going to die. You have to appreciate them.

When you're young, you don't think you're gonna die. But I realized at a very young age that I might not make it. A lot of people came out maimed. I'm grateful that I made it out alive, so I value all the time I have.

I learned that sometimes there's not a damn thing you can do. There's no reason to explain why somebody else got killed and you didn't. It's not up to us to decide that. And it's not your fault. There's a lot of survivor's guilt among Vietnam veterans: "Why'd I make it?" It's not your decision. It's the rules of fate. Fate put you here, and fate took the other guy away. Live with it.

With my cancer in remission, I'm loving life. I realized when I was nineteen years old how precious time was. But now, with my grandchildren and my kids, there's so much more to live for.

JOHN HOWE

ALBANY, NEW YORK

STAFF SARGEANT, UNITED STATES ARMY, VIETNAM

In the summer of 1999, I returned to Vietnam. I went as one of three veterans who were subjects of a documentary film about the stress put on Vietnam veterans and their families. My son went with me.

I had always thought I lost my youth in Vietnam. But being there made me realize I didn't lose my youth in Vietnam. My youth lives on. You teach your children well, and they become your youth. I have some very strong feelings about what I did: I acted with honor. The trip reinforced my knowledge of myself. I may have made mistakes, but I never brought dishonor upon my family's name.

I made one of those mistakes outside a village near Nui Ba Den, the Mountain of the Black Virgin. The producers of the movie wanted us to go back to places where we had been involved in serious ground combat. So I went to that village.

We were in our holes one night, roughly four hundred meters away from this village, and we started getting mortar fire. They woke me up—must have been 3:00 A.M.—and gave me a set of coordinates. I plotted out the direction for our mortars, the distance, the elevation, and so on, then gave the order to fire. Little did I think to remember that the sight on the mortar was divided. We had the old sights, not the new ones, and the old sights were divided into halves, a north half and a south half. So when I gave the fire command, which included all the information I'd just plotted, I didn't say facing north or facing south. I should have said north; they set the gun up facing south. And they fired three rounds into the village. Then they fired another three rounds into the village. The next morning the villagers came out with their dead dogs and cats and one little dead baby.

I've lived with that all my life. That was a mistake. That was *my* mistake. The guys firing the guns didn't make that mistake, I made it. I was the man in charge. And I've felt very badly about that over the years.

I haven't totally forgiven myself, but God has forgiven me. Yeah, God has made me feel better sometimes. I have not put it behind me. There's still the what-if: What if I didn't do that? It's like a cop who kills a kid. Does he ever forgive himself? But I handle it. Sometimes I handle it well. Sometimes I don't. I see little kids sometimes, and I think about it—I thought about it particularly when I was over there and I went back to that same village.

When I went back, I felt better about it. Now I know what it was. It was a reasonable mistake. A guy's tired in the middle of the night, he's gotten almost no sleep, he gets his directions wrong. I know that, when all is said and done, I did my job. I did my job.

I did two tours in Vietnam. Afterward I was stationed in Europe for three and a half years, then was assigned to the 101st Airborne Division at Fort Campbell, Kentucky. And then they found out I had asthma very bad, and I left the Army. I went to school, got my undergraduate degree.

I don't know if most folk understand the level of sheer uselessness that one can feel when he drinks. In '75, '76, I was drinking maybe a quart a day. Yeah, a quart of scotch. Chivas Regal, a very expensive habit. As a matter of fact, at one point in time I was drinking Royal Salute, which is a twenty-one-year-old Chivas. It goes down like baby's milk.

I'd started going back to church, but I slacked off. I had a marriage that was disintegrating, and I began to chase wild women and that kind of stuff. I could work every day, that was no problem. But I finally got to a point where I decided I had enough. I knew if I didn't do something to change my life, I was going to end up dead. So finally I kind of settled down. I ended up getting a divorce from my first wife and met the current love of my life, the true love of my life. She was the one who influenced me to go back to church full-time. And she was the one who finally said to me, "The hard liquor's pickling your brain."

I never joined Alcoholics Anonymous. I never went to a meeting. I just stopped drinking. One day I just said, "That's it." That was in 1980. I still drink wine—if there's a birthday, I'm down for a couple of glasses of champagne. Or an exceptional piece of filet mignon and a nice Bordeaux, they go well together. But it may be weeks or months before I have my next glass. My drinking is under control. If it wasn't, I'd be in trouble.

There were times I had terrible nightmares. The most common was about that village where we fired the mortars with the wrong coordinates. I had another recurring nightmare about being in a helicopter and it went down.

I got to the point where I almost snapped. I got to the point where one day somebody said something to me and I found myself rummaging in my old footlocker looking for my Gerber Mark I fighting knife.

I can't even remember what it was that set me off. My wife called a white friend of mine, Sam Nappi. I was seething.

So Sam came over and said, "John, where are you going?"

I said, "I'm going to kill that fucking bastard."

"Are you sure you want to do that?"

"Yeah, I want to fucking do it. It's going to feel good."

"You do that, you'll go to jail."

"Fuck it."

So he finally stands up and he says, "I'll tell you what. You bring your big fucking black ass over here and try to go on through that door, and you're going to take me with you." And my wife says, "Honey, please. Please. Please."

She told me I had to find some help. So I went to the vet center in Syracuse, where we were living at the time, and I told them, "I've got to talk to somebody, because I'm either gonna kill somebody or I'm gonna end up dead myself." So they took me right away, and they began to talk to me. It's been instrumental in me keeping my sanity. I'll tell you, if it wasn't for the vet centers, a lot of guys would be in trouble.

A big thing was my return to spiritualism. Going back to church is one thing, but this is going back to understanding that there's a higher being and that my destiny is not formed by myself. I have choices, and I make decisions, but I have to make them based on the guidance that I get from a higher power. I think of the psalm, "Yea, though I walk through the valley of the shadow of death, I will fear no evil." I think of another verse of Scripture: Acts of the Apostles, chapter 6, verse 3. There's a dispute among the Christians, and Paul says, Brothers, select from among you "seven men full of honest report, full of the Holy Ghost and wisdom." Let them take care of this business, and we will give ourselves to "the ministry of the word."

I have *physically* done harm in this world. Some people can't say that, but I know that I've *physically* done harm. I have hurt people, and I've taken human life. Now I give back, in service. I'm not redeeming myself, I'm not replacing the lives that I've taken or undoing the pain that I've caused, but I am helping to make the world a little better. I spend a lot of time in the community. I go to schools and talk about Vietnam. I'm involved with the Boy Scouts.

You went and you killed some people. Okay. But it was a soldier who was at the foot of the cross who said, "Truly this man was a Son of God." It was a soldier, a protector. More than just being an attacker, you're a protector. The military has changed, and they're now doing things that I think about—peacekeeping and humanitarian aid. We didn't do those things thirty years ago; we just went out and killed people. I had a sign I used to hang outside my hooch. It was written on the side of a C-ration box: "This is the mortar platoon, home of high angle hell. You call, they fall." That's the way we were. They've changed that now in the military.

My recurring nightmares about Vietnam have ended. But when I was back in Vietnam for the film, I had a real bad dream. Oh, God. I was in a firefight. And a guy ran at me with a bayonet, and he hit me in my gut. I just screamed. I ended up going to my son's room and sleeping there with him. It was that bad.

That entire trip my son looked out for me. He covered my back. This kid would not let anything happen to me.

ED JACKSON

TIPP CITY, OHIO

STAFF SERGEANT, UNITED STATES ARMY AIR FORCES, WORLD WAR II

Mike and I don't talk about the wars. I don't want him to know the gory details of what I went through, and I don't think he wants me to know the gory details of what he went through. So you just don't talk about it. There's some people that like to talk about that kind of stuff; I'm one of them that don't.

I'll tell you, when I got out of the service, I was so glad to be done with that type of life that I never gave it much thought after that. I never go camping, because to me that's just going back and doing something I had to do when I was in the service.

One of my sons, the one that's next to Mike in age, loves to camp. He and his wife and their two boys, who were both Eagle Scouts, they camp, camp, camp, camp, camp. My idea of going camping is finding an air-conditioned motel room someplace and eating in a restaurant. I'm serious. I had all the camping I wanted when I was missing in action.

When my own kids were in Boy Scouts, they'd go on the camp-outs, and the father was supposed to go. And I would go. But when I had to go to the bathroom, I'd come back home and use the bathroom and brush my teeth. They used to get a kick out of that. They couldn't understand why all the other dads would stay there and I'd excuse myself and jump in the car, drive into town, and be back in a couple of hours.

I like luxury. Air-conditioning and a good steak. Champagne.

And I just like peace and quiet. I don't enjoy going out where there's some kind of a demonstration. If there's something like that going on, whether it's right-to-life or whatever it is, I won't go. And I'm for right-to-life, but I don't attend none of their functions. I don't want to get involved in demonstrating.

Maybe I would've if I hadn't been in the war. I don't know. I can be perfectly happy sitting out on my front porch doing nothing, just listening to the birds.

HOWARD BAUGH SR.

Midlothian, Virginia
Captain, United States Army Air Forces, World War II

The Ninety-ninth and 332nd had thirty-two pilots shot down or forced down in enemy territory who became prisoners of war. One came back and reported that when he was being interrogated by the German intelligence officer, he was asked, "Why do you people fight so hard for a country that treats you so badly?" He probably didn't have a good answer. I didn't give that question a whole lot of thought at the time, and I don't think the other guys did either. There's been some reflection on it since, of course.

I was fighting for my country, our country. This was our country. It was ours as much as anybody else's. We paid taxes just like everybody else. Same rates, too. We paid the same fare to get on the streetcar and had to ride in the back.

We never considered ourselves second-class citizens. Other people did. We didn't. We didn't think we were lacking in intelligence or leadership or any of the other things that the Army thought African Americans didn't have.

We were doing what we had to do and what we thought was right to do. Looking back on it now, I still think it was the right thing to do.

HOWARD BAUGH JR.

Airline Pilot
Plantation, Florida
Captain, United States Air Force, Vietnam

While attending Tennessee State University in Nashville, Howard L. Baugh Jr. participated in the school's ROTC program, which his father commanded. Upon graduation in 1965 at the age of twenty-one, he was commissioned a second lieutenant in the Air Force and soon entered pilot training at Williams Air Force Base, Arizona. The plane he would eventually fly was the KC-135, a four-engine jet designed to refuel other airplanes in midflight.

Assigned to the Forty-second Air Refueling Squadron at Loring Air Force Base in Maine, he served two temporary-duty tours in Southeast Asia as copilot on a KC-135 crew that flew out of Thailand. "Fighters take off so loaded down with armament that they don't have a whole lot of fuel. So what they do is they get to altitude, then we fill 'em up before they go off to the strike zone. They go off and drop the ordnance, then come back to us for post-strike fuel so they can make it home to their base."

The Baugh family had moved to Nashville in 1959, when public facilities—schools, movie theaters, rest rooms—were still segregated.

In Nashville, I saw people who were impressed by my dad's uniform and people who never saw my dad, never saw any of us. We'd move around and through, and people never even knew we were there. That was part of the culture at the time: We were invisible. My dad was a successful black man. Successful black men don't make the news. So he was invisible.

But I didn't focus on that. I focused on the fact that there were a lot of folks who looked at my dad with a great deal of racial pride. Even though he doesn't think that he was doing anything, when he'd walk around in the uniform with wings on his lapel, he was a role model. In a place where most blacks were confined to menial jobs, to find out there were black men flying fighter aircraft gave people a feeling that if he can do it, I can do it, too.

I have a tie clasp that's a P-51 with the tail painted red to make it look like the Tuskegee Airmen's distinctive red tails. I got it about ten years ago from a guy who's also a United Airlines pilot. He found out that my father was a Tuskegee Airman, and he researched my dad's history in the organization and gave me the clasp. I have worn it ever since. It's part of my uniform.

One reason I wear it is to bring awareness to the history of the Tuskegee Airmen. History's important. It really is. You've got to know where you've been.

I see my dad as a pioneer. He says he was just doing a job and a lot of it was just survival, but I don't see it that way. I think he's a hero. As an aviator, I'm proud that my dad was an aviator. But he has been a tremendous role model for us all—my brothers and me—throughout our lives.

I want my father to get credit, I want him to get his due. I'm incredibly proud of him, and I want everybody else to know that I'm proud of him. What he has done is monumental. The thing that I am most proud of in my life is the fact that I'm his son.

GREG CAMP

COLUMBUS, GEORGIA

CAPTAIN, UNITED STATES ARMY, VIETNAM

In the mid-eighties I was stationed at Fort Lewis, Washington. One of my kids was in Cub Scouts, and I went with a group of them one time to the state capital. And there was some guy standing out there with a mobile Vietnam Wall. I'd never seen it. I said, "What is that?"

"That's the Vietnam Wall."

I was in civilian clothes, but I had short hair, so he asked me if I was in the Army. I said yes. "Did you serve in Vietnam?" I said yes. And he said, "Thank you, man."

I thought, "That's the first time anybody's ever said something like that to me."

I've been to the Wall in D.C. a few times. It's sobering. I look for people I know. There's a lot of them, not necessarily that died in my unit when I was there, but classmates of mine, friends of mine, people I know who were killed there. You go and find their name on the Wall.

You see a name etched there, it's like a magnet. It draws you to your connection with that person, your memory of him.

In the summer of 1970, I went to a wedding in upstate New York. A bunch of West Point classmates were in the wedding, all of us just back from Vietnam. One of the guys had been in the 101st Airborne and was the roommate at West Point of this other classmate of ours who had been killed literally days before this wedding.

At the time he was still listed as missing in action, because they had not recovered his body. I can't remember for the life of me whether that was because it was in deep, deep jungle or what it was. But Jim Llewellyn knew without a shadow of a doubt that Donnie Workman, his roommate and our classmate, was dead.

Jim Llewellyn and I drove west together after the wedding—my next assignment was at Fort Riley, Kansas; he was due at another base out west. On the way we stopped off at St. Louis and saw Donnie's mother. Jimmy had stayed at her home before, and he said, "I just have to see her. I have to hug her."

We were there an hour, maybe. She served us iced tea, something like that, lemonade. She showed us his room. She lived in an apartment or town house, and his room was almost like a museum to him. At this point, maybe a week after he'd been killed, all his mother had was, "Your son's missing in action." They still haven't identified his body, they still haven't declared him a KIA. But based on what Llewellyn's told me—and Llewellyn was still in Vietnam when it happened—he's dead. We know he's dead.

And yet his mother, as any mother would be, is absolutely convinced that he has escaped: "His Ranger School training is keeping him alive, and he's gonna show up. The reason that they haven't found him yet is because he's trying to fight his way through all the jungle and the enemy soldiers."

And we're sitting there listening to her cling to this hope that we know is futile. We weren't gonna tell her that her son was dead. For one thing, that's not our job. That's the Army's job. But Llewellyn and I looked at each other with—I don't know what kind of look. I don't know how to describe it. But it was pain, agony. We knew that she didn't really believe it, but what mother is not going to hang on to every hope that her son is alive, until there is no more hope?

What we felt—and Jimmy much more than me—was that she was looking to us to encourage her hope: "Yeah, that's right. We were in Ranger School together. We learned how to escape and evade."

But we weren't going to encourage it. So we sat there. Our silence was probably an indicator to her that we didn't share her hope.

And so every time I go to the Wall, if I see Donnie Workman's name there, that's exactly what comes to mind. I knew him for four years at West Point, and we became close friends at Ranger School. But I don't think of those things. I don't think of the fact that he was one of the regimental commanders at West Point or that he was captain of the lacrosse team. Every time I see his name, I just remember his mother, as you would any mother, and that vain hope that her son was still alive.

JIM COYNE SR.

Manahawkin, New Jersey
Technical Sergeant, United States Army, World War II

When I knew that Jimmy would be going off to Vietnam, the first thing I thought was "Hey, Lord, protect my son. Not only my son—protect them all." And I knew that was impossible. I remember the day we saw him off at Newark Airport. He was going to California, which was the last stop in the U.S.A. before going out to Vietnam. It was a hard day for me. I kept my feelings inside. I told myself, "You gotta show up for him."

I remember Jimmy at the top of the stairs before he entered the plane. He gave me a wave. Inside, I felt the same feeling I had when

I left to fight. I thought then, "I'm never coming back here," and I looked off the boat to see Jersey City one last time. When Jim waved, I thought I might never see him again. It was a *long* time before I would realize that Jimmy was gonna make it. I guess I could tell from the letters we got. Jimmy was a good kid.

My experience in war wasn't all that different from Jim's. It was a different experience because it was different people, but when you undergo gunfire, I don't think there's a difference. You keep your head down, take care of yourself. Any young man in any war—the first thing you have to do is take care of yourself. Not as an individual, as part of the unit. You've got the people there to save your life. Some guys had no fear, no fear at all. I wasn't one of them.

I don't think anybody really *wanted* to be in the Army if they were there a couple of days. But after all the years I've been out of the Army, I still have a feeling that it was the right thing to do.

I don't think about the war too much now. But sometimes I close my eyes and I see the Army. I see my friend who was killed in Sicily. Anthony.

He was about Jimmy's height, had dark hair—Italian. If he walked through the door right now, I'd remember him.

And when I go to bed at night, first I bless myself. Then I cross myself again, and I bless the men and boys who aren't with us. I say, "For those who were left behind."

JIM COYNE JR.

HIGH SCHOOL GUIDANCE COUNSELOR AND ATHLETICS COACH
WAYNE, NEW JERSEY
FIRST LIEUTENANT, UNITED STATES ARMY, VIETNAM

James J. Coyne Jr., born in 1946, entered the Army as a second lieutenant after completing his bachelor's degree at Niagara University, where he had been enrolled in ROTC.

Jim arrived in Vietnam in 1969 to join the Fourth Infantry

Division as a communications and reconnaissance officer. "The Americans hired Vietnamese to do everything. They worked in the PXs, they were hired as maids, as food-service people. Initially, I was suspicious of civilians, but they just grew on you. You saw them every day. Whenever you were out on the road they had service stands. Very few Americans spoke the language, but we all knew everything was one dollar. A can of soda was a dollar, and it was always Coca-Cola, so it was probably stolen soda that you were paying for. If you needed a cold soda, what the hell is a dollar?"

When Reagan got elected and said the war is not over until the POWs are returned, Vietnam vets, including me, picked up on that. I went to Washington a few times to lobby. I met some family members of POWs/MIAs.

The more that I investigated the issue, the more I was certain these people got screwed. After Nixon got reelected in '72, he needed a big positive, what with Watergate hanging over his head. The formal treaty signing with Vietnam was in January 1973, and by April of 1973, when 591 Americans were released, Nixon said now all our prisoners are home. I think he knew that wasn't true. What happened to the 500 guys that got shot down over Laos? Only nine Americans came out of Laos; you can't tell me all the rest of them died. The more I studied the problem, the more I read, the more I researched, the more I was convinced that a lot of people got the wool pulled over their eyes. Back in '85, '86, we were convinced that those people were alive. Now? There's just too much time gone by.

On my right wrist, I wear a bracelet. It's made of tin, and the top is red, with silver lettering that says "Sergeant Peter R. Cressman, 2/5/73, Laos, USAF." Even though the war officially ended the last week of January, Peter was up over Laos a few days later intercepting radio signals when his plane was shot down. Peter's home of record was Wayne, New Jersey.

After his plane was downed, the Army Security Agency tracked North Vietnamese radio traffic saying that they had taken four survivors from this aircraft and were marching them north toward the

Vietnam border, out of Laos. When Americans got to the site two mornings after the crash, they only found four bodies on the plane, although there had been eight crew members. So my question was, what happened to the other four? Were they killed? Their bodies were not in the aircraft, they were not around the aircraft. And why is there this suspicious North Vietnamese radio intercept saying they were marching four Americans from this site toward the Vietnamese border? What happened to Peter Cressman?

I met the Cressman family at a meeting in Washington. They were among the militants who weren't believing what the government was telling them. The government was saying, "We are doing all we can," and basically what "all we can" meant was accepting the boxes of bones the Vietnamese sent back to them.

Eventually what happened in the Cressman case was, they found one tooth that matched Peter Cressman's dental records, and they asked the Cressman family to accept that one tooth as proof that their son was dead. The Cressman family refused to do that. Unfortunately, Peter's mother, who led the fight for so long, died in 1997. And when I was told she had died, I was so sad, because she fought for so long to try and find out what happened to her son, and she died without ever knowing.

MAS TAKAHASHI

Torrance, California

Technical Sergeant, United States Army, World War II

We were fighting to be recognized as Americans. We were trying to show that we were just as American as the next guy.

You can say, "Why would you be going to fight for your country when it put you in camp?" But it wasn't that. It was for after. You figured it would be better for everybody if you went. And it did turn out to be better for everybody that we went.

It opened up all kinds of doors for the Japanese Americans.

When I got back to California after the war, job opportunities were still limited. Most Japanese became gardeners or had grocery stores or gas stations. I went to work driving a truck for a while; then I worked at a gas station. The Issei, our parents, weren't allowed to own land or become citizens until 1952. But you look at what Japanese Americans are today. You got generals. You got high executives. You got doctors. You got everything.

Now they're trying to publicize what they call the "no-no boys," the draft resisters. They put down no/no when they had to sign the questionnaire—whether you're loyal to the country and whether you want to go in the service. They're trying to make heroes out of them, which I don't think is right. Not when all the guys were getting killed and wounded overseas. It might have been one of their relatives. They could have gone and helped.

When Vietnam came, all I know is, people are protesting, and then here Scott's overseas. I couldn't understand what they were protesting.

I guess a lot of parents didn't want their kids to go. So they either went to Canada or protested. But the way I see it, if you get drafted, that means your country needs you. Right or wrong—you can't be a judge of that. I didn't know anything about why we were fighting in Vietnam. I still don't know why. All I know is, if you get drafted, it's an obligation. You've got to go.

A lot of people still don't know about the Nisei soldiers *or* the camps.

Even teachers don't know. My niece's daughter wrote a paper on the camps, and her teacher refused to believe it. The teacher says, "This is not true," and she wouldn't accept the paper.

We finally got reparations. That was a struggle for the NCRR—the National Coalition for Redress and Reparation—and everybody. A lot of people were saying no, it's not gonna happen. But Elma and I, we kept going to the meetings. We kept going to candlelight parades. We kept trying to raise funds. We had a hard time. Then, finally, it started to get rolling, and we were able to send people to Washington.

I was happy when it passed. I feel now they're kind of giving you a pardon for putting you in camp.

We each got a letter from the president and twenty thousand dollars. But the ones who lost everything—the Issei—didn't get anything, because they were dead.

A standard thing when one Nisei visits another is that the conversation comes around to "What camp were you in?" It's something to talk about, not just hello and good-bye.

I went to the VA one time, and they asked me on some form if I was ever in jail. I said, "Yeah. I was in a concentration camp. U.S. concentration camp."

There's stuff you lost that you can't replace. You lost your freedom. You can't put a money value on that.

SCOTT TAKAHASHI

GARDENA, CALIFORNIA

SERGEANT, UNITED STATES ARMY, VIETNAM

As a Christmas present for me about five years ago, my stepson's wife did an embroidery of a section of the Vietnam Wall. It's from a preexisting pattern that is sold, and it comes with actual names from the Wall. Since I have a number of friends and relatives on the Wall, she managed to put those names in among the names that came with the pattern. She had it framed before she gave it to me.

I had no idea what the gift was before I unwrapped it. When I did, it was pretty overwhelming. It's still powerful.

I keep it displayed in the living room, and it's an important piece of our house. Anyone who visits will see it.

Certainly the most important person on it is my cousin, Douglas Yuki. His birthday is the Fourth of July. I still see my aunt, his mom.

He was about five months older than me and very bright. He didn't have to go to Vietnam. He had a full scholarship to Harvey Mudd College, and his lottery number was 200. But he enlisted.

I was already in Vietnam, so I never got to talk to him about why he enlisted, but I tried to warn him in letters—not in letters to him directly, but I wrote to my mother that I didn't think it was a good idea for him to go. He was more focused in life than I was. He was an Eagle Scout. I don't know, from the people that I was with, I just couldn't picture him over there.

I wasn't home very long when he was killed. I went to the funeral. I don't talk to my aunt and uncle about it. I never have, and I don't think that's something I want to bring up.

Isaac Hosaka, a kid I played football with, often comes to mind, too, just because I still live in the same town. I remember having coffee with him in the bowling-alley coffee shop. He did two tours; this was between them. He told me he was going back.

The one person who died in our unit is on the embroidery.

Leonard Sugimoto is the brother of someone I went out with while I was in high school.

Ernie Mitchell is a guy I was in a junior-high-school band with.

I've seen the Wall in Washington a couple of times.

It's impossible not to be emotional there. It touches deep inside your soul. You wonder who died over there. Maybe the guy who was going to find the cure for the common cold.

And there were so many.

TONY RIVAS SR.

San Antonio, Texas

Seaman First Class, United States Navy, World War II

On March 31, 1945, while its guns were bombarding Okinawa in preparation for the Marine landing there, the Indianapolis *was set upon by a kamikaze airplane. Nine men were killed in an area of the ship Tony had left only minutes before.*

Following the attack, Tony requested shore duty. "They already had me for about two years—I was an old-timer—so I could put in for it. The ship was going to San Francisco for an overhaul, and I thought I would get shore duty in San Francisco. They messed me up and assigned me to Guam."

He was on Guam when the Indianapolis *was torpedoed—just a week before the* Enola Gay *flew its mission over Hiroshima. The ship sank in twelve minutes, taking over three hundred men down with her. Eight hundred crewmen survived the sinking, but because naval authorities failed to notice the ship missing, some five hundred of them succumbed to sharks, exposure, and waterlogged life jackets during four days on the open sea before rescue vessels finally arrived.*

I found out about the sinking of the *Indianapolis* from a guy who worked for Nimitz.

Nimitz was in Guam, and this guy came to me and said, "Tony, did you know that they sunk the ship?"

I said, "What ship?"

"The *Indianapolis.*"

I knew before all the rest of the people. It sank on July 30, but they didn't announce it until later, after everybody had celebrated the end of the war.

They sent several of the survivors to Leyte and other ones to Guam. I went to see my friend in the hospital—Santos Peña was his name. He saw me, and then he began crying just like a little baby. He was all blisters.

"*¿Qué pasó?*"

"Oh, I had it bad. I was in the water for four nights. The first day everybody was singing and hollering. We said, 'We'll be saved by tomorrow.' The second day, man, I'm telling you, you could see the sharks coming."

There were two guys named Sanchez on my ship. There was

Little Sanchez and Big Sanchez. Big Sanchez was kind of a rough guy, so the one I used to get together with was Little Sanchez. We used to call him "Cantínflas" because he acted like Cantínflas, the comedian in Mexico. He had a tattoo of the Lady of Guadalupe on his chest. He died when the ship went down. I asked for him, and they told me he didn't make it.

Big Sanchez survived, and when I saw him in the hospital, he said when he was on the raft, he thought some guy was sleeping on the side of it. And he went and grabbed him and pulled him up. There was no body below the chest—the sharks ate it.

Sanchez said he heard voices telling him to go in the water, to go underneath the ocean, that there was a lot of beer there, a lot of watermelons. He said, "I wanted to jump. And then I heard a voice telling me, 'Please do not do that. Please, please don't do it. Don't jump overboard.' And then suddenly I saw this big light coming right in my face. I said, 'What the hell? A star's coming. Maybe it's God.' " No. It was the Navy with boats picking people up. And they grabbed him by the arms to take him aboard the ship.

They gave Captain McVay a court-martial, and then a lot of people bothered him because they said that they lost all their sons, their brothers on account of him. But it wasn't on account of him. They wanted to put the blame, everything, on the captain. For years he was receiving notes and receiving letters all the time. So he got a gun and killed himself.

I went and visited the captain in the hospital in Guam, to say hello and talk to him. I said, "Captain McVay, my name is Tony Rivas."

He said, "What do you do here?"

"I have shore duty."

"Oh, you're lucky," he says. "You're lucky."

They get a meeting of survivors of the *Indianapolis* every two years. But I don't feel comfortable going. It says "survivors." That doesn't include me.

I feel real bad because I lost a lot of my buddies. Once in a while, I think about them and I feel like I'm going to cry, but I don't. My wife says that I cry inside of me. I don't cry in front of her, I don't cry in front of my children. But I do feel bad.

I should have been there with them. I don't know what happened to save me—from the kamikaze, from the ship sinking. Maybe it was my mother always praying. She was always praying to the Virgin of Guadalupe.

Peña lives in Tucson now. He told me that once in a while he goes outside to his porch and he starts crying, remembering. He'll hear them talking.

I especially think about it if I see something in the newspaper or on TV about the *Indianapolis.* It gets into my system and it hurts. It hurts me a lot.

I wish I would have gone with them, my friends, buddies.

RICHARD RIVAS

School Guidance Counselor
San Antonio, Texas
Specialist Fourth Class, United States Army, Vietnam

The youngest veteran in this book, Ricardo M. Rivas was born in 1950.

Drafted in 1970, he went to Vietnam in May 1971, when, owing to Richard Nixon's policy of Vietnamization, most of the traffic was going the other way. In-country, he found matters in a state of flux. "We were moving so much around that our duties changed constantly. The infantry was leaving, and the Army was going to different bases to pick up people for different assignments."

He served with four outfits during his tour, at various times working as a helicopter mechanic, a security guard, and a helicopter gunner.

"Vietnam made me a better person. I learned more about death and about living than I would have known if I had not been there.

I appreciate life a lot more. I appreciate my parents. For me, every day is a holiday."

I had a friend named Joe Silva, but this guy wanted so much to be a Marine, we used to call him "Marine." But Marine didn't pass the physical to go into the Marines; he was a little bit overweight. So he and I got drafted into the Army at the same time.

Marine was the type of guy that was a leader. He was the gung-ho guy. He was the guy that wanted to go to Vietnam. He was the one that was gonna do everything to save the country. He became the leader of our group, and we used to follow him. We looked up to him, a bunch of us green guys going with him.

We were inducted on September 16, 1970, Mexican Independence Day, and we went to basic together at Fort Lewis, Washington. I think we got there at two o'clock in the morning. And as soon as we got off the bus, there was all kinds of racket. It was chaos. Basic training lasted eight weeks, and it was chaos for the first six.

I was just trying to follow everybody. Living in the barrio, sometimes you have to know how to survive. It was, like, "We have to make it. There's nothing that's gonna break us."

Marine was more experienced than the rest of us. I had never seen a drill sergeant. But Marine always wanted to be there with them, so he read a lot of books, he talked to a lot of veterans. And he knew: "They're gonna do this drill, they're gonna do that." That helped us, being with somebody that had some of the answers. He kept saying, "Don't worry, guys. You'll make it through." He taught us how to survive in the Army.

We finished basic, and from there we split up for AIT. He went into the infantry. I went to Fort Eustis, Virginia, to learn to be a helicopter mechanic. It was a long training—maybe sixteen weeks. Infantry AIT was eight weeks, I think. And when Joe finished AIT, he went in-country.

He didn't last long.

I was home on leave when he came back. I saw him in the coffin with his uniform on. I'm not sure how he died.

He was buried at Fort Sam. I had finished AIT and was waiting to go overseas; this was my first view of a casualty—before I left. That's when it hit me: "I don't think I'm gonna make it back." If I saw this guy, my hero, being killed over there, how would I make it?

Going through the Internet a couple of months ago, I saw a website called "The Virtual Wall," and his name was on it. And I made peace with him, saying, "Thanks a lot for helping us through basic training. Thanks a lot for the things you did for us."

XX

"We are flawed by nature."

WARS PAST, PRESENT, AND FUTURE

In 1926, when Congress first recognized Armistice Day—what we now call Veterans Day—in commemoration of the agreement that ended World War I, it declared that November 11, 1918, "marked the cessation of the most destructive, sanguinary, and far-reaching war in human annals and the resumption by the people of the United States of peaceful relations with other nations, which we hope may never again be severed. . . ."

Three-quarters of a century after Congress expressed that hope, how tragically naive it seems to have believed there could ever be a "war to end all wars," as World War I was once known. Yet when the Cold War concluded, we allowed ourselves to believe that it had been the war to end all wars. We knew in 1991 that prior victories in prior wars had led us to delusions of eternal peace, but now that we had won the "long, twilight struggle" to which John Kennedy had called us, what was left to win? History had come to an end; mankind had chosen, once and for all, its optimal organizing principles. Civilization had dawned anew.

That brave new millennium lasted all of a decade, of course. Four hijacked jetliners forced us to adjust our eyes to the twilight once more.

PERRY POLLINS

LEXINGTON, MASSACHUSETTS

CORPORAL, UNITED STATES MARINE CORPS, WORLD WAR II

A lot of people in this day and age solve problems by words and money. David and I solve problems by putting our life on the line.

I'm a member of the Marine Corps League, and I sit down among these people. Now, some of them have been to Desert Storm. Some of them have never seen combat at all. But I was in the Marine Corps at a period of time when this country really needed a Marine Corps. I witnessed some things as a Marine that nobody in their life, other than fellow Marines, experienced.

It was frightening, and it was an achievement, a mental and physical achievement. And I look at all these other guys—and I've talked to majors and colonels, officers and noncoms—who didn't experience these things, and they dress up in their blues, and I call 'em wannabes. Oh, they show me a lot of respect. And when they parade, and The President's Own marches by—that's what they call the Marine Corps band—I give them *mucho* credit. But everybody's not equal. There are major differences between what people have done.

I know my son went through a lot, and I know I did. I know my boyhood neighbor Tom Drummond did. That's for sure.

I never had a set of blues, and I never really wanted them. In Massachusetts the way they make many of the license plates is, number, number, number, number, letter, letter. And the letters on mine, purely by happenstance, are RA. That RA is ideal for me, because that means raggedy-ass. I was a raggedy-ass Marine.

I went to fight a war to preserve the nation. It might sound as if I'm bragging. I'm sorry. I'm bragging. I did. Like a lot of people did in those days.

What came after the Marine Corps was something that I expected. I went to college. I studied all my various subjects to get a degree. I got out of college, and I went to work for this company,

I went to work for that company. I had good experiences, and it was interesting.

But by comparison to those slightly over two years, it was minor. Sure. I made money working at something I enjoyed doing. But, for the love of Pete, in the Marine Corps I put my life on the line. I was scared half out of my wits—I must've repeated the Twenty-third Psalm a couple hundred thousand times. But I withstood it. I did my job. I didn't win any medals, but I did what I was expected to do.

The experiences I had in the Marine Corps were just excellent. I met top-rate people and had an adventure that few people could ever expect to have. And we won, and I'm alive to tell about it.

It's that pure and simple. I'm not a complicated person.

MICKEY HUTCHINS

Concord, North Carolina
First Lieutenant, United States Army, Vietnam

The realization that my dad was at D-Day didn't hit until I was probably well into my teens, and just on a very superficial level. I only learned the details of what my dad had done a few years ago. My daughter was doing a school paper—the general subject was to be World War II. And the more she looked at the war, the more she ended up focusing on D-Day. When she sat Dad down, there was not much way he was gonna weasel out of it.

During my discussions with my daughter about D-Day, we realized something that I think I'd known intuitively but hadn't voiced: that on that one day—and you could almost pinpoint, maybe not *one* hour, but a few hours on that one day—the history of the twentieth century turned. To realize that Dad was at D-Day was powerful stuff.

We must somehow figure out how to remember the hard lessons of war, while preparing future generations to understand how to maintain peace. I'm not sure I know how to do that, to be honest. There's not much of a blueprint there in all of history. We know what it is to wage war—we do it better or worse from time to time. We seemed to have a pretty good grasp on it by the end of World War II and when we prosecuted the Gulf War, but we certainly fell down on the job in Korea and Vietnam. We've got war colleges. We've got the various military academies. We've devoted substantial resources to learning what it takes to wage war, and, if called upon, we can do it with the best in the world. We've never really looked at the other side of the coin: What does it take to wage peace?

Maybe the closest we've ever come was the Marshall Plan, and even that was controversial at the time. It's a tough thing. It's sort of like what I ran into on occasions in Vietnam when I held my fire—you see something coming at you that you know is potentially threatening, and maybe even potentially lethal, but you don't react in a lethal way or necessarily even a defensive way. In order to have peace, there's little doubt in my mind that we will have to take risks that make us feel vulnerable—and, in fact, more than make us *feel* vulnerable, actually *make* us vulnerable—and I have a real hard time reconciling myself to that. There's got to be a method of getting along with our neighbors in the world without having to resort to war.

One of the lessons I learned in Vietnam is that there's good and bad in everybody, and the right set of circumstances can bring out either the good or the bad. I really believe that within the heart of every man is the capacity for any sin you care to name, including murder. We are flawed by nature. We are imperfect material and can't expect to make a perfect world from it.

On my nephew's twenty-first birthday, he was lamenting the fact that he hasn't been in the military and he couldn't identify with all that. And I said, "You know, the whole reason we did this was so you wouldn't have that experience." But I am pragmatic enough to realize that there are parts of the world where brute force is the only thing that's truly understood.

After 9/11 there was a part of me that asked the question "Should we try to follow the teachings of the Bible and turn the other cheek?" I have little doubt that is what God would prefer us to do. However, everything I have experienced in life, especially during my time in Vietnam, is screaming at me that the only thing that will bring any response from terrorists is lethal force. I wish I could see some other way, but I fear that the only way we will ever have true peace and security is by a "Pax Americana." Even if we achieve that, it will be at the price of a heartsickness of the nation when we realize what we've done—we will have the same reaction as Elijah after slaying the Prophets of Baal.

I wish there would be a way to wage peace instead of war. It's sort of a self-fulfilling prophecy: If you make war plans, it's amazing how frequently you end up going to war. If you make peace plans, does the same thing happen?

MAX HUTCHINS

CONCORD, NORTH CAROLINA
FIRE CONTROLMAN FIRST CLASS, UNITED STATES NAVY, WORLD WAR II

I thought during the war about what the Bible says about killing. I felt like it was wrong to take a life but that it was the right thing to do under the circumstances. It was a situation that God had put us into, and we had to protect ourselves. That's what I was fighting for, to keep the war from coming to the United States. I didn't want it to hit the people here, particularly my family.

I think God tests people, and the war could have been a test for our country. I've always felt like God has a purpose for everything, and I think He had a purpose for that war. I don't know what it was and don't know if we'll ever know in this life. But the evil that was being shown by Hitler and Mussolini had to be overcome in some way. This was the way to do it, and I think it was part of God's plan.

The Bible talks about wars and rumors of wars, and there have been wars from the very beginning of time. I don't think we'll know peace until Christ returns. We're all greedy—the human heart is where all the problems come from.

I don't think we'll ever know peace until Christ returns. I don't think it's humanly possible.

GREG CAMP

COLUMBUS, GEORGIA

CAPTAIN, UNITED STATES ARMY, VIETNAM

[Song Be, South Vietnam]
7 Dec 1969
Pearl Harbor Day

Dear Dad,

I guess our family hasn't progressed too far in the last 28 years. You endured the surprise attack on Pearl Harbor 28 years ago today and so far we've had 3 mortar attacks on my Landing Zone today. Is it too much for us to hope that your grandson will not have to endure the same in another 28 years? If history is any indicator of the future then it is doubtful Timmy will fare much better than us. Plato once said, "Only the dead have seen the end of war," and so far he's been right. But as long as there is a God in Heaven there is hope that wars will end. That's about all we can do, is hope and pray and keep our heads down.

Your son,
Greg

XXI

"I didn't let myself worry about it."

PAUL WALMSLEY

PAUL WALMSLEY

RETIRED AIR-CONDITIONING AND REFRIGERATION CONTRACTOR
CAMPTI, LOUISIANA
STAFF SERGEANT, UNITED STATES ARMY, WORLD WAR II

After their breakout from the Normandy hedgerows in late July 1944, Allied ground forces advanced so swiftly across France and Belgium that they soon were outrunning their supply lines. Matériel of all kinds grew scarce, but no commodity was more coveted than gasoline. At the end of August, George Patton's Third Army, the fastest of all the Allied outfits, had to pull up and wait five days after a requisition for four hundred thousand gallons was answered with a shipment of 31,975. "My men can eat their belts," Patton complained, "but my tanks have gotta have gas."

There was plenty of gas in liberated France, but Allied supplies were still being unloaded way back where the campaign had begun, in Normandy, three hundred miles behind Third Army's spearhead. In between, the French railway system lay in shambles, just as Allied bombing commanders had intended. Some gasoline was flown to Patton—by pilots like Bill Perkins—but most of it had to be moved by truck. One convoy after another plied French roads, but the truckers could deliver to Third Army and the rest of the

Allied forces only a small fraction of the million gallons a day they needed to keep moving.

Patton wasn't the only Allied commander clamoring for more gasoline. At the direction of Supreme Allied Commander Dwight Eisenhower, the attacking armies were arrayed along a broad front. To the north and west were the British and Canadian forces of the Twenty-first Army Group, led by Bernard Montgomery. To the south and east was the American Twelfth Army Group, led by Omar Bradley and made up of First Army, commanded by Courtney Hodges, on its left flank and Patton's force on its right. Ike's strategy had as much to do with holding together an alliance as with seizing territory, but the Anglo-American partnership was put to the test by Montgomery and Patton, both of whom repeatedly petitioned Eisenhower to be anointed leader of a concentrated, fatal stab to Germany's heart, and to be granted the resources to deliver it. Gasoline may have been hard to come by as Eisenhower sought to manage the war, but he faced no shortage of ego among his talented but vexing subordinates.

Ike held firm until September, when Montgomery presented him with his imaginative Market-Garden plan, designed to put British tanks in Berlin within weeks. Eager to establish a bridgehead over the Rhine, Eisenhower finally agreed to put Allied supplies at Monty's disposal. As the fiasco unfolded in Arnhem, Patton, his men, and his thirsty tanks were forced to take up defensive positions. They would not go back on the offensive for a month and a half.

The cutoff of Patton's gasoline underlies one of the lasting "what-ifs" of the Second World War. Lines of supply behind Third Army were overextended in September 1944, to be sure, but in front of it German forces were crumbling. By November, however, when Third Army's gasoline spigot was opened once again, the Germans had had time to regroup. They mounted a fierce defense of their homeland and even managed a counterattack, in the Battle of the Bulge, that nearly proved catastrophic to the Allies' cause.

But was it the time to regroup that differentiated the faltering

German soldiers of the summer from the staunch fighters of the late fall, winter, and early spring? Or was it the territory at issue? In the summer, the Germans were fighting to hold territory they had occupied; once the Allies had crossed France, the Germans were fighting to keep invaders from their home. Had the battle been taken to the Fatherland in September would its defenders have closed ranks, as they did later? Or would summer's disarray have persisted, leaving Third Army an open road to the führer's bunker?

No one can know what would have happened had Patton, instead of Montgomery, been armed with the knife to stab Germany's heart. But it is *known that Montgomery was given the opportunity to end the war in 1944, that he squandered it, and that the war lasted another seven grueling months.*

Born in 1920, Paul S. Walmsley served under General Patton in the 777th Antiaircraft Artillery Automatic Weapons Battalion.

I'm different from most people in a lot of ways.

For one thing, a lot of medicine works backwards on me from what it does on others. Tranquilizers are supposed to calm people down. They do the exact opposite with me. They run me crazy. And pain. What pain that most people just almost would be screaming with, I more or less ignore. I just put up with it.

I've always been able to accept what has happened a lot easier than anybody else I've ever seen. Even when my wife died. She was in and out of the hospital nineteen months before she died, and damn near every night she spent in the hospital, I was there with her. She knew she was dying, and we talked about it. And she accepted it, and I accepted it, because we done everything we could, and there wasn't anything else we could do.

I know how serious stomach cancer is. I know I've got it, and I've accepted it, and I'll do what I can about it, and that's it. Either I'll get over it or I won't.

My philosophy my whole life, even when I was a kid, was that worrying about something does no good at all. I just trained myself, if there's something bad happening or gonna happen, if I can do something to stop it, I do it. If I can't, I won't worry about it.

I seen a lot of dead bodies overseas, but it wasn't hard for me. I've just always been able to accept things like that.

My father died when I was seventeen years old—he wasn't but fifty-seven. I had one brother that was a year older than me, and I had two sisters younger and one brother younger. Of course, they had no such thing as survivor's benefits back then. He had a couple small insurance policies, and that was all.

So, like a lot of boys at that time, I had to quit school and go to work and help my mother raise the younger kids. I was driving a gasoline truck at night, and I made seven dollars a week. Then, later on, I made ten dollars a week. That was for seven days.

I joined the National Guard for a source of extra income. We had one drill a week and two weeks' summer camp. We got a dollar a week for each drill and a dollar a day when we was in camp.

It was the 204th Coast Artillery then—it was an antiaircraft unit, a regiment of the Louisiana National Guard. Battalion regimental headquarters was in Shreveport, and A, B, C, and D Batteries was in Shreveport. There was one battery from Ruston and one from Many; others were scattered out over the northwest part of Louisiana. Battery H was in Natchitoches.

We began to suspect 'long about '36 that there was gonna be another war. I believed there would be, and most of the people that I knew believed there would be. We could see newsreels at the movies, especially after Hitler invaded Czechoslovakia. My thought was, I'd be in it whether I was in the National Guard or not, because I was exactly the right age.

In the summer of 1940, we had our notice that we were gonna be mobilized on January the sixth, 1941, for one year of full-time service. And in January we were sent to Camp Hulen, Texas. That's at Palacios, down about a hundred miles south of Houston.

When the war started on December the seventh, we got word late, about three or four o'clock in the afternoon. I was the battery commander's driver then. And the first thing they did was, they started running around and rounding up everybody who had an Army truck driver's license, me being one of 'em.

They gathered up every truck they could find in the whole camp. They were Chevrolet 4×4 trucks and GMC two-and-a-half-ton trucks. They loaded up everybody, just a driver in each one of those trucks, and we left about eight o'clock. It was after dark. We had no idea where we was going. We were each just a driver on a truck in a convoy, and that's all.

It took us all night long to get from Camp Hulen to Fort Sam Houston, in San Antone. They fed us breakfast at Fort Sam Houston; we hadn't even had supper the night before. Then we got back on the trucks and drove to some Army depot they had way out in the country somewhere. And we loaded all of those trucks up with pyramidal tents, these big Army tents that eight people stayed in.

We then drove the trucks back to Camp Hulen. It was after dark, the night of December the eighth, and I just had time to park that truck and go get on a truck the rest of my unit was loaded up on. We left the trucks with the tents there—I have no idea what they did with them. We convoyed all night long from Camp Hulen till we got to Houston the next morning. We drove our vehicles up on railroad flatcars and got them lashed down. Then we got in the troop-carrying cars, and the train left out of Houston.

It was raining and cloudy. We not only didn't know where we were going, we didn't even know what direction we were going till about three days later. The train stopped, and on the side of the track, the snow was piled up above the windows on the car. We was in Flagstaff, Arizona.

We stayed there about a day, and then we lit out again. They were sending us to the West Coast to go to the Philippines, I found out later. When we got to San Diego, we unloaded off of the train and went to the Marine base there, and, other than a few guards on the gate and a few Marines, it was empty. All of the Marines had been put on ships and was headed for the Philippines. We were headed there, too, but we stayed in the Marine barracks till they could get us some guns.

About four or five days later, here come all the Marines back. They got 'em on ships and started, and then realized they might as well shoot 'em as to send 'em to the Philippines. There was no hope for the Philippines. So they brought them back, and then they got us our guns, and we set up antiaircraft positions on top of the roof of the Consolidated Aircraft factory around Coronado Island.

There were a lot of people back then said, "Thank God for Hitler," because he was the reason they was looking for shipyard workers and all kinds of stuff like that. San Diego about doubled in size overnight, from the Navy people coming out there and the Marines that were already there, and all the shipyard workers and aircraft-factory workers.

Of course, the shipyard workers were paid much more than the servicemen. There was a lot of friction between the civilian workers and the servicemen out there because of the difference in pay.

They had one company up somewhere around Riverside, California, a small company making some essential part of the shipbuilding—I don't even remember what it was. They had something like six or seven hundred employees that got their jobs all at once. And they built a private railroad spur up to this factory just for the purpose of hauling this material down to the shipyards.

Everybody who worked in that factory was exempt from the draft because they were in an essential industry. And they were being paid two dollars an hour, while a private in the Army was paid one dollar a day.

Anyhow, the ones working on this private railroad decided that two dollars an hour wasn't enough. They wanted three dollars an hour, so they went on strike. That shows how greedy people can get. They were making two dollars an hour for no telling how many hours a day, and probably getting time-and-a-half overtime. Back then a bank president made, I believe, five thousand dollars a year. Of big banks. And these workers were making way more money than that.

So when they went on strike and shut the railroad down, the Army nationalized the railroad, drafted every one of 'em in the Army right then—within a day or two—and put 'em back at their same jobs on the railroad at a dollar a day.

We were glad to hear it.

There was a Navy base at Coronado, and they sent me to communications school there. So instead of being a driver, I became a communications sergeant.

I stayed in San Diego until early in '43, when they assigned me, our first sergeant, and two platoon sergeants to a cadre. The first sergeant was Sergeant Lester Gimbert, and one of the platoon sergeants was Charlie Settle. They were all from Natchitoches. Frank Mondello was over there. He was from Powhatan, which is about eight miles north of Natchitoches.

We formed a nucleus of a new unit, and they shipped us to Fort Sheridan, Illinois. That's where we met the 777th Antiaircraft Artillery Battalion, and we were Battery D. We started training the recruits; I trained the radio operators. We had half-tracks, and each half-track had four .50-caliber machine guns mounted on it.

We went on maneuvers in Tennessee in the middle of the winter, '43–'44. And after maneuvers was over, they sent us to Camp Davis, North Carolina, and we stayed there a couple of weeks, I guess while they were deciding where to send us next. I got a one-week leave from Camp Davis. Everybody did, to go home for one last time, because we knew then we was going overseas.

I was glad to be home. Naturally I hated to leave my mother

with those small kids by herself. But I had to. I just made sure that the kids was all right and that she was getting by all right. She was a good cook, and we had a big garden and two cows. I milked the cows and worked in the garden when I was home. And I had my allotment that I sent her.

When I left, there wasn't anything emotional about it for me. I just hugged her. She was crying, naturally. But I wasn't.

I knew there wasn't anything I could do about me having to leave, because I had to leave, and I knew I had to leave, and she knew I had to leave.

We went overseas to England in April of '44 on the *Nieuw Amsterdam,* a converted luxury liner. We landed at Glasgow, and then we were shipped down in southern England. We were given new half-tracks and guns and ammunition, and we set up around an air base for antiaircraft protection. We shot down some planes there.

We were scheduled for the D-Day invasion—the unit was all packed up and ready to go. But just maybe three or four days before June the sixth, they had a sudden change of plan. By then they had located these V-1 buzz bombs the Germans had over on the Channel coast, and they knew the Germans would be sending them over the coast of Dover, where the Channel is the narrowest. So they took us out of the invasion and sent us up to get in line with where those things were gonna fly on the way to London. And sure enough, right after the invasion started, they started sending them things over. We shot a bunch of them down.

After it got to where the buzz bombs weren't much of a threat anymore, they pulled us out and on July the eighteenth we went to France and was attached to the Sixth Armored Division, which soon got attached to the Third Army. And that's when we started.

When we landed on Omaha Beach, it was a mess. There wasn't the large numbers of bodies there like they said there was on D-Day, but there were still a lot of them laying around, because our people were still being killed there—we only had twelve miles in from the beach, and the Germans had artillery within range of the whole beachhead.

We didn't stay on the beach. We went right in to the front lines and set up to protect the units that were already there. We passed through St.-Lô. It was nothing but a pile of masonry. That was done by the American bombers.

The twenty-fifth of July is when they started what they call the "breakout from the hedgerows." We were first attached to what they called the "division trains." That was a trucking outfit that was hauling supplies.

The day of the breakout, from daylight in the morning, the sky was filled with B-17s, B-24s, B-25s, and B-26s. From horizon to horizon, as far as you could see, the sky was full of planes going to bomb the German lines. I was the communications sergeant, so I rode in the Battery D headquarters half-track. There was me and the driver and the first sergeant and the captain in there. Being as it was the headquarters track, we had just one .50-caliber machine gun on it; I'd usually man the gun when we was moving. Either that or sometimes I'd relieve the driver and let him get a little rest, because I was the only other one in the half-track that could drive it.

That first night we was in a convoy. We had to stay close, because we couldn't use any regular lights. They had these little blackout lights on the vehicles—they had a purple-colored lens with shutters down over it. If you looked low enough behind it, you could see that light. But if you got your eye up, you couldn't see a thing. We drove all night long, slow, maybe five miles an hour. Our units were dispersed among the convoy, so no matter what part of it the Germans tried to attack, there'd be antiaircraft units close to it.

The driver had drove all night, and I took over before we got to Avranches early in the morning. The First Army had already captured the town, but they went on, and the Germans come back in. There was a single bridge across the river that was at Avranches, and I was driving when we was crossing it. We were trying to stay spread out on the bridge—let one vehicle get most of the way across before the next would start onto it. I was about a quarter of the way on the bridge, and the vehicle on the other end was almost off, when this German plane come over, and the first bomb he dropped didn't miss the bridge very far. And then there was about two or three of them planes circling around trying to bomb the bridge, because that was the only bridge across that river.

I floorboarded that half-track. The captain, he woke up and he says, "Stop, stop!"

I says, "Stop, hell. I'm getting off this damn bridge."

What worried me even more than the bombs was some First Army antiaircraft units down below the bridge. This was one of these steel-superstructure bridges, and they was firing right through that superstructure. Some of them shells couldn't have missed the top of our vehicle by no more than a couple of feet. You could see the machine-gun tracer bullets as they went by. I got off of that bridge.

On the other side of the bridge, there was dead people laying everywhere, mostly German, but a lot of dead Americans, too. And Lester Gimbert, the first sergeant, looked off to the side, and there was an American soldier that he knew, a boy from Natchitoches, laying there. He recognized his face when we went by. I didn't know the boy, but he was a good friend of Lester's.

He was there on the side of the road, dead, and his feet were sticking out in the street a little ways. They were about twice the size of a normal foot. Vehicles—tanks, trailers, half-tracks—had run over them and mashed 'em flat. They couldn't help it; these were narrow streets. His feet were sticking out in the road, and there just wasn't room to go around him.

He didn't feel it anyhow.

After the supply trucks unloaded, we drove back to Omaha Beach and picked up another load of supplies and turned around and drove back. The Sixth Armored Division had pushed all the Germans back into Brest; we met 'em just outside of it.

The Sixth Armored Division didn't try to capture Brest. They brought in the Second and Twenty-ninth Infantry Divisions to encircle Brest and hold it. Then they took us off of the division-train escort and put us as antiaircraft support with the division artillery. And we went from Brest over to just outside of Lorient. The Germans had a submarine base at St.-Nazaire, south of Lorient.

The artillery hit that submarine base. And then, a couple of days after that, the rest of the tank units caught up with us after they got through being relieved by those infantry divisions.

They had a big sloping hillside where we were, and the division commander, General Grow, lined up all the tanks—three or four battalions of them—in rows up on that hillside. I was with the artillery, which was set up down at the bottom of the hill, ahead of the tanks. And everybody zeroed all their guns on Lorient, which the Germans held. And then he had a memorial service for the men who were killed during the advance on Brest. They fired a three-volley salute, just like they do at a graveside, but they fired the shells into the German positions. And just as the third shot was fired, they blew taps over the radio and loudspeakers. Then, after taps, they started firing again. They must've fired well over a hundred volleys in there.

At that time blacks and whites were separated in the Army—there weren't mixed units. And we had a 155-millimeter artillery battery there, and it was all black. And they had a great big old black guy. He was the gunner, and he'd stand there with the lanyard in his hand. And to fire an artillery gun, you just snatched the lanyard real hard. That was the same as pulling the trigger.

When he got the order to fire, he'd say, "Mr. Hitler, count your men!" And he'd snatch that lanyard.

The first man who got killed in my battery was named Donaldson. His basic job was radio repairman, but he was a radio operator, too—there were radios in all the vehicles. He was one of the ones I trained in Fort Sheridan.

Our half-track was D-6, and D-3 was the platoon half-track he was riding in. One morning I got a call over the radio: "D-3 disabled, out of action, casualty Donaldson." That's all they said: "casualty Donaldson." So I called them back on the radio, and that was still all I could get out of them: "casualty Donaldson." That didn't tell me if he was hurt or killed. It was the policy not to give out information in the clear on the radio.

A little later on, I got in touch with the platoon leader, and they said he was killed. What he was, he was real tall. They had little zip-out openings in the canvas cover of the half-track, and one of them was in the front over that machine gun—you could stand up through it and fire out the side. He didn't like to sit down under that canvas, he liked to stand, and most of him stuck up out of there, he was so tall. And what happened, a German plane dropped a bomb in front of that half-track. The bomb didn't hit the half-track, but it blew a big crater in the road. And before the driver could stop, the half-track run in the crater and turned over and threw Donaldson in underneath it and fell on top of him and mashed him.

My attitude was, I knew it could happen and was gonna happen to some people, and there was nothing I could do about it. So I didn't let myself worry about it.

After we went to Lorient, we headed over towards the eastern part of France, and we came through what they call the Falaise Cauldron. That was where they trapped the German Seventh Army. You couldn't hardly put your foot on the ground without stepping on a dead German. The units I was with didn't do it to them; we just passed through there.

Nancy, France, is where we were headed for. It's near the Moselle River, not too far from Germany.

There were pockets of Germans everywhere. We just bypassed them. They'd be holding a town; our tanks would shell the buildings, and then we'd keep on going and leave 'em there. Very seldom did anyone actually get on the ground and fight.

Everybody that I was ever in contact with liked the tactics that Patton used. He didn't believe in stopping and sitting there and fighting it out. If the Germans wanted to stay there and fight, let 'em fight each other. Just go on by 'em, or go through 'em.

We captured German prisoners that would tell us they just couldn't understand. At night they'd go to bed thirty miles in front of the closest American unit. The next morning they'd be ten miles behind. We went forty miles many a night.

Nancy is where we stopped. The whole Army was stopped, to give all the gasoline that they could to Montgomery to try his wingding thing up in Holland. He was gonna go straight through to Berlin, and he didn't go anywhere.

There wasn't no written, official notice of it, but we knew that's what was happening. I'm sure Third Army headquarters knew what it was, and it filtered its way down. We certainly knew we didn't have any gasoline. We got a little bit, enough to do what running around had to be done just staying in place. But we didn't get enough to where we could mount any kind of drive.

Before they took away the gasoline, we really thought the war was almost over. And I guarantee you one thing: If the Third Army had got the supplies and gasoline that they diverted to Montgomery, the war would've been over before Christmas, because there wasn't nothing to stop us. We could have been in Berlin in a week.

Montgomery got two American airborne units, the 101st and Eighty-second Divisions, assigned to him, and he also had the British First Airborne Division. The British paratroopers were supposed to take Arnhem, but one battalion into that town was all they got. Then a big British force was supposed to drive north into Arnhem.

The Americans done their part of the job good. They captured what they was supposed to capture—the two main towns on the road into Arnhem. And they kept the road open. But the British didn't come up that road fast enough. The British theory was, "If I'm gonna step on that spot, first I'm gonna stand here, I'm gonna look at it a while, and then I'm gonna step on it. And then I'm gonna look at the next spot a while, and then I'm gonna step on *it.*" That was their philosophy of how to fight a war.

Now, they were really some good soldiers. They were brave soldiers. But their leadership is what was wrong.

The American philosophy—Patton's philosophy—was to go. Go over 'em, under 'em, around 'em. It don't matter, just go, as quick as possible. Don't even think about it—just go on and do it. And it worked. And really, I believe it caused less casualties that way than the way the British did it.

If they hadn't held us back, the war would've been over before Christmas. Because when we stopped in Nancy, the Germans didn't stop us. We just didn't have no gas.

When we were moving, we'd find a house and we'd ask if they had a place for us to stay. Most of them had a lot of spare room in the house, because their men were all gone, either killed or fighting somewhere or prisoners. I know we stopped in one French town after we left Nancy. Me and my half-track driver, we had our bedrolls, and we hadn't slept in a bed since we left England.

So we asked this lady—yeah, she had a room we could sleep in. And she had a featherbed about fifteen inches deep. We got on that doggone featherbed, and neither one of us could sleep. You'd just sink down in it—I felt like I was gonna smother. I got out and got on the floor, and my driver did, too. Most of what sleeping we did while we were over there would be sitting up in the half-track, or I'd just kind of lay down a little bit and go to sleep right close to the radio, where I'd hear it if somebody said anything. That bed was just too soft.

When we were gonna be set up in positions for a few days, we'd have a switchboard, and we'd string a field telephone line out to each gun position and use that instead of radio, because the Germans had radio directional findings. Well, we had 'em, too. You didn't stay on that radio long, because they could zero in on you, and here'd come an eighty-eight after you.

One time I was patching a wire that was broke, up on a telephone pole or a tree. I forget which it was—we used trees, and if there were poles, we used them. I could hear guns going off everywhere and bullets going through the air. I didn't know there was anybody aiming directly at me.

But somebody in a unit not too far away seen a German sniper shooting at me, and he killed him. He killed the German, and he reported it, how brave I was to stay up there, and that's how I got a Bronze Star.

I wasn't brave at all. I just didn't know I was being shot at. Hell, I would have stayed anyhow, because I didn't have no choice.

We stayed in Nancy until November the seventh, and then we took off again.

As soon as they got word of the Battle of the Bulge, the first thing they did, they sent the 101st Airborne in there to try to hold Bastogne. And they were surrounded. Then, from all that I've seen about it in books and on TV, Eisenhower was looking for somebody that could go rescue Bastogne. Patton volunteered, even though we were a hundred miles from Bastogne, going the opposite direction. We were in what they call the Battle of the Saar Basin.

I think it was December the nineteenth when we just turned around, completely around, the whole Third Army, and started toward Bastogne. The Sixth Armored Division was on one road, and the Fourth Armored was over on another road five or six miles away. Bastogne was kind of a hub. We would run into Germans all along the way; we'd whip 'em or capture 'em and just keep on going. We were on the move day and night.

On the way up toward Bastogne, every so often we had to stop and chop the ice out from underneath the jeeps with an ax. All that exhaust was partially melting the snow, and the slush would sling up underneath the jeeps and refreeze. And you'd be driving down the road like being in a big block of ice. That's how cold it was. Of course, the half-tracks were higher off the ground than the jeeps, but we had to chop it off the half-tracks some, too.

I had my feet and my hands half frozen quite a few times. About the only way to halfway get warm was when we stopped for a little bit. The half-track had a big muffler, and it'd get real hot. And you'd get out there and hold your hands around that muffler or stick your foot up on the muffler and try to warm up a little bit.

One time I tried to shave. I used my bayonet for shaving—I'd sharpen up the last few inches of it. So I got out of the half-track and I put my canteen cup on top of that muffler and got the water good and hot and got lathered up. And I just made one scrape down one side of my face, and they hollered, "Move out."

I had to jump up in the back of the half-track with that lather. And we hadn't gone fifty feet till that lather was just froze all over my face. I had to take my fingers and break it off.

The artillery was in action every day, regardless. While everybody else was sitting there resting, the artillery was up as far as the American lines were, shelling the German positions. We were with the artillery. We stayed with them all the time.

The Germans had plenty of planes into '45; they just didn't have any gasoline to put in 'em. When we captured Mühlhausen, Germany, they had a German airfield, and they had Ju 88s, which was a German twin-engine bomber. They must've had a hundred of them lined up side by side in two or three rows. The engines on those planes had never run. There never had been a bit of oil or gasoline put in 'em, just brand-new planes with nothing to fly 'em. This was getting along towards the end of the war, probably February, maybe March.

Mühlhausen was not far from where we captured the Buchenwald concentration camp. We had heard about the concentration camps—there was a few little articles in the *Stars and Stripes*—but we didn't know it for sure until we saw it.

I got there I guess the next day after it was actually captured.

They had disposed of some of the bodies then. They had bulldozers, and they just dug a big ditch and pushed 'em in and covered 'em up with dirt. But there was still a lot of them laying around.

And some of the live ones, it was hard to see how they could still be alive. Their arms would be an inch or two around—no meat on their arms at all. And they'd be sunk in between their ribs.

But the Americans cleared them out pretty fast. They set up a big tent somewhere—probably put IVs on a lot of them. And probably a lot of them went ahead and died, too.

I talked to a few of them. They were mostly Poles, and I didn't know any Polish. There was one or two there that could talk a little French. Of course, they were all real upset and crying. Being from Louisiana, I knew enough French for them to understand me, but they didn't talk slow enough for me to understand them. If I was talking to an ordinary Frenchman, I could slow him down and make him take time to pronounce the words. But these people couldn't slow down. They wanted to tell how they felt and what they'd been through, and they wanted to tell it real fast.

One word that they did say, though, was the German word for dead: *tot.* I could understand that.

There was a line of scaffolds up at the camp. There was just a long bar; each end was resting on top of a post. They had maybe eight long ropes on the bar, and a trapdoor underneath each rope. They would put their head in the noose and stand 'em on that trapdoor and spring the trapdoor, and they'd drop about ten feet until they'd hit the end of the rope, and that'd break their neck. And then they'd undo 'em down below and pull the rope back up for somebody else.

Right underneath the trapdoors was a hallway, and when the bodies dropped, they dropped right down in front of the ovens. And evidently they'd just unhook 'em and put 'em on these tables they had, which were like hospital gurneys. The tables were the same height as the ovens, and it looked like what they would do is just roll 'em up and slide the bodies off into the oven, and then take the gurney back for another one.

Those ovens were big, massive, masonry things. They were still hot enough when we got there that you could put your hand on them, but you had to get it off in a hurry. The fires was out, but there was still ashes in them. So they done that right up to the end.

They made all the German people that lived in the town go through and look, too, because some of them didn't believe that was going on. I've seen films since then that say Patton ordered that.

If I hadn't seen it, it would've been hard for me to believe that anybody could do something like that. But I know it happened because I seen it. I didn't read it in the paper. I didn't hear it on the radio or see it on TV. I know it happened because I seen it with my own eyes.

Like I said earlier, I've always been able to not let things like that bother me. I don't like it. I hate it. I wished it'd never happened. If there was any way I could have kept it from happening, I would have. But once it happened, there wasn't a damn thing I could do about it. So why let it worry me?

A lot of the Americans wanted to get away. A lot of them wouldn't even go look. But most of them had my same attitude, I guess. We done all we could to prevent it, but we couldn't. Anyhow, by that time most all of us had seen so many dead people that it really didn't have any effect on us.

One thing I'm very happy with: I made it through the war without having to shoot somebody that I know of. I may have, but I didn't know it. Our battery got credit for shooting down twenty-one German planes. Of course, we probably shot down a lot of 'em that we didn't get credit for.

But if I was shooting at a plane and that plane come down, I didn't know if I hit it or if somebody else that was shooting at it hit it. Nobody knew. I'm just glad I didn't actually have to point my gun at somebody and shoot him. I would have if I had to, but I'm glad I didn't.

I just don't think I would like killing people, regardless of how bad they were. The German soldiers that we captured seemed like pretty decent people. They were doing something they were told they had to do, and they didn't have any choice.

Now, for just a little while after the war was over, they put me and the half-track driver as security at a hospital over there. They had a lot of displaced persons in there that was sick and had been wounded. I captured an SS colonel in that hospital.

This German colonel, he didn't have a uniform on, but one of the patients in the hospital had been a prisoner at a concentration camp, and this colonel was in the SS unit in charge of that camp. And this patient pointed him out to me. So I took my rifle over there, and I collared him. I told him to sit on the ground with his hands up. I didn't point my rifle right at him, but I kept it where he knew I could get it pointed at him right quick. I told the half-track driver to call battalion headquarters, and they sent somebody to pick him up.

They put him in jail. I don't know what happened after that—they tried him and executed him, most likely. If he would've tried to run, I would've executed him right there. But I'm glad I didn't.

While we were at Bastogne, we were down in the basement of a bombed-out building one night, and there was one German plane come over and dropped one bomb. We knew it fell pretty close—we could hear it. So me and the half-track driver decided we'd go out and see what that bomb hit. We walked out, and there was this great big hole in the middle of the street, and it was the darnedest smell you ever smelled coming out of that hole. It smelled like a brewery.

So we walked over and looked down in there, and we could see racks with bottles on 'em. It was a wine cellar. Originally there was an entrance into it from the building we were in, but the Belgian people that owned it, when they found out that their country was gonna be occupied by Germans, they bricked up that entrance.

So the Germans never did find it. But when they dropped that bomb, *we* found it. We had a little trailer that we pulled behind the half-track with our duffel bags and all that stuff in it. They called it a quarter-ton trailer—it was about like one of these U-Haul trailers. Well, we took all them duffel bags out and tied 'em on the outside of the half-track and on top of the trailer and all kind of places, and we filled that trailer up with champagne and wine—mostly champagne.

We knew the war wasn't gonna last all that much longer, so we agreed then that we would not drink a drop of it until the war was over. And we kept our promise—we didn't touch it.

The night the war was over, we broke it out.

I didn't like wine. I would drink beer and a whiskey and Coke or something like that, but very little, because I just didn't like it. But I made up my mind I was gonna drink that champagne. So I got drunk on the stuff. And for about four or five days, I could be laying down asleep and just turn my head over to the other side, and the whole room would go whirling around.

It was worth it. That was May the eighth, 1945, and that's the last time I ever got drunk.

HEADQUARTERS
777TH AA AUTO WPNS BN
APO 403, U S ARMY

8 MAY 1945

GENERAL ORDERS
NUMBER 9

TO THE OFFICERS AND ENLISTED MEN OF THE 777TH ANTIAIRCRAFT ARTILLERY AUTOMATIC WEAPONS BATTALION

This battalion will cease hostilities at 0001 hours 9 May 1945 due to the complete capitulation of our German enemies.

To all of you, of all ranks, I extend my heartiest thanks for your outstanding performance of duty these many weary months of combat. From the beaches of Normandy to the junction of our victorious American and Russian Armies, through Avranches, Brittany, the Loire, the Saar, Bastogne, Luxembourg, the Rhineland, and the heart of Saxony, you have continually fought in such a manner as to excite the admiration and earn the respect of all men. It is an honor to be a member of this unit.

In this hour of triumph, let us all thank God for His blessing, and pray for a just and lasting peace. Let us not forget our friends who have sacrificed themselves that we might live. I am proud to have been permitted to command such a magnificent body of men.

JOSEPH H. TWYMAN, JR.
Lieutenant Colonel
Commanding

I was hoping Sandy wouldn't be going to Vietnam a second time. After he got trained as a medic and went to work in the hospital in Corpus Christi, I thought he'd be there till his hitch was up. Well, I think he did, too, but we both got fooled.

Before he left to go back overseas, I gave him the only advice that I could give anybody that was gonna go into that situation: Whatever your job is, do it as good as you can; and don't take any more chances than you have to, but take all the chances you have to, to do your job. That was my attitude.

At the time I was working for Walgreen. I was servicing the air-conditioning, refrigeration, and cooking equipment in about thirty stores, and we were living in Houston. We didn't live a mile from the Hobby Airport.

So me and his mother took him over to catch the plane. After we got through, instead of going home, we come back to the Gulf Freeway, and we were going downtown for something. And as we got on the freeway, the plane he was on took off and flew right over us.

She started crying, and I tried to console her, telling her he was gonna be all right and all that jazz. I thought he would probably have maybe the same luck I had. I hoped he would, but if he didn't, there wasn't anything I could do about it. I was trying to convince her he would be all right. And I believed he would be, because I didn't want to believe anything else.

If the United States had gone into Vietnam with the same resolve that we went into World War II with, the North Vietnamese would have been defeated in six months or less. The policy to me seemed to be, "If he hits me with one fist, I'll hit him with one fist. If he hits me with both of 'em, I'll hit him with both of 'em. If he kicks me with one foot, I'll kick him back." In other words, just go so far, don't go no farther. "If they kill fifty of our soldiers, we'll kill fifty of theirs."

Hell, the way I look at it, if they kill fifty of our soldiers, we should kill ten thousand of theirs, or every one we can.

I worked until I was seventy-five. As long as I was out working every day, from 1945 until 1995, I was so tired I didn't have time to let what happened overseas bother me. I could push it aside. But from '95 on, I just can't push it aside anymore. I try to, but I can be driving down the road sometimes, and all of a sudden, I hear a radio message: "casualty Donaldson." I dream about it at night, too, and it seems like I'm still right there in that half-track on the radio taking that message. Other dreams I'm in places like up on that telephone pole or on that bridge.

I remember all the chances I had to not come back. I had a lot less chance to get through it than I did to not get through it, and I got the chance that was the least. Now, why, I don't know. It's either that I was never in the wrong place at the right time or the right place at the wrong time, one or the other.

I talked to doctors at the VA, and they gave me some kind of doggone sleeping pills to take. But, like I tell you, tranquilizers make me completely goofy, so I didn't take them, because I knew what they'd do. Then they gave me medicines for depression. I'm not depressed. I remember things, but I'm not depressed about them.

I wish I couldn't remember. But since I got where I can't work, things just keep coming back to me—and there ain't nothing I can do about it.

My memory's so doggone good. Like I told you to start with, I'm different from a lot of people in a lot of ways.

XXII

"You can't help but care for your family."

SANDY WALMSLEY

SANDY WALMSLEY

Retired Air-conditioning and Refrigeration Contractor
Natchitoches, Louisiana
Hospital Corpsman Second Class, United States Navy, Vietnam

As Allied ground forces advanced during World War II, field hospitals, situated not far to their rear, advanced with them. During the war in Vietnam, with no front lines and with large, permanent, relatively secure American bases scattered throughout the combat zone, the American military was able to establish a web of stationary, well-equipped hospitals, placed so that Dustoff pilots never had to go far to reach one. The average time from a serviceman's wounding until his arrival at a medical facility had been 10.5 hours in World War II and 6.3 in Korea; in Vietnam it was 2.8. Some casualties arrived at hospitals no more than twenty minutes after taking their hit.

Before evacuation, wounded servicemen were under the care of enlisted men trained to give first aid. Army "medics" and Marine "corpsmen"—members of the Navy's Hospital Corps who were attached to Marine outfits—walked the same ground, got stuck in the same mud, were pinned down in the same firefights as the grunts who called them "Doc." Medics and corpsmen served in other capacities in Vietnam—as hospital orderlies and as base-camp sanitation supervisors, to name two. But if they were tramping through the jungles with infantrymen, they bore two main responsibilities: to watch over the general health of their charges—by seeing, for instance, that they took their malaria pills—and to begin the treatment of men injured in battle.

Bandaging wounds, stanching bleeding, easing pain with an injection of morphine, medics and corpsmen worked to stabilize the condition of men who had been hurt and to prepare them for transport. If a firefight claimed a number of casualties, the medic or corpsman performed triage on them.

The nature of wounds sustained by American servicemen in Vietnam shifted over the course of the war. In 1966, 43 percent of wounds were caused by small-arms fire and a virtually identical portion by mines and booby traps. Four years later, after the enemy's tactics had changed from direct confrontation to slow attrition, small arms accounted for only 17 percent of American wounds while mines and booby traps were responsible for 80. But the concern of medics and corpsmen for the men in their care remained constant. Approximately 1,300 Army medics and 690 Navy corpsmen were killed in Vietnam. Twelve medics and four corpsmen received the Congressional Medal of Honor.

John Howe, speaking of a friend, says that combat medics "have this propensity for absorbing the pain around them." That description fits Sandy G. Walmsley, born in 1947, who saw combat first as an ordinary seaman, then as a corpsman attached to a grunt unit in the First Marine Division.

As a kid I asked my dad questions about the war. He would tell me places that he went; he said that they liberated a cellar of wine and all got drunk at the war's end. But I never remember him getting into any action details. "I was just one of the guys. I ran the radio," is about all he would tell me.

I knew he was a communications sergeant in the Army and in the war. And before I went to Vietnam and saw what war was all about, I figured he was a noncombatant—communications was pretty well safe, like a clerk's job. He gave me no reason to believe that he was in combat. By the time I got back, I knew that he had seen combat because of what I had seen. Yes, radio operators were one of the prime targets of the enemy. Probably right up there with medics and hospital corpsmen.

And I began to realize my dad must have experienced some similar things to what I did, because combat is combat. I don't care what your character is and what your strength is and what your weaknesses are, the crucible of battle creates similar circumstances in all generations. I've even got to looking at some of the PBS specials, and they've talked about some of the Roman soldiers and how they possibly suffered PTSD symptoms back then, only they may have called it something else.

He was the first one I talked to about some of my experiences. I'd ask him, "Pop, have you ever seen people killed?" Usually when I'd been drinking. He really did not know the extent to which I was addicted—either that or as a father he was in denial. I don't think to this day he would accept it, even though I did tell him. "Congratulations, your son is an alcoholic"—he would not let himself believe that. That's just the father in him, I guess.

But he would not answer me, not directly anyway. I would say the first time he ever mentioned anything as far as he being personally involved in combat was three or four years ago. And slowly but surely he would start coming out with a few details.

It makes me feel better to have him open up. It gives me a closer feeling to him—as father and son, and as fellow veterans—to know that we have this shared history. I think you'll find that most Vietnam sons idolize what our fathers did in World War II. And we feel that we let ourselves and everyone down because we could not reach the magnitude of what they accomplished.

To this day I would like to feel like I was a part of something that did some good and that was for a right reason. But you don't get that out of all the discussions about Vietnam. You get everything that was wrong with it and everything we did wrong. In other words, we feel like failures. Whereas our fathers were national heroes for doing something that was unquestionably good, something that needed to be stood up for and done, we don't get that sense—at least I don't, personally and privately—out of the Vietnam experience.

I've seen programs that said, "Yes, you contributed to the demise of Communism in that area for that period of time." But to me it's so pitifully little that you get into the question of what would've been right to do. Here's what we did wrong; what would've been right? There's no end of debate. Even among ourselves, there is disagreement:

"We should've never been there. The protesters were right. We should've joined them and gotten us all out of there a lot sooner than we did."

"No, we should've gone in and bombed the whole damn North off the face of the map. Nuked 'em if we had to. Not given a damn what Communist China said they would do." The Douglas MacArthur approach—if we had only.

Well, we don't know what would've happened if we had only, because we didn't. We might've gotten into a nuclear exchange.

I am against war. I am against even the hatred of one human being for another, because war is all it leads to. But if you have to fight a war, it will save more in the long run to fight it to win. Get it over with. If you're going to do it, do it. If you're not, don't do it. But don't ever do it halfway.

The first things they would ask when we would come up on an enemy base camp—normally the enemy would be gone by that time—were, "How many weapons?" "Are there any bodies?" It was like brownie points—the more weapons you could account for, the more enemy bodies you could account for, the better the little brownie points that were handed out.

Meaning what? I got the inkling that there was a pressure to give big counts. "Give us some success here." It was almost a pressure to produce results even if you didn't have any. "Give us something."

But after you finished the mission, it wouldn't be a month later that that same base camp was taken over again by the enemy, because you had no means of securing it long-term. So it might be three months later you had the same job to do over again, which was extremely frustrating.

There was no measurable, permanent success in what you were doing. There was no clear-cut end goal that said, "Here is where we're going. Here is what we're doing for victory." It was just an endless take one hill, abandon it, take another one, abandon it, go back to the first one, take it again, abandon it again. There was no sense of closure or end to it. And after a while there was no sense of patriotism about what you were doing.

It hurt me so bad when my son told me that he wanted to join the armed forces. Young men don't know any better; they don't know what's waiting for them. Patriotism is a wonderful thing. I would fight and die for this country right here on this shore, right now. But when you've been through it, you see the bigger scheme of things. I can see now why mothers cry. Their sons go off to war like lambs to slaughter.

In a lot of ways, that's what we were. We were patriotic, we were young, we were innocent. And in a lot of ways, we were stupid. We went believing in what we were fixing to do, and we were slaughtered—emotionally, mentally, physically.

Some of the lucky ones are dead.

I started at the University of Houston in the summer of '65, right after I graduated from high school. I was trying to work and pay my way and promptly came up with failing grades. The next thing I knew, I had a draft notice in the mail. I mean, it was boom, boom, boom. It was quick.

I reported to the induction center, which was in one of the federal buildings in downtown Houston. The induction center was on the same floor as the recruiters' offices, so there in that narrow hallway, in addition to the line of people reporting for induction, there were three lines of people waiting to see the recruiters. The longest line was the Air Force. The shortest line was the Army. And kind of in between was the Navy. I don't know where the Marines were—I guess they had their own place somewhere on another floor.

I was standing in the line for induction; I had my notice in my hand. And a guy came out of the Navy recruiting office. He was ten years older than me. He was overweight, bald. And for some reason we caught each other's eye—I guess I looked like a lost puppy. He said, "I see you're in the wrong line."

I said, "What do you mean?"

"Look, go in this line and show the Navy recruiter your induction notice. He just cut a deal for me." He said, "Don't think, do it. You'll thank me. It might save your life."

I said, "What have I got to lose?"

So I got in that line, and I went in there, and the Navy recruiter looked at my notice. He said, "Got drafted, didn't you?"

I said, "Yeah."

"You want me to get you out of this?"

"Hell, yeah."

"You ready to leave in the morning to go to boot camp in the Navy?"

"Yeah."

"Good answer."

So instead of being drafted into the Army, I had volunteered to go into the Navy.

Navy boot camp is a walk in the woods compared to Army basic training and Marine Corps boot camp. See, we trained right next door to Camp Pendleton, and sometimes at midnight, one or two in the morning, you would hear a company of Marines out there, still training because they didn't get it right during the day. And they stayed there until they got it right.

We went through what to do aboard a ship, and we did running and calisthenics. But I would say a good 70 to 75 percent of our training consisted of learning how to march so we could look real good for our parents at graduation exercises.

After we graduated, two of us were assigned to a fire-support ship called the USS *Carronade.* They flew us to a little place called Vung Tau, and from there they sent communications out to the ship. And the ship said, "We're fixing to go on operation. We don't have time to come in. Put 'em on something and send 'em out."

So they found out there was a PT boat going out that direction, and they boated us on out.

The section leader came up and got us. And we hadn't been aboard but a few minutes when the ship's intercom sounded: "General quarters. All hands man your battle stations," and they rang the bell. The next thing I know, we're buckled up belowdecks and we're going somewhere.

We stayed for hours that way. And finally word starts filtering down: "Hey, we're going on something called Deckhouse III. It's up the Mekong Delta. Pass it on."

Deckhouse III was the name of the mission. There were six of them, and—I believe I'm remembering correct—I was on three of them while I was aboard ship.

They kept naming it Deckhouse I, II, III, and so on because it was more or less the same mission over and over again: a fire-support mission in support of a troop sweep to clean out the Vietcong.

I was just a seaman recruit, which meant they could use me anywhere. I wasn't trained to do anything, so I just brought food to the guys and swabbed decks and sat there and made sure I was available when needed. They weren't about to put somebody like me on a rocket launcher; we were the gofers.

After about four months, they looked at my records and saw

that during my short tenure at the University of Houston, I had taken engineering. It was electrical engineering, but to those down in the engineering department, "engineering" was all they needed to know. The next thing I knew, I was an engineer. A fireman. What they call in the Navy a "snipe."

I descended into hell. I had never been down there before—"authorized personnel only." All of a sudden, I was an authorized personnel. When they opened that door to the engine room, there was noise and heat and a real pungent diesel smell like you have never smelled in your life. And for the next three months, that was my abode for twelve hours each day.

We had thermometers that we kept in our pockets, and they stayed pegged at about 140 degrees. We were required to take so much water and so many salt tablets every hour. We had to sign a book, and they had to watch us take 'em. We had to wear earplugs for the noise. It was senseless to try to talk, so we learned hand signals.

I read gauges and charted 'em. Checked dipsticks on oil levels to make sure they were right, checked valves to make sure they were in the proper position. I never was more hot, miserable, dirty, and had such a bad mental attitude as during those three months that I was in that place.

What got me out of there was a beautiful directive from the fleet commander all the way back in California that said all ships in our fleet would have what was termed a hospital-corpsman striker. In other words, somebody who was interested in medicine and wanted to be a corpsman, and who would be designated for on-the-job training by the hospital corpsman already assigned to the ship. See, big ships had doctors who were commissioned officers. Smaller ships like ours had a hospital corpsman chief, NCO in rank, and he ran a small hospital bay.

The directive was just put out there for those who were interested. Volunteers. And so, "Yeah, I'm interested." Anything to get out of this hole.

There was another boy down there that was also interested, but they could only take one. So the chief said, "I want each one of y'all to sit down and write me a little so-many-page essay on why you want this job."

I sat down and wrote mine, and I was just honest with him: "I'm getting sick down in this hellhole. I'm gonna die down here. And I promise I'll do my very best." The other guy told me later he wrote down a bunch of bullshit about being in the medical field before and how he was the best man for the job and common sense dictates that you should choose me and not that other rotten dude.

The chief accepted me. Oh, the best day of my life is when he looked at me and he said, "Go get a bath." I had stayed covered with grease down in that hole—you couldn't help it. And I scrubbed. I scrubbed until I got all that stuff off.

He began to show me what to do. He taught me how to give shots, how to draw blood. I got to go with him on some of his trips that he made into the hospitals when we would go ashore and see how a hospital operated.

He became more than just a mentor. He became almost a second father to me. He was older—his career was just about over—and he pulled enough rank aboard ship that he made it a lot nicer for me and gave me a new lease on life.

It was a six-month period that I trained aboard ship. Then I left the ship in Hong Kong and flew to San Diego for Hospital Corps School.

They were in need of more hospital corpsmen because they were being killed at such a high rate. That's hindsight. At the time I didn't realize that.

Hospital Corps School, at Balboa Hospital in San Diego, was a four- or five-month course, very intense, and compacted into ten- and twelve-hour days of study and testing. They put us through lifesaving techniques, personal hygiene, suturing. They taught us how to do pressure points, bandaging, CPR, splinting. All the things that we'd need to do in order to sustain life on a battlefield till the person could be transported to a proper medical facility.

When I finished the schooling, I was assigned to the hospital at the naval air station in Corpus Christi, Texas. Probably about 80 to 90 percent of patients there were casualties from Vietnam—it was one of the receiving points for United States Marine Corps casualties and Navy casualties. Every kind imaginable.

They had a burn ward at Corpus Christi, which was, to me, the most horrendous place in the world. I worked in it for a short while; I couldn't work there too long. Probably the most pitiful place that you ever want to work is any kind of burn ward.

The majority of patients were helicopter crewmen who had crashed. Most of the helicopters were magnesium-based in their foundation, and magnesium burns very, very intensely when it's ignited. So if they were shot down or they crashed, almost inevitably the helicopters would burn, and you'd have some fierce casualties—third-degree burns over 50 to 75 percent of their bodies before they could extract them from those helicopters.

It was a terrible, terrible thing to witness. Most of them, if they did survive, would be scarred for the rest of their life and severely handicapped. It took months of intensive care to get them on the road to recovery.

In one section of the burn ward, down at the end, they had a huge portable scrub tank, a swimming pool. And they had a device that had a sling arm on it and a harness. And they would put the patients in that harness and swing them over and let them down into that pool.

The tank was filled with warm saline water that had a sterile solution in it. Of course, they drained it and refilled it and made it ready for each patient that came there.

The old infected tissue had to be scrubbed away or they were going to die from the infection. Then dressings were applied to the new tissue and they'd be brought back to the ward. It had to heal in sections and layers. It was easier to work with them in the tank than it was just laying on a bed; they were buoyant in the water, so all parts of their body were accessible. In the pool would be a technician in shorts, and he would have nylon scrub brushes and antiseptic.

I never got into the water with them and actually debrided the wounds, but I was present when it was done. I would go to their bedside and help get them onto the gurney and bring them to the pool and help hoist them over. It was terrible, because they only had to experience it once to know it was pure hell. They would be given massive doses of morphine.

You'd hear the poor people start screaming down in the ward when the nurse would come in with the morphine drip, because they knew what they were getting ready for. This had to be done usually once a week—sometimes every three or four days, depending on the severity of the burns and the infection that had set in. Several of them asked to be killed rather than brought down there.

Most that weren't too badly burned were thankful later that they were made to go through the experience, because once they were healed, then they just had the scars inside their heads to deal with.

They were salvageable. They just didn't know it at the time.

My next orders read to go from Corpus Christi to Guam, and it was a good chance I could serve the rest of my time at the naval hospital there handling the medevac system. What happened my dad does not know. I believe I told it to him one time, right after I came back, but I think he chose to forget about it, because it was incomprehensible to him that I would do such a thing.

My best friend was named David Overstreet. We met at Corps School, and we became closer than brothers. When we got through with school, we both went to Corpus Christi and served at the hospital there. When our orders came, and mine were to go to Guam, David's were to go to the Third Marine Division in Vietnam.

He wanted to go. He was all gung ho. He believed in what he was doing, probably as strongly as anyone in our class, and he wanted to save lives. He wanted to do something with his life that made a mark. He was that type of individual. If he found out something you needed, he would quietly and privately go behind your back and make sure it got done for you. He didn't want to be known as the one who did it; he would do it privately.

We had another, older corpsman there with us. How Joe ever got in the service, I'll never know. He had some type of palsy—part of his eye drooped, and part of his mouth drooped because of the loss of muscle control. Plus, he had a wife and three small children. It was incomprehensible to me that when his orders came, they were for First Marine Division in Da Nang.

When he got those orders, his wife had a nervous breakdown, and they had to put her in the hospital. He asked for a hardship reversal of orders. They would not give it to him. He should not have gotten those kind of orders, and the old man at the hospital, the one in command, was trying to help him out. But the old man's superiors said, "The orders stand." And when they give such a decision, that's it, there's no appeal. Joe was going.

I asked my boss, "What is the relief that this man can get?"

He said, "The only option is if someone would trade orders with him. As long as they got a body going over there, they'll be satisfied."

I said, "If my friend David can do stuff like that, damn it, I can, too." David was always my hero.

So I went to the old man. I said, "Look, I'm a single man. I've got a friend going to Vietnam. I'd rather go with him than go to Guam. Trade these orders."

He said, "Joe's gonna find out about it."

"Just make sure I'm gone before he does."

"You are crazier than a betsy bug."

"Maybe. But I'm single. I have no brothers or sisters and no close ties to any girlfriend or anything. Trade orders before I change my mind."

And he did. He had the clerk take care of it while I was sitting there in his office. He said, "Good luck to you. I still think you're crazy. More than that, I don't think I'm gonna see you again."

Everybody had been pulling for Joe. They had all given depositions. Even the civilian hospital where his wife was put had sent a letter saying it was causing a hardship.

So I figured my one good strike at life had been done, and I was happy to have done it. I would still do it again to this day. I'd still be crazy as a betsy bug, but it's something I wanted to do, and, like David, I didn't want anybody to know about it. I'm sure afterwards they told him what had happened—you had a right to know, eventually, who traded orders with you. But the news came down right as I was leaving, and all he knew was he had got his orders reversed.

He was talking to his wife on the phone at the hospital last I saw of him, and he was the happiest man. He gave me the thumbs-up—everything was going to be okay.

That made me feel so good.

Before going overseas we went to the Field Medical Service School, five weeks at Camp Pendleton, which prepared you directly for the battlefront. They did as good a job as they knew how. But how can an old Marine drill sergeant that takes us for five weeks convey to us his full knowledge of what it's like to be in combat? He told us things we needed to know to stay alive in adverse situations. How to duck, how to cover, how to hide, how to dodge.

He scared us one night. About two o'clock in the morning, he got us up and he started firing off blank rounds and got us confused, and the only way out was over a cliff. We didn't know what was below, but every one us dove off of it, because we had no choice the way he drove us. It turned out it was only about a ten- or twelve-foot drop into a nice sandpit. And he said, "That's what it's like to be confused in the middle of the night in a firefight; that's when you end up killing your own men. Make sure you know where everybody is in the middle of that situation. You get out of position on a perimeter, you're dead." And he said, "You think I'm kidding"—because he had lost men that way himself.

We thought he was the meanest asshole on the face of the earth, because he drove us those five weeks unmercifully. But handing out the diplomas, he broke down and cried. In front of every one of us.

Big old, burly, scarred-up-where-he-had-been-wounded Marine. He could've retired from the Corps, but he said, "I wouldn't be here if it wasn't for hospital corpsmen. I'll stay here as long as I have to, to help you guys save lives and to live yourself. Because you have no idea. I have done all I can to get you ready, but you're gonna wake up soon."

After he finished talking and handing out the certificates, he grinned and got out of the way, and the door to the galley was open. And on all the tables in there were pitchers of ice-cold beer. He said, "It's on Sarge." We started drinking, and some didn't stop till 0800 the next morning, when we were due out at the tarmac to get on the jet and fly to Da Nang. He kept the pitchers coming as long as we could drink 'em. In other words, enjoy yourselves while you can, because . . .

We wondered about his crying—did he do that for every class? But I think it was heartfelt. It's said that the casualty rate for hospital corpsmen in combat in Vietnam was one of the highest for any group in the United States services—way above 50 percent. Knowing what I know now, could I do what this old sergeant did? That's intense—training these boys for five weeks and sending them off, knowing half of 'em are gonna be killed or wounded, no ifs, ands, or buts.

It's a rule that they let you acclimatize in-country before they send you out on operations, but the night before my flight landed in late November of '68, the last healthy corpsman of our company was killed in an ambush. There was one other, but he was slightly wounded and was staying back treating guys at the base camp. So when I got in, I was it.

I was proud of my medical insignia and dressed up in all my best. We were fixing to go out on a patrol to pick up the bodies from the ambush. And the first thing the old gunnery sergeant did was come up and look at me and shake his head and reach up and rip the caduceus off my collar. He rubbed some dirt on me and he said,

"Son, if you want to live beyond sunset, you will dress like a Marine. You will walk like one and you will smell like one. If I had let you go out there the way you were dressed, you wouldn't last a day."

He had to check me out on my weapon before he issued it to me, a .45 side arm. I'd never had a .45 in my hand in my life. He was drinking a beer and smoking a cigar when he talked to me, and he said, "Wait a minute." And he finished his beer, and he walked out there about forty yards and set his can down on the dirt. Everything was open and safe—we were out on the far end of the camp.

And he said, "Okay, Doc. You've got to at least squeeze off a couple of rounds and show me you know how to shoot this." And I sighted—with one hand. He said, "Whoa. Whoa. Whoa. Two hands." He showed me how to cuff the other hand underneath and hold it steady. And he shook his head and backed away, and I sighted down that thing.

In the meantime I was so tense I already had the safety off and was squeezing the trigger. And that trigger got enough tension on it so the gun went off. Because I wasn't expecting to shoot just yet, it scared me, and so I squeezed it again, before I finally let my finger go. The first shot hit that can on the bottom rim and knocked it up in the air about ten feet. The second round hit the can in the air and blew it backwards about twenty feet.

The look on his face was worth a million dollars. He said, "Damn. You been pulling my leg. Who taught you how to shoot like that?" And I just did the old blowing on the end of the thing and put on the safety and holstered it. I never told him any different. Those were the luckiest shots on the face of the earth, and that was the last time I ever shot that thing.

All the other guys were ready to go; I was the last one. The corpsman who was slightly wounded made me up a first-aid pack. I didn't even know how to tag a guy. He said, "You're gonna find 'em dead, and you're gonna have to tag 'em. Make sure they're dead. They're gonna be, but you have to do it officially, like a coroner. The tag is self-explanatory; just fill in the blanks. The guys will help you."

And so I went out there, and there were—oh, I forget how many dead. The only one that I ever remember in any detail was the corpsman. I felt silly trying to take a pulse on him. Rigor mortis had set in a long time ago; I estimated from what they told me that he'd been dead probably about eight hours. And I filled in the tag—name, unit, cause of death, time of death. Attached it on the front of his torso, where they could see it. I don't know if they could read it—my writing was shaky, and all my tags were wet because on the way in I had slipped off the rice paddy and fallen into the muck. But I tagged him, and we bagged him.

And, oh, this guy was big. He was heavy. He was over two hundred pounds easy. He shouldn't have passed the physical to even get there. But we had to carry him about five hundred yards across the rice-paddy area to the road where the half-track was waiting to take him back to the morgue. That was a load, and it was a hot day. We hauled him all the way across that rice paddy and loaded him up on the vehicle, and by the time we got there, I was shaking so hard. It wasn't even necessarily off of physical exertion. I was scared. It started hitting me then that this is a dead body. I had never been around a dead body before in my whole life. And it stank.

When you go out on your first patrol and you see your first man blown away, it's like a slap right in the face. You say, "Damn, this is real."

It was my job to make sure the men stayed as healthy as possible. I brought foot powders, and I made sure the men brought an extra pair of socks. They traveled on their feet; if their feet go, they're no good. So they'd all get mad at me. But as soon as we knew the perimeter was secure, the first thing I made them do was take their boots off and change their socks. And even if they had to use canteen water, I insisted they wash their socks—they could hang 'em on their backpacks and let 'em dry. And when we stopped again, I made them change socks again.

I was responsible for about thirty Marines, a platoon. Actually, sometimes I was responsible for the whole company, because there was a shortage of corpsmen.

The relationship between Marines and corpsmen was really inculcated in you at Field Medical Service School in Camp Pendleton.

That was for five weeks. The Marines caught it from the time they went through boot camp: "The hospital corpsman is your only hope for survival if you're wounded. You take care of him, he'll take care of you." And then you're both put into the combat situation, and the relationship just naturally happens.

You bond together, and you learn to serve together and trust each other, and with trust comes a certain amount of affection and closeness. It's just something that happens in a human situation. Maybe not in absolutely every case. I'm sure you can find a Marine somewhere who curses the corpsmen, who has a bad attitude because he got wounded and he thought maybe one didn't do his job. There's oddities like that in every situation.

But by and large they trusted you with their lives, and they took care of you, too. It was a very close bond. It was set up to be that way, and it was consummated in battle.

If there was a situation where it became your life or theirs, they would do what they had to in order to protect you. I wasn't personally witness to an example, but there are Congressional Medal of Honor winners who threw themselves on hand grenades to save corpsmen.

They'd make sure that I got my foxhole dug, because I'd be too damn tired to do it. They'd make sure I got food. They'd encourage me to keep going if I was tired. They'd carry me if they had to. Big brother, little brother. You're gonna look out after your little brother, and you're gonna make sure that he gets protected. He's kept as much out of harm's way as possible. And in reciprocation—it's called "Corpsman up."

When a corpsman hears a Marine call "Corpsman up" in a bad situation, he does not have to go out there. He does not have to. They will order guns up to advance on the enemy. They will not order a hospital corpsman to go forward. Ninety percent of the cases, he chose to do that.

It is not unusual to have heard stories of corpsmen actually placing their bodies in the line of fire to protect the man they were treating. Why they do it, I don't know. They just do it. Men have for ages done what afterwards was called heroic—they call it foolish if they live to speak about it—to protect their fellow man and to come to his aid. The Marines have almost a shame if they leave any bodies on the battlefield. Why? They're not ordered to do that. There's no order anywhere that says you shall not leave, under pain of prosecution and court-martial, the body of your fallen comrade on the field. Well, the North Vietnamese did that, too. They risked their lives to pull bodies out of combat situations. So it's a human trait.

There was one incident that reminds me we're not very far apart when you consider the overview of the family of man. We were coming back from one patrol. Thank God we had made no contact with the enemy, but we were worn out. We were tired. It was getting late in the afternoon. Home was in sight, and we were happy to be going in that direction.

We were walking in a downward spiral around a mountain toward our base camp. For some odd reason, somebody said, "Hey, guys, look." We had a view of the mountain opposing ours, and there on the other mountain was an enemy platoon headed in a spiral upward. They had their dark khaki uniforms on, which meant they were NVA regulars.

We were too far apart to engage each other in small-arms fire, and yet we were close enough for both sides to recognize that they were North Vietnamese and we were Marines—if we could see them, they could see us; we're all trained to be observant. And Billy Maxwell took his M-16 and held it up in the air above his head. And the guy at the lead of the NVA patrol did the same thing with his AK-47. Both of them held them there for about thirty seconds, looking at each other. And then both of them lowered their weapons, and we just went on our way.

We had mortars, and I know they always carried small mortars. We could've had a battle. Nobody knew but us, and nobody knew but them. We never reported it. We went back home, and I'm sure they did, too. It had been a long day at the office, and we just let it be.

It was the strangest thing, and it got me thinking on a broader scale: They're people, too. And they get weary. And they get tired.

Oliver and Ritchie became buddies at Marine boot camp at Camp Pendleton. Went to Vietnam together, were assigned to our company. Fought like cats and dogs. You'd never know they were buddies for all the fussing and cussing they gave each other. But it was just that type of relationship; they were really close.

Oliver was walking point one day. We heard some enemy fire, and then our guns were called up for support fire. Then I heard somebody screaming, "Get your ass back here." And then they called, "Corpsman up." And I went up to the edge of a little open area—maybe fifty yards of open space before the trees started again. I was there with Billy Maxwell. I said, "Max, what happened?"

He said, "Damn it, Oliver got hit. And Ritchie had to go out there."

If Ritchie would have stayed where he was with the rest of them, he would have been safe. But it was his buddy, so before anyone knew what was happening, he was tearing ass out there. And that's why they yelled, "Get your ass back here." And Ritchie went down, too.

I could see one of the bodies draped over a log up at the other side of the clearing. And I said, "Damn," because normally you'd get into a low crawl to cross a clearing, but there was no crawling to be done here—they had to be gotten to pretty quick.

Billy said, "Well, Doc, it's your call."

I said, "We have to see about them. There may be a chance that one of 'em is alive." The one who was across the log, I could see the dark hair on him. That meant that that was Ritchie. So Oliver had to be down on the ground somewhere around him.

This was the only time I ever took charge of a combat situation. When things got quiet, I yelled, "Fellas, this is Doc. Do y'all think y'all can give me some cover fire without killing my ass?"

"Yeah, Doc. We can do it."

I said, "Do y'all know where I am?"

"Yeah, we hear you."

I said, "I'm gonna risk it. I'm gonna hold my hand up so y'all know where I am."

"Okay, we see you."

"Okay, fellas, on three. One—" and on two I got up and started running. And I heard some of 'em start cussing, and they started firing. Ain't one of 'em hit me.

I never ran so hard and low and fast in my life. I got about fifteen feet from Ritchie, and I did the old face-forward slide into second base—just threw myself forward with all four and went on in in a cloud of dust. I came up about five feet short, crawled the rest of the way to the log. I got down behind it so I wouldn't be in any line of fire.

Now I could see Oliver. He was off to the left of Ritchie in some vegetation. Ritchie was draped over the log.

I knew he was dead from back there, but as I got right on him, I said, "Maybe he's just holding position," because, for all the world, his rifle was at the ready, and his hands were on it, and his head was cocked down the sights; it's just his helmet had come off. But he wasn't moving, and he didn't acknowledge my presence. So I grabbed him by the collar and pulled him over. And when I pulled him over—and in my dreams I still see this again and again, me pulling him over, pulling him over, pulling him over—his eyes were wide open, and right between his eyes, as if surgically placed, was a bullet hole. There was no exit wound anywhere in his head, not even any torn skin. You could not have gone up and drawn it better with a pencil.

I knew he had died instantly.

I could hear gurgling from Oliver over in the bushes. I went to him and turned him over, and he had a through-and-through wound right in the heart area, which made him the hardest in the world to do CPR on. I could tell that the round had impacted several of his ribs. He had an exit wound through one broken rib in the back.

He didn't have a lot of external bleeding. I knew he was bleeding internally. There's a kind of a pooling and a firm feel to the stomach area that's indicative of internal bleeding, as if a balloon is being filled. I bandaged him as good as I could on both the entrance and exit wounds. I found just a faint, faint pulse on him. And then it went away as I was feeling it. It died out.

So I said, "Well, if his heart has been pumping, he may not have had brain damage yet." I turned him over very gently, being careful myself to stay low behind that log, and I started giving him CPR. In the meantime they were securing the area around me, and some of them started coming up as far as I was.

I asked anyone if they knew CPR, and one of the corporals said yeah. I said, "Look, you do the breaths, I'll do the compression." I didn't have any whole blood, but I had a bottle of saline solution, of all things, on me. I didn't normally carry one, but I had that and an IV set. And what I needed was volume to get his blood pressure back up and restore his heartbeat.

I figured I had a chance, so we kept at it for about ten minutes. I stopped long enough to try to start an IV in his wrist, but his veins had collapsed, and I didn't have a big needle where I could go deep enough to find an artery—all they gave us was these little butterfly needles.

They had taught us out of textbooks—they didn't have dummies to use—how to do a cut-down. And normally you do it where there's a big vein, and that would be in the ankle. So I stripped his boots off and his socks off, and you could see a big flat blue line under his skin, which was his main vein in the inside part of the ankle.

So I went ahead and got my bayonet out. I had sharpened the point, and I carried it strapped to my right leg. And I remember saying something like, "God, please help me on this, because I don't know what the hell I'm doing." Meanwhile I was showing the other guy what to do to continue the CPR. The CPR was being done in a crude manner, but it was keeping enough volume going to hopefully prevent brain damage. And I was working as fast as I could to do this cut-down.

You just make the incision alongside the vein. You break the skin and fascia tissue underneath, and you peel it back any way you can. And there's your vein exposed right there. And then you can manipulate the vein with your fingers and get that needle started, which I did. And I taped it up real good, and I reached up enough to hang that IV bottle on a branch above me. And I turned that flow wide open, and we started getting some good volume in him, and then his heartbeat started restoring.

I was going places now. I said, "Man, we've got a real chance here."

And then the guy that was doing the breaths said, "Doc, I can't get no more in. Something's wrong." And I went and tried, and his airway was blocked. For whatever reason, I don't know. It was just blocked solid, and I couldn't see anything in his mouth that had blocked it.

Before, what encouraged me was he hadn't turned quite as ashen as they normally turn when they're dying. But now his fingernails started turning that ashen color, which meant he wasn't getting oxygen good enough.

They'd also shown us in a textbook how to do a tracheotomy. So I said, "I'm not sure about this, but it's the only chance this guy has." And they did not give us tracheotomy kits. They didn't exist back then for us. They taught us how to do a tracheotomy with a ballpoint pen.

So I asked somebody did they have a ballpoint pen, and one of the sergeants had one. I unscrewed it and threw away the top part, threw away the ink and the spring and just used the bottom barrel part. And I cut a bigger hole in the bottom where the ink comes out. I was nervous as hell. My hands were shaking. I put his head back like they showed us to expose his windpipe. I had the men support his head, and I counted the rings below the Adam's apple like they showed us so I wouldn't destroy his voice box. And I said, "If I don't have it, I'm close enough." I had to go quick.

And I got that bayonet and I said, "Please don't let me kill this man." And I put that point across there, and I pushed, and it broke the skin, but that's all it did. There was no bleeding, because his blood had all pooled. And I said, "That's not enough. You're gonna have to do more." And so I gathered everything I had, and I pushed a little bit harder, and that thing popped right through. You could feel it when it went into the space in the windpipe. And I left it there and turned it sideways and got the barrel from the pen like they taught us and put it in alongside and pushed. And that thing went in perfect, right into his windpipe, and I felt a slight whoosh of air go in there as his lungs started accepting the air. And I went ahead and taped it in place, like they told us to do.

And then all I had to do was blow on that pen and make his chest go up and down. He still wasn't breathing on his own, but I was feeling his pulse, and it was starting to return. He even moaned a little bit. And they said, "Doc, it's getting late. You want a medevac on this one?"

I said, "Have you got the area secure?"

"There are Marines walking around here. It should be okay."

I stood up and I let somebody else take over the respiration, because I was exhausted. They said, "Doc, we need a decision. It's getting dark."

It was my call. That's what astounded me. I was an E4, and the guy that was asking me this is a captain in the Marine Corps, the company commander. He's asking me is it okay to go ahead. That's just the way it was: In a combat medical situation, the hospital corpsman had the say-so on whether to bring a medevac helicopter in or not.

I said, "Captain, bring him in. I think we can save him." And he got on his radio, I mean right away. He contacted Da Nang, which was about twelve miles away, and gave our position, and they started the medevac in.

This whole time, I'd been up walking around adjusting his IV, taking over the puffs, keeping the CPR going. I forget how long it took that chopper to get out there, but he finally did. We didn't have time to clear a landing zone for him, so he hovered overhead and he sent down a gurney. We got the man laid down very gently in that gurney, got the straps across him. I hung the IV on it, made sure it didn't fall out.

The guy in the chopper started to winch up. We got the gurney shoulder high and were just fixing to let go of it when rifle rounds went off. *Crack, crack-crack, crack, crack, crack.* It was an AK-47. It had a specific sound. Everybody knew it wasn't an M-16 on the perimeter.

All of the Marines had relaxed when that chopper came in. But there was one enemy soldier who had stayed behind, just beyond where we secured the perimeter. He killed the man in the doorway of the chopper outright. He hit the hydraulic lines on the chopper. He wounded the copilot. The door-gunner on the other side was able to get some rounds off, but the chopper was in an emergency situation. The gunner cut the strap and dropped the gurney back down. There was no way they could get that man up.

Everything fell to the ground—us, the gurney, and everything, because we were diving for cover. We didn't know what the hell was happening. We'd thought the perimeter had been secured. That's what you do when you bring in a medevac—you secure the perimeter. And we had told them it wasn't a hot zone. So the helicopter just wasn't under a heightened state of readiness.

We could hear that helicopter struggling—we were hoping it wouldn't come down on top of us. The helicopter turned away, and we could see something coming out underneath it. What it was, was hydraulic fluid. And you've got to have hydraulic fluid to fly one of those things. There was frantic radioing going on between our radioman and the chopper, and the chopper and the base. The pilot couldn't find anyplace to set it down—it was too dense—so his only hope was to make the base twelve miles away, and he was fighting those controls for all he was worth.

He was about halfway there, and the radio signal went dead. I found out later that all the hydraulic fluid had leaked out and he crashed, and everybody was killed—there were five on board that day. Oliver died shortly afterward.

Everyone said, "Doc, it's okay." They all told me they did the what-ifs, too. But to this day I can't help but feel responsible for the deaths of seven men—I count both on the ground, too.

It's very easy to say, "Don't think that way." And maybe it's healing if you can find a way not to. But you carry the guilt of stuff like this so many years. It was a toss of the coin. I told them, "If I had said, 'No, I don't believe this man'll make it,' those men on the chopper would have never been—" But the guys stopped me and said, "Doc, if we would've done our job and cleared the perimeter deep enough, it wouldn't have happened either."

So I guess we all felt enough guilt that day. That was a lonely night. We had to spend it with those two dead bodies there.

I still have that dream about Ritchie, turning him over—just the way it happened—turn and see his face again and again and again. Maybe once a week, maybe sometimes two or three times a week, depending if I'm under stress. I have no reason or rhyme to the thing. Of course, when I drank a lot, I could drown some of it out for a while. But it never completely left me.

I'll be truthful. There are some days I make it through most of the day without the Vietnam War being in the forefront of my mind. But I can tell you it's never more than a heartbeat away.

After it all happened, I found out that the lieutenant was putting me in for a Bronze Star. He was needing me to sign it, and that was the only time I ever confronted him. I said, "Lieutenant, you take that piece of paper, you roll it, and you shove it up your ass. I do not in any essence feel like a hero. I feel like a bum."

And the rest of the guys that were around me knew exactly what I was talking about, because you couldn't have given any of them a medal that day. They were feeling guilty about not securing the perimeter, and they were feeling even more guilty that there was a whole platoon—almost a whole company—there, and one enemy soldier brought down a helicopter and was responsible for that many lives. One. And then they didn't get him. We never got him.

I didn't feel like I had done anything successful. It was my job to keep people alive. And when you don't do that, you don't feel like you've done your job. I would have felt a lot better if that guy had gotten out of there and lived, if I could have returned him to his family, even if he would have been a little brain-damaged. He would have been alive and been able to enjoy his daughters and his sons and his nephews and whatever.

We can't know it all. I probably would have felt guilty had I told them not to come. The man would have died, and I'd have felt guilty about that.

One thing they did tell us at Corps School is, "Do your best to separate yourself from the situation. If you have to be clinically cold, do that. If you have to be uncaring, go that route rather than become involved with people that you're treating."

I never did like that theory.

If you're in the medical profession, you do care. And even those who say they can accomplish that detachment, I don't think they're telling the truth, to themselves or other people.

Being that close to it in an ongoing situation, death is a strange character to deal with. It's okay to go to your uncle's funeral every ten years. But when you wake up every morning not knowing who you're gonna treat today that may die, it does something to you. These are men that you've served with, that you've gotten mad with, that you've chewed out because they didn't do certain things.

It's a family situation. You can't help but care for your family. And it devastates. It takes a toll that thirty years or fifty years does not necessarily erase.

It was only a few days after Oliver and Ritchie were killed that I was wounded. We were on an operation, and I took a round in the sole of my left foot. It lodged at the top of the ankle.

When it happened, I was lying close to the ground with my

hands stretched past my head. I had a cartridge belt on with canteens on both sides, and both canteens got bullet holes through the bottom, and both caps on those canteens were shot off. So it had to be just the luckiest series of shots in the world, to impact both those canteens, go all the way through, bust the caps out of them, and still miss my arms and torso. The fire was raking across in a steady stream. Any one of the rounds could've impacted in the main part of my body. Could have killed me deader than a hammer.

I went away from there thanking God in a big way.

I was medevacked to First Med in Da Nang. I stayed there three days stabilizing; then they put me on what we call the "Freedom Bird" with a bunch of other wounded fellas. And I did not honestly feel like I was leaving until I saw the coast of Vietnam disappear completely out that plane window. And it dawned on me that I was going home.

I went to Japan for just a short while and eventually went on to Corpus Christi, where they did debridement and closure and physical therapy. I was there almost five months. I was on crutches, with a cast on my leg, but when I started to get my strength back, I volunteered to work so I could stay busy. I was able to do some stuff at sick call. I didn't mind doing it. After all, it was my old stamping ground before I went overseas.

I had to use a cane for a couple of years after that, until I got used to everything. I haven't used a cane since.

I lost about three-quarters to an inch of height in my left leg. And that made for complications in the back later, because everything wound up out of kilter.

I wear regular tennis shoes when I'm just banging around and I don't have far to go. If I'm going a long way, I have shoes that have a brace on them, and they have a measured lift inside. They're custom-made to fit, because I've got pressure points in my foot that are real sensitive. I can still go all day on my feet, but I pay the price at night if I do that. Arthritis and pain, edema. A lot of swelling.

It's funny. Last night I had a dream about playing basketball, and I was healed and I was actually slam-dunking. I never could do that even when I was well, but I guess the mind wishes strange things.

I ran track when I was in high school. I loved to run. Oh, I could run all day. I was fast, too, especially in the short-distance events. And for years after getting hurt, I had dreams of running and being completely whole again. Of course, there'd be the wake-up and the disappointment. And like everybody falls into, I felt sorry for myself. The pity pot for a long time.

But I met other veterans who went through a whole lot more than I did. And I began to grow up and realize with their help that there were a lot of things I could still do. I was alive, and I could fairly well function. And even though some of the things you don't forget, maybe forever, you accept what you are. There might be a lot of pain, but you do learn to work with what you have.

David Overstreet was killed doing what David did best, going after someone in trouble when he didn't have to. Alan, a mutual friend, told me what happened; he was there to identify David's body and take the report from a lieutenant who saw the action. They were just coming over a rise and headed down when the enemy set off an ambush, shooting the point man. The rest of the Americans scattered off the trail and were returning fire.

Apparently the enemy had several snipers in the trees—you set up in three different directions and you've got a triangle kill zone. That's what they'd trapped these Marines in. And David could see the man still moving. Of course, you know what that man was: He was bait. A lot of times they didn't kill them outright. They'd wound them in some type of clearing where they'd have a good field of fire. And David should've known better, because we'd been told about stuff like that. But his heart overruled his head, and before they could stop him, he headed down. He couldn't stand seeing the man wounded. And just before he got there, they caught him, Alan said, right under the earlobe. That's a helluva shot, at a perfect kill point. David just folded up. He was dead before he touched the ground and didn't feel a thing.

Oddly enough, they were able to locate and eliminate the snipers, and the man he was going after lived.

I didn't know David had been killed until six months or so after it happened. He wrote me a letter, I think the day before he died. It didn't catch up to me until a month after I was all the way back to Corpus Christi.

There were only two or three left there that knew us mutually, and they knew that my best friend had been killed, but they just could not bring themselves to tell me until I got that letter. One of them was a nurse, a lieutenant. I guess it was because I kept talking about him: "When he gets out, we're gonna do this, we're gonna do that."

There were old editions of *Stars and Stripes* laying around everywhere, but for some reason there was one edition I couldn't find. When the lieutenant saw that letter come in from him, it started working on her pretty bad. I'm sure she thought, "We got to tell this guy sooner or later." So when she delivered the letter to me, she let me read it first, and then she gave me that *Stars and Stripes.*

She just handed it to me. "Here's that issue that you didn't see." I had a feeling what it was. I was reading his letter, she brought me the *Stars and Stripes,* she had tears in her eyes. You can put two and two together. I went straight to the obituaries, and he was listed there: KIA. She was crying. She said, "I just couldn't—"

I said, "That's okay. It happens."

It didn't affect me then. I was home and talking to my mother. I was telling her the circumstances of it, and I said, "He's dead." All of a sudden, it was a fact. It was actually true.

We had planned to start off our life together after Vietnam. Pretty dumb idea, thinking of it now, but the government had a reclaim-the-horses program in Colorado or Montana somewhere, where they'd give you acreage and all the wild horses you could gather in. We were gonna start a horse farm.

It was one of those foolish, boyish things. But we would have attempted it, knowing David. Because whatever he said he was gonna do, he usually did.

We had made a promise that we would name our children after each other. My wife was wondering why I was crying when our son was born. I said, "You named the girls, I'm naming this one." I did let her give him his first name, Christopher, but I insisted that David be his middle name, and he's always been known as David.

That was in 1979. It took me a long time, but I kept that promise. That was a good feeling. It's like a part of him lived on.

At first, alcohol seemed to work pretty good at numbing the pain in both places: the physical pain and the mental anguish. Pain medication—pills—did the same.

Going through the VA system, all you had to do was look like you needed something for pain, and you would get it without even asking. What can you say? They felt like they owed it to you. I could've refused it anytime I wanted. But I just continued to medicate to put these memories out, to keep them from coming to the forefront, where they hurt.

I would switch back and forth. When I could not get the pills, I would use the alcohol. I rarely did both at the same time.

Actually, the alcohol was a lot more devastating than the pills. Even though I was addicted to the medication, at least I had a better quality of family life with that than with the alcohol. The alcohol would put me out of control completely.

It came to a head about four years ago. I thank God that I found two individuals at the Veterans Administration Hospital who helped me realize that it was an issue and that it did need to be addressed. Because my family would be what they call codependent and would make excuses.

Around that same time, though, my wife finally started to give hints that she was getting ready to leave. I think a woman has to be brave like that. In an addict's mind, there's nothing wrong in your family life. You can't see the destruction you're causing, because you're concentrating so much on yourself and your own pain that you're not there for them.

For many years I was not there. I did the best I could, and I guess the kids will admit that I didn't harm them in any way, but I didn't help them a lot in any way either. In other words, I wasn't the dad that I could've been if I had decided to do this a lot earlier.

I have not had a drink, I have not taken any drugs, for almost four years now. I still have the strain. I still have the memories. But I know now that in the long run the alcohol and drugs only add a couple more problems to what you already have. And I am free now to address my problems in a manner that I could not before.

Recovery has been beautiful.

War changes almost everyone who's concerned with it—in some way, to some degree—for the rest of their lives.

You've got to remember that the purpose of an army in wartime will never change. It's to kill other people. You can do statistics, you can do logistics, you can market it any way you want, but the bottom line is to destroy other human lives. That is what an army is all about, and that's what a soldier is trained to do or give support to. What I did was put pieces back together.

We've got to slaughter other human beings. It takes being involved in war to realize the very simple fact that there's something wrong with this.

I remember one hill I saw. A battle had gone on there before we arrived, and it was all bombed out and cratered. They had done some helicopter extractions.

On the top of this hill, there was a charred tree that was left with one branch off to the side of it. And all around the tree was a burn area in a circle, and little pieces of glass and metal lying all over the ground, and a charred half of a pilot's seat lying off to the side.

A helicopter had crashed at that site not a day before, right on top of that tree. The wreckage had been somewhat cleaned up. But whoever cleaned it up had left something there. On that branch out to the side was a rib cage; I knew anatomy, so I recognized it as human. A rib cage, just the bones—no flesh, no legs, no coccyx. The helicopter had burned so severely that it consumed everything of the man inside except that portion, which happened to land on that tree and hang on that branch. Nobody put it there. It was just so striking to whoever had to come there and clean that mess up that they left it. It was a stark witness to what had happened on that hill. It gave a clear message how horrendous war can be.

"How would you feel," people ask me, "if you actually met the little son of a bitch that shot you?" Well, in the first place, he probably never saw me. I don't know if it would have made any difference; he probably could have killed me better if he had. But guess what? We would have killed him if we saw him. I've seen beyond the futility of that now. I would be friends with him, as strange as it may seem.

He was in a time and place doing his job just like I was. I only wish we could find a different way of coming to grips with things rather than armed conflict. Why don't we play chess over territory? What makes people kill other people in an armed situation on a national basis? What does that? If we could come to grips with that compulsion, we'd be a lot wiser a civilization.

If we could send everybody up in a spaceship and let them take a look at how delicate and beautiful the earth is, we might change a few minds. War is a terrible crucible to go through. I wouldn't wish it on anyone, not in this generation or any to come.

I'm fortunate to be where I am at this particular time. I wake up every morning, and I feel happy that I can breathe and I'm alive and I've got a chance. I'm not rich monetarily. But if I use some of the experiences and lessons that I've learned, then I can be rich in other ways. If I can pass them on to other people and give them something from it, I can be rich in the best way.

GLOSSARY OF MILITARY TERMS

I-A

Draft status: fit for military service.

II-S

Draft status: deferred as full-time student.

IV-F

Draft status: unfit for service.

AAA

Antiaircraft artillery.

Abrams, Creighton (1914–1972)

General in command of U.S. forces in Vietnam, 1968–1972.

Air Corps

Name of the Army's aviation arm from 1926 to 1941; although the name was changed in June 1941 to Army Air Forces, many still refer to the wartime entity as the Air Corps. The Air Force became a separate armed service in 1947.

AIT

Advanced individual training; phase of Army training, specific to a soldier's military occupational specialty (MOS), that follows basic.

AK-47
Soviet-designed rifle used by VC/NVA. Captured AK-47s were also used by American personnel.

Alphabet
To ensure accurate voice communications, military personnel use a standardized set of words to express the letters of the alphabet. During Vietnam, the U.S. armed forces used the same alphabet in use today: Alpha, Bravo, Charlie, Delta, Echo, Foxtrot, Golf, Hotel, India, Juliet, Kilo, Lima, Mike, November, Oscar, Papa, Quebec, Romeo, Sierra, Tango, Uniform, Victor, Whiskey, X-Ray, Yankee, Zulu. The World War II alphabet was: Able, Baker, Charlie, Dog, Easy, Fox, George, How, Item, Jig, King, Love, Mike, Nan, Oboe, Peter, Queen, Roger, Sugar, Tare, Uncle, Victor, William, X-Ray, Yoke, Zebra.

AO
Area of operations.

Arc Light
Code name for raids conducted by Air Force B-52 bombers, 1965–1973, mostly over South Vietnam, but also in Cambodia, Laos, and North Vietnam. Used to support ground operations and to cut enemy lines of supply.

Army Air Forces
Name of Army's aviation arm from 1941 until 1947, when it became a separate armed service, the United States Air Force.

ARVN ("AR-vin")
Army of the Republic of Vietnam (the South Vietnamese army).

AWOL ("A-wall")
Absent without leave.

Beaucoup
"Much, many"; slang (from French).

Buffalo Soldiers
Members of all-black United States Army regiments formed after the Civil War.

C&C
Command and control.

Casualties
Servicemembers killed, wounded, captured, or missing in action; the number of casualties is often confused with the number only of those killed in action.

Charlie
Vietcong; from the military alphabet's designation for VC: Victor Charlie. Also used to refer to the enemy in general, including NVA.

Charlie Company
C company. Companies are identified by letter; Charlie is the military alphabet's designation for C.

Chicken plate
Chest armor.

ChiCom
Chinese Communist.

Chinook
U.S. helicopter used for transport of troops and cargo.

CIDG
Civilian Irregular Defense Group; forces composed of South Vietnamese ethnic minorities, mostly Montagnards, organized by U.S. Special Forces.

Claymore
U.S. antipersonnel mine, placed on the ground, detonated either by remote command or by trip wire; Vietcong and NVA used homemade versions.

CO
Commanding officer.

Commo
Communications.

Company-grade officer
Second lieutenant, first lieutenant, or captain in the Army, Air Force, or Marine Corps.

CP
Command post.

C rations
Canned food issued for consumption in the field; eaten hot or cold.

D+1
The day after an operation's beginning. Also, D+2, D+3, etc.

D-Day
The day any operation begins. Used also to designate specifically the first day of the invasion of Normandy, June 6, 1944.

DEROS ("DEE-roase")
Date Eligible to Return from Overseas (sometimes rendered as Date of Estimated Return from Overseas); since personnel were sent to Vietnam for a limited period of time, usually a year (thirteen months for most Marines), each knew his DEROS. Also used as a verb, to describe a person's departure at the end of his tour.

Deuce and a half
Two-and-a-half-ton truck.

DI

Drill instructor. Noncommissioned officer who trains new recruits in the Marine Corps or Navy.

DMZ

Demilitarized Zone; strip separating North and South Vietnam.

DUKW ("DUCK")

Amphibious landing vehicle manufactured by General Motors; name is an acronym composed of GM designations for its design.

DZ

Drop zone.

E4

Enlisted pay grade 4; equivalent to an Army or Marine Corps corporal.

Eighty-eight

Eighty-eight-millimeter German artillery weapon.

Executive officer

Officer second in command of a unit.

FAC ("FACK")

Forward air controller.

Field-grade officers

Major, lieutenant colonel, or colonel in the Army, Air Force, or Marine Corps.

Flak

Antiaircraft fire; contraction from German *Fliegerabwehrkanone,* aircraft-defense cannon.

Fort Sam (Houston)

Army installation in San Antonio, Texas.

Frag

Fragmentation grenade.

Fragging

The wounding, murder, or attempted murder of an officer by his troops in Vietnam, usually for perceived incompetence or overzealousness. Term refers to the fragmentation grenade often used in the attack, but applies to any such attack, regardless of weapon.

Gatling gun

Machine gun with rotating set of barrels; although out of use for nearly a century, the Gatling gun was updated during Vietnam, with the weapon's hand crank replaced by a motor capable of firing six thousand rounds per minute.

Gunship

A heavily armed helicopter in Vietnam; also applies to heavily armed fixed-wing aircraft and heavily armed boats used in riverine operations.

Half-track

Armored personnel carrier with two front tires and caterpillar tracks in the rear.

Ho Chi Minh (1890–1969)

North Vietnamese Communist leader.

Ho Chi Minh Trail

Network of roads extending from North Vietnam south through eastern Laos and Cambodia with numerous spurs extending into South Vietnam. Used by VC/NVA to move supplies and personnel into South Vietnam.

Hooch

Any type of small dwelling in Vietnam.

Huey

Any one of several models of the UH-1 helicopter (UH = utility helicopter). Most common helicopter employed by U.S. and allied forces in Vietnam. Used for a variety of functions, including troop transport, medical evacuation, command and control, and fire support.

I Corps

The U.S. military divided South Vietnam into four tactical zones (from north to south): I Corps ("EYE-kore"), II Corps, III Corps, IV Corps.

In-country

In Vietnam.

Intel

Intelligence.

Kamikaze

Japanese for "Divine Wind," after typhoon that destroyed invading Mongol navy in 1281. One of the Japanese pilots who attempted the suicidal crash of their aircraft into an American ship, 1944–1945.

KIA

Killed in action.

Klick

Kilometer.

KP

Kitchen police.

LCM

Landing craft, mechanized; used for amphibious landings.

Liberty Ship

Transport ship mass-produced in U.S. during World War II.

Listening post
Forward watch position.
LP
Listening post.
LST
Landing ship, tank; large vessel used for amphibious landing of personnel, tanks, and other equipment.
LZ
Landing zone.
LZ X-ray
Landing zone during the Battle of Ia Drang, 1965.
M-14
Standard rifle used by U.S. infantry when the Vietnam War began.
M-16
Lighter successor to M-14.
MACV ("MACK-VEE")
Military Assistance Command, Vietnam: interservice headquarters that commanded all military operations in South Vietnam and its coastal waters. More distant naval operations and air strikes over North Vietnam were commanded directly by the U.S. Pacific Command in Hawaii.
McChord
Air Force base near Seattle.
Medevac
Medical evacuation.
MIA
Missing in action.
Mike-mike
Millimeter. "Mike" is the word for M in the military alphabet; "mike-mike" refers to the abbreviation for millimeter: "mm."
Montagnards
French for "mountain people." People indigenous to Vietnam's Central Highlands.
MOS
Military occupational specialty. Signifies the specific kind of work assigned to a servicemember.
MP
Military police, military police officer.
Napalm
Compound of gasoline and petroleum jelly used as an incendiary.

NCO

Noncommissioned officer. Corporal or sergeant in the Army or Marine Corps; sergeant in the Air Force; petty officer in the Navy.

Ninety-day wonder

An officer during World War II commissioned after an abbreviated course of Officer Candidate School.

NVA

North Vietnamese Army.

OCS

Officer Candidate School.

Old man

A unit's commanding officer.

OSS

Office of Strategic Services; World War II intelligence organization, precursor of the Central Intelligence Agency.

Point

Leading position on a patrol.

POW

Prisoner of war.

PTSD

Post-traumatic stress disorder.

Puff (the Magic Dragon)

AC-47 aircraft; modification of C-47 transport plane for use in Vietnam as a gunship in support of ground operations. Aircraft's civilian designation is DC-3.

Punji stakes

Sharpened bamboo stakes used by Vietcong to create antipersonnel traps; sometimes smeared with excrement to induce infection.

Purple Heart

Award given to any servicemember wounded or killed in battle.

PX

Post exchange; general store at a military facility.

RA

Regular Army; the standing army (i.e., draftees were not Regular Army).

Rack

Bed.

R&R

Rest and recuperation; short period of rest for which service personnel are transported away from the area of combat.

REMF ("REMPH")
Rear-echelon motherfucker.
Republic of Vietnam
South Vietnam.
Revetment
Masonry or steel covering of an earthen embankment.
RPG
Rocket-propelled grenade, also known as the B-40; weapon used by the VC/NVA.
RTO
Radio-telephone operator.
Seabees
Navy construction forces (after initials CB, "construction battalion").
Sea-Tac
Seattle Tacoma airport.
SEAL
Elite Navy commando; a contraction of "Sea, Air, Land" to signify that SEALs operate in all environments.
Shake-and-bake
School attended by enlisted personnel to become noncommissioned officers; the equivalent of OCS for NCOs.
Short
Having little time left before one's tour in Vietnam was scheduled to end.
Sitrep
Situation report.
Spec-4
Specialist fourth class; Army rank equal in pay grade to corporal but without command responsibility.
Special Forces
Elite organization in the U.S. Army; known also as the Green Berets, for their distinctive headgear.
SS
Schutzstaffel (German for "Protective Echelon"); elite Nazi military organization. The SS ran the death and concentration camps and conducted mass-murder "actions." *Waffen* (Armed) SS units served in combat.
Stalag
Contraction of *Stammlager* (German for base camp).
Stars and Stripes
Daily newspaper of the U.S. armed forces.

Steel pot
Helmet.
Tan Son Nhut
Large U.S. and South Vietnamese air base near Saigon; also served as a commercial airport.
TDY
Temporary duty.
Tommy gun
Thompson submachine gun; a lightweight automatic weapon.
Tracer
Shell filled with phosphorus that leaves a visible trail as it travels toward its target. Tracers are placed among regular automatic-weapon rounds to assist in directing fire.
Track
Half or fully tracked armored personnel carrier.
VC
Vietcong.
VFW
Veterans of Foreign Wars; after the American Legion, the largest U.S. veterans' service organization.
Vietcong
American term for South Vietnamese guerrillas; contraction of "Vietnamese Communists."
Walking fire
Moving fire gradually across a given area.
The Wall
Vietnam Veterans Memorial in Washington, D.C.
War Relocation Authority
U.S. government organization established in 1942 to administer the evacuation of Japanese Americans from the West Coast.
Westmoreland, William (1914–)
General in command of U.S. forces in Vietnam, 1964–1968.
Whiskey India Alpha
See "alphabet" above.
White phosphorus
Smoke-producing substance used for marking targets; also used to create a smoke screen and as an incendiary.
Willie Pete
White phosphorus; based on World War II military alphabet.

The World
The United States (to military personnel in Vietnam).
WPA
Works Progress Administration, Work Projects Administration; New Deal employment program.
XO
Executive officer.
Zero
Japanese fighter plane.

NOTES

CHAPTER I, MIKE NOVOSEL SR.

Introduction. John Costello, *The Pacific War 1941–1945* (New York: Quill, 1982), 547–553. Williamson Murray and Allan R. Millett, *A War to Be Won: Fighting the Second World War* (Cambridge, Massachusetts, and London, England: The Belknap Press of Harvard University Press, 2000), 503–508. Richard Natkiel, Text by Robin L. Sommer, *Atlas of World War II* (New York: Barnes & Noble Books, 1985), 136–137.

A detailed explanation of the circumstances by which "Dustoff" became the permanent code name for helicopter medical evacuation in Vietnam may be found at *http://psysim.www7.50megs.com/html/dustoff.htm.* A differing account appears in an official history of Army medicine in Vietnam (Major General Spurgeon Neel, *Vietnam Studies: Medical Support of the U.S. Army in Vietnam 1965–70* [Washington, D.C.: Department of the Army, 1991, first printed 1973], 72–73), but Mike Novosel Sr. credits the story told on this website by Si Simmons, a Dustoff veteran.

Mike Novosel Sr. has written his own book: *Dustoff: The Memoir of an Army Aviator* (Novato, CA: Presidio Press, 1999).

CHAPTER II, MIKE NOVOSEL JR.

Introduction. Neel, *Medical Support,* 51, 69.

CHAPTER III, LEGACIES OF NATION AND FAMILY

Sonny Dunbar. Introduction. Bernard C. Nalty, *Strength for the Fight: A History of Black Americans in the Military* (New York: The Free Press, 1986), 136–139, 199.

John Howe. Introduction. Lt. Col. (Ret.) Michael Lee Lanning, *The African-American Soldier: From Crispus Attucks to Colin Powell* (Secaucus, New Jersey: Citadel Press, 1999), 263, 268.

CHAPTER IV, PEARL HARBOR AND THE GULF OF TONKIN

Introduction. "On January 2, 1963 . . ." Neil Sheehan, *A Bright Shining Lie: John Paul Vann and America in Vietnam* (New York: Random House, 1988), 201–265. "On March 8, 1965 . . ." John S. Bowman, genl. ed., *The Vietnam War Day by Day* (New York: Barnes & Noble Books, 1989), 64–65.

Chronology of Tonkin Gulf incidents and resolution: Marvin E. Gettleman, Jane Franklin, Marilyn B. Young, and H. Bruce Franklin ed., *Vietnam and America: The Most Comprehensive Documented History of the Vietnam War,* 2d ed. (New York: Grove Press, 1995), 250–252. A. J. Langguth, *Our Vietnam: The War 1954–1975* (New York: Simon & Schuster, 2000), 299–307. Spencer C. Tucker, ed., *Encyclopedia of the Vietnam War: A Political, Social, and Military History* (New York: Oxford University Press, 1998), s.v. "Tonkin Gulf Incidents (1964)" and "Tonkin Gulf Resolution (1964)," both by Edwin E. Moise, 405–406. Bowman, *Day by Day,* 44, 166.

Tony Rivas Sr. Introduction. *Encyclopedia Britannica 2002,* s.v. "Works Progress Administration."

CHAPTER V, JOINING AND TRAINING

Ed Jackson. "They said I could get shell shock . . ." "And once again, they said . . ." According to the book *World War II: America at War 1941–1945,* by Norman Polmar and Thomas B. Allen (New York: Random House, 1991, p. 725), draftees at the beginning of the war were required to have "at least half of 32 natural teeth." Jeff Charleston, of the Center of Military History in Washington, D.C., explains the rule: "Dentures can get lost in combat and can't be easily replaced. You have to be able to chew your food." After checking a number of sources, however, including the Center of Military History and the National Center for Post Traumatic Stress Disorder, my research assistant, Rebecca Webber, could find no confirmation that bad teeth had ever been connected, however spuriously, to susceptibility to combat trauma. Yet Ed Jackson clearly recalls being handed such an explanation twice, in two different locations, by two sets of authorities. The theory must have had some currency at the time.

Howard Baugh Sr. Inception of Tuskegee program. Lynn M. Homan and Thomas Reilly, *The Tuskegee Airmen,* Images of America Series (Charleston, SC: Arcadia Publishing, 1998), 7–8. Nalty, *Strength,* 138–139.

Chapter VI, John Mace

Introduction. Murray and Millett, *A War,* 463–471. Natkiel and Sommer, *Atlas,* 180–183. Gerhard Weinberg, *A World at Arms: A Global History of World War II* (New York: Cambridge University Press, 1994), 765–771.

"It only takes a bomb . . ." John Mace spoke these words five and a half months before the felling of the World Trade Center.

Chapter VIII, First Blood

John Howe. Introduction. Bowman, *Day by Day,* 119–120. Tucker, *Encyclopedia,* s.v. "Tet Offensive Overall Strategy (1968)," 395, and "Tet Offensive: the Sài Gòn Circle (1968)," 396–399, both by David T. Zabecki.

John Howe. "Elbert R. Perry" is a pseudonym. Unless otherwise noted, all names in this book—with the exception of those in Chapter X (see chapter introduction)—are real.

Perry Pollins. Introduction. Costello, *Pacific War,* 502–503.

Mike Perkins. Introduction. Tucker, *Encyclopedia,* s.v. "United States: Special Forces," 434–435, by Richard L. Kiper, Harve Saal, and Spencer C. Tucker; s.v. "Civilian Irregular Defense Group," 74–75, by David M. Berman. Harry G. Summers Jr., *Vietnam War Almanac* (New York, New York and Oxford, England: Facts on File Publications, 1985), s.v. "Special Forces," 316–317. *Vietnam Studies: U.S. Army Special Forces 1961–1971,* CMH Publication 90-23 (Washington, D.C.: Department of the Army, 1989; first printed 1973), 4–15. Available at *http://www.army.mil/cmh-pg/books/Vietnam/90-23/90-23C.htm.*

Max Hutchins. Introduction. Murray and Millett, *A War,* 420–423. Weinberg, *A World,* 686–687.

Mickey Hutchins. Introduction. Tucker, *Encyclopedia,* s.v. "Territorial Forces," by Clayton D. Laurie, 395.

CHAPTER IX, DOING BATTLE

Tony Rivas, Sr. Introduction. Crew count on the *Indianapolis:* Richard F. Newcomb, *Abandon Ship! The Saga of the U.S.S.* Indianapolis, *the Navy's Greatest Sea Disaster,* with an introduction and afterword by Peter Maas (New York: HarperCollins, 2000; originally New York: Henry Holt, 1958), 110. Aleutian campaign. Costello, *Pacific War,* 307, 404–406. Elizabeth-Anne Wheal, Stephen Pope, and James Taylor, *A Dictionary of the Second World War* (New York: Peter Bedrick Books, 1990), s.v. "Aleutian Islands," 10. *Dictionary of American Fighting Ships,* Vol. III (Washington, D.C.: Navy Department, Office of the Chief of Naval Operations, Naval History Division, 1968), s.v. "Indianapolis (CA-35)," 434, as transcribed by Haze, Gray and Underway, a website specializing in naval history: *http://www.hazegray.org.*

Steve Kraus. Introduction. Rebecca Webber's correspondence with Dr. Gary Solis, Chief of Oral History, Marine Corps Historical Center, Washington. Summers, *Almanac,* s.v. "DMZ (Demilitarized Zone)," 144. Harry G. Summers Jr., introduction and epilogue by Stanley Karnow, *Historical Atlas of the Vietnam War* (Boston and New York: Houghton Mifflin, 1995), 96–97. Tucker, *Encyclopedia,* s.v. "Demilitarized Zone (DMZ)," by Brent Langhals, 97.

Ed Jackson. Introduction. Murray and Millett, *A War,* 304–335. Richard Overy, *Why the Allies Won* (New York and London: W. W. Norton & Company, 1995), 101–133.

CHAPTER X, COMRADES

Mike Perkins. "Marty Green" is a pseudonym.

Jim Coyne Sr. Introduction. Murray and Millett, *A War,* 299. Weinberg, *A World,* 437–440.

CHAPTER XI, AL TARBELL

Introduction. Murray and Millett, *A War,* 438–443. Natkiel and Sommer, *Atlas,* 180–181. Cornelius Ryan, *A Bridge too Far* (New York: Simon &

Schuster, 1974; reprint, New York: Popular Library, 1977). Wheal, Pope, and Taylor, *Dictionary,* s.v. "Arnhem," 29–30.

For information concerning the Allied landing at Anzio see the introduction to Arthur Way's recollections, p. 351.

"When we get over Holland . . ." In his description of the crash of this plane into the waters of Schouwen Island, along the Netherlands coast, Cornelius Ryan quotes Lieutenant James Megellas, of Al Tarbell's outfit (*Bridge,* 168). Bill Perkins, piloting one of the C-47s that carried the 82nd Airborne to Holland that day, also witnessed the plane's demise. "I was flying right wing man at that time. Up to my right and slightly above me, one of my roommates, Captain Bohannan, was leading another flight. And I happened to look up, and I saw his aircraft was on fire." The paratroopers, identifiable by their olive-drab parachutes, managed to bail out to safety, as did the crew chief, using the white parachute issued to airmen. But Bohannan and the rest of the crew perished. "I watched him, and he went right on into the estuary with a big splash."

Chapter XII, Mike Tarbell

Introduction. Summers, *Almanac,* s.v. "Airmobile Operations," 75–76. Tucker, *Encyclopedia,* s.v. "Airmobility," 9–10, by John L. Bell. Richard P. Weinert Jr., *A History of Army Aviation—1950–1962,* ed. Susan Canedy, TRADOC Historical Monograph Series, gen. ed. Henry O. Malone and John L. Romjue (Fort Monroe, Virginia: Office of the Command Historian, United States Army Training and Doctrine Command, 1991), 181–183. Available at: *http://www-tradoc.army.mil/historian/pubs/aahist/.*

"We have a term . . ." A poem well known to infantrymen begins: "I am the Infantry—Queen of Battle! For two centuries I have kept our Nation safe, Purchasing freedom with my blood. To tyrants, I am the day of reckoning; to the oppressed, the hope for the future. Where the fighting is thick, there am I . . . *I am the Infantry! FOLLOW ME!*" On website of Fort Benning: *http://www.benning.army.mil/fbhome/followme/default.htm.*

"We worked with the Koreans . . ." Four nations sent combat troops to Vietnam in aid of the Americans and South Vietnamese. In 1969, at the peak strength of the "Free World Military Forces," these personnel numbered 48,869 from South Korea, 11,568 from Thailand, 7,672 from Australia, and 552 from New Zealand. (Summers, *Almanac,* s.v. "Free World Military Forces, 173; Tucker, *Encyclopedia,* s.v. "Free World Assistance Program," by Arthur T. Frame, 140–141).

Chapter XIV, Fighting, Killing, Dying

Introduction. For a discussion of killing in war, see Lieutenant Colonel Dave Grossman, *On Killing: The Psychological Cost of Learning to Kill in War and Society* (Boston, New York, London: Little Brown and Company, 1995). Grossman examines the particular burden borne by Vietnam veterans in the section "Killing in Vietnam: What Have We Done to Our Soldiers?"

Perry Pollins. Introduction. Costello, *Pacific War,* 497.

Greg Camp. Introduction. Langguth, *Our Vietnam,* 563–571. Tucker, *Encyclopedia,* s.v. "Cambodia," by Arnold R. Isaacs, 53–56, and "Cambodian Incursion," by John D. Root, 57–59.

Chapter XV, Enemies and Allies

Greg Camp. Introduction. Harry G. Summers Jr., Colonel of Infantry, *On Strategy: A Critical Analysis of the Vietnam War* (Novato, California: Presidio, 1982), 1.

Walter Kraus. Tokyo Rose. "Tokyo Rose" was the collective name given by American servicemen to fourteen female announcers who broadcast to them from Japan. One of the women, Iva Toguri d'Aquino, returned to her native America after the war and was convicted of treason. Sentenced to ten years in prison, she served six years with time off for good behavior. Gerald Ford issued her pardon in 1977.

Mike Jackson. Introduction. *Department of Defense Dictionary of Military and Associated Terms: Joint Terminology Master Database as of 10 June 1998* (Washington, D.C.: U.S. Government Printing Office), 388.

Richard Recendez. Introduction. Summers, *Almanac,* s.v. "Iron Triangle," 207–208.

Arthur Way. Introduction. Murray and Millett, *A War,* 381–382, 385.

Chapter XVI, Gene Swanson

Introduction. Costello, *Pacific War,* 542–547, 566, 577–578. Murray and Millet, *A War,* 510–513. Weinberg, *A World,* 886. "One recent history . . ." Murray and Millet, *A War,* 520. Role of Third Marine Division at Iwo Jima: Rebecca Webber's correspondence with Patrick Osborn, Archivist, Modern Military Records, The National Archives and Records Administration.

Chapter XVII, Gary Swanson

Introduction. Kennedy Slogan: "Died, Walt Rostow," in "Milestones," *Time,* February 24, 2003, 17. "Called for black Americans to have patience . . ." Taylor Branch, *Parting the Waters: America in the King Years 1954–63* (New York: Simon and Schuster, 1988), 235. Chronology of antiwar movement: Tucker, *Encyclopedia,* s.v. "Antiwar Movement, United States," 18–19. College draft deferment: Summers, *Almanac,* s.v. "Draft," 146.

Chapter XVIII, Life After War

Vince Way. Interstitial material about Agent Orange. Summers, *Almanac* s.v. "Agent Orange," 66–68. Tucker, *Encyclopedia* s.v. "Defoliation," 95, "Herbicides," 170–171, "RANCH HAND, Operation (1961–1971)," 345–346, all by Charles J. Gaspar.

Chapter XIX, Remembering and Forgetting

Introduction. Statements from the American Battle Monuments Commission appear on the website *WWWIIMemorial.com.*

Tony Rivas Sr. Introduction. Newcomb (with Maas), *Abandon,* xii, 93, 174.

Chapter XX, Wars Past, Present, and Future

Greg Camp. "Only the dead . . ."

In his famous "farewell address" to West Point on May 12, 1962, Douglas MacArthur exhorted the cadets to take as the "very obsession of [their] public service" the values embodied in "three hallowed words": "duty, honor, courage." He went on: "This does not mean that you are warmongers. On the contrary, the soldier above all other people prays for peace, for he must suffer and bear the deepest wounds and scars of war. But always in our ears ring the ominous words of Plato, that wisest of all philosophers: 'Only the dead have seen the end of war.'"

Because of MacArthur's address, these "ominous words" have become familiar ones among the American military. Greg Camp, whose letter of December 7, 1969, includes the saying, arrived at West Point two years after MacArthur spoke there. The maxim has spread also to the broader culture, here and abroad: it appears as an epigraph in at least two recent books about war and one recent film, and may be seen in a permanent display at the Imperial War Museum in London.

After Greg sent me this letter, I looked to find the specific work of Plato in which the quotation appears. The most reliable collections of quotations—

Bartlett's, Columbia, Oxford—do not include it, but it appears in a few others, with attribution only to "Plato," not to any specific work. Paging through an English translation of Plato's complete works, I found nothing resembling the quotation.

I E-mailed classicists at a number of universities around the country. None could provide a citation offhand. Several generously took the time to research the question. One of them, Chuck Hagen of California Polytechnic State University, searched not just Plato but the entire ancient Greek canon without finding any words that could have yielded the quotation. Others came up just as empty-handed.

Bernard Duffy, also of Cal Poly, who has co-edited a collection of MacArthur's speeches, alerted me to a website attributing the saying to George Santayana, the American philosopher and critic. I contacted the Santayana Edition, a group of scholars engaged in editing a complete edition of Santayana's works for the MIT Press, and was referred to a work by Santayana entitled *Soliloquies in England,* first published in 1922. In the chapter "Tipperary," the narrator assays the mood among veterans of the recently completed Great War: "[T]he poor fellows think they are safe! They think that the war—perhaps the last of all wars—is over!

"Only the dead are safe; only the dead have seen the end of war."

David Lupher, of the University of Puget Sound, surmised that MacArthur read Santayana's work and eventually came to misremember its author. I would add that the original mistake may have been MacArthur's, or it may have been the doing of a lesser mortal, whose error, along with the quotation, somehow made its way to the general. Whoever made the switch, it probably occurred because Santayana is considered in some respects a Platonist and in 1927 published a work entitled *Platonism and the Spiritual Life.*

The provenance of the words does not detract from their import, nor from the extraordinary wisdom of a twenty-three-year-old soldier writing to his father from a tiny firebase in Southeast Asia.

Chapter XXI, Paul Walmsley

Introduction. Murray and Millett, *A War,* 434–439. Weinberg, *A World,* 760–761. Ryan, *A Bridge,* 61–86. Naktiel and Sommer, *Atlas,* 179. Charles M. Province, *Patton's Third Army: A Daily Combat Diary* (New York: Hippocrene Books, 1992), 27–84. Author's correspondence with Mr. Province. "My men can eat their belts . . ." Ryan, *A Bridge,* 69. Caleb Carr, the novelist and military historian, offers an emphatic indictment of Eisenhower and the broad-front strategy in his essay "VE Day—November

11, 1944" (Robert Cowley, ed., *What If 2: Eminent Historians Imagine What Might Have Been* [New York: G.P. Putnam's Sons, 2001], by Caleb Carr, 333–343). Murray and Millett, on the other hand, argue that realities of politics and supply lines made victory unattainable in 1944 (*A War,* 435).

"All the Marines had been put on ships . . ." Chuck Melson, chief historian of the Marine Corps, notes that responsibility to relieve the Philippines would have fallen to the Army or Navy, not the Marine Corps. However, he says, the Marine Corps did mount a relief expedition to Wake Island only to call it back when commanders realized the troops would not arrive in time to prevent the island's capture by the Japanese. Paul Walmsley died on December 19, 2001, before I could follow up with him on this point, or on the following matter of the railroad strike.

"They had one company . . ." I have been unable to confirm Paul Walmsley's account of the railroad strike. Other records of labor unrest during World War II describe the Army's takeover and operation of rail facilities until the disputes were settled, not the drafting of striking workers.

Chapter XXII, Sandy Walmsley

Introduction. Neel, *Medical Support,* 49–58. Tucker, *Encyclopedia,* s.v. "Medicine, Military," by Jack McCallum, 260–262, "Medics and Corpsmen," by Pia C. Heyn, 262.

"Billy Maxwell" is a pseudonym.

ACKNOWLEDGMENTS

My thanks go first to the forty men who tell their stories here. Without exception, they were unstinting with their time and their recollections, willing to speak plainly even about events whose remembrance opened wounds that decades have not healed. I'm grateful to all of them for their abundant patience in explaining war to an author untutored by the hard experience of it. I am honored to know them.

Four men appear in this book posthumously: World War II veterans Jim Coyne Sr., Sonny Dunbar, and Paul Walmsley, and Vietnam veteran Mickey Hutchins. I am saddened at the passing of them all but find Mickey's untimely death the most distressing. The world was cheated of an extraordinarily thoughtful and articulate voice when he died; I was cheated of a provocative and trustworthy new friend. My thanks go also to Ethel Coyne, Jim Sr.'s widow, for her assistance and encouragement.

I interviewed a number of veterans whose compelling stories I was unable to fit into this one volume. All were generous with their time and candor; I regret that I was unable to put their words to good use. They are Ben and Jerry Carson of Oregon, Albert and Bill Garbett of Ohio, Elwood and Floyd Kitchen of Utah and

Oregon, Jack and Tom Hanton of California and Virginia, Bert, Jack, and Paul Jolis of New York and California, Duane and Brock Lilly of Illinois, James E. and James G. Violante of New Jersey. My gratitude as well to the many other veterans who contacted me with interest in the project.

I thank Bernard Edelman for his permission to use poetry of Michael Davis O'Donnell as the book's epigraph. Also Tom Galvin for allowing me to include his tributes to the Novosels.

I was lucky to have the help of talented people in this book's preparation. By her hard work and her genuine interest in people, Linda Poggetti guided me toward many of the men who appear in these pages. Rebecca Webber proved endlessly resourceful and intelligent in checking even the most obscure of facts. Mary Ellen Feinberg of Arctype Professional Services provided idiomatic, precise transcriptions of dozens of hours of interviews. I'm also grateful for the contributions of John Dean Alfone, Alexandra Cann, and Shravanti Reddy.

Rebecca and I called upon many experts kind enough to assist in making the book as accurate as possible. With apologies to any I've omitted, they are (in no particular order): Terry Charman of London's Imperial War Museum, Thomas Figueria and Corey Brennan of Rutgers University, Bernard Duffy and Chuck Hagen of California Polytechnic Institute, David Reeve of the University of North Carolina, David Lupher of the University of Puget Sound, Kristine Frost of the Santayana Edition, Aaron Belkin and Nathaniel Frank of the Center for the Study of Sexual Minorities in the Military, Steve Ralls of the Servicemembers Legal Defense Network, Patrick Deer of New York University, Lesley Smith of George Mason University, Mike Province of the Patton Society, Perrie Ballantyne of the University of Melbourne, Patrick Osborn and Kenneth D. Schlessinger of the National Archives and Records Administration, Captain Joe Kloppel of the United States Marine Corps, Staff Sergeant Jeremy Cheek and Dieter Smith-Christmas of the Marine Corps Museum at Quantico, Robert J. Cressman of the Naval Historical Center, Robert V. Aquilina, Charles Smith,

Gary Solis, and Chuck Melson of the Marine Corps Historical Center, Jeff Charleston, Jeffrey Clarke, and Robert Wright of the Center of Military History, Jack A. Green of the Naval Historical Center, Z. Frank Hanner of the National Infantry Museum, Alyce Burton of the Selective Service System, Raymond Emory of the Pearl Harbor Survivors Association, Pearl Harbor veteran Richard Fiske, Daniel Martinez of the National Park Service Pearl Harbor Memorial, Ensign David Luckett of the Office of Navy Chief of Information, Bob Babcock for information about the Fourth Infantry Division, Laurie Smith of the Walter Reed Medical Center, Brett Stolle of the Air Force Museum, John Greenwood of the Office of the Surgeon General of the Army, Fleming Bell of the Institute of Government at the University of North Carolina, Robert Anzuoni of the Eighty-second Airborne Division Museum, Milton Leitenberg of the Center for International and Security Studies, Daniel Peterson of the First Armored Division Museum, Joe Hitt of the Public Affairs Office at Fort Lewis, Mark Megehee of the Field Artillery Museum, David Kanatawakhon-Maracle of the University of Western Ontario, John Duvall and Patrick Tremblay of the Airborne and Special Operations Museum, Nguyen Thi Nga of the University of Michigan, Richard Weiner of University, and Con Thien survivor Richard Camacho. Also W. J. McCoy, Julia Annas, Claudia Baracchia, Gail Fine, Bernard Suzanne, Nathan Bradshaw, William Taylor, Adil Sarghini, Mark S. Morgan, Valerie Hoffman, Gregory J. Hagge, Nilu Dorschner, Billy Colewell, Roger Roscoe, Neil Keating, Leonard Linton, Dale Ahlquist, Cindy Ulrich, Ginny Sayre, Jill Swiecichowski, Mary Slupe, Mary C. Pickering, Adam Katz, Kim Melchor, Bob Sherman, Celia Stratton, Russell S. Hansen, Ed Borkowski, John Marsh, Frederick J. Shaw, Eric Newton, Jim Griffiths, Daniel W. Brumbaugh, Doug Blake, and Thomas S. Abler. And some people whose names I know either incompletely or not at all: Sergeant Mailes, Chief Sharrard, Dustoff 69, and staff at Fort Benning, the U.S. Army Airborne School, the American Merchant Marine Museum, and the Dayton and Montgomery County Public

Library. My good friend Rob Spencer, a physician who lives in Concord, New Hampshire, helped me understand a medical issue. And I'm grateful to Victor Bers, of the Yale Classics Department, less for answering my question than for remembering me after nearly thirty years.

The enthusiasm of my editor, Mauro DiPreta, for this project never flagged; neither did his deft direction ever fail to improve it. No matter what I needed, his assistant, Joelle Yudin, did not miss a beat in providing it. I'm lucky to have formed a partnership with a diligent, skilled agent, Craig Kayser, whose interest made this book possible and whose steady support helped get it done.

All the aforementioned have only added to this book. All shortcomings and errors are mine alone.

My good fortune is my family. I'm happy that my mother knew of this project before she died, but sorrowful that she is not here to see its completion. I'm thankful for the love of my sister and my brothers; for the indulgence of my son, who in his young life has spent far too many Sunday afternoons without his father; and for Amy, constant and wise, who makes possible all good things.